D0886336

CHILDREN'S
DAILY
PRAYER

for the School Year 2018–2019

Margaret Burk
and Vivian E. Williams

LTP

LITURGY
TRAINING
PUBLICATIONS

Nihil Obstat
Reverend Mr. Daniel G. Welter, JD
Chancellor
Archdiocese of Chicago
October 16, 2017

Imprimatur
Very Reverend Ronald A. Hicks
Vicar General
Archdiocese of Chicago
October 16, 2017

The *Nihil Obstat* and *Imprimatur* are official declarations that the material is free from doctrinal or moral error, and thus is granted permission to publish in accordance with c. 827. No legal responsibility is assumed by the grant of this permission. No implication is contained herein that those who have granted the *Nihil Obstat* and *Imprimatur* agree with the content, opinions, or statements expressed.

The Scripture quotations are from the *New Revised Standard Version Bible: Catholic Edition* copyright © 1993 and 1989 by the National Council of the Churches of Christ in the U.S.A. Used by permission. All rights reserved.

Excerpts from the English translation of *The Liturgy of the Hours* © 1973, 1974, 1975, International Commission on English in the Liturgy (ICEL); excerpts from the English translation of *The Roman Missal* © 2010, ICEL. All rights reserved.

Blessing prayer for birthdays adapted from *Book of Blessings*, additional blessings for use in the United States, © 1968, United States Conference of Catholic Bishops, Washington, DC. Used with permission.

Many of the concepts and guidelines, as well as various prayer services offered in this book, were originally conceived and developed by Dr. Sofia Cavalletti, Ms. Gianna Gobbi, and their collaborators. Theological underpinnings and many elements of these prayer services were first documented in Cavalletti's foundational books including, *The Religious Potential of the Child* and *The Religious Potential of the Child Age 6–12*.

Liturgy Training Publications acknowledges the significant contribution made by Elizabeth McMahon Jeep to the development of *Children's Daily Prayer*. Ms. Jeep worked tirelessly for more than fifteen years to help this resource become the essential annual prayer resource for children and their parents, teachers, and catechists. We are indebted to her for her authorship and guidance.

CHILDREN'S DAILY PRAYER 2018–2019 © 2018 Archdiocese of Chicago: Liturgy Training Publications, 3949 South Racine Avenue, Chicago, IL 60609; 800-933-1800; orders@ltp.org; fax 800-933-7094. All rights reserved. See our website at www.LTP.org.

The cover art is by Mikela Prevost, and the interior art is by Paula Wiggins © LTP. Paper Clip image by Babich Alexander, used under license from Shutterstock.com. This book was edited by Margaret Brennan; Michael A. Dodd was the production editor; Juan Alberto Castillo was the designer and production artist.

Printed in the United States of America.

ISBN 978-1-61671-386-7

CDP19

CONTENTS

CONTENTS

The editors appreciate your feedback.
E-mail: cdp@ltp.org.

INTRODUCTION

UNDERSTANDING THE ORDER OF PRAYER

Children's Daily Prayer is a form of the Liturgy of the Hours, adapted for children. It is based on the Church's tradition of Morning Prayer. A selected psalm is prayed for several weeks at a time. The readings for the daily prayers have been chosen to help children become familiar with significant themes and major stories in Scripture. The Sunday reading is always the Gospel of the day. Reflection questions for silent meditation or group conversation follow the reading.

For schools and homeschooling families, this book provides an order of prayer for each day of the school year (Prayer for the Day). For religious education settings, it provides prayer services for once a week (Prayer for the Week). Not every prayer element in the order of prayer will be useful in every situation. From the elements listed below, you can choose the ones that will be most effective for your group, setting, and time available.

OPENING

This gives the context for the Scripture reading and, when space allows, introduces the saint to be remembered that day. It also indicates when a particular theme or focus will be followed for the week. Sometimes difficult words or concepts in the reading are explained.

SIGN OF THE CROSS

An essential ritual action Catholics use to begin and end prayer. By making the Sign of the Cross, we place ourselves in the presence of the Father, the Son, and the Holy Spirit. Young children may need to practice making the Sign of the Cross.

PSALM

Praying the psalm is central to Morning Prayer. You may use the short version on the prayer page or the longer version on the Reproducible Psalms pages.

READING OR GOSPEL

Daily Scripture texts have been carefully selected to help children "walk through the Bible," and become familiar with the great stories and themes of Salvation History. By following a story or exploring a theme for several days, the children experience how God has spoken to us through the words of Scripture and also through particular people and events in history. They begin to see how people have cooperated with God in bringing about God's Kingdom on earth, and to realize their role in this great work. The Prayer for the Week always uses the Sunday Gospel.

FOR SILENT REFLECTION

This is designed to be a time of silence so the children can ponder the Scripture they have heard and experience the value of silence in prayer. You might prefer to use this question at another time for a discussion about the reading or for journal writing. You may want to substitute your own instruction and questions. In either case, some silence should be kept after the Scripture.

CLOSING PRAYER

This prayer element begins with intercessions and ends with a brief prayer related to the liturgical season. In preparing for daily prayer, children can write the intercessions for the day and include relevant events to school and classroom life, as well as the world. They can also be encouraged to offer their own intentions spontaneously. You may choose to end with the Our Father.

PRAYER SERVICES

Children need to learn that the Church's prayer forms are rich and varied. We have the celebration of the Eucharist, and traditional prayers such as the Rosary. We also have a long tradition of other forms of prayer, such as the Liturgy of the Hours, which emphasizes the psalms, or the Liturgy of the Word, which focuses on Holy Scripture. Additional prayer services are offered in this book for specific liturgical times, memorials, feasts, or solemnities. (Check the table of contents.) You may prefer to use one of these instead of the Prayer for the Day. Consider using these prayer services when the whole school gathers to celebrate a season. You might add an entrance procession and children and adults can do the ministerial roles.

GRACE BEFORE MEALS AND PRAYER AT DAY'S END

In order to instill in children the habit of prayer, use these prayers before lunch or at the end of the day.

PSALMS AND CANTICLES

Additional psalms and canticles (liturgical songs from the Bible, e.g., the Magnificat) are provided at the end of the book, and you will find many more in your Bible. Substitute these for any of the psalm excerpts in the prayer services or pray these with the children at any time a different choice is better for what is happening in your classroom community.

HOME PRAYERS

Children enjoy connecting their classroom and home lives. The Home Prayers offer a wonderful catechetical tool and resource for family prayer. You may photocopy these pages to send home.

CREATING A SACRED SPACE AND TIME FOR PRAYER

Children and adults benefit from having a consistent time for prayer. Where possible, it is helpful to the formation of prayer life to have a "sacred space," that is a designated place or table with religious objects such as the Bible, a cross, a beautiful cloth that reflects the color of the liturgical season. The introductions to each liturgical season will offer specific ideas on how to do the following:

1. Use the language in the introduction to help the children understand the character of the time.

2. Look for practical suggestions for how to celebrate the liturgical time in a classroom setting:

   - how to arrange a sacred space within the classroom
   - what colors and objects to use in the sacred space
   - what songs to sing in each liturgical time
   - suggestions for special prayers for that liturgical time and how best to introduce them to children
   - help with adapting ideas from this book to special circumstances, especially for catechists who meet with students once a week.

HOW CHILDREN PRAY

THE YOUNGEST CHILDREN

Children are natural liturgists and theologians. Young children (up until age 6) will pray simple but profound acclamations when they are given a real opportunity to hear the Word of God or to experience the language of signs found in our liturgy. Their spontaneous prayers most often reflect their understanding of the Word of God, their thanksgiving for God's goodness, and the joy they receive in their relationship with Christ. Here are some examples of prayers collected by catechists: "Thank you, Lord, for the light!" (a 3-year-old); "Thank you

TIPS FOR GIVING CHILDREN A GREATER ROLE IN PRAYER

This book is intended to be used by children. It will help them become familiar with being leaders of prayer and will form them in the habit of daily prayer.

1. Ideally daily prayer takes place at the beginning of the day in individual classrooms. Consider inviting the children to work in groups to prepare and lead the prayer in your classroom. The group can take on the roles of leader, psalmist, Scripture reader, and perhaps, music leader for the *Alleluia*. An intercessor might compose and lead a few petitions, and then invite the class to add individual ones.

2. If it is necessary to begin the prayer over the public address system, consider doing only the opening and Sign of the Cross over the loud speaker. Then invite the individual classrooms to continue the prayer in their own setting.

3. If you wish to lead the whole prayer over the public address system, consider inviting children from the various grades to do the roles listed in the first paragraph.

4. To help the younger children learn to lead prayer, consider inviting older children to lead in the lower grade classrooms as mentioned in paragraph one.

5. Invite your older students to help orient the younger ones to the prayer service. The older ones can help the younger ones practice the readings and compose intercessions so that eventually the younger ones can lead prayer in their own classrooms.

for everything!" (a 4-year-old); "I love you!" (a 3-year-old); and "I want to take a bath in your light" (a 4-year-old). These prayers point to the young child's ability to appreciate the greatest of realities: life in relationship with God.

When praying with these "little ones," it is best to proclaim the Scripture (explaining difficult words in advance to help their understanding) and then to ask one or two open-ended questions to help them to reflect on what the passage is saying to them. If you then invite them to say something to Jesus about what they've heard, you may be surprised at what comes out of the mouths of those budding little theologians!

PRAYING WITH OLDER CHILDREN

Older children (ages 6–12) begin to appreciate the gift of prayer language. We should go slowly and use a light touch, though. When they're younger, give them one beautiful phrase ("Our Father, who art in heaven") that they can begin to appreciate and love. As they grow you can add a second phrase, then a third. But make sure that they understand the words they are using, and encourage them to pray slowly.

Older children also enjoy leading prayer and composing their own prayers. If you give them each a small prayer journal and give them time to write in it, they will produce meaningful prayers and little theological drawings (particularly if you give them time to write and draw right after reading Scripture together).

PSALMS

The psalms offer a treasure trove of prayer language. Consider praying with one or two verses at a time. You could write one or two verses onto an unlined index card and display it up on your prayer table. You can invite older children to copy them into their prayer journals. But remember to go over each word with the class, asking them to reflect on what the prayer wants to say to God. Children need time to explore the rich implications in their prayer. Also, psalms may be sung or chanted (after all, they were written as songs). Perhaps a parish cantor or choir member would lead a sung version of the psalm once in a while. At least the refrain might be sung on one note.

MUSIC IN PRAYER

It is a fact that the songs we sing in church are all prayers, so include singing in your classroom prayer life. What a wonderful difference it makes! Don't be shy, and don't worry about how well you sing. Even if you don't think you have a good voice, children will happily sing with you. So go ahead and make a joyful noise! Children enjoy the chance to lift their voices to God. You may even have a few gifted singers in the class who can help you lead the singing.

The best music to use in the classroom is what your parish sings during the Sunday liturgy. You might incorporate the Penitential Act ("Lord Have Mercy, Christ Have Mercy, Lord Have Mercy") in Lent, the refrain of the Gloria in Easter, the Gospel Acclamation (Alleluia), even a chanted Our Father. But any songs, hymns, or chants that your parish sings would be a good choice. Your parish music director or diocesan director of music can be good resources.

Also, in the introductions to each liturgical time, you will find a wealth of music suggestions.

ART AS PRAYER

Once in a while suggest the children draw a picture after having heard the Scripture reading. Their drawings often reveal their joy and love in ways that language can't always express. Some children are more visual than verbal. Drawing allows them to lengthen and deepen their enjoyment of prayer time.

Don't give the children assignments or themes for these "prayer" drawings, and don't offer a lot of fancy art supplies or media. The best, most reverent drawings come from children who are simply invited to draw something that has to do with what they have just heard in the Scripture reading, something to do with the Mass, or anything to do with God. These open-ended suggestions allow the Holy Spirit room to enter into the children's work.

PRAYER CANNOT BE EVALUATED

This book is most often used in school or religious education programs. In these settings, teachers are often required to give children a grade in religion. However, prayer is not class work and teachers and catechists who have any choice in the matter should make certain **not to give the children a grade for prayer!** Prayer expresses an inner, mysterious reality, for which teachers can provide the environment. Prayer is a person's conversation with God. Consider Jesus' teaching on prayer (Matthew 6:5–13) or take a close look at his parable of the Pharisee and the tax collector (Luke 18:9–14). We don't want the children to pray for the benefit of a grade or praise from the teacher; but rather, we want them to pray from their feeling of relationship with a listening God.

JOY

In all you do with the children, feel free to communicate your joy to them, especially your joy in praying. Joy is a great sign of the presence of Christ. If you take pleasure in your students' company, they will understand that they are precious children of God. If you take pleasure in your work, they will understand that work is a beautiful gift. If you listen to them and take their words seriously, you will be incarnating Christ, who so valued children. Perhaps you will be the initial prayer leader and model that role. Something to model is a relaxed attitude when things go wrong (e.g., someone begins the Scripture too early). Try to give simple, clear directions ahead of time and then correct the situation as gently as possible. While you must keep order in your classrooms and an atmosphere of dignity in prayer, don't be afraid of a little silliness at times. Both laughter and tears are signs of the presence of the Holy Spirit.

ABOUT THE AUTHORS

Vivian E. Williams holds her master of arts degree in pastoral studies, with a concentration in word and worship, from Catholic Theological Union in Chicago. She formerly served as liturgy director for the St. Giles Family Mass Community in Oak Park, Illinois (eighteen years); a Catholic school teacher (twenty-five years); and a parish catechist (ten years). Vivian still writes and speaks on topics related to liturgy, ministry, and catechesis. She is the author of *Classroom Prayer Basics* (Oregon Catholic Press), coauthor of the *When Children Gather* series (GIA Publications, Inc.), and a contributor to *Sourcebook for Sundays, Seasons and Weekdays 2012 & 2013* (Liturgy Training Publications). Her experiences include eight summers in Lithuania leading seminars for religion teachers. Margaret Burk has a masters of arts degree in communication from Michigan State University and has done additional study at Catholic Theological Union. She completed three hundred hours of certification in the Catechesis of the Good Shepherd training and has been a catechist for over twenty years.

ABOUT THE ARTISTS AND THE ART

The cover art is by illustrator Mikela Prevost. Prevost received her BA in painting from the University of Redlands, California, and her MFA from California State Fullerton. She and her husband have three children. Much of her work focuses on children, making her a fitting artist for this book. Her artistic rendering of children leading prayer and praying together in the classroom captures the spirit and intent of this annual resource.

The interior art is by Paula Wiggins, who lives and works in Cincinnati. At the top of the page for each day's prayer, you will find a little picture that reflects on the liturgical time. During Ordinary Time in the autumn, a sturdy mustard tree with tiny seeds blowing from it reminds us of the parable of the mustard seed. For Advent we find the familiar Advent wreath. During the short season of Christmas Time, there is a manger scene with sheep and a dove.

As we begin counting Ordinary Time, we find an oyster shell with pearls—an image for the parable of the pearl of great price. During Lent, bare branches remind us of this time of living simply, without decoration and distraction, so that we can feel God's presence. During Easter Time, we find the empty tomb in the early dawn of the first Easter. And as we return to Ordinary Time after Pentecost, a beautiful grape vine reminds us of Jesus' parable of the vine and the branches.

At the beginning of each new liturgical time, special art accompanies the Grace before Meals and Prayer at Day's End, and you will find appropriate scenes for the various prayer services throughou the year. Finally, notice the harps accompanying the psalms, reminding us that these prayers were originally sung. The incense on the pages of canticles pictures the way we want our prayers to rise to God.

A NOTE ABOUT COPIES

As a purchaser of this book, you have permission to duplicate only the Reproducible Psalms pages, the Grace before Meals and Prayer at Day's End pages, the Prayer Services, and the Home Prayer pages; these copies may be used only with your class or group; and the Home Prayer pages may be used only in the students' households. You may not duplicate the psalms or prayers unless you are using them with this book. Other parts of this book may not be duplicated without the permission of Liturgy Training Publications or the copyright holders listed on the copyright page.

INSTRUCTIONS FOR PRAYER FOR THE DAY AND WEEK

FOR THE WHOLE GROUP

All of us participate in the prayer each day by lifting our hearts and voices to God. When the leader begins a Scripture passage by saying, "A reading from the holy Gospel according to . . . ," we respond "Glory to you, O Lord." At the conclusion of the Gospel, we say, "Praise to you, Lord Jesus Christ." At the conclusion of other Scripture readings, we say, "Thanks be to God." We offer our prayers and our intentions to God. When we conclude a prayer we say, "Amen."

Amen means: "Yes! I believe it is true!" Let your "Amen" be heard by all.

FOR THE LEADER

1. Find the correct page and read it silently. Parts in bold black type are for everyone. All others are for you alone.

2. Practice reading your part aloud, and pronounce every syllable clearly. The parts marked with ◆ and ✚ are instructions for what to do. Follow the instructions but do not read them or the headings aloud. If you stumble over a word, repeat it until you can say it smoothly.

3. Pause after "A reading from the holy Gospel according to . . . " so the class can respond. Pause again after "The Gospel of the Lord." Remember to allow for silence when the instructions call for it, especially after the Gospel and after reading the questions "For Silent Reflection."

4. Pause after "Let us bring our hopes and needs to God . . . " so that individuals may offer their prayers aloud or in silence. After each petition, the group responds, "Lord, hear our prayer."

5. When you make the Sign of the Cross, use your right hand and do it slowly and reverently, first touching your forehead ("In the name of the Father"), next just below your chest ("and of the Son"), then your left shoulder ("and of the Holy Spirit"), and finally your right shoulder ("Amen").

6. At prayer time, stand in the front of the class straight and tall. Ask the students to use their reproducible sheet of psalms for reading their part. Read slowly and clearly.

IF THERE ARE TWO LEADERS

One leader reads the Reading or Gospel while the other reads all of the other parts. Practice reading your part(s). Both leaders should stand in front of the class during the entire prayer.

Remember to read very slowly, with a loud, clear voice.

ORDINARY TIME, AUTUMN

Psalm for Sunday, August 12—Friday, September 21

Psalm 66:1–3a, 5, 8, 16–17

LEADER: Make a joyful noise to God, all the earth.

ALL: **Make a joyful noise to God, all the earth.**

LEADER: Make a joyful noise to God, all the earth;
sing the glory of his name;
give to him glorious praise.
Say to God, "How awesome are
your deeds!"

ALL: **Make a joyful noise to God, all the earth.**

Short version: use above only; Long version: use above and below.

SIDE A: Come and see what God has done;
he is awesome in his deeds
among mortals.
Bless our God, you peoples;
let the sound of his praise be heard.

SIDE B: Come and hear, all you who fear God,
and I will tell you what
he has done for me.
I cried aloud to him,
And he was extolled with my tongue.

ALL: **Make a joyful noise to God, all the earth.**

ORDINARY TIME, AUTUMN

Psalm for Sunday, September 23—Friday, October 19

Psalm 145:2–3, 4–5, 10–11

LEADER: I will praise your name for ever, LORD.

ALL: **I will praise your name for ever, LORD.**

LEADER: Every day will I bless you,

and I will praise your name for ever
and ever.
Great is the LORD and greatly
to be praised;
his greatness is unsearchable.

ALL: **I will praise your name for ever, LORD.**

Short version: use above only; Long version: use above and below.

SIDE A: One generation shall laud your works
to another, and shall declare your
mighty acts.
On the glorious splendor of your majesty,
and on your wondrous works,
I will meditate.

SIDE B: All your works shall give thanks to you,
O LORD, and all your faithful shall
bless you.
They shall speak of the glory of your
kingdom, and tell of your power.

ALL: **I will praise your name for ever, LORD.**

CHILDREN'S DAILY PRAYER 2018–2019 © 2018 Archdiocese of Chicago: Liturgy Training Publications, 3949 South Racine Avenue, Chicago IL 60609. All rights reserved. Orders: 800-933-1800 or www.LTP.org. Scripture excerpts are taken from *The New Revised Standard Version Bible: Catholic Edition,* © 1989, Division of Christian Education of the National Council of the Churches of Christ in the United States of America. Used with permission. All rights reserved.

ORDINARY TIME, AUTUMN; ADVENT

ORDINARY TIME, AUTUMN

Psalm for Sunday, October 21—Friday, November 30

Psalm 98:1, 2–3, 3–4

LEADER: The LORD has made known his victory.

ALL: **The LORD has made known his victory.**

LEADER: O sing to the LORD a new song,
  for he has done marvelous things.
  His right hand and his holy arm have
  gained him victory.

ALL: **The LORD has made known his victory.**

Short version: use above only; Long version: use above and below.

SIDE A: The LORD has made known his victory;
  he has revealed his vindication in the
  sight of the nations.
  He has remembered his steadfast love
  and faithfulness to the house of Israel.

SIDE B: All the ends of the earth have seen the
  victory of our God.
  Make a joyful noise to the LORD,
  all the earth; break forth into joyous
  song and sing praises.

ALL: **The LORD has made known his victory.**

ADVENT

Psalm for Sunday, December 2—Sunday, December 23

Psalm 85:4a, 8, 10–11, 12–13

LEADER: Restore us again,
  O God of our salvation!

ALL: **Restore us again,
  O God of our salvation!**

LEADER: Let me hear what God the LORD
  will speak,
  for he will speak peace to his people,
  to his faithful, to those who turn to
  him in their hearts.

ALL: **Restore us again, O God of our
  salvation!**

Short version: use above only; Long version: use above and below.

SIDE A: Steadfast love and faithfulness will meet;
  righteousness and peace will kiss
  each other.
  Faithfulness will spring up from
  the ground,
  and righteousness will look down
  from the sky.

SIDE B: The LORD will give what is good,
  and our land will yield its increase.
  Righteousness will go before him,
  and will make a path for his steps.

ALL: **Restore us again,
  O God of our salvation!**

 CHILDREN'S DAILY PRAYER 2018–2019 © 2018 Archdiocese of Chicago: Liturgy Training Publications, 3949 South Racine Avenue, Chicago, IL 60609. All rights reserved. Orders: 800-933-1800 or www.LTP.org. Scripture excerpts are taken from *The New Revised Standard Version Bible: Catholic Edition,* ©1989, Division of Christian Education of the National Council of the Churches of Christ in the United States of America. Used with permission. All rights reserved.

REPRODUCIBLE PSALMS
CHRISTMAS TIME; ORDINARY TIME, WINTER

CHRISTMAS TIME

Psalm for Sunday, January 6—Sunday, January 13

Psalm 96:1–2a, 2b–3, 5b–6, 11a

LEADER: Let the heavens be glad and the
earth rejoice!

ALL: **Let the heavens be glad and the
earth rejoice!**

LEADER: Sing to the LORD a new song;
sing to the LORD, all the earth.
Sing to the LORD; bless his name.

ALL: **Let the heavens be glad and the
earth rejoice!**

Short version: use above only; Long version: use above and below.

SIDE A: Tell of his salvation from day to day.

Declare his glory among the nations,
his marvelous works among all
the peoples.

SIDE B: The LORD made the heavens.
Honor and majesty are before him;
strength and beauty are in his sanctuary.

ALL: **Let the heavens be glad and the
earth rejoice!**

ORDINARY TIME, WINTER

Psalm for Monday, January 14—Tuesday, March 5

Psalm 23:1–3a, 3b–4, 5, 6

LEADER: I shall dwell in the house of the LORD my
whole life long.

ALL: **I shall dwell in the house of the LORD my
whole life long.**

LEADER: The LORD is my shepherd,
I shall not want.
He makes me lie down in
green pastures;
he leads me beside still waters;
he restores my soul.

ALL: **I shall dwell in the house of the LORD my
whole life long.**

Short version: use above only; Long version: use above and below.

SIDE A: He leads me in right paths
for his name's sake.
Even though I walk through the
darkest valley,
I fear no evil; for you are with me;
your rod and your staff—
they comfort me.

SIDE B: You prepare a table before me
in the presence of my enemies;
you anoint my head with oil;
my cup overflows.

ALL: **I shall dwell in the house of the LORD my
whole life long.**

CHILDREN'S DAILY PRAYER 2018–2019 © 2018 Archdiocese of Chicago: Liturgy Training Publications, 3949 South Racine Avenue, Chicago IL 60609. All rights reserved. Orders: 800-933-1800 or www.LTP.org. Scripture excerpts are taken from *The New Revised Standard Version Bible: Catholic Edition*, © 1989, Division of Christian Education of the National Council of the Churches of Christ in the United States of America. Used with permission. All rights reserved.

REPRODUCIBLE PSALMS
LENT; EASTER TIME

LENT

Psalm for Wednesday, March 6—Wednesday, April 17

Psalm 34:4–5, 6–7, 16–17, 18–19

LEADER: The LORD saves the crushed in spirit.

ALL: **The LORD saves the crushed in spirit.**

LEADER: I sought the LORD, and he answered me,
and delivered me from all my fears.
Look to him, and be radiant;
so your faces shall never be ashamed.

ALL: **The LORD saves the crushed in spirit.**

Short version: use above only; Long version: use above and below.

SIDE A: This poor soul cried, and was heard by
the LORD,
and was saved from every trouble.
The angel of the LORD encamps
around those who fear him, and
delivers them.

SIDE B: The face of the LORD is against evildoers,
to cut off the remembrance of them
from the earth.
When the righteous cry for help,
the LORD hears,
and rescues them from all
their troubles.

ALL: **The LORD saves the crushed in spirit.**

LEADER: The LORD is near to the brokenhearted,
and saves the crushed in spirit.
Many are the afflictions of the righteous,
but the LORD rescues them from
them all.

ALL: **The LORD saves the crushed in spirit.**

EASTER TIME

Psalm for Sunday, April 21—Friday, May 10

Psalm 105:1–2, 3–4, 6–7

LEADER: Let the hearts of those who seek the
LORD rejoice.

ALL: **Let the hearts of those who seek the
LORD rejoice.**

LEADER: O give thanks to the LORD, call on
his name,
make known his deeds among
the peoples.
Sing to him, sing praises to him;
tell of all his wonderful works.

ALL: **Let the hearts of those who seek
the LORD rejoice.**

Short version: use above only; Long version: use above and below.

SIDE A: Glory in his holy name;
let the hearts of those who seek the
LORD rejoice.
Seek the LORD and his strength;
seek his presence continually.

SIDE B: O offspring of his servant Abraham,
children of Jacob, his chosen ones.
He is the LORD our God;
his judgments are in all the earth.

ALL: **Let the hearts of those who seek
the LORD rejoice.**

CHILDREN'S DAILY PRAYER 2018–2019 © 2018 Archdiocese of Chicago: Liturgy Training Publications, 3949 South Racine Avenue, Chicago, IL 60609. All rights reserved. Orders: 800-933-1800 or www.LTP.org. Scripture excerpts are taken from *The New Revised Standard Version Bible: Catholic Edition*, © 1989, Division of Christian Education of the National Council of the Churches of Christ in the United States of America. Used with permission. All rights reserved.

EASTER TIME

Psalm for Sunday, May 12—Sunday, June 9

Psalm 118:1–2, 4, 22–24, 25–27a

LEADER: The stone that the builders rejected
has become the chief cornerstone.

ALL: **The stone that the builders rejected
has become the chief cornerstone.**

LEADER: O give thanks to the LORD, for he is good;
his steadfast love endures forever!
Let Israel say,
"His steadfast love endures forever."
Let those who fear the LORD say,
"His steadfast love endures forever."

ALL: **The stone that the builders rejected
has become the chief cornerstone.**

Short version: use above only; Long version: use above and below.

SIDE A: The stone that the builders rejected
has become the chief cornerstone.
This is the LORD's doing;
it is marvelous in our eyes.
This is the day that the LORD has made;
let us rejoice and be glad in it.

SIDE B: Save us, we beseech you, O LORD!
O LORD, we beseech you,
give us success!
Blessed is the one who comes in the name
of the LORD.
We bless you from the house
of the LORD.
The LORD is God,
and he has given us light.

ALL: **The stone that the builders rejected
has become the chief cornerstone.**

ORDINARY TIME, SUMMER

Psalm for Monday, June 10—Friday, June 21

Psalm 85:8–9, 10–11, 12–13

LEADER: The LORD speaks of peace to his people.

ALL: **The LORD speaks of peace to his people.**

LEADER: Let me hear what God the LORD
will speak,
for he will speak peace to his people,
to his faithful, to those who turn to
him in their hearts.
Surely his salvation is at hand for those
who fear him,
that his glory may dwell in our land.

ALL: **The LORD speaks of peace to his people.**

Short version: use above only; Long version: use above and below.

SIDE A: Steadfast love and faithfulness will meet;
righteousness and peace will kiss
each other.
Faithfulness will spring up from
the ground,
and righteousness will look down
from the sky.

SIDE B: The LORD will give what is good,
and our land will yield its increase.
Righteousness will go before him,
and will make a path for his steps.

ALL: **The LORD speaks of peace to his people.**

CHILDREN'S DAILY PRAYER 2018–2019 © 2018 Archdiocese of Chicago: Liturgy Training Publications, 3949 South Racine Avenue, Chicago IL 60609. All rights reserved. Orders: 800-933-1800 or www.LTP.org. Scripture excerpts are taken from *The New Revised Standard Version Bible: Catholic Edition,* © 1989, Division of Christian Education of the National Council of the Churches of Christ in the United States of America. Used with permission. All rights reserved.

ORDINARY TIME AUTUMN

SUNDAY, AUGUST 12 — FRIDAY, NOVEMBER 30

AUTUMN ORDINARY TIME

THE MEANING OF ORDINARY TIME

Times and seasons on our liturgical calendar, in contrast to the secular calendar, are valued in a different, altogether new way. Our Christian calendar even has a different shape! Instead of a rectangle, we draw all the days of a year in a circle. Instead of marking off times according to the weather, we celebrate those great moments when God reveals a great love for us in marvelous and mysterious ways.

Our liturgical calendar has four primary seasons. Advent (the four weeks before Christmas); Christmas; Lent (the six weeks before Easter); Easter (which extends for fifty days after Easter through Pentecost) but, the longest part of the calendar is called Ordinary Time.

Ordinary Time is thirty-three or thirty-four weeks a year. It is called "Ordinary Time" because the weeks are numbered. The Latin word *ordinalis*, which refers to numbers in a series and stems from the Latin word *ordo*, from which we get the English word *order*. Ordinary time is therefore "ordered time." Calling it "Ordered Time" reminds us of God's great plan for creation. There was a specific time for the creation of light, planets, water, earth, plants, animals, and humankind. Ordinary Time begins after Christmas, continues until Ash Wednesday when it stops for Lent and Easter, then picks up again after Pentecost Sunday and runs through the summer and autumn until the beginning of Advent. Each Sunday in Ordinary Time has a number and the numbers increase each week.

During autumn Ordinary Time, there are weekly themes for the Scripture readings. Some of the themes help us to understand qualities of our faith: importance of community, friendship, keeping the Sabbath holy, prayer, service and the great commandment to love God and love one another. In these weeks, the readings cover a historical spectrum of Scripture.

From the New Testament, we will read parables or stories that Jesus told. With moral parables in week twenty-one, like The Sower, The Wicked Tenants, and The Barren Fig Tree, Jesus teaches us about the consequences of our behavior.

From the Old Testament we will read beautiful passages about Wisdom in the Book of Sirach. We will read from the Book of Genesis and wonder at the marvelous story of Creation. We will spend three weeks on the story of Moses who was one of the greatest heroes in the Old Testament. God chose Moses to lead the Hebrew people out of slavery in Egypt. During their escape and on their long journey through the deserts, the people met many challenges: the Egyptian army, lack of food and water, hostile tribes. But God was always with them and taking care of them. One of the greatest gifts God gave to the Hebrew people and to people of all time is the Gift of the Law: the Ten Commandments, which give clear instructions on how people can live together in peace.

As we come to the end of Ordinary Time and prepare for Advent in the thirty-third and thirty fourth weeks, the theme is, "Who is Jesus?" Jesus is: Messiah, Savior of Israel, Son of Man, Lord of the Sabbath, Teacher and Healer, Good Shepherd, and Christ the King!

PREPARING TO CELEBRATE ORDINARY TIME IN THE CLASSROOM

SACRED SPACE

You want the prayer table or space to be in a place where the children will see it often and perhaps go to it in their free moments. If you can have a separate prayer table it should not be too small, perhaps a coffee table size. You may wish to buy one or two inexpensive cushions to place before your prayer table so that children will feel invited to sit or kneel there. The essential things for the prayer table are a cross or crucifix (unless one is on the wall), a Bible, a substantial candle and a cloth of liturgical color. Cover the prayer table with a plain green cloth or one that mixes green with other Autumn colors. Large table napkins or placemats work, or remnants from a sewing store. Green, the color of hope and life, is the color of Ordinary Time. If you can, set the Bible on a bookstand. Point out the candle beside the Bible, and remind them that Jesus said, "I am the Light of the world" (John 8:12). You might light the candle, open the Bible, and read that verse to the class. Other objects you might want to include are a simple statue of Mary (September 8), images of angels (Archangels, September 29 and Guardian, October 2), an image of St. Francis or the children's pets (October 4), a rosary (October 7). Use natural objects, too, like flowers, dried leaves or small gourds. If there is the space, pictures of loved ones who have died would be appropriate in November.

MOVEMENT AND GESTURE

Consider reverencing the Word of God in the Bible by carrying it in procession. Place a candle ahead of it and perhaps carry wind chimes as it moves through the room. At the prayer space the processors turn and the Bible is raised. The class reverences with a profound bow (a bow from the waist) then the bible and candle are placed and the chimes are silenced. Also consider reverencing the Crucifix or a Cross near September 14, the Triumph of the Cross. Take the crucifix from the wall (or use another one) and carry it in procession at the beginning of prayer in a similar manner or take the cross to each child and let them kiss it or hold it or make a head bow before it.

FESTIVITY IN SCHOOL AND HOME

For Ordinary Time in autumn, *Children's Daily Prayer* provides several special prayer services to use in the classroom—or with larger groups like the whole school—to celebrate the beginning of the school year, to pray for peace (on September 11) and to honor Our Lady of the Rosary (October 7). The Home Prayer pages can be duplicated for the students to take home and share with their families: Morning Prayer for Families Departing for the Day; Home Prayer for All Saints and All Souls, called Celebrating the Saints; Remembering the Dead; and a Meal Prayer for Thanksgiving. At the end of this time you will find a Home Prayer page for praying with an Advent wreath. It's placed at the end of Ordinary Time so you won't forget to send it home with the students *before* the First Sunday of Advent.

SACRED MUSIC

One of the best ways to help the children enter into the special qualities of this or any liturgical time is by teaching them the Sunday music of their parish. Teach the children (or invite the school music teacher, parish music director or a choir member/ cantor to do it) how your church sings her "Alleluia!" See what songs and hymns the children know and love. For example, in Ordinary Time, consider "For the Beauty of the Earth," and "Make Me a Channel

of Your Peace." Learn and sing just a good refrain. Singing is an integral part of how we pray.

PRAYERS FOR ORDINARY TIME

During this season, take some time to discuss the meaning of the various intercessions of the Our Father with the children in your class. In particular, discuss the Kingdom of God—that time of peace and justice proclaimed by and fulfilled in Jesus. Ask what it means for God's Kingdom to come. Go through the prayer one intercession at a time asking what each means. Explore with them what Jesus is teaching us about how we should pray: We ask for God's name to be treated as blessed and holy, for the coming of the Kingdom of God, for God's will to be accomplished on earth, for our "daily bread," for forgiveness, and for strength in the face of temptation.

A NOTE TO CATECHISTS

Because you meet with your students once a week, you may wish to use the Prayer for the Week pages. These weekly prayer pages contain an excerpt from the Sunday Gospel and will help to prepare the children for Mass. Sometimes, though, you may wish to substitute the Prayer for the Day if it falls on an important solemnity, feast, or memorial of the Church (Our Lady of the Rosary, October 7, for example). In this introduction, you will see the suggestions for your prayer space. You may have to set up a prayer space each time you meet with your group. Think in advance about where to place it, have all your materials in one box and always set it up in the same place.

GRACE BEFORE MEALS

FOR ORDINARY TIME • AUTUMN

LEADER:

Lord, you gift us with your love in so many ways.

ALL: We praise you and thank you!

✠ All make the Sign of the Cross.

In the name of the Father, and of the Son, and of the Holy Spirit. Amen.

LEADER:

Father, Son, and Spirit,
you bring us joy
through your abundant grace.
As we gather to share this meal,
may we be grateful for the
loving people who prepared it
every step of the way.
We thank all those in lands far from us
and those nearby who
helped grow, nurture, package,
transport, store, and cook our food.
We bless these brothers and sisters
as we bless each other here,
for you created all of us in
your image of goodness and love.
May this meal nourish our bodies
to give you glory and to build your Kingdom.
We ask this through Jesus Christ, our Lord.

ALL: Amen.

✠ All make the Sign of the Cross.

In the name of the Father, and of the Son, and of the Holy Spirit. Amen.

PRAYER AT DAY'S END

FOR ORDINARY TIME • AUTUMN

LEADER:

God of all wisdom,
we offer back to you
all that we have done today
through the gift of your gentle Spirit.

ALL: For your love is in our hearts!

✝ All make the Sign of the Cross.

In the name of the Father, and of the Son, and of the Holy Spirit. Amen.

LEADER:

We are grateful for
the signs and wonders of this day,
for the ordinary events and its surprises,
big and small.
We thank you for the
loving people who surround us.
May we continue to reflect your goodness
to others in your name.
We ask this through your beloved Son, Jesus.

ALL: Amen.

✝ All make the Sign of the Cross.

In the name of the Father, and of the Son, and of the Holy Spirit. Amen.

PRAYER SERVICE
BEGINNING OF THE YEAR FOR SCHOOL STAFF

Seek volunteers to lead this prayer service. You may involve up to seven leaders (as marked below). The fourth leader will need a Bible for the Scripture passage. Choose hymns for the beginning and ending if you wish.

FIRST LEADER:

We gather in Christ's name
to celebrate all of God's children.
Let us ask the Holy Spirit for guidance
as we begin our journey again with them.

◆ Gesture for all to stand.

Together we enter this time of prayer as we make the Sign of the Cross.

✝ All make the Sign of the Cross.

> **In the name of the Father, and of the Son, and of the Holy Spirit. Amen.**

SECOND LEADER:

Spirit of God,
enlighten our minds
as we begin another school year, for
these children are gifts of new life.
Draw us closer to all
that is good and true
so that through us
all that they see
is you.
We ask this through Christ our Lord.

Amen.

THIRD LEADER:

Spirit of your Son Jesus,
grant us your wisdom and
integrity each and every day,
for you are the breath of all
that is holy.

CHILDREN'S DAILY PRAYER 2018–2019, © 2018 Archdiocese of Chicago: Liturgy Training Publications. All rights reserved. Orders: 800-933-1800 or www.LTP.org.

Refresh us with ideas that
inspire our youth with your energy
and enthusiasm.
We ask this in Christ's name.

Amen.

◆ Gesture for all to sit.

FOURTH LEADER: Romans 8:31b–35, 37–39
A reading from the Letter of Paul to Romans.

◆ Read the Scripture passage from the Bible.

The Word of the Lord.

◆ All observe silence.

FIFTH LEADER:

◆ Gesture for all to stand.

Let us bring our hopes and needs to God as we pray from the Opening Prayer of our Church leadership as they embarked on the Second Vatican Council. Our response will be: **Guide us with your love.**

For light and strength to know your will,
to make it our own,
and to live it in our lives,
we pray to the Lord.

ALL: Guide us with your love.

For justice for all;
enable us to uphold the rights of others;
do not allow us to be misled by ignorance
or corrupted by fear or favor,
we pray to the Lord.

ALL: Guide us with your love.

Unite us to yourself in the bond of love
and keep us faithful to all that is true,
we pray to the Lord.

ALL: Guide us with your love.

May we temper justice with love,
so that all our discussions and reflections
may be pleasing to you, and earn the reward
promised to good and faithful servants,
we pray to the Lord.

ALL: Guide us with your love.

SIXTH LEADER:
Let us pray as Jesus taught us:
Our Father . . . Amen.

◆ Pause and then say:
Let us offer one another the sign of
Christ's peace.

◆ All offer one another a sign of peace.

SEVENTH LEADER:
Let us pray:
God, our Creator,
your presence through the
Holy Spirit strengthens us
for the days ahead.
Guide us with your patience
and compassion as we
mentor our future leaders in Christ.

Amen.

✝ All make the Sign of the Cross.

In the name of the Father, and of the Son, and of the Holy Spirit. Amen.

PRAYER SERVICE
BEGINNING OF THE YEAR FOR STUDENTS

This prayer service may be led by the eighth grade students or by older students. The third and fifth leaders will need a Bible for the passages from Matthew and Luke. Take time to help the third and fifth leaders practice the readings. You may wish to sing "This Little Light of Mine" as the opening and closing songs. If the group will sing, prepare someone to lead the songs.

FIRST LEADER:
We are embarking on a journey together
in this brand new school year.
As we look ahead at all that this year
might reveal,
let us remember Jesus,
who will walk beside us every step of the way.

SONG LEADER:
Let us begin by singing the first few verses of
our song.

◆ Gesture for all to stand, and lead the first few
verses of the song.

SECOND LEADER:

✢ All make the Sign of the Cross.

**In the name of the Father, and of the
Son, and of the Holy Spirit. Amen.**

Let us pray:
God our Creator,
we were made in
your image and likeness.
Help us to be gentle with
ourselves and each other
as we mature this year with your grace.

CHILDREN'S DAILY PRAYER 2018–2019, © 2018 Archdiocese of Chicago: Liturgy Training Publications. All rights reserved. Orders: 800-933-1800 or www.LTP.org.

Guide us in our studies and help us develop
with knowledge and maturity.
We ask this through Christ our Lord.

Amen.

> ◆ Remain standing and sing Alleluia.

THIRD LEADER: Matthew 5:14–16
A reading from the holy Gospel according
to Matthew.

> ◆ Read the Gospel passage from the Bible.

The Gospel of the Lord.

> ◆ All sit and observe silence.

FOURTH LEADER:

> ◆ Gesture for all to stand.

Let us bring our hopes and needs to God as we
pray, Let your light shine through us.

ALL: Let your light shine through us.

Help us to show honor and respect
to all those who teach and coach us,
we pray to the Lord.

ALL: Let your light shine through us.

Guide us with your counsel, Lord,
when we are frustrated with our studies,
we pray to the Lord.

ALL: Let your light shine through us.

Help us to take care of our
minds and bodies
so that we give you glory in
everything we do,
we pray to the Lord.

ALL: Let your light shine through us.

Help us to remember all that we learn
so that we can apply it to our lives
in the months and years ahead,
we pray to the Lord.

ALL: Let your light shine through us.

FIFTH LEADER: Luke 6:31–36
Let us listen to what Jesus teaches
to his disciples:

A reading from the holy Gospel according
to Luke.

> ◆ Read the Gospel passage from the Bible.

The Gospel of the Lord.

SIXTH LEADER:
Let us pray:
O God,
we know you are with us on this journey.
Help us to love one another
as you love us.
Guide us with your light of mercy and justice.
May we be considerate with our friends
and respectful of all who lead us.
Help us to learn and grow in your
wisdom throughout this year.
We ask this through Christ our Lord.

Amen.

> ✝ All make the Sign of the Cross.
>
> **In the name of the Father, and of the
> Son, and of the Holy Spirit. Amen.**

SONG LEADER:
Please join in singing the final verses of our
closing song.

HOME PRAYER
MORNING PRAYER FOR FAMILIES DEPARTING FOR THE DAY

The Catechism of the Catholic Church calls the family the "domestic church" where children are first introduced to the faith (CCC, 2204 and 2225). A blessing is a prayer that acknowledges and thanks God for the good things in our lives and asks God to be with us. When the household gathers in the morning, perhaps at breakfast, a parent, grandparent, or other adult may lead this blessing.

The longer prayer can be used on one of the first days of school and other special occasions. At other times, you may just want to bless the child with the Sign of the Cross on the forehead and a "God bless you" as he or she leaves for school.

✚ All make the Sign of the Cross.

In the name of the Father, and of the Son, and of the Holy Spirit. Amen.

LEADER:

We each have important things
to do today, and so we ask God's blessing.
We go to school and to work.
We learn and play.
We praise and thank God for each other
and for the love we share.
We ask God to be with those
who are lonely or sick
or without basic needs.
We ask this in Jesus' name.

All: Amen.

LEADER:

Holy God,
giver of all good gifts,
walk with us today,
guide our words and our actions,
and keep us on the path of truth.
Bring us back together in peace
at the end of this day.
We ask this through Christ our Lord.

✚ The Leader makes the Sign of the Cross on one person's forehead saying:

"God bless you and keep you today."

ALL: Amen.

CHILDREN'S DAILY PRAYER 2018–2019, © 2018 Archdiocese of Chicago: Liturgy Training Publications, 3949 South Racine Avenue, Chicago, IL 60609. All rights reserved. Orders: 800-933-1800 or www.LTP.org. Scripture excerpts are taken from *The New Revised Standard Version Bible: Catholic Edition*, Division of Christian Education of the National Council of the Churches of Christ in the United States of America. Used with permission. All rights reserved.

PRAYER FOR THE WEEK
WITH A READING FROM THE GOSPEL FOR **SUNDAY, AUGUST 12, 2018**

OPENING

Today we hear Jesus say that he is the "bread of life." Bread is essential nourishment for people all over the world. By comparing himself to bread, Jesus reveals that he is essential to our spiritual life and to the life of the world. By following his example, listening to his Word, and receiving him in Holy Communion, we nourish our spiritual life and we help to bring his life to everyone around us.

◆ All make the Sign of the Cross.

In the name of the Father, and of the Son, and of the Holy Spirit. Amen.

PSALM   (For a longer psalm, see page xi.) Psalm 66:1–3a

Make a joyful noise to God, all the earth.

Make a joyful noise to God, all the earth.

Make a joyful noise to God, all the earth;
   sing praise to the glory of his name;
   give to him glorious praise.
Say to God, "How awesome are your deeds!"

Make a joyful noise to God, all the earth.

◆ All stand and sing **Alleluia.**

GOSPEL   John 6:47–51

A reading from the holy Gospel according to John.

Jesus said, "Very truly, I tell you, whoever believes has eternal life. I am the bread of life. Your ancestors ate the manna in the wilderness, and they died. This is the bread that comes down from heaven, so that one may eat of it and not die. I am the living bread that came down from heaven. Whoever eats of this bread will live forever; and the bread that I will give for the life of the world is my flesh."

The Gospel of the Lord.

◆ All sit and observe silence.

FOR SILENT REFLECTION

Think about this silently in your heart. How are you nourished when you when you pray or when you receive Holy Communion?

CLOSING PRAYER

Let us pray to God for our needs and the needs of others: our family, neighborhood, and the world. For each need we say, "Lord, hear our prayer."

◆ All may add their own prayers here.

Let us pray: **Our Father . . . Amen.**

Holy God, we thank you for Jesus,
who cares for us
and gives us all that we need.
Help us to receive his love and his life.
Help us to bring his life to others, so that
we all may live in happiness and peace.
We ask this in Jesus' name.

Amen.

◆ All make the Sign of the Cross.

PRAYER FOR
MONDAY, AUGUST 13, 2018

OPENING

This week we look at what the Bible tells us about forming a good community. A community is a group of people who share something in common. As we begin the school year, we are a community of students, teachers, staff, and parents who seek to be helpful and caring toward each other.

✚ All make the Sign of the Cross.

In the name of the Father, and of the Son, and of the Holy Spirit. Amen.

PSALM
(For a longer psalm, see page xi.) Psalm 66:1–3a

Make a joyful noise to God, all the earth.

Make a joyful noise to God, all the earth.

Make a joyful noise to God, all the earth;
  sing praise to the glory of his name;
  give to him glorious praise.
Say to God, "How awesome are your deeds!"

Make a joyful noise to God, all the earth.

◆ All stand and sing **Alleluia.**

GOSPEL
Mark 3:13a, 14, 19b–20, 31–35

A reading from the holy Gospel according to Mark.

Jesus went up the mountain and called to him those whom he wanted. And he appointed twelve, whom he also named apostles, to be with him, and to be sent out to proclaim the message. Then he went home; and the crowd came together again, so that they could not even eat. Then his mother and his brothers came; and standing outside, they sent to him and called him. A crowd was sitting around him; and they said to him, "Your mother and your brothers and sisters are outside, asking for you." And he replied, "Who are my mother and my brothers?" And looking at those who sat around him, he said, "Here are my mother and my brothers! Whoever does the will of God is my brother and sister and mother."

The Gospel of the Lord.

◆ All sit and observe silence.

FOR SILENT REFLECTION

Think about this silently in your heart. Jesus made everyone feel welcome. How can you do that?

CLOSING PRAYER

Let us pray to God for our needs and the needs of others: our family, neighborhood, and the world. For each need we say, "Lord, hear our prayer."

◆ All may add their own prayers here.

Let us pray: **Our Father . . . Amen.**

Holy God, make us a community
who care for one another,
share with those in need,
and proclaim your love to all.
We ask this in Jesus' name.

Amen.

✚ All make the Sign of the Cross.

OPENING

The early Christians were a close community. They "had all things in common," which means they shared everything equally. Today is the memorial of St. Maximilian Kolbe, a Polish Franciscan who hid Jews from the Nazis. When he was arrested and placed in a concentration camp he volunteered to die in place of another man who had a wife and children.

✛ All make the Sign of the Cross.

In the name of the Father, and of the Son, and of the Holy Spirit. Amen.

PSALM
(For a longer psalm, see page xi.) Psalm 66:1–3a

Make a joyful noise to God, all the earth.

Make a joyful noise to God, all the earth.

Make a joyful noise to God, all the earth;
    sing praise to the glory of his name;
    give to him glorious praise.
Say to God, "How awesome are your deeds!"

Make a joyful noise to God, all the earth.

READING
Acts 2:38, 43–47

A reading from the Acts of the Apostles.

Peter said to them, "Repent, and be baptized every one of you in the name of Jesus Christ so that your sins may be forgiven; and you will receive the gift of the Holy Spirit. Awe came upon everyone, because many wonders and signs were being done by the apostles. All who believed were together and had all things in common; they would sell their possessions and goods and distribute the proceeds to all, as any had need. Day by day, as they spent much time together in the temple, they broke bread at home and ate their food with glad and generous hearts, praising God and having the goodwill of all the people. And day by day the Lord added to their number those who were being saved.

The Word of the Lord.

◆ All observe silence.

FOR SILENT REFLECTION

Think about this silently in your heart. How well do you share with others in your class or family?

CLOSING PRAYER

Let us pray to God for our needs and the needs of others: our family, neighborhood, and the world. For each need we say, "Lord, hear our prayer."

◆ All may add their own prayers here.

Let us pray: **Our Father . . . Amen.**

Holy God, help us to be like the early Christians who praised you by sharing with one another and doing good and kind deeds.
May we be joyful and generous.
We ask this in Jesus' name.

Amen.

✛ All make the Sign of the Cross.

WEDNESDAY, AUGUST 15, 2018

OPENING

Today is the Solemnity of the Assumption of the Blessed Virgin Mary, a Holy Day of Obligation. We celebrate that Mary has gone before us, body and soul, into heaven. Mary said "yes!" to being Jesus' mother and to keeping God's commandment to love her neighbor as herself. Today we celebrate her with joy.

✛ All make the Sign of the Cross.

In the name of the Father, and of the Son, and of the Holy Spirit. Amen.

PSALM (For a longer psalm, see page xi.) Psalm 66:1–3a

Make a joyful noise to God, all the earth.

Make a joyful noise to God, all the earth.

Make a joyful noise to God, all the earth;
   sing praise to the glory of his name;
   give to him glorious praise.
Say to God, "How awesome are your deeds!"

Make a joyful noise to God, all the earth.

◆ All stand and sing **Alleluia.**

GOSPEL Luke 1:40–46

A reading from the holy Gospel according to Luke.

When Elizabeth had heard Mary's greeting, the infant leaped in her womb, and Elizabeth, filled with the Holy Spirit, cried out in a loud voice and said, "Most blessed are you among women, and blessed is the fruit of your womb. And how does it happen to me, that the mother of my Lord should come to me? For at the moment the sound of your greeting reached my ears, the infant in my womb leaped for joy. Blessed are you who believed that what was spoken to you by the Lord would be fulfilled."

And Mary said: "My soul proclaims the greatness of the Lord; my spirit rejoices in God my Savior."

The Gospel of the Lord.

◆ All sit and observe silence.

FOR SILENT REFLECTION

Think about this silently in your heart. How does Mary proclaim God's greatness?

CLOSING PRAYER

Let us pray to God for our needs and the needs of others: our family, neighborhood, and the world. For each need we say, "Lord, hear our prayer."

◆ All may add their own prayers here.

Let us pray: **Hail Mary, full of grace,**

the Lord is with you.
Blessed are you among women,
and blessed is the fruit of your womb, Jesus.

Amen.

✛ All make the Sign of the Cross.

OPENING

St. Paul is very specific about what the Ephesians [ee-FEE-zhuhnz] need to do as followers of Jesus to create a good community. He focuses on how they interact and treat each other. Listen to what he encourages them to do, and to what he says to avoid. His advice applies to us as well as to the early Christians.

✛ All make the Sign of the Cross.

In the name of the Father, and of the Son, and of the Holy Spirit. Amen.

PSALM (For a longer psalm, see page xi.) Psalm 66:1–3a

Make a joyful noise to God, all the earth.

Make a joyful noise to God, all the earth.

Make a joyful noise to God, all the earth;
   sing praise to the glory of his name;
   give to him glorious praise.
Say to God, "How awesome are your deeds!"

Make a joyful noise to God, all the earth.

READING Ephesians 4:25–27, 29–32

A reading from the Letter of Paul to the Ephesians.

So then, putting away falsehood, let all of us speak the truth to our neighbors, for we are members of one another. Be angry but do not sin; do not let the sun go down on your anger, and do not make room for the devil. Let no evil talk come out of your mouths, but only what is useful for building up, as there is need, so that your words may give grace to those who hear. And do not grieve the Holy Spirit of God, with which you were marked with a seal for the day of redemption. Put away from you all bitterness and wrath and anger and wrangling and slander, together with all malice, and be kind to one another, tenderhearted, forgiving one another, as God in Christ has forgiven you.

The Word of the Lord.

◆ All observe silence.

FOR SILENT REFLECTION

Think about this silently in your heart. What can you say or do to create community in your class?

CLOSING PRAYER

Let us pray to God for our needs and the needs of others: our family, neighborhood, and the world. For each need we say, "Lord, hear our prayer."

◆ All may add their own prayers here.

Let us pray: **Our Father . . . Amen.**

Holy God, make us a community
who care for one another,
share with those in need, and
proclaim your love to all.
We ask this in Jesus' name.

Amen.

✛ All make the Sign of the Cross.

PRAYER FOR
FRIDAY, AUGUST 17, 2018

OPENING

This week we have reflected on how a Christian community acts and cares for its members. It is not always easy to kind, or honest, or generous. St. Paul tells us to "stand firm in the Lord" and to rejoice in the hard work. He has confidence in the Ephesians [ee-FEE-zhuhnz], and God has confidence in us.

✚ All make the Sign of the Cross.

In the name of the Father, and of the Son, and of the Holy Spirit. Amen.

PSALM   (For a longer psalm, see page xi.) Psalm 66:1–3a

Make a joyful noise to God, all the earth.

Make a joyful noise to God, all the earth.

Make a joyful noise to God, all the earth;
  sing praise to the glory of his name;
  give to him glorious praise.
Say to God, "How awesome are your deeds!"

Make a joyful noise to God, all the earth.

READING   Philippians 4:1, 4–5a, 7–9

A reading from the Letter of Paul to the Philippians.

Therefore, my brothers and sisters, whom I love and long for, my joy and crown, stand firm in the Lord in this way, my beloved. Rejoice in the Lord always; again I will say, Rejoice. Let your gentleness be known to everyone. And the peace of God, which surpasses all understanding, will guard your hearts and your minds in Christ Jesus. Finally, beloved, whatever is true, whatever is honorable, whatever is just, whatever is pure, whatever is pleasing, whatever is

commendable, if there is any excellence and if there is anything worthy of praise, think about these things. Keep on doing the things that you have learned and received and heard and seen in me, and the God of peace will be with you.

The Word of the Lord.

◆ All observe silence.

FOR SILENT REFLECTION

Think about this silently in your heart. What have you learned this week about being a member of a Christian community?

CLOSING PRAYER

Let us pray to God for our needs and the needs of others: our family, neighborhood, and the world. For each need we say, "Lord, hear our prayer."

◆ All may add their own prayers here.

Let us pray: **Our Father . . . Amen.**

Holy God, we rejoice that you have called us to be your holy people.
May we always try to follow Jesus in our words and our actions.
We ask this in Jesus' name.

Amen.

✚ All make the Sign of the Cross.

OPENING

Bread, a common food, is an important part of our diet. Jesus uses the metaphor of bread to help people understand how necessary it is to have a relationship with him. He is our spiritual food. He nourishes us with his own life so that we will have eternal life with him and with the Father.

✛ All make the Sign of the Cross.

In the name of the Father, and of the Son, and of the Holy Spirit. Amen.

PSALM

(For a longer psalm, see page xi.) Psalm 66:1–3a

Make a joyful noise to God, all the earth.

Make a joyful noise to God, all the earth.

Make a joyful noise to God, all the earth;
sing praise to the glory of his name;
give to him glorious praise.
Say to God, "How awesome are your deeds!"

Make a joyful noise to God, all the earth.

◆ All stand and sing **Alleluia.**

GOSPEL

John 6:51, 56–57

A reading from the holy Gospel according to John.

Jesus said, "I am the living bread that came down from heaven. Whoever eats of this bread will live forever; and the bread that I will give for the life of the world is my flesh. Those who eat my flesh and drink my blood abide in me, and I in them. Just as the living Father sent me, and I live because of the Father, so whoever eats me will live because of me. This is the bread that came down from heaven, not like that which your ancestors ate, and they died. But the one who eats this bread will live forever."

The Gospel of the Lord.

◆ All sit and observe silence.

FOR SILENT REFLECTION

Think about this silently in your heart. Jesus says he will abide in us and we in him. Abide means "to remain." How can you remain in Jesus?

CLOSING PRAYER

Let us pray to God for our needs and the needs of others: our family, neighborhood, and the world. For each need we say, "Lord, hear our prayer."

◆ All may add their own prayers here.

Let us pray: **Our Father . . . Amen.**

Most loving God,
thank you for the gift of your Son Jesus
who revealed how close you are to us.
Keep us always in your care.
We ask this in Jesus' name.

Amen.

✛ All make the Sign of the Cross.

OPENING

This week we will look at the theme of being a friend. In today's reading from the Book of Exodus, we hear that God speaks to Moses like a friend. Today is the memorial of St. Bernard, a French abbot who wrote many important papers on the Church. He is called a "Doctor" or "wise teacher" of the Church.

✠ All make the Sign of the Cross.

In the name of the Father, and of the Son, and of the Holy Spirit. Amen.

PSALM (For a longer psalm, see page xi.) Psalm 66:1–3a

Make a joyful noise to God, all the earth.

Make a joyful noise to God, all the earth.

Make a joyful noise to God, all the earth;
   sing praise to the glory of his name;
   give to him glorious praise.
Say to God, "How awesome are your deeds!"

Make a joyful noise to God, all the earth.

READING Exodus 3 3:7a, 9–11b

A reading from the Book of Exodus.

Now Moses used to take the tent and pitch it outside the camp, far off from the camp; he called it the tent of meeting. When Moses entered the tent, the pillar of cloud would descend and stand at the entrance of the tent, and the LORD would speak with Moses. When all the people saw the pillar of cloud standing at the entrance of the tent, all the people would rise and bow down, all of them, at the entrance of the tent. Thus the LORD used to speak to Moses face to face, as one speaks to a friend.

The Word of the Lord.

◆ All observe silence.

FOR SILENT REFLECTION

Think about this silently in your heart. Why is it important to talk to a friend "face to face"?

CLOSING PRAYER

Let us pray to God for our needs and the needs of others: our family, neighborhood, and the world. For each need we say, "Lord, hear our prayer."

◆ All may add their own prayers here.

Let us pray: **Our Father . . . Amen.**

Most loving God,
we yearn for you to speak to us
as a friend.
We ask you to teach us how listen
and show us what to do and say
that will keep our friendship strong.
We ask this in Jesus' name.

Amen.

✠ All make the Sign of the Cross.

OPENING

Today is the memorial of Pope Pius X who lowered the age for First Communion from twelve years to seven years old. Our Scripture tells us that Holy Wisdom, a name for God, makes us "friends of God" and sometimes prophets! St. Pius listened to Holy Wisdom when he allowed younger children to receive Holy Communion.

✚ All make the Sign of the Cross.

In the name of the Father, and of the Son, and of the Holy Spirit. Amen.

PSALM   (For a longer psalm, see page xi.) Psalm 66:1–3a

Make a joyful noise to God, all the earth.

Make a joyful noise to God, all the earth.

Make a joyful noise to God, all the earth;
  sing praise to the glory of his name;
  give to him glorious praise.
Say to God, "How awesome are your deeds!"

Make a joyful noise to God, all the earth.

READING   Wisdom 7:7–9b, 10, 27de

A reading from the Book of Wisdom.

Therefore I prayed, and understanding was given me; I called on God, and the spirit of wisdom came to me. I preferred her to scepters and thrones, and I accounted wealth as nothing in comparison with her. Neither did I liken to her any priceless gem, because all gold is but a little sand in her sight. I loved her more than health and beauty, and I chose to have her rather than light because her radiance never ceases. She renews all things; in every genera-tion she passes into holy souls and makes them friends of God, and prophets.

The Word of the Lord.

◆ All observe silence.

FOR SILENT REFLECTION

Think about this silently in your heart. Who do you know who has great understanding and wisdom? What can you learn from that person?

CLOSING PRAYER

Let us pray to God for our needs and the needs of others: our family, neighborhood, and the world. For each need we say, "Lord, hear our prayer."

◆ All may add their own prayers here.

Let us pray: **Our Father . . . Amen.**

Holy Wisdom, we ask that you
come to us during this school year.
Help us to be good friends to one another.
Make us wise in our studies,
kind in our words and deeds,
and always open to your guidance.
We ask this in Jesus' name.

Amen.

✚ All make the Sign of the Cross.

OPENING

Like most of us, Jesus knew many people but had only a few very close friends. Among these good friends were Lazarus and his sisters, Mary and Martha. When Lazarus died Jesus came to his tomb. Jesus was overcome with sadness and cried.

✚ All make the Sign of the Cross.

In the name of the Father, and of the Son, and of the Holy Spirit. Amen.

PSALM   (For a longer psalm, see page xi.) Psalm 66:1–3a

Make a joyful noise to God, all the earth.

Make a joyful noise to God, all the earth.

Make a joyful noise to God, all the earth;
   sing praise to the glory of his name;
   give to him glorious praise.
Say to God, "How awesome are your deeds!"

Make a joyful noise to God, all the earth.

◆ All stand and sing **Alleluia.**

GOSPEL   John 11:1, 3–4b, 11b, 17, 32, 35–36

A reading from the holy Gospel according to John.

A certain man was ill, Lazarus of Bethany, the village of Mary and her sister Martha. So the sisters sent a message to Jesus, "Lord, he whom you love is ill." But when Jesus heard it, he said, "This illness does not lead to death." He told them, "Our friend Lazarus has fallen asleep, but I am going there to awaken him." When Jesus arrived, he found that Lazarus had already been in the tomb for four days. When Mary came where Jesus was and saw him, she knelt at his feet and said to him, "Lord, if you had been here, my brother would not have died." He said, "Where have you laid him?" They said to him, "Lord, come and see." Jesus began to weep. So, the Jews said, "See how he loved him!"

The Gospel of the Lord.

◆ All sit and observe silence.

FOR SILENT REFLECTION

Think about this silently in your heart. How do you help a friend who is sad?

CLOSING PRAYER

Let us pray to God for our needs and the needs of others: our family, neighborhood, and the world. For each need we say, "Lord, hear our prayer."

◆ All may add their own prayers here.

Let us pray: **Our Father . . . Amen.**

Holy and loving God,
we thank you for the gift of friendship.
May we always remember that Jesus
is our friend and is always with us.
May we be a good friend to others.
We pray in Jesus' name.

Amen.

✚ All make the Sign of the Cross.

OPENING

Friends often give things to one another. Jesus is willing to give his life for his friends. Today is the memorial of St. Rose of Lima [LEE-muh] who lived in Peru. She was a great friend to poor children and to the sick. She made her home into a hospital for them.

✝ All make the Sign of the Cross.

In the name of the Father, and of the Son, and of the Holy Spirit. Amen.

PSALM
(For a longer psalm, see page xi.) Psalm 66:1–3a

Make a joyful noise to God, all the earth.

Make a joyful noise to God, all the earth.

Make a joyful noise to God, all the earth;
   sing praise to the glory of his name;
   give to him glorious praise.
Say to God, "How awesome are your deeds!"

Make a joyful noise to God, all the earth.

◆ All stand and sing **Alleluia.**

GOSPEL
John 15:12–15, 17

A reading from the holy Gospel according to John.

Jesus said, "This is my commandment, that you love one another as I have loved you. No one has greater love than this, to lay down one's life for one's friends. You are my friends if you do what I command you. I do not call you servants any longer, because the servant does not know what the master is doing; but I have called you friends, because I have made known to you everything that I have heard from my Father. I am giving you these commands so that you may love one another."

The Gospel of the Lord.

◆ All sit and observe silence.

FOR SILENT REFLECTION

Think about this silently in your heart. How do people "lay down their lives," that is, make sacrifices for their friends?

CLOSING PRAYER

Let us pray to God for our needs and the needs of others: our family, neighborhood, and the world. For each need we say, "Lord, hear our prayer."

◆ All may add their own prayers here.

Let us pray: **Our Father . . . Amen.**

Loving and holy God,
help us to love others as you love us.
Help us to be good and true friends
to one another.
Help us to be kind to all we meet today.
We ask this in Jesus' name.

Amen.

✝ All make the Sign of the Cross.

OPENING

Today is the feast of St. Bartholomew [bahr-THAHL-uh-myoo], one of the Twelve Apostles and a friend of Jesus. Being a Christian means being a loving person even toward strangers. In the Scripture, Gaius [GUY-uhs] is commended for being a good friend to fellow Christians and for telling the truth about Jesus.

✚ All make the Sign of the Cross.

In the name of the Father, and of the Son, and of the Holy Spirit. Amen.

PSALM   (For a longer psalm, see page xi.) Psalm 66:1–3a

Make a joyful noise to God, all the earth.

Make a joyful noise to God, all the earth.

Make a joyful noise to God, all the earth;
  sing praise to the glory of his name;
  give to him glorious praise.
Say to God, "How awesome are your deeds!"

Make a joyful noise to God, all the earth.

READING   3 John 1:1–6a

A reading from the Third Letter of John.

To the beloved Gaius, whom I love in truth. Beloved, I pray that all may go well with you and that you may be in good health, just as it is well with your soul. I was overjoyed when some of the friends arrived and testified to your faithfulness to the truth, namely how you walk in the truth. I have no greater joy than this, to hear that my children are walking in the truth. Beloved, you do faithfully whatever you do for the friends, even though they are strangers to you; they have testified to your love before the church.

The Word of the Lord.

◆ All observe silence.

FOR SILENT REFLECTION

Think about this silently in your heart. How can we be friends with people we do not know?

CLOSING PRAYER

Let us pray to God for our needs and the needs of others: our family, neighborhood, and the world. For each need we say, "Lord, hear our prayer."

◆ All may add their own prayers here.

Let us pray: **Our Father . . . Amen.**

God our Father,
you call us to act in friendship
with all people, even those we do not know.
In friendship we pray for those in need,
and for those who are sick and suffering,
whether near or far away.
We pray this in Jesus' name.

Amen.

✚ All make the Sign of the Cross.

PRAYER FOR THE WEEK

OPENING

Today Jesus reminds us that his words bring life to us. They show us the way to eternal life, that is, to life with God here on earth, and one day, with him in heaven. Jesus warns people that they will not understand him nor stay with him unless they have faith in God the Father.

✚ All make the Sign of the Cross.

In the name of the Father, and of the Son, and of the Holy Spirit. Amen.

PSALM
(For a longer psalm, see page xi.) Psalm 66:1–3a

Make a joyful noise to God, all the earth.

Make a joyful noise to God, all the earth.

Make a joyful noise to God, all the earth;
 sing praise to the glory of his name;
 give to him glorious praise.
Say to God, "How awesome are your deeds!"

Make a joyful noise to God, all the earth.

◆ All stand and sing **Alleluia.**

GOSPEL
John 6:63b–69

A reading from the holy Gospel according to John.

Jesus said, "The words that I have spoken to you are spirit and life. But among you there are some who do not believe." For Jesus knew from the first who were the ones that did not believe, and who was the one that would betray him. And he said, "For this reason I have told you that no one can come to me unless it is granted by the Father." Because of this many of his disciples turned back and no longer went about with him. So Jesus asked the twelve, "Do you also wish to go away?" Simon Peter answered him, "Lord, to whom can we go? You have the words of eternal life. We have come to believe and know that you are the Holy One of God."

The Gospel of the Lord.

◆ All sit and observe silence.

FOR SILENT REFLECTION

Think about this silently in your heart. Do you ever want to "walk away" from following Jesus by not being kind or truthful or loving?

CLOSING PRAYER

Let us pray to God for our needs and the needs of others: our family, neighborhood, and the world. For each need we say, "Lord, hear our prayer."

◆ All may add their own prayers here.

Let us pray: **Our Father . . . Amen.**

Deepen our faith in you, O God.
Help us follow Jesus more closely.
Help us to be like Peter, and to know
that Jesus is the "Holy One" who calls us
to be his disciples.
We ask this in Jesus' name.

Amen.

✚ All make the Sign of the Cross.

OPENING

This week we hear some of Jesus' stories called "parables." Jesus knew people liked to listen to stories. Parable stories always tell us something about God and God's Kingdom. Usually Jesus compares the Kingdom of God to familiar everyday things to help us understand. Today is the memorial of St. Monica. She is the mother of St. Augustine. Her prayers helped him turn away from sin.

✚ All make the Sign of the Cross.

In the name of the Father, and of the Son, and of the Holy Spirit. Amen.

PSALM   (For a longer psalm, see page xi.) Psalm 66:1–3a

Make a joyful noise to God, all the earth.

Make a joyful noise to God, all the earth.

Make a joyful noise to God, all the earth;
    sing praise to the glory of his name;
    give to him glorious praise.
Say to God, "How awesome are your deeds!"

Make a joyful noise to God, all the earth.

◆ All stand and sing **Alleluia.**

GOSPEL   Mark 4:1a, 11a, 30bc, 31–32

A reading from the holy Gospel according to Mark.

Such a very large crowd gathered around him that he got into a boat on the sea and sat there, while the whole crowd was beside the sea on the land. He began to teach them many things in parables. And he said to them, "With what can we compare the kingdom of God, or what parable will we use for it? It is like a mustard seed, which, when sown upon the ground, is the smallest of all the seeds on earth; yet when it is sown it grows up and becomes the greatest of all shrubs, and puts forth large branches, so that the birds of the air can make nests in its shade."

The Gospel of the Lord.

◆ All sit and observe silence.

FOR SILENT REFLECTION

Think about this silently in your heart. How can you help the seed of God's Kingdom grow in our school?

CLOSING PRAYER

Let us pray to God for our needs and the needs of others: our family, neighborhood, and the world. For each need we say, "Lord, hear our prayer."

◆ All may add their own prayers here.

Let us pray: **Our Father . . . Amen.**

Help us hear the parables
with new ears, O God.
We know they can teach us
about how to live and
how to build your Kingdom on earth.
We ask this in Jesus' name.

Amen.

✚ All make the Sign of the Cross.

OPENING

Today is the memorial of St. Augustine, a Doctor of the Church. As a young man he led an immoral life. His mother, St. Monica, prayed constantly for him to change his way of life, and he did. We understand that our loving God will not destroy us, but we can destroy ourselves if we continually choose to sin. Today's parable shows the wickedness of greed.

✚ All make the Sign of the Cross.

In the name of the Father, and of the Son, and of the Holy Spirit. Amen.

PSALM
(For a longer psalm, see page xi.) Psalm 66:1–3a

Make a joyful noise to God, all the earth.

Make a joyful noise to God, all the earth.

Make a joyful noise to God, all the earth;
sing praise to the glory of his name;
give to him glorious praise.
Say to God, "How awesome are your deeds!"

Make a joyful noise to God, all the earth.

◆ All stand and sing **Alleluia.**

GOSPEL
Mark 12:1–3, 5b, 6a, 7ac, 9

A reading from the holy Gospel according to Mark.

Then Jesus began to speak to them in parables. "A man planted a vineyard; then he leased it to tenants and went to another country. When the season came, he sent a slave to the tenants to collect from them his share of the produce of the vineyard. But they seized him, and beat him, and sent him away empty-handed. Then he sent another, and that one they killed. And so it was with many others. He had still one other, a beloved son. Finally he sent him to them, saying, 'They will respect my son.' But those tenants said to one another, 'Come, let us kill him, and the inheritance will be ours.' What then will the owner of the vineyard do? He will come and destroy the tenants and give the vineyard to others."

The Gospel of the Lord.

◆ All sit and observe silence.

FOR SILENT REFLECTION

Think about this silently in your heart. Who do you think the "beloved son" mentioned in the parable might be?

CLOSING PRAYER

Let us pray to God for our needs and the needs of others: our family, neighborhood, and the world. For each need we say, "Lord, hear our prayer."

◆ All may add their own prayers here.

Let us pray: **Our Father . . . Amen.**

Loving God, our Father,
thank you for the many gifts
you have given to us.
May we always be grateful for
your generous love.

Amen.

✚ All make the Sign of the Cross.

PRAYER FOR
WEDNESDAY, AUGUST 29, 2018

OPENING

Some parables, like ones we hear today, are very short but have great meaning. The Kingdom is compared to a "treasure" and a "pearl," which have great value. And the Kingdom of Heaven is also compared to a net that catches all kinds of fish. Listen for what image speaks to you. Today is the memorial of the Passion of St. John the Baptist.

✚ All make the Sign of the Cross.

In the name of the Father, and of the Son, and of the Holy Spirit. Amen.

PSALM
(For a longer psalm, see page xi.) Psalm 66:1–3a

Make a joyful noise to God, all the earth.

Make a joyful noise to God, all the earth.

Make a joyful noise to God, all the earth;
   sing praise to the glory of his name;
   give to him glorious praise.
Say to God, "How awesome are your deeds!"

Make a joyful noise to God, all the earth.

◆ All stand and sing **Alleluia.**

GOSPEL
Matthew 13:2–3a, 44–48

A reading from the holy Gospel according to Matthew.

Such a very large crowd gathered around Jesus that he got into a boat on the sea and sat there, while the whole crowd was beside the sea on the land. And Jesus told them many thing in parables, saying: "The kingdom of heaven is like treasure hidden in a field, which someone found and hid; then in his joy he goes and sells all that he has and buys that field. "Again, the kingdom of heaven is like a merchant in search of fine pearls; on finding one pearl of great value, he went and sold all that he had and bought it. "Again, the kingdom of heaven is like a net that was thrown into the sea and caught fish of every kind; when it was full, they drew it ashore, sat down, and put the good into baskets but threw out the bad."

The Gospel of the Lord.

◆ All sit and observe silence.

FOR SILENT REFLECTION

Think about this silently in your heart. Make a short parable by finishing this sentence with a modern day image: The Kingdom of God is like . . .

CLOSING PRAYER

Let us pray to God for our needs and the needs of others: our family, neighborhood, and the world. For each need we say, "Lord, hear our prayer."

◆ All may add their own prayers here.

Let us pray: **Our Father . . . Amen.**

Help us to listen to your word, O God.
Give us ears to hear your message
so that we may build your Kingdom
on earth.

Amen.

✚ All make the Sign of the Cross.

OPENING

Today's parable reminds us that we don't know when we will go to God. We have to live each day well by loving God, our neighbor, and ourselves. Being human, we sometimes choose not to love and sometimes we just forget. Jesus says we need to be aware and alert each day.

✝ All make the Sign of the Cross.

In the name of the Father, and of the Son, and of the Holy Spirit. Amen.

PSALM
(For a longer psalm, see page xi.) Psalm 66:1–3a

Make a joyful noise to God, all the earth.

Make a joyful noise to God, all the earth.

Make a joyful noise to God, all the earth;
   sing praise to the glory of his name;
   give to him glorious praise.
Say to God, "How awesome are your deeds!"

Make a joyful noise to God, all the earth.

◆ All stand and sing **Alleluia.**

GOSPEL
Mark 13:32–35a, 36

A reading from the holy Gospel according to Mark.

Jesus said: "But about that day or hour no one knows, neither the angels in heaven, nor the Son, but only the Father. Beware, keep alert; for you do not know when the time will come. It is like a man going on a journey, when he leaves home and puts his slaves in charge, each with his work, and commands the doorkeeper to be on the watch. Therefore, keep awake— for you do not know when the master of the house will come, in the evening, or at midnight, or at cockcrow, or at dawn, or else he may find you asleep when he comes suddenly."

The Gospel of the Lord.

◆ All sit and observe silence.

FOR SILENT REFLECTION

Think about this silently in your heart. What helps you to live God's law of love?

CLOSING PRAYER

Let us pray to God for our needs and the needs of others: our family, neighborhood, and the world. For each need we say, "Lord, hear our prayer."

◆ All may add their own prayers here.

Let us pray: **Our Father . . . Amen.**

Loving God, help us
to be awake and alert to your will each day.
May we always be ready to meet you.
We ask this in Jesus' name.

Amen.

✝ All make the Sign of the Cross.

PRAYER FOR
FRIDAY, AUGUST 31, 2018

OPENING

Jesus uses the example of a fig tree in today's parable. Just as a fig tree bears fruit, God wants us to bear fruit through our words and good deeds. The fruit will be a more just and peaceful world. Jesus is the gardener, and his teachings are like fertilizer that helps us to grow in our Christian life.

✚ All make the Sign of the Cross.

In the name of the Father, and of the Son, and of the Holy Spirit. Amen.

PSALM   (For a longer psalm, see page xi.) Psalm 66:1–3a

Make a joyful noise to God, all the earth.

Make a joyful noise to God, all the earth.

Make a joyful noise to God, all the earth;
   sing praise to the glory of his name;
   give to him glorious praise.
Say to God, "How awesome are your deeds!"

Make a joyful noise to God, all the earth.

◆ All stand and sing **Alleluia.**

GOSPEL   Luke 13:1–3acd, 6–9

A reading from the holy Gospel according to Luke.

Then Jesus told this parable: "A man had a fig tree planted in his vineyard; and he came looking for fruit on it and found none. So he said to the gardener, 'See here! For three years I have come looking for fruit on this fig tree, and still I find none. Cut it down! Why should it be wasting the soil?' The gardener replied, 'Sir, let it alone for one more year, until I dig around it and put manure on it. If it bears fruit next year, well and good; but if not, you can cut it down.'"

The Gospel of the Lord.

◆ All sit and observe silence.

FOR SILENT REFLECTION

Think about this silently in your heart. What helps you grow in your faith?

CLOSING PRAYER

Let us pray to God for our needs and the needs of others: our family, neighborhood, and the world. For each need we say, "Lord, hear our prayer."

◆ All may add their own prayers here.

Let us pray: **Our Father . . . Amen.**

Loving God, you are like a patient gardener.
You want us to bear good fruit
and you give us what we need to grow.
Help us to grow stronger in our faith
and more loving in our actions.
We ask this in Jesus' name.

Amen.

✚ All make the Sign of the Cross.

PRAYER SERVICE
FOR THE CARE OF CREATION ON SEPTEMBER 1

In 2015 Pope Francis declared September 1 to be a world-wide day of prayer for the care of creation. His encyclical Laudato Si' (Praised Be) *is subtitled* On Care for Our Common Home. *Using the words of St. Francis, he compares the earth, our common home, to a "sister with whom we share our life and a beautiful mother who opens to embrace us." For this prayer service, divide the class into two groups. This could be girls and boys or another simple division of voices to pray the Canticle of St. Francis. Song suggestions are "All Creatures of Our God and King," "Joyful, Joyful, We Adore Thee," or another hymn that honors creation.*

ALL

O Most High, all-powerful, good Lord God,
to you belong praise, glory,
honor and all blessing.

GROUP I

Be praised, my Lord, for all your creation
and especially for our Brother Sun,
who brings us the day and the light;
he is strong and shines magnificently.
O Lord, we think of you when we look
at him.

GROUP II

Be praised, my Lord, for Sister Moon,
and for the stars
which you have set shining and lovely
in the heavens.

GROUP I

Be praised, my Lord,
for our Brothers Wind and Air
and every kind of weather
by which you, Lord,
uphold life in all your creatures.

GROUP II

Be praised, my Lord, for Sister Water,
who is very useful to us,
and humble and precious and pure.

GROUP I

Be praised, my Lord, for Brother Fire,
through whom you give us light in the darkness:
he is bright and lively and strong.

GROUP II

Be praised, my Lord,
for Sister Earth, our Mother,
who nourishes us and sustains us,
bringing forth
fruits and vegetables of many kinds
and flowers of many colors.

GROUP I

Be praised, my Lord,
for those who forgive for love of you;
and for those
who bear sickness and weakness
in peace and patience
you will grant them a crown.

GROUP II

Be praised, my Lord, for our Sister Death,
whom we must all face.
I praise and bless you, Lord,
and I give thanks to you,
and I will serve you in all humility.

ALL

O Most High, all-powerful, good Lord God,
to you belong praise, glory, honor and all
blessing. Amen.

PRAYER FOR THE WEEK

OPENING

Jesus followed the Jewish laws intended to keep people "undefiled," that is to keep them pure and holy. Because he and his disciples were often on the road they could not always wash before eating as the law required. Jesus reminds us that the need to eat is more important than a law, and that what really defiles us is evil in our hearts.

✚ All make the Sign of the Cross.

In the name of the Father, and of the Son, and of the Holy Spirit. Amen.

PSALM   (For a longer psalm, see page xi.) Psalm 66:1–3a

Make a joyful noise to God, all the earth.

Make a joyful noise to God, all the earth.

Make a joyful noise to God, all the earth;
sing praise to the glory of his name;
give to him glorious praise.
Say to God, "How awesome are your deeds!"

Make a joyful noise to God, all the earth.

◆ All stand and sing **Alleluia.**

GOSPEL   Mark 7:1–3ab, 5, 14–15, 21ab

A reading from the holy Gospel according to Mark.

Now when the Pharisees and some of the scribes who had come from Jerusalem gathered around him, they noticed that some of his disciples were eating with defiled hands, that is, without washing them. (For the Pharisees, and all the Jews, do not eat unless they thoroughly wash their hands.) So the Pharisees and the scribes asked him, "Why do your disciples not live according to the tradition of the elders, but eat with defiled hands?" Then he called the crowd again and said to them, "Listen to me, all of you, and understand: there is nothing outside a person that by going in can defile, but the things that come out are what defile. For it is from within, from the human heart, that evil intentions come."

The Gospel of the Lord.

◆ All sit and observe silence.

FOR SILENT REFLECTION

Think about this silently in your heart. Do you have any habit that "defiles" you, that is, that keeps you from being holy?

CLOSING PRAYER

Let us pray to God for our needs and the needs of others: our family, neighborhood, and the world. For each need we say, "Lord, hear our prayer."

◆ All may add their own prayers here.

Let us pray: **Our Father . . . Amen.**

God, help us to follow Jesus,
our model for holiness,
who spoke the truth with compassion.
We ask this in Jesus' name.

Amen.

✚ All make the Sign of the Cross.

OPENING

This week we will hear Scriptures that teach us about wisdom. To have wisdom means to have the qualities of knowledge and good judgment. Today's Scripture is a well-known passage that reminds us that we experience different things at different times in life. The writer is asking us to trust in God at all times and seasons.

✛ All make the Sign of the Cross.

In the name of the Father, and of the Son, and of the Holy Spirit. Amen.

PSALM
(For a longer psalm, see page xi.) Psalm 66:1–3a

Make a joyful noise to God, all the earth.

Make a joyful noise to God, all the earth.

Make a joyful noise to God, all the earth;
sing praise to the glory of his name;
give to him glorious praise.
Say to God, "How awesome are your deeds!"

Make a joyful noise to God, all the earth.

READING
Ecclesiastes 3:1a, 2–4, 5b–8, 11a

A reading from the Book of Ecclesiastes.

For everything there is a season: a time to be born, and a time to die; a time to plant, and a time to pluck up what is planted; a time to kill, and a time to heal; a time to break down, and a time to build up; a time to weep, and a time to laugh; a time to mourn, and a time to dance; a time to embrace, and a time to refrain from embracing; a time to seek, and a time to lose; a time to keep, and a time to throw away; a time to tear, and a time to sew; a time to keep silence, and a time to speak; a time to love, and a time to hate; a time for war, and a time for peace. God has made everything suitable for its time.

The Word of the Lord.

◆ All observe silence.

FOR SILENT REFLECTION

Think about this silently in your heart. What "time" is it in your life?

CLOSING PRAYER

Let us pray to God for our needs and the needs of others: our family, neighborhood, and the world. For each need we say, "Lord, hear our prayer."

◆ All may add their own prayers here.

Let us pray: **Our Father . . . Amen.**

O God, our Holy Wisdom,
give us the qualities of wisdom.
Help us to trust in you at all times:
when we are happy and when we are sad;
when we succeed and when we fail;
when we are with family and friends,
and when we are alone.
We ask this in Jesus' name.

Amen.

✛ All make the Sign of the Cross.

PRAYER FOR
WEDNESDAY, SEPTEMBER 5, 2018

OPENING

Today is St. Mother Teresa's feast day. She ministered to India's poor and dying by taking them off the streets and making their final days comfortable. In our Scripture, St. Luke suggests wisdom means not judging others until we've judged ourselves. We need to see our own flaws clearly before we point out flaws in others.

✛ All make the Sign of the Cross.

In the name of the Father, and of the Son, and of the Holy Spirit. Amen.

PSALM (For a longer psalm, see page xi.) Psalm 66:1–3a

Make a joyful noise to God, all the earth.

Make a joyful noise to God, all the earth.

Make a joyful noise to God, all the earth;
　　sing praise to the glory of his name;
　　give to him glorious praise.
Say to God, "How awesome are your deeds!"

Make a joyful noise to God, all the earth.

◆ All stand and sing **Alleluia.**

GOSPEL Luke 6:39–42

A reading from the holy Gospel according to Luke.

Jesus told them a parable: "Can a blind person guide a blind person? Will not both fall into a pit? A disciple is not above the teacher, but everyone who is fully qualified will be like the teacher. Why do you see the speck in your neighbor's eye, but do not notice the log in your own eye? Or how can you say to your neighbor, 'Friend, let me take out the speck in your eye,' when you yourself do not see the log in your own eye? You hypocrite, first take the log out of your own eye, and then you will see clearly to take the speck out of your neighbor's eye."

The Gospel of the Lord.

◆ All sit and observe silence.

FOR SILENT REFLECTION

Think about this silently in your heart. Why is it important to avoid judging others?

CLOSING PRAYER

Let us pray to God for our needs and the needs of others: our family, neighborhood, and the world. For each need we say, "Lord, hear our prayer."

◆ All may add their own prayers here.

Let us pray: **Our Father . . . Amen.**

Faithful and just God,
only you know what is in each person's heart.
We pray for wisdom in our relationships.
Help us to see each other with the eyes of love,
and to be kind, patient, and caring.
We ask this in Jesus' name.

Amen.

✛ All make the Sign of the Cross.

OPENING

The writer of Sirach [SEER-ack] advises us not to judge our friends too quickly or too harshly. A wise person asks questions before breaking up with a friend to see if the evil we hear about is a lie, or slander, or just a mistake. If someone does speak evil, we are advised to forgive because this is what God wants.

✚ All make the Sign of the Cross.

In the name of the Father, and of the Son, and of the Holy Spirit. Amen.

PSALM
(For a longer psalm, see page xi.) Psalm 66:1–3a

Make a joyful noise to God, all the earth.

Make a joyful noise to God, all the earth.

Make a joyful noise to God, all the earth;
     sing praise to the glory of his name;
     give to him glorious praise.
Say to God, "How awesome are your deeds!"

Make a joyful noise to God, all the earth.

READING
Sirach 19:6, 9, 12–16

A reading from the Book of Sirach.

Never repeat gossip, and you will lose nothing at all. Have you heard something? Let it die with you. Question your friend—he may not have done it; and if he did, he may not do it again. Question your neighbor—he may not have said it; and if he did, he may not say it again. Question your friend—often it may be slander; every story you must not believe. Then, too, a man can slip and not mean it; who has not sinned with his tongue? Question your neighbor before you break with him; thus will you fulfill the law of the Most High.

The Word of the Lord.

◆ All observe silence.

FOR SILENT REFLECTION

Think about this silently in your heart. What can you do to help your classroom be a fair and happy place for each person?

CLOSING PRAYER

Let us pray to God for our needs and the needs of others: our family, neighborhood, and the world. For each need we say, "Lord, hear our prayer."

◆ All may add their own prayers here.

Let us pray: **Our Father . . . Amen.**

O God, our Holy Wisdom,
give us the qualities of wisdom
so that we will judge things correctly
and know when and how
to speak and act.
We ask this in Jesus' name.

Amen.

✚ All make the Sign of the Cross.

OPENING

St. Paul uses a metaphor, that is a comparison, about how to fight against real evil like bullying and malicious gossip. He tells us that we need to put on the "armor of God," carry "the shield of faith," and the "sword of the Spirit." Jesus' teachings are that armor, faith in Jesus is the shield, and God's word is the sword.

✝ All make the Sign of the Cross.

In the name of the Father, and of the Son, and of the Holy Spirit. Amen.

PSALM   (For a longer psalm, see page xi.) Psalm 66:1–3a

Make a joyful noise to God, all the earth.

Make a joyful noise to God, all the earth.

Make a joyful noise to God, all the earth;
  sing praise to the glory of his name;
  give to him glorious praise.
Say to God, "How awesome are your deeds!"

Make a joyful noise to God, all the earth.

READING   Ephesians 6:10–11, 14–18a

A reading from the Letter of Paul to the Ephesians.

Be strong in the Lord and in the strength of his power. Put on the whole armor of God, so that you may be able to stand against the wiles of the devil. Stand and fasten the belt of truth around your waist, and put on the breastplate of righteousness. As shoes for your feet put on whatever will make you ready to proclaim the gospel of peace. With all of these, take the shield of faith, with which you will be able to quench all the flaming arrows of the evil one. Take the helmet of salvation, and the sword of the Spirit, which is the word of God. Pray in the Spirit at all times in every prayer and supplication.

The Word of the Lord.

◆ All observe silence.

FOR SILENT REFLECTION

Think about this silently in your heart. What do you need to stand up to in school, at home, or in the neighborhood? Pray for the Spirit to help you.

CLOSING PRAYER

Let us pray to God for our needs and the needs of others: our family, neighborhood, and the world. For each need we say, "Lord, hear our prayer."

◆ All may add their own prayers here.

Let us pray: **Our Father . . . Amen.**

O God, our Holy Wisdom,
we pray that we can be strong
in the fight against evil and wrongdoing.
We trust that you will give us what we need
to live in truth, peace, and love.
We ask this in Jesus' name.

Amen.

✝ All make the Sign of the Cross.

PRAYER FOR THE WEEK
WITH A READING FROM THE GOSPEL FOR **SUNDAY, SEPTEMBER 9, 2018**

OPENING

Jesus' teaching about God's love is not just for the Jews but for all people. He leaves Galilee and travels into Gentile, or non-Jewish, territory to teach. Jesus' power and authority is seen in the miracles he accomplishes. The Decapolis area had ten cities in it.

✝ All make the Sign of the Cross.

In the name of the Father, and of the Son, and of the Holy Spirit. Amen.

PSALM   (For a longer psalm, see page xi.) Psalm 66:1–3a

Make a joyful noise to God, all the earth.

Make a joyful noise to God, all the earth.

Make a joyful noise to God, all the earth;
  sing praise to the glory of his name;
  give to him glorious praise.
Say to God, "How awesome are your deeds!"

Make a joyful noise to God, all the earth.

◆ All stand and sing **Alleluia.**

GOSPEL   Mark 7:31–37

A reading from the holy Gospel according to Mark.

Then Jesus returned from the region of Tyre, and went by way of Sidon towards the Sea of Galilee, in the region of the Decapolis. They brought to him a deaf man who had an impediment in his speech; and they begged him to lay his hand on him. Jesus took him aside in private, away from the crowd, and put his fingers into his ears, and he spat and touched his tongue. Then looking up to heaven, he sighed and said to him, "Ephphatha, [EHF-uh-thuh]" that is, "Be opened." And immediately his ears were opened, his tongue was released, and he spoke plainly. Then Jesus ordered them to tell no one; but the more he ordered them, the more zealously they proclaimed it. They were astounded beyond measure, saying, "He has done everything well; he even makes the deaf to hear and the mute to speak."

The Gospel of the Lord.

◆ All sit and observe silence.

FOR SILENT REFLECTION

Think about this silently in your heart. Why did Jesus order them not tell that the deaf man could now hear and speak?

CLOSING PRAYER

Let us pray to God for our needs and the needs of others: our family, neighborhood, and the world. For each need we say, "Lord, hear our prayer."

◆ All may add their own prayers here.

Let us pray: **Our Father . . . Amen.**

Heal us, O God,
and fill us with your grace.
We ask this in Jesus' name.

Amen.

✝ All make the Sign of the Cross.

35

OPENING

This week we will look at the many ways God feeds and nourishes us. Today we hear how God is like a shepherd who provides physical and spiritual feeding for his flock. We can think of God's grace and Jesus' teaching as the spiritual food that nourishes us.

✜ All make the Sign of the Cross.

In the name of the Father, and of the Son, and of the Holy Spirit. Amen.

PSALM   (For a longer psalm, see page xi.) Psalm 66:1–3a

Make a joyful noise to God, all the earth.

Make a joyful noise to God, all the earth.

Make a joyful noise to God, all the earth;
   sing praise to the glory of his name;
   give to him glorious praise.
Say to God, "How awesome are your deeds!"

Make a joyful noise to God, all the earth.

READING   Ezekiel 34:11, 13b–16ace

A reading from the Book of the
prophet Ezekiel.

For thus says the Lord GOD: I myself will search for my sheep, and will seek them out. I will bring them into their own land; and I will feed them on the mountains of Israel, by the watercourses, and in all the inhabited parts of the land. I will feed them with good pasture, and the mountain heights of Israel shall be their pasture; there they shall lie down in good grazing land, and they shall feed on rich pasture on the mountains of Israel. I myself will be the shepherd of my sheep, and I will make them lie down, says the Lord GOD. I will seek the lost, and I will bring back the strayed, and I will bind up the injured, and I will strengthen the weak. I will feed them with justice.

The Word of the Lord.

◆ All observe silence.

FOR SILENT REFLECTION

Think about this silently in your heart. What are some of the ways the shepherd cares for his flock that you heard in the reading?

CLOSING PRAYER

Let us pray to God for our needs and the needs of others: our family, neighborhood, and the world. For each need we say, "Lord, hear our prayer."

◆ All may add their own prayers here.

Let us pray: **Our Father . . . Amen.**

Holy God,
when we are hurt or frightened,
or feeling lost,
help us to remember that you care for us
as a shepherd cares for his flock.
Thank you for your great love and tender care.

Amen.

✜ All make the Sign of the Cross.

OPENING

Today is called the National Day of Remembrance and Mourning, when we remember the tragic events of September 11, 2001. In our Scripture reading, we hear how Jesus takes care of the hungry crowd who had come to hear his teaching.

✛ All make the Sign of the Cross.

In the name of the Father, and of the Son, and of the Holy Spirit. Amen.

PSALM   (For a longer psalm, see page xi.) Psalm 66:1–3a

Make a joyful noise to God, all the earth.

Make a joyful noise to God, all the earth.

Make a joyful noise to God, all the earth;
    sing praise to the glory of his name;
    give to him glorious praise.
Say to God, "How awesome are your deeds!"

Make a joyful noise to God, all the earth.

◆ All stand and sing **Alleluia.**

GOSPEL   Mark 6:34–35b, 36–37a, 38, 41–42a, 44

A reading from the holy Gospel according to Mark.

As Jesus went ashore, he saw a great crowd; and he had compassion for them, because they were like sheep without a shepherd; and he began to teach them many things. When it grew late, Jesus' disciples came to him and said, "Send them away so that they may go into the surrounding country and villages and buy something for themselves to eat." But he answered them, "You give them something to eat." They said to him, "Are we to go and buy two hundred denarii worth of bread?" And he said to them, "How many loaves have you? Go and see." When they had found out, they said, "Five, and two fish." Taking the five loaves and the two fish, he looked up to heaven, and blessed and broke the loaves, and gave them to his disciples to set before the people; and he divided the two fish among them all. And all ate and were filled. Those who had eaten the loaves numbered five thousand men.

The Gospel of the Lord.

◆ All sit and observe silence.

FOR SILENT REFLECTION

Think about this silently in your heart. How do you imagine the people felt when everyone was fed?

CLOSING PRAYER

Let us pray to God for our needs and the needs of others: our family, neighborhood, and the world. For each need we say, "Lord, hear our prayer."

◆ All may add their own prayers here.

Let us pray: **Our Father . . . Amen.**

Good and generous God,
we thank you for feeding us.
We thank you for your love.

Amen.

✛ All make the Sign of the Cross.

PRAYER SERVICE
NATIONAL DAY OF SERVICE AND REMEMBRANCE ON SEPTEMBER 11

Prepare two leaders and a reader for this service. Perhaps someone can serve as a music leader for an appropriate gathering song and the "Alleluia." Another option is to toll a bell several times or strike a singing bowl. The Gospel should be marked with ribbon or a bookmark in the Bible. You might consider lighting a candle before the Gospel is read.

LEADER 1:

✚ All make the Sign of the Cross.

> **In the name of the Father and of the Son and of the Holy Spirit.**

Let us pray:
Holy God,
we pray for all who died
on September 11, 2001,
and we pray for their grieving families.
We turn to you for the courage
to be peacemakers and servants
to all people in the world.
We ask this in Jesus' name.

ALL: Amen.

◆ All stand and sing **Alleluia**.

READER   Luke 6:36–37
A reading from the holy Gospel according
to John.

◆ Proclaim the Gospel passage from the Bible.

The Gospel of the Lord.

LEADER 2
Let us pause and ask ourselves what it is we
can we do to serve God's people and
be Christ's peacemakers.

◆ Allow a minute of silence.

Our response to the intercessions is, "Lord,
hear our prayer."

May we always find a peaceful way to resolve
arguments, we pray . . .

May the hearts and minds of terrorists be
healed, we pray . . .

May we let go of our feelings of anger, hurt,
or revenge, we pray . . .

May we look for ways to serve the poor and
lonely, we pray . . .

May we notice one another's needs and do
what we can to help, we pray . . .

May those we love who have died be received
in heaven, we pray . . .

May those we love who are ill receive the
healing they need, we pray . . .

We ask this in the name of Jesus.

All: Amen.

Let us offer one another a sign of Christ's
peace.

◆ All offer one another a sign of peace.

And may God bless us,

✚ All make the Sign of the Cross.

protect us from all evil,
and bring us to everlasting life.

ALL: Amen.

CHILDREN'S DAILY PRAYER 2018–2019, © 2018 Archdiocese of Chicago: Liturgy Training Publications. All rights reserved. Orders: 800-933-1800 or www.LTP.org.

OPENING

Today we hear of Jesus' sharing the bread and cup of wine at the Passover meal he celebrated with his disciples. We experience being fed by Jesus' body and blood each time we are at Mass. Today is the memorial of the Most Holy Name of Mary.

✚ All make the Sign of the Cross.

In the name of the Father, and of the Son, and of the Holy Spirit. Amen.

PSALM
(For a longer psalm, see page xi.) Psalm 66:1–3a

Make a joyful noise to God, all the earth.

Make a joyful noise to God, all the earth.

Make a joyful noise to God, all the earth;
> sing praise to the glory of his name;
> give to him glorious praise.
Say to God, "How awesome are your deeds!"

Make a joyful noise to God, all the earth.

◆ All stand and sing **Alleluia.**

GOSPEL
Mark 14:12a, 12c–13a, 16–24

A reading from the holy Gospel according to Mark.

On the first day of Unleavened Bread, his disciples said to him, "Where do you want us to go and make the preparations for you to eat the Passover?" So Jesus sent two of his disciples, saying to them, "Go into the city." So the disciples set out and went to the city, and found everything as he had told them; and they prepared the Passover meal. While they were eating, he took a loaf of bread, and after blessing it he broke it, gave it to them, and said, "Take; this is my body." Then he took a cup, and after giving thanks he gave it to them, and all of them drank from it. He said to them, "This is my blood of the covenant, which is poured out for many."

The Gospel of the Lord.

◆ All sit and observe silence.

FOR SILENT REFLECTION

Think about this silently in your heart. How can you show your gratitude for Jesus' gift of himself in Holy Communion?

CLOSING PRAYER

Let us pray to God for our needs and the needs of others: our family, neighborhood, and the world. For each need we say, "Lord, hear our prayer."

◆ All may add their own prayers here.

Let us pray: **Our Father . . . Amen.**

We give you thanks, O God,
for the gift your son Jesus,
whose teachings nourish our spirits,
and whose Body and Blood sustain us
on our journey through life.

Amen.

✚ All make the Sign of the Cross.

OPENING

After Jesus rose from the dead he appeared to the disciples to comfort them and give some instructions. Peter represents the whole Church, which includes us. Jesus wants all of us to feed his sheep. Since we are all Jesus' sheep we must feed one another. Today is the memorial of St. John Chrysostom.

✝ All make the Sign of the Cross.

In the name of the Father, and of the Son, and of the Holy Spirit. Amen.

PSALM   (For a longer psalm, see page xi.) Psalm 66:1–3a

Make a joyful noise to God, all the earth.

Make a joyful noise to God, all the earth.

Make a joyful noise to God, all the earth;
    sing praise to the glory of his name;
    give to him glorious praise.
Say to God, "How awesome are your deeds!"

Make a joyful noise to God, all the earth.

◆ All stand and sing **Alleluia.**

GOSPEL   John 21:14–17

A reading from the holy Gospel according to John.

This was now the third time that Jesus appeared to the disciples after he was raised from the dead. When they had finished breakfast, Jesus said to Simon Peter, "Simon son of John, do you love me more than these?" He said to him, "Yes, Lord; you know that I love you." Jesus said to him, "Feed my lambs." A second time Jesus said to him, "Simon son of John, do you love me?" He said to him, "Yes, Lord; you know that I love you." Jesus said to him, "Tend my sheep." Jesus said to him the third time, "Simon son of John, do you love me?" Peter felt hurt because he said to him the third time, "Do you love me?" And Peter said to him, "Lord, you know everything; you know that I love you." Jesus said to him, "Feed my sheep."

The Gospel of the Lord.

◆ All sit and observe silence.

FOR SILENT REFLECTION

Think about this silently in your heart. Why do you think Jesus asked Peter the same question three times?

CLOSING PRAYER

Let us pray to God for our needs and the needs of others: our family, neighborhood, and the world. For each need we say, "Lord, hear our prayer."

◆ All may add their own prayers here.

Let us pray: **Our Father . . . Amen.**

Loving God,
help us to remember that we show our love for you
by caring for one another
and feeding those in need.

Amen.

✝ All make the Sign of the Cross.

OPENING

St. Paul gives surprising advice to the Church. Feed your enemies! Give them something to drink! This will help us overcome evil with good as Jesus did. Today is the feast of the Exaltation of the Holy Cross. The cross is a sign of how Jesus overcame evil so we celebrate it!

✦ All make the Sign of the Cross.

In the name of the Father, and of the Son, and of the Holy Spirit. Amen.

PSALM   (For a longer psalm, see page xi.) Psalm 66:1–3a

Make a joyful noise to God, all the earth.

Make a joyful noise to God, all the earth.

Make a joyful noise to God, all the earth;
   sing praise to the glory of his name;
   give to him glorious praise.
Say to God, "How awesome are your deeds!"

Make a joyful noise to God, all the earth.

READING   Romans 12:9–10, 14, 16, 18, 19a, 20–21

A reading from the Letter of Paul to the Romans.

Let love be genuine; hate what is evil, hold fast to what is good; love one another with mutual affection; outdo one another in showing honor. Bless those who persecute you; bless and do not curse them. Live in harmony with one another; do not be haughty, but associate with the lowly; do not claim to be wiser than you are. If it is possible, so far as it depends on you, live peaceably with all. Beloved, never avenge yourselves, No, if your enemies are hungry, feed them; if they are thirsty, give them some-thing to drink; for by doing this you will heap burning coals on their heads. Do not be over-come by evil, but overcome evil with good.

The Word of the Lord.

◆ All observe silence.

FOR SILENT REFLECTION

Think about this silently in your heart. Why would Jesus want us to be good to our enemies?

CLOSING PRAYER

Let us pray to God for our needs and the needs of others: our family, neighborhood, and the world. For each need we say, "Lord, hear our prayer."

◆ All may add their own prayers here.

Let us pray: **Our Father . . . Amen.**

We pray, O loving God,
for our love to be genuine,
and for the courage to be kind
and generous, even to our enemies.
We ask this in Jesus' name.

Amen.

✦ All make the Sign of the Cross.

PRAYER FOR THE WEEK

WITH A READING FROM THE GOSPEL FOR **SUNDAY, SEPTEMBER 16, 2018**

OPENING

Jesus insists that only by following his teachings will humankind be saved. This doesn't just mean we'll go to heaven. It means, if we do God's work, we'll save the world from hunger and war and other evils. Sometimes we will suffer, as Jesus did, if we do and say the right thing.

✚ All make the Sign of the Cross.

In the name of the Father, and of the Son, and of the Holy Spirit. Amen.

PSALM   (For a longer psalm, see page xi.) Psalm 66:1–3a

Make a joyful noise to God, all the earth.

Make a joyful noise to God, all the earth.

Make a joyful noise to God, all the earth;
 sing praise to the glory of his name;
 give to him glorious praise.
Say to God, "How awesome are your deeds!"

Make a joyful noise to God, all the earth.

◆ All stand and sing **Alleluia.**

GOSPEL   Mark 8:31–35

A reading from the holy Gospel according to Mark.

Then Jesus began to teach them that the Son of Man must undergo great suffering, and be rejected by the elders, the chief priests, and the scribes, and be killed, and after three days rise again. He said all this quite openly. And Peter took Jesus aside and began to rebuke him. But turning and looking at his disciples, he rebuked Peter and said, "Get behind me, Satan! For you are setting your mind not on divine things but

on human things." Jesus called the crowd with his disciples, and said to them, "If any want to become my followers, let them deny themselves and take up their cross and follow me. For those who want to save their life will lose it, and those who lose their life for my sake, and for the sake of the gospel, will save it."

The Gospel of the Lord.

◆ All sit and observe silence.

FOR SILENT REFLECTION

Think about this silently in your heart. Is there something we need to do or say even though someone might not like it?

CLOSING PRAYER

Let us pray to God for our needs and the needs of others: our family, neighborhood, and the world. For each need we say, "Lord, hear our prayer."

◆ All may add their own prayers here.

Let us pray: **Our Father . . . Amen.**

Help us do your work, O God.
Give us the courage to
take up our cross and follow Jesus
so we can continue his mission
to save all God's people.
We ask this in Jesus' name.

Amen.

✚ All make the Sign of the Cross.

OPENING

In the Book of Deuteronomy [doo-ter-AH-nuh-mee], Moses gives Israel what we call the Greatest Commandment. Moses emphasizes how important this particular Commandment is to making "things go well" as they are about to enter the promised land.

✚ All make the Sign of the Cross.

In the name of the Father, and of the Son, and of the Holy Spirit. Amen.

PSALM
(For a longer psalm, see page xi.) Psalm 66:1–3a

Make a joyful noise to God, all the earth.

Make a joyful noise to God, all the earth.

Make a joyful noise to God, all the earth;
    sing praise to the glory of his name;
    give to him glorious praise.
Say to God, "How awesome are your deeds!"

Make a joyful noise to God, all the earth.

READING
Deuteronomy 5:1a; 6:1ac, 3b, 5–9

A reading from the Book of Deuteronomy.

Moses convened all Israel, and said to them: Now this is the commandment the LORD your God charged me to teach you to observe in the land that you are about to cross into and occupy, so that it may go well with you, and so that you may multiply greatly in a land flowing with milk and honey. You shall love the LORD your God with all your heart, and with all your soul, and with all your might. Keep these words that I am commanding you today in your heart. Recite them to your children and talk about them when you are at home and

when you are away, when you lie down and when you rise. Bind them as a sign on your hand, fix them as an emblem on your forehead, and write them on the doorposts of your house and on your gates.

The Word of the Lord.

◆ All observe silence.

FOR SILENT REFLECTION

Think about this silently in your heart. What does it mean to love God with your whole heart?

CLOSING PRAYER

Let us pray to God for our needs and the needs of others: our family, neighborhood, and the world. For each need we say, "Lord, hear our prayer."

◆ All may add their own prayers here.

Let us pray: **Our Father . . . Amen.**

We wish to love you completely, O God, and obey your Commandments faithfully. Give us the courage we need to love you with all our heart, all our mind, and all our soul. We ask this in Jesus' name.

Amen.

✚ All make the Sign of the Cross.

OPENING

The second Great Commandment about loving our neighbor came from the Book of Leviticus in the Old Testament. Jesus knew the Hebrew Scriptures and taught both Great Commandments, love of God and of our neighbor.

✦ All make the Sign of the Cross.

In the name of the Father, and of the Son, and of the Holy Spirit. Amen.

PSALM   (For a longer psalm, see page xi.) Psalm 66:1–3a

Make a joyful noise to God, all the earth.

Make a joyful noise to God, all the earth.

Make a joyful noise to God, all the earth;
   sing praise to the glory of his name;
   give to him glorious praise.
Say to God, "How awesome are your deeds!"

Make a joyful noise to God, all the earth.

◆ All stand and sing **Alleluia.**

GOSPEL   Luke 10:25–28

A reading from the holy Gospel according to Luke.

Just then a lawyer stood up to test Jesus. "Teacher," he said, "what must I do to inherit eternal life?" He said to him, "What is written in the law? What do you read there?" He answered, "You shall love the Lord your God with all your heart, and with all your soul, and with all your strength, and with all your mind; and your neighbor as yourself." And he said to him, "You have given the right answer; do this, and you will live."

The Gospel of the Lord.

◆ All sit and observe silence.

FOR SILENT REFLECTION

Think about this silently in your heart. Why must we love ourselves before we can love our neighbor?

CLOSING PRAYER

Let us pray to God for our needs and the needs of others: our family, neighborhood, and the world. For each need we say, "Lord, hear our prayer."

◆ All may add their own prayers here.

Let us pray: **Our Father . . . Amen.**

God of love,
you sent Jesus to teach us
how we should live.
Like the lawyer in today's Gospel,
may we seek to love you with our whole heart
and to love others as we love ourselves.
We ask this in Jesus' name.

Amen.

✦ All make the Sign of the Cross.

OPENING

The lawyer in the Gospel has just mentioned the two Great Commandments, and now he tests Jesus by asking who is our neighbor. Loving God may seem easier than loving our neighbor who might be a stranger or someone mean. Today and tomorrow we'll hear Jesus' answer in the parable of the Good Samaritan. The Jews and the Samaritans had a long history of hatred and rarely dealt with one another.

✛ All make the Sign of the Cross.

In the name of the Father, and of the Son, and of the Holy Spirit. Amen.

PSALM   (For a longer psalm, see page xi.) Psalm 66:1–3a

Make a joyful noise to God, all the earth.

Make a joyful noise to God, all the earth.

Make a joyful noise to God, all the earth;
    sing praise to the glory of his name;
    give to him glorious praise.
Say to God, "How awesome are your deeds!"

Make a joyful noise to God, all the earth.

◆ All stand and sing **Alleluia.**

GOSPEL   Luke 10:29–32

A reading from the holy Gospel according to Luke.

The lawyer wanting to justify himself, asked Jesus, "And who is my neighbor?" Jesus replied, "A man was going down from Jerusalem to Jericho, and fell into the hands of robbers, who stripped him, beat him, and went away, leaving him half dead. Now by chance a priest was going down that road; and when he saw him, he passed by on the other side. So likewise a Levite, when he came to the place and saw him, passed by on the other side."

The Gospel of the Lord.

◆ All sit and observe silence.

FOR SILENT REFLECTION

Think about this silently in your heart. Are you ever like the priest or the Levite? Is there someone you refuse to deal with? Why?

CLOSING PRAYER

Let us pray to God for our needs and the needs of others: our family, neighborhood, and the world. For each need we say, "Lord, hear our prayer."

◆ All may add their own prayers here.

Let us pray: **Our Father . . . Amen.**

Good and generous Father,
you wish for people to live as one family.
Help us to love our neighbor as
we love ourselves,
and to care for everyone, especially
those in need.
We ask this in Jesus' name.

Amen.

✛ All make the Sign of the Cross.

OPENING

Today we hear the second part of the parable of the Good Samaritan. Jesus says showing mercy is one way to love our neighbor. Today is the memorial of 103 people martyred in Korea in the 1800s. We remember St. Andrew Kim Tae-gŏn, a priest, and St. Paul Chŏng Ha-Sang, a layperson, and their Companions.

✛ All make the Sign of the Cross.

In the name of the Father, and of the Son, and of the Holy Spirit. Amen.

PSALM   (For a longer psalm, see page xi.) Psalm 66:1–3a

Make a joyful noise to God, all the earth.

Make a joyful noise to God, all the earth.

Make a joyful noise to God, all the earth;
  sing praise to the glory of his name;
  give to him glorious praise.
Say to God, "How awesome are your deeds!"

Make a joyful noise to God, all the earth.

◆ All stand and sing **Alleluia.**

GOSPEL   Luke 10:33–37

A reading from the holy Gospel according to Luke.

"But a Samaritan while travelling came near him; and when he saw him, he was moved with pity. He went to him and bandaged his wounds, having poured oil and wine on them. Then he put him on his own animal, brought him to an inn, and took care of him. The next day he took out two denarii, gave them to the inn-keeper, and said, 'Take care of him; and when I come back, I will repay you whatever more you spend.' Which of these three, do you think, was a neighbor to the man who fell into the hands of the robbers?" He said, "The one who showed him mercy." Jesus said to him, "Go and do likewise."

The Gospel of the Lord.

◆ All sit and observe silence.

FOR SILENT REFLECTION

Think about this silently in your heart. How do you show mercy to your classmates?

CLOSING PRAYER

Let us pray to God for our needs and the needs of others: our family, neighborhood, and the world. For each need we say, "Lord, hear our prayer."

◆ All may add their own prayers here.

Let us pray: **Our Father . . . Amen.**

Merciful God,
we pray that we will learn to
be like the Samaritan.
Help us to see those who are in need
and to respond to them as best we can.
Help us not be afraid to reach out to others
with mercy and care.

Amen.

✛ All make the Sign of the Cross.

OPENING

Today is the feast of St. Matthew, an Apostle and Gospel writer. Matthew wrote his Gospel for the Jews to convince them Jesus was the expected Messiah from the family of King David. In our reading today, St. Paul tells us what to do, and not do, if we love God and our neighbor. Loving our neighbor is the way we show we love God.

✜ All make the Sign of the Cross.

In the name of the Father, and of the Son, and of the Holy Spirit. Amen.

PSALM

(For a longer psalm, see page xi.) Psalm 66:1–3a

Make a joyful noise to God, all the earth.

Make a joyful noise to God, all the earth.

Make a joyful noise to God, all the earth;
   sing praise to the glory of his name;
   give to him glorious praise.
Say to God, "How awesome are your deeds!"

Make a joyful noise to God, all the earth.

READING

Ephesians 4:22a, 24, 31–32; 5:1–2

A reading from the Letter of Paul to the Ephesians.

You were taught to put away your former way of life and to clothe yourselves with the new self, created according to the likeness of God in true righteousness and holiness. Put away from you all bitterness and wrath and anger and wrangling and slander, together with all malice, and be kind to one another, tenderhearted, forgiving one another, as God in Christ has forgiven you. Therefore be imitators of God, as beloved children, and live in love, as Christ loved us and gave himself up for us, a fragrant offering and sacrifice to God.

The Word of the Lord.

◆ All observe silence.

FOR SILENT REFLECTION

Think about this silently in your heart. Forgiving means to stop feeling angry with someone or to stop blaming someone. Whom do you need to forgive?

CLOSING PRAYER

Let us pray to God for our needs and the needs of others: our family, neighborhood, and the world. For each need we say, "Lord, hear our prayer."

◆ All may add their own prayers here.

Let us pray: **Our Father . . . Amen.**

Holy God,
in Baptism we became a new creation,
and we received the light of Christ.
May we remember that we bear Christ-likeness
and seek to act as he would act.
We ask this in Jesus' name.

Amen.

✜ All make the Sign of the Cross.

PRAYER FOR THE WEEK

WITH A READING FROM THE GOSPEL FOR **SUNDAY, SEPTEMBER 23, 2018**

OPENING

In today's Gospel we hear the disciples arguing about who was the greatest among them. Jesus challenges them. To teach them a lesson, he uses the example of a little child.

✚ All make the Sign of the Cross.

In the name of the Father, and of the Son, and of the Holy Spirit. Amen.

PSALM   (For a longer psalm, see page xi.) Psalm 145:2–3

I will praise your name for ever, LORD.

I will praise your name for ever, LORD.

Every day I will bless you,
   and praise your name forever and ever.
Great is the LORD, and greatly to be praised;
   his greatness is unsearchable.

I will praise your name for ever, LORD.

◆ All stand and sing **Alleluia.**

GOSPEL   Mark 9:30–31a, 32–37

A reading from the holy Gospel according to Mark.

Jesus and his disciples passed through Galilee. He did not want anyone to know it; for he was teaching his disciples. But they did not understand what he was saying and were afraid to ask him. Then they came to Capernaum; and when Jesus was in the house he asked them, "What were you arguing about on the way?" But they were silent, for on the way they had argued with one another who was the greatest. He sat down, called the twelve, and said to them, "Whoever wants to be first must be last

of all and servant of all." Then he took a little child and put it among them; and taking it in his arms, he said to them, "Whoever welcomes one such child in my name welcomes me, and whoever welcomes me welcomes not me but the one who sent me."

The Gospel of the Lord.

◆ All sit and observe silence.

FOR SILENT REFLECTION

Think about this silently in your heart. Why do you think Jesus would choose a little child to teach his disciples?

CLOSING PRAYER

Let us pray to God for our needs and the needs of others: our family, neighborhood, and the world. For each need we say, "Lord, hear our prayer."

◆ All may add their own prayers here.

Let us pray: **Our Father . . . Amen.**

Holy and loving God,
we pray that we may always remember
that you care for the least among us—the
children, the poor, and the needy.
May we welcome them as we would
welcome you.

Amen.

✚ All make the Sign of the Cross.

48

OPENING

For the next two weeks, we will hear beautiful commentaries on the first Genesis creation story from the Book of Sirach [SEER-ack]. Sirach is one of the Bible's wisdom books that gives instructions on right attitudes and good living. Today's passage praises all the good things God filled the earth with.

✝ All make the Sign of the Cross.

In the name of the Father, and of the Son, and of the Holy Spirit. Amen.

PSALM
(For a longer psalm, see page xi.) Psalm 145:2–3

I will praise your name for ever, LORD.

I will praise your name for ever, LORD.

Every day I will bless you,
  and praise your name forever and ever.
Great is the LORD, and greatly to be praised;
  his greatness is unsearchable.

I will praise your name for ever, LORD.

READING
Sirach 16:24–30

A reading from the Book of Sirach.

Listen to me, my child, and acquire knowledge, and pay close attention to my words. I will impart discipline precisely and declare knowledge accurately. When the Lord created his works from the beginning, and, in making them, determined their boundaries, he arranged his works in an eternal order, and their dominion for all generations. They neither hunger nor grow weary, and they do not abandon their tasks. They do not crowd one another, and they never disobey his word.

Then the Lord looked upon the earth, and filled it with his good things. With all kinds of living beings he covered its surface, and into it they must return.

The Word of the Lord.

◆ All observe silence.

FOR SILENT REFLECTION

Think about this silently in your heart. What are some of the good things and people with which God has filled your life?

CLOSING PRAYER

Let us pray to God for our needs and the needs of others: our family, neighborhood, and the world. For each need we say, "Lord, hear our prayer."

◆ All may add their own prayers here.

Let us pray: **Our Father . . . Amen.**

Most powerful Creator God,
thank you for inviting us to be your partner
in caring for your beautiful creation.
Show us how we can care for the earth
and all that is in it.
We ask this in Jesus' name.

Amen.

✝ All make the Sign of the Cross.

PRAYER FOR
TUESDAY, SEPTEMBER 25, 2018

OPENING

Sirach says creation shows God's glory, power, and wisdom. God creates everything to function just as it should. All of creation, not just human beings, do God's will.

✛ All make the Sign of the Cross.

In the name of the Father, and of the Son, and of the Holy Spirit. Amen.

PSALM
(For a longer psalm, see page xi.) Psalm 145:2–3

I will praise your name for ever, Lord.

I will praise your name for ever, Lord.

Every day I will bless you,
  and praise your name forever and ever.
Great is the Lord, and greatly to be praised;
  his greatness is unsearchable.

I will praise your name for ever, Lord.

READING
Sirach 42:15–17, 21–22

A reading from the Book of Sirach.

I will now call to mind the works of the Lord, and will declare what I have seen. By the word of the Lord his works are made; and all his creatures do his will. The sun looks down on everything with its light, and the work of the Lord is full of his glory. The Lord has not empowered even his holy ones to recount his marvelous works, which the Lord the Almighty has established so that the universe may stand firm in his glory. He has set in order the splendors of his wisdom; he is from all eternity one and the same. Nothing can be added or taken away, and he needs no one to be his counselor.

How desirable are his works and how sparkling they are to see!

The Word of the Lord.

◆ All observe silence.

FOR SILENT REFLECTION

Think about this silently in your heart. What things in the world do you think "sparkle" with God's splendor?

CLOSING PRAYER

Let us pray to God for our needs and the needs of others: our family, neighborhood, and the world. For each need we say, "Lord, hear our prayer."

◆ All may add their own prayers here.

Let us pray: **Our Father . . . Amen.**

Most powerful Creator God,
thank you for inviting us to be your partner
in caring for your beautiful creation.
Show us how we can care for the earth
and all that is in it.
We ask this in Jesus' name.

Amen.

✛ All make the Sign of the Cross.

OPENING

Sirach tells us the sky is the pride of the places above the earth. The writer, like many early people, may have believed the sky was solid like a roof so he calls it a "vault." However, the sun gets the most praise as a powerful creation that reflects the greatness of God. Today is the memorial of Sts. Cosmos and Damien, Martyrs.

✦ All make the Sign of the Cross.

In the name of the Father, and of the Son, and of the Holy Spirit. Amen.

PSALM   (For a longer psalm, see page xi.) Psalm 145:2–3

I will praise your name for ever, Lord.

I will praise your name for ever, Lord.

Every day I will bless you,
   and praise your name forever and ever.
Great is the Lord, and greatly to be praised;
   his greatness is unsearchable.

I will praise your name for ever, Lord.

READING   Sirach 42:15; 43:1–5; 42:22

A reading from the Book of Sirach.

I will now call to mind the works of the Lord, and will declare what I have seen. The pride of the higher realms is the clear vault of the sky, as glorious to behold as the sight of the heavens. The sun, when it appears, proclaims as it rises what a marvelous instrument it is, the work of the Most High. At noon it parches the land, and who can withstand its burning heat? A man tending a furnace works in burning heat, but three times as hot is the sun scorching the mountains; it breathes fiery vapors, and its bright rays blind the eyes. Great is the Lord who made it; at his orders it hurries on its course. How desirable are his works and how sparkling they are to see!

The Word of the Lord.

✦ All observe silence.

FOR SILENT REFLECTION

Think about this silently in your heart. Give thanks for the gifts of the sun: light, warmth, growth.

CLOSING PRAYER

Let us pray to God for our needs and the needs of others: our family, neighborhood, and the world. For each need we say, "Lord, hear our prayer."

✦ All may add their own prayers here.

Let us pray: **Our Father . . . Amen.**

Creator God,
all of creation praises you.
The sky with its sun of day and stars of night proclaim your glory.
We too give you thanks and praise
for your wonderful creation.

Amen.

✦ All make the Sign of the Cross.

PRAYER FOR
THURSDAY, SEPTEMBER 27, 2018

OPENING

Today is the memorial of St. Vincent de Paul, a French priest who devoted himself to caring for the poor. Many parishes have a St. Vincent de Paul society that takes donations of household items, food, and money to give to the poor. In our Scripture the author of Sirach describes the moon as "festal" that is, a sign of celebration.

✛ All make the Sign of the Cross.

In the name of the Father, and of the Son, and of the Holy Spirit. Amen.

PSALM
(For a longer psalm, see page xi.) Psalm 145:2–3

I will praise your name for ever, LORD.

I will praise your name for ever, LORD.

Every day I will bless you,
   and praise your name forever and ever.
Great is the LORD, and greatly to be praised;
   his greatness is unsearchable.

I will praise your name for ever, LORD.

READING
Sirach 42:15; 43:6–8; 42:22

A reading from the Book of Sirach.

I will now call to mind the works of the Lord, and will declare what I have seen. By the word of the Lord his works are made; and all his creatures do his will. It is the moon that marks the changing seasons, governing their times, their everlasting sign. From the moon comes the sign for festal days, a light that wanes when it completes its course. The new moon, as its name suggests, renews itself; how marvelous it is in this change, a beacon to host on high, shining in the vault of the heavens!

How desirable are his works and how sparkling they are to see!

The Word of the Lord.

◆ All observe silence.

FOR SILENT REFLECTION

Think about this silently in your heart. Think about the beautiful light the full moon makes on a dark night, and give God thanks and praise.

CLOSING PRAYER

Let us pray to God for our needs and the needs of others: our family, neighborhood, and the world. For each need we say, "Lord, hear our prayer."

◆ All may add their own prayers here.

Let us pray: **Our Father . . . Amen.**

Holy Lord God, creator of all,
we thank for the beauty of the night sky,
and for the light of the moon and the stars.
We praise you for the gift of light that shines
forth and reminds us of your majesty.

Amen.

✛ All make the Sign of the Cross.

OPENING

The stars are praised as a "glittering array" and a rainbow as a "glorious arc." Remember, the book Sirach is one of the Bible's wisdom books that helps us learn to be wise in our attitudes and behaviors. The author has an attitude of awe toward God's creation. We remember St. Wenceslaus, a king who tried to help his whole country believe in Jesus Christ.

✙ All make the Sign of the Cross.

In the name of the Father, and of the Son, and of the Holy Spirit. Amen.

PSALM
(For a longer psalm, see page xi.) Psalm 145:2–3

I will praise your name for ever, LORD.

I will praise your name for ever, LORD.

Every day I will bless you,
  and praise your name forever and ever.
Great is the LORD, and greatly to be praised;
  his greatness is unsearchable.

I will praise your name for ever, LORD.

READING
Sirach 42:15; 43:9–12; 42:22

A reading from the Book of Sirach.

I will now call to mind the works of the Lord, and will declare what I have seen. By the word of the Lord his works are made; and all his creatures do his will. The glory of the stars is the beauty of heaven, a glittering array in the heights of the Lord. On the orders of the Holy One they stand in their appointed places; they never relax in their watches. Look at the rainbow, and praise him who made it; it is exceedingly beautiful in its brightness. It encircles the sky with its glorious arc; the hands of the Most High have stretched it out. How desirable are his works and how sparkling they are to see!

The Word of the Lord.

◆ All observe silence.

FOR SILENT REFLECTION

Think about this silently in your heart. Have you ever seen a "glittering array" of stars? Say a prayer of thanks and praise for the stars.

CLOSING PRAYER

Let us pray to God for our needs and the needs of others: our family, neighborhood, and the world. For each need we say, "Lord, hear our prayer."

◆ All may add their own prayers here.

Let us pray: **Our Father . . . Amen.**

Creator God,
we thank for the gift of the stars.
As a star guided the shepherds and wise men
to you in Bethlehem many years ago,
may we be guided by the light of your word.

Amen.

✙ All make the Sign of the Cross.

PRAYER FOR THE WEEK

WITH A READING FROM THE GOSPEL FOR **SUNDAY, SEPTEMBER 30, 2018**

OPENING

Jesus teaches many lessons today. He warns the disciples not to judge others. Courtesy toward those who follow Jesus, whether friends or not, will be rewarded. Finally, we have a responsibility to be good examples for the "little ones," Jesus' loving name for those who follow him.

✦ All make the Sign of the Cross.

In the name of the Father, and of the Son, and of the Holy Spirit. Amen.

PSALM   (For a longer psalm, see page xi.) Psalm 145:2–3

I will praise your name for ever, LORD.

I will praise your name for ever, LORD.

Every day I will bless you,
   and praise your name forever and ever.
Great is the LORD, and greatly to be praised;
   his greatness is unsearchable.

I will praise your name for ever, LORD.

✦ All stand and sing **Alleluia.**

GOSPEL   Mark 9:38–42

A reading from the holy Gospel according to Mark.

John said to him, "Teacher, we saw someone casting out demons in your name, and we tried to stop him, because he was not following us." But Jesus said, "Do not stop him; for no one who does a deed of power in my name will be able soon afterward to speak evil of me. Whoever is not against us is for us. For truly I tell you, whoever gives you a cup of water to drink because you bear the name of Christ will by no means lose the reward. If any of you put a stumbling block before one of these little ones who believe in me, it would be better for you if a great millstone were hung around your neck and you were thrown into the sea."

The Gospel of the Lord.

✦ All sit and observe silence.

FOR SILENT REFLECTION

Think about this silently in your heart. Are you courteous to all of your classmates?

CLOSING PRAYER

Let us pray to God for our needs and the needs of others: our family, neighborhood, and the world. For each need we say, "Lord, hear our prayer."

✦ All may add their own prayers here.

Let us pray: **Our Father . . . Amen.**

Help us be Jesus' "little ones," dear God.
Help us overcome any meanness
or contempt for anyone in our class or school.
Bless us with an inclusive and courteous heart.
We ask this in Jesus' name.

Amen.

✦ All make the Sign of the Cross.

OPENING

We continue to explore the Book of Sirach's comments on Genesis' first story of Creation. The author sees God's power and splendor in the wind and thunder and storms. Today is the memorial of St. Thérèse of the Child Jesus, a Doctor, or Wise Teacher, of the Church.

✤ All make the Sign of the Cross.

In the name of the Father, and of the Son, and of the Holy Spirit. Amen.

PSALM   (For a longer psalm, see page xi.) Psalm 145:2–3

I will praise your name for ever, Lord.

I will praise your name for ever, Lord.

Every day I will bless you,
  and praise your name forever and ever.
Great is the Lord, and greatly to be praised;
  his greatness is unsearchable.

I will praise your name for ever, Lord.

READING   Sirach 42:15a; 43:13, 15–19; 42:22

A reading from the Book of Sirach.

I will now call to mind the works of the Lord, and will declare what I have seen. By his command he sends the driving snow and speeds the lightening of his judgment. In his majesty he gives the clouds their strength, and the hailstones are broken in pieces. The voice of his thunder rebukes the earth; when he appears the mountains shake. At his will the south wind blows; so do the storm from the north and the whirlwind. He scatters the snow like birds flying down, and its descent is like locusts alighting. The eye is dazzled by the beauty of its whiteness, and the mind is amazed as it falls. He pours frost over the earth like salt, and icicles form like pointed thorns. How desirable are his works and how sparkling they are to see!

The Word of the Lord.

◆ All observe silence.

FOR SILENT REFLECTION

Think about this silently in your heart. What in nature reveals God's power to you?

CLOSING PRAYER

Let us pray to God for our needs and the needs of others: our family, neighborhood, and the world. For each need we say, "Lord, hear our prayer."

◆ All may add their own prayers here.

Let us pray: **Our Father . . . Amen.**

Most powerful Creator God,
may we learn to respect and care
for all of creation.
We pray for all those who have experienced natural disasters from flood, fire, or wind.
May they be safe and free from harm.

Amen.

✤ All make the Sign of the Cross.

OPENING

We celebrate the memorial of the Holy Guardian Angels today. The verses in Sirach were written about four hundred years after the Creation story in the Book of Genesis. In these verses the author praises two states of water, solid ice and liquid mist.

✦ All make the Sign of the Cross.

In the name of the Father, and of the Son, and of the Holy Spirit. Amen.

PSALM   (For a longer psalm, see page xi.) Psalm 145:2–3

I will praise your name for ever, LORD.

I will praise your name for ever, LORD.

Every day I will bless you,
   and praise your name forever and ever.
Great is the LORD, and greatly to be praised;
   his greatness is unsearchable.

I will praise your name for ever, LORD.

READING   Sirach 42:15; 43:19–22; 42:22

A reading from the Book of Sirach.

I will now call to mind the works of the Lord, and will declare what I have seen. By the word of the Lord his works are made; and all his creatures do his will. The cold north wind blows, and ice freezes on the water; it settles on every pool of water, and the water puts it on like a breastplate. He consumes the mountains and burns up the wilderness, and withers the grass like fire. A mist quickly heals all things; the falling dew gives refreshment from the heart. How desirable are his works and how sparkling they are to see!

The Word of the Lord.

◆ All observe silence.

FOR SILENT REFLECTION

Think about this silently in your heart. Ask your guardian angel to guide and protect you.

CLOSING PRAYER

Let us pray to God for our needs and the needs of others: our family, neighborhood, and the world. For each need we say, "Lord, hear our prayer."

◆ All may add their own prayers here.

Let us pray: **Our Father . . . Amen.**

Let us say the prayer to our Guardian Angels:
Angel of God,
my guardian dear,
to whom his love commits me here,
ever this day be at my side
to light and guard,
to rule and guide.

Amen.

✦ All make the Sign of the Cross.

OPENING

Today we hear the author of the Book of Sirach speak of the sea with its islands and sea monsters! Remember that the writer lived long ago, and yet he realized that the seas and oceans held many marvelous creatures!

✝ All make the Sign of the Cross.

In the name of the Father, and of the Son, and of the Holy Spirit. Amen.

PSALM   (For a longer psalm, see page xi.) Psalm 145:2–3

I will praise your name for ever, LORD.

I will praise your name for ever, LORD.

Every day I will bless you,
    and praise your name forever and ever.
Great is the LORD, and greatly to be praised;
    his greatness is unsearchable.

I will praise your name for ever, LORD.

READING   Sirach 42:15; 43:23–26; 42:22

A reading from the Book of Sirach.

I will now call to mind the works of the Lord, and will declare what I have seen. By the word of the Lord his works are made; and all his creatures do his will. By his plan he stilled the deep and planted islands in it. Those who sail the sea tell of its dangers, and we marvel at what we hear. In it are strange and marvelous creatures, all kinds of living things, and huge sea monsters. Because of him each of his messengers succeeds, and by his word all things hold together. How desirable are his works and how sparkling they are to see!

The Word of the Lord.

◆ All observe silence.

FOR SILENT REFLECTION

Think about this silently in your heart. Say a prayer of thanks for the oceans and seas, and all of the life that they provide.

CLOSING PRAYER

Let us pray to God for our needs and the needs of others: our family, neighborhood, and the world. For each need we say, "Lord, hear our prayer."

◆ All may add their own prayers here.

Let us pray: **Our Father . . . Amen.**

Most powerful Creator God,
thank you for the waters that cover the earth.
Thank you for the gifts from the sea:
fish that feed us;
shells and rocks that
delight us.
Water is essential to all life.
Show us how we can care for the gift
of water in all of its forms.
We ask this in Jesus' name.

Amen.

✝ All make the Sign of the Cross.

OPENING

Today is the memorial of St. Francis Assisi, who died in 1226. He is known for his great love of God's creation. He even called the sun "brother," and the moon, "sister." The author of Sirach reminds us that human beings have been given the gift of God's own image as well as authority over the earth.

✝ All make the Sign of the Cross.

In the name of the Father, and of the Son, and of the Holy Spirit. Amen.

PSALM   (For a longer psalm, see page xi.) Psalm 145:2–3

I will praise your name for ever, LORD.

I will praise your name for ever, LORD.

Every day I will bless you,
 and praise your name forever and ever.
Great is the LORD, and greatly to be praised;
 his greatness is unsearchable.

I will praise your name for ever, LORD.

READING   Sirach 42:15; 17:1–3, 6b–7, 12; 42:22

A reading from the Book of Sirach.

I will now call to mind the works of the Lord, and will declare what I have seen. By the word of the Lord his works are made; and all his creatures do his will. The Lord created human beings out of earth, and makes them return to it again. He gave them a fixed number of days, but granted them authority over everything on the earth. He endowed them with strength like his own, and made them in his own image. Ears and a mind for thinking he gave them. He filled them with knowledge and understanding, and showed them good and evil. He established with them an eternal covenant, and revealed to them his decrees. How desirable are his works and how sparkling they are to see!

The Word of the Lord.

◆ All observe silence.

FOR SILENT REFLECTION

Think about this silently in your heart. How should we act and speak if we believe we are made in God's own image?

CLOSING PRAYER

Let us pray to God for our needs and the needs of others: our family, neighborhood, and the world. For each need we say, "Lord, hear our prayer."

◆ All may add their own prayers here.

Let us pray: **Our Father . . . Amen.**

Loving God,
we praise you and thank you
for all of creation, but most especially
for the gift of human life, which you created
in your image.

Amen.

✝ All make the Sign of the Cross.

OPENING

We often take the beauty and power of creation for granted. The writer of the Book of Sirach, reminds us that "God is all" and more powerful than anything in the universe. We are advised to have an attitude of wonder and awe at the many desirable and sparkling works of God.

✚ All make the Sign of the Cross.

In the name of the Father, and of the Son, and of the Holy Spirit. Amen.

PSALM

(For a longer psalm, see page xi.) Psalm 145:2–3

I will praise your name for ever, LORD.

I will praise your name for ever, LORD.

Every day I will bless you,
  and praise your name forever and ever.
Great is the LORD, and greatly to be praised;
  his greatness is unsearchable.

I will praise your name for ever, LORD.

READING

Sirach 43:27–30a, 31–33; 42:22

A reading from the Book of Sirach.

We could say more but could never say enough; let the final word be: "God is all." Where can we find the strength to praise him? For he is greater than all his works. Awesome is the Lord and very great, and marvelous is his power. Glorify the Lord and exalt him as much as you can, for he surpasses even that. Who has seen God and can describe him? Or who can extol him as he is? Many greater things than these lie hidden, for I have seen but a few of his works. For the Lord has made all things, and to the godly he has given wisdom. How desirable are his works and how sparkling they are to see!

The Word of the Lord.

◆ All observe silence.

FOR SILENT REFLECTION

Think about this silently in your heart. What are one or two of God's creation that you can appreciate more and thank God for this week?

CLOSING PRAYER

Let us pray to God for our needs and the needs of others: our family, neighborhood, and the world. For each need we say, "Lord, hear our prayer."

◆ All may add their own prayers here.

Let us pray: **Our Father . . . Amen.**

Your creation, O Lord, reveals
your greatness and love.
And yet, we know you are greater still.
We look forward to the day
when you will be all in all,
and all creation will praise you!

Amen.

✚ All make the Sign of the Cross.

OPENING

Jesus knew that little children have the faith and trust that is needed to enter the Kingdom of God. The disciples didn't understand this. They saw children as unimportant and wasting Jesus' time. Jesus scolded his disciples. Listen to what Jesus says to the disciples about little children in today's reading.

✝ All make the Sign of the Cross.

In the name of the Father, and of the Son, and of the Holy Spirit. Amen.

PSALM
(For a longer psalm, see page xi.) Psalm 145:2–3

I will praise your name for ever, LORD.

I will praise your name for ever, LORD.

Every day I will bless you,
 and praise your name forever and ever.
Great is the LORD, and greatly to be praised;
 his greatness is unsearchable.

I will praise your name for ever, LORD.

◆ All stand and sing **Alleluia.**

GOSPEL
Mark 10:13–16

A reading from the holy Gospel according to Mark.

People were bringing little children to him in order that he might touch them; and the disciples spoke sternly to them. But when Jesus saw this, he was indignant and said to them, "Let the little children come to me; do not stop them; for it is to such as these that the kingdom of God belongs. Truly I tell you, whoever does not receive the kingdom of God as a little child will never enter it." And he took them up in his arms, laid his hands on them, and blessed them.

The Gospel of the Lord.

◆ All sit and observe silence.

FOR SILENT REFLECTION

Think about this silently in your heart. What do you think are the special qualities that Jesus sees in little children?

CLOSING PRAYER

Let us pray to God for our needs and the needs of others: our family, neighborhood, and the world. For each need we say, "Lord, hear our prayer."

◆ All may add their own prayers here.

Let us pray: **Our Father . . . Amen.**

Loving God, help us to appreciate
the openness and kindness of little children.
Help us to remain as faithful and loving
as they are.
We want to help build your Kingdom.
Thank you for reminding us
once again what is most important.

Amen.

✝ All make the Sign of the Cross.

60

OPENING

Jesus spoke often about the importance of service: service to God and service to one another. To give service means to help, to give aid, to take care of. When the disciples argued about such as things as who was most important or who did the best work, Jesus reminded them that service, humility, and kindness are what God wants most from us.

✚ All make the Sign of the Cross.

In the name of the Father, and of the Son, and of the Holy Spirit. Amen.

PSALM   (For a longer psalm, see page xi.) Psalm 145:2–3

I will praise your name for ever, LORD.

I will praise your name for ever, LORD.

Every day I will bless you,
   and praise your name forever and ever.
Great is the LORD, and greatly to be praised;
   his greatness is unsearchable.

I will praise your name for ever, LORD.

◆ All stand and sing **Alleluia.**

GOSPEL   Mark 9:33–37

A reading from the holy Gospel according to Mark.

Jesus and his disciples came to Capernaum; and when Jesus was in the house he asked them, "What were you arguing about on the way?" But they were silent, for on the way they had argued with one another who was the greatest. He sat down, called the twelve, and said to them, "Whoever wants to be first must be last of all and servant of all." Then he took a little child and put it among them; and taking it in his arms, he said to them, "Whoever welcomes one such child in my name welcomes me, and whoever welcomes me welcomes not me but the one who sent me."

The Gospel of the Lord.

◆ All sit and observe silence.

FOR SILENT REFLECTION

Think about this silently in your heart. Is there someone you can help today? Who can you be of service to today?

CLOSING PRAYER

Let us pray to God for our needs and the needs of others: our family, neighborhood, and the world. For each need we say, "Lord, hear our prayer."

◆ All may add their own prayers here.

Let us pray: **Our Father . . . Amen.**

Dear Lord,
we get carried away thinking about ourselves.
Help us to think less about ourselves
and more about helping other people.
We ask this in Jesus' name.

Amen.

✚ All make the Sign of the Cross.

OPENING

Today is the memorial of St. Denis who was bishop of Paris during the third century and martyred for his Christian faith. He is the patron saint of France. In Jesus' time, little children were not considered very important. The disciples thought that blessing all the children that parents brought to Jesus was taking up too much of his time. But Jesus scolded the disciples.

◆ All make the Sign of the Cross.

In the name of the Father, and of the Son, and of the Holy Spirit. Amen.

PSALM   (For a longer psalm, see page xi.) Psalm 145:2–3

I will praise your name for ever, Lord.

I will praise your name for ever, Lord.

Every day I will bless you,
   and praise your name forever and ever.
Great is the Lord, and greatly to be praised;
   his greatness is unsearchable.

I will praise your name for ever, Lord.

◆ All stand and sing **Alleluia.**

GOSPEL   Mark 10:13–16

A reading from the holy Gospel according to Mark.

People were bringing little children to him in order that he might touch them; and the disciples spoke sternly to them. But when Jesus saw this, he was indignant and said to them, "Let the little children come to me; do not stop them; for it is to such as these that the kingdom of God belongs. Truly I tell you, whoever does not receive the kingdom of God as a little child will never enter it." And he took them up in his arms, laid his hands on them, and blessed them.

The Gospel of the Lord.

◆ All sit and observe silence.

FOR SILENT REFLECTION

Think about this silently in your heart. Jesus wants children to come to him because he loves children in a very special way. Do you know that Jesus loves you?

CLOSING PRAYER

Let us pray to God for our needs and the needs of others: our family, neighborhood, and the world. For each need we say, "Lord, hear our prayer."

◆ All may add their own prayers here.

Let us pray: **Our Father . . . Amen.**

Kind and loving God,
thank you for knowing
and seeing the goodness of children.
We trust that you love us
and hold us in your care always.

Amen.

◆ All make the Sign of the Cross.

OPENING

Jesus' disciples frequently did what most of us often do; think of ourselves first. And Jesus was always reminding them that following him was not about gaining praise and glory for themselves but about serving others.

✚ *All make the Sign of the Cross.*

In the name of the Father, and of the Son, and of the Holy Spirit. Amen.

PSALM   (For a longer psalm, see page xi.) Psalm 145:2–3

I will praise your name for ever, LORD.

I will praise your name for ever, LORD.

Every day I will bless you,
 and praise your name forever and ever.
Great is the LORD, and greatly to be praised;
 his greatness is unsearchable.

I will praise your name for ever, LORD.

◆ *All stand and sing* **Alleluia.**

GOSPEL   Mark 10:35–40a

A reading from the holy Gospel according to Mark.

James and John, the sons of Zebedee, came forward to Jesus and said to him, "Teacher, we want you to do for us whatever we ask of you." And Jesus said to them, "What is it you want me to do for you?" And they said to him, "Grant us to sit, one at your right hand and one at your left, in your glory." But Jesus said to them, "You do not know what you are asking. Are you able to drink the cup that I drink, or be baptized with the baptism that I am bap-tized with?" They replied, "We are able." Then Jesus said to them, "The cup that I drink you will drink; and with the baptism with which I am baptized, you will be baptized; but to sit at my right hand or at my left is not mine to grant."

The Gospel of the Lord.

◆ *All sit and observe silence.*

FOR SILENT REFLECTION

Think about this silently in your heart. Whom could you do one nice thing for today?

CLOSING PRAYER

Let us pray to God for our needs and the needs of others: our family, neighborhood, and the world. For each need we say, "Lord, hear our prayer."

◆ *All may add their own prayers here.*

Let us pray: **Our Father . . . Amen.**

Generous God,
you have blessed us with so many gifts.
Help us to stop thinking so much
about ourselves.
Fill our hearts with gratitude
and help us to joyfully serve others.

Amen.

✚ *All make the Sign of the Cross.*

OPENING

St. Paul traveled to Galatia [guh-LAY-shuh] (which was the area we now call Turkey). He preached the good news about Jesus, and many people became Christians. Paul taught the Galatians [guh-LAY-shuhnz] the "Great Commandment." And he warned them what would happen if they did not follow it.

✦ All make the Sign of the Cross.

In the name of the Father, and of the Son, and of the Holy Spirit. Amen.

PSALM

(For a longer psalm, see page xi.) Psalm 145:2–3

I will praise your name for ever, LORD.

I will praise your name for ever, LORD.

Every day I will bless you,
  and praise your name forever and ever.
Great is the LORD, and greatly to be praised;
  his greatness is unsearchable.

I will praise your name for ever, LORD.

READING

Galatians 5:13–15; 6:10a,15ab

A reading from the Letter of Paul to the Galatians.

You were called to freedom, brothers and sisters; only do not use your freedom as an opportunity for self-indulgence, but through love become slaves to one another. For the whole law is summed up in a single commandment, "You shall love your neighbor as yourself." If, however, you bite and devour one another, take care that you are not consumed by one another. So then, whenever we have an opportunity. Let us work for the good of all. As for those who will follow this rule—peace be upon them, and mercy.

The Word of the Lord.

◆ All observe silence.

FOR SILENT REFLECTION

Think about this silently in your heart. Why do you think there is one Great Commandment that Paul says all Christians must follow?

CLOSING PRAYER

Let us pray to God for our needs and the needs of others: our family, neighborhood, and the world. For each need we say, "Lord, hear our prayer."

◆ All may add their own prayers here.

Let us pray: **Our Father . . . Amen.**

Understanding and compassionate God, sometimes it is really hard to love others. Help us to keep trying to make peace with one another even when it is difficult. Help us to trust that you always stand with us, even when things feel difficult.

Amen.

✦ All make the Sign of the Cross.

OPENING

Today is the feast of Our Lady of Aparecida, which is celebrated as a national holiday in Brazil. The basilica that houses the statue, a dark-skinned image of Our Lady, is one of the largest churches in the world. St. Peter, the leader of the early Church, wrote, traveled, and preached to the early Christian communities. Listen to the advice he gives people in today's reading.

✜ All make the Sign of the Cross.

In the name of the Father, and of the Son, and of the Holy Spirit. Amen.

PSALM
(For a longer psalm, see page xi.) Psalm 145:2–3

I will praise your name for ever, LORD.

I will praise your name for ever, LORD.

Every day I will bless you,
   and praise your name forever and ever.
Great is the LORD, and greatly to be praised;
   his greatness is unsearchable.

I will praise your name for ever, LORD.

READING
1 Peter 4:8–11

A reading from the First Letter of Peter.

Above all, maintain constant love for one another, for love covers a multitude of sins. Be hospitable to one another without complaining. Like good stewards of the manifold grace of God, serve one another with whatever gift each of you has received. Whoever speaks must do so as one speaking the very words of God; whoever serves must do so with the strength that God supplies, so that God may be glori-fied in all things through Jesus Christ. To him belong the glory and the power forever and ever. Amen.

The Word of the Lord.

◆ All observe silence.

FOR SILENT REFLECTION

Think about this silently in your heart. How does loving, being kind, and serving one another make the world better?

CLOSING PRAYER

Let us pray to God for our needs and the needs of others: our family, neighborhood, and the world. For each need we say, "Lord, hear our prayer."

◆ All may add their own prayers here.

Let us pray: **Our Father . . . Amen.**

Loving God,
you have given each of us talents.
You ask us to use these talents to serve others.
We want to contribute in making
the world a better place.
Give us good people who can show us
how to use our talents in service to others.
We ask this in the name of Jesus.

Amen.

✜ All make the Sign of the Cross.

PRAYER SERVICE
MEMORIAL OF OUR LADY OF THE ROSARY

Prepare eight leaders for this service. The third and fourth leaders will need Bibles for the Scripture passages and may need help practicing the readings. You may wish to begin by singing "The Servant Song" and end with "We Have Been Told." If the group will sing, prepare a song leader.

FIRST LEADER:
May the grace and peace of our Lord Jesus Christ be with us, now and forever.

Amen.

SECOND LEADER:
Today we celebrate Mary,
the Mother of our Lord Jesus,
whose life of holiness always pointed
toward Christ our Savior.
And today we honor her with this feast
in thanksgiving for the Rosary
that highlights the mysteries of
the life and Death of our Messiah.
May we say "yes" to God
as she did throughout her life.
We ask this through Christ our Lord.

Amen.

◆ All stand and sing **Alleluia.**

THIRD LEADER: Luke 1:39–45
A reading from the holy Gospel according to Luke

◆ Read the passage from a Bible.

The Gospel of the Lord.

Response: **Praise to you, Lord Jesus Christ.**

CHILDREN'S DAILY PRAYER 2018–2019, © 2018 Archdiocese of Chicago: Liturgy Training Publications. All rights reserved. Orders: 800-933-1800 or www.LTP.org.

FOURTH LEADER: Luke 1:46–56

A reading from the holy Gospel according to Luke

◆ Read the passage from a Bible.

The Gospel of the Lord.

Response: Praise to you, Lord Jesus Christ.

◆ All sit and observe silence.

FIFTH LEADER:

Lord Jesus,
your Mother's life
was centered around you.
Through the gift of the Rosary,
we can reflect on the key events
in your life filled with
joy, sorrow, and glory.
Guide us toward living as fully
as Mary did as we meditate on
your mysteries.
In your name we pray.

Amen.

SIXTH LEADER:

Together let's pray one decade of
the Rosary in honor of this
feast of our Mother Mary:
Hail Mary, full of grace
the Lord is with you,
blessed are you among women
and blessed is the fruit of your womb, Jesus.
Holy Mary, Mother of God,
pray for us sinners,
now and at the hour of our death.

Amen.

Glory be to the Father,
and to the Son,
and to the Holy Spirit.

Amen.

SEVENTH LEADER:

Loving Jesus,
fill our hearts with the same
loving response as Mary had
when the angel Gabriel asked her
to be the Mother of our Lord.
May we be mindful of how you
also remained faithful to God's will
through the tragedies and joys
of your life.
Help us to be vessels of your grace.
We ask this through Christ our Lord.

Amen.

EIGHTH LEADER:

May the love of God,

✝ All make the Sign of the Cross.

Father, Son, and Holy Spirit,
keep us connected with the help of
our Mother Mary,
now and forever.

Amen.

PRAYER FOR THE WEEK

OPENING

Today's Gospel reading is challenging. A young man questions Jesus about how to be a good disciple. But when Jesus says that he must give up something he loves, the young man finds it too difficult and turns away.

✛ All make the Sign of the Cross.

In the name of the Father, and of the Son, and of the Holy Spirit. Amen.

PSALM
(For a longer psalm, see page xi.) Psalm 145:2–3

I will praise your name for ever, LORD.

I will praise your name for ever, LORD.

Every day I will bless you,
   and praise your name forever and ever.
Great is the LORD, and greatly to be praised;
   his greatness is unsearchable.

I will praise your name for ever, LORD.

◆ All stand and sing **Alleluia.**

GOSPEL
Mark 10:17–18a, 19a, 20–23, 25

A reading from the holy Gospel according to Mark.

As Jesus was setting out on a journey, a man ran up and knelt before him, and asked him, "Good Teacher, what must I do to inherit eternal life?" Jesus said to him, "You know the commandments." He said to Jesus, "Teacher, I have kept all these since my youth." Jesus, looking at him, loved him and said, "You lack one thing; go, sell what you own, and give the money to the poor; then come, follow me." When the man heard this, he was shocked and went away grieving, for he had many possessions. Then Jesus looked around and said to his disciples, "How hard it will be for those who have wealth to enter the kingdom of God!" It is easier for a camel to go through the eye of a needle than for someone who is rich to enter the kingdom of God."

The Gospel of the Lord.

◆ All sit and observe silence.

FOR SILENT REFLECTION

Think about this silently in your heart. Why do you think it is important to share what we have with others who have less?

CLOSING PRAYER

Let us pray to God for our needs and the needs of others: our family, neighborhood, and the world. For each need we say, "Lord, hear our prayer."

◆ All may add their own prayers here.

Let us pray: **Our Father . . . Amen.**

Dear God, help us to be generous.
Help us to see the needs of others
and be willing to share what we have.
We ask this in Jesus' name.

Amen.

✛ All make the Sign of the Cross.

OPENING

Today is the memorial of St. Teresa of Avila, who lived in Spain in the sixteenth century. St. Teresa joined the order of Carmelite nuns and committed herself to a life of poverty. She was a great writer and was one of the first women to be named Doctor of the Church. Our readings this week focus on the Sabbath, which is that day of the week that is reserved to honor God by prayer and rest.

✚ All make the Sign of the Cross.

In the name of the Father, and of the Son, and of the Holy Spirit. Amen.

PSALM
(For a longer psalm, see page xi.) Psalm 145:2–3

I will praise your name for ever, LORD.

I will praise your name for ever, LORD.

Every day I will bless you,
    and praise your name forever and ever.
Great is the LORD, and greatly to be praised;
    his greatness is unsearchable.

I will praise your name for ever, LORD.

READING
Exodus 20:1, 8–11

A reading from the Book of Exodus.

Then God spoke all these words: remember the sabbath day, and keep it holy. Six days you shall labor and do all your work. But the seventh day is a sabbath to the LORD your God; you shall not do any work—you, your son or your daughter, your male or female slave, your livestock, or the alien resident in your towns. For in six days the LORD made heaven and earth, the sea, and all that is in them, but rested the seventh day; therefore the LORD blessed the sabbath day and consecrated it.

The Word of the Lord.

◆ All observe silence.

FOR SILENT REFLECTION

Think about this silently in your heart. How do you and your family observe Sunday, the Sabbath day for Christians?

CLOSING PRAYER

Let us pray to God for our needs and the needs of others: our family, neighborhood, and the world. For each need we say, "Lord, hear our prayer."

◆ All may add their own prayers here.

Let us pray: **Our Father . . . Amen.**

Dear God, our lives are very busy.
We have school and sports
and extracurricular activities.
Our parents work hard and often long hours.
Help us to commit to follow
your commandment to keep the Sabbath holy.

Amen.

✚ All make the Sign of the Cross.

PRAYER FOR
TUESDAY, OCTOBER 16, 2018

OPENING

St. Margaret Mary Alacoque, a French nun in the seventeenth century, had visions of Jesus that led her to promote devotion to the Most Sacred Heart of Jesus. Today is her memorial. With today's reading we continue thinking about the importance of times of rest, not only for people but for the land also.

✦ All make the Sign of the Cross.

In the name of the Father, and of the Son, and of the Holy Spirit. Amen.

PSALM   (For a longer psalm, see page xi.) Psalm 145:2–3

I will praise your name for ever, LORD.

I will praise your name for ever, LORD.

Every day I will bless you,
   and praise your name forever and ever.
Great is the LORD, and greatly to be praised;
   his greatness is unsearchable.

I will praise your name for ever, LORD.

READING   Leviticus 25:1–5

A reading from the Book of Leviticus.

The LORD spoke to Moses on Mount Sinai, saying: Speak to the people of Israel and say to them: When you enter the land that I am giving you, the land shall observe a sabbath for the LORD. Six years you shall sow your field, and six years you shall prune your vineyard, and gather in their yield; but in the seventh year there shall be a sabbath of complete rest for the land, a sabbath for the LORD: you shall not sow your field or prune your vineyard. You shall not reap the after growth of your harvest

or gather the grapes of your unpruned vine: it shall be a year of complete rest for the land.

The Word of the Lord.

◆ All observe silence.

FOR SILENT REFLECTION

Think about this silently in your heart. God told Moses that the land should observe a Sabbath, or rest, for the Lord. Why is that important?

CLOSING PRAYER

Let us pray to God for our needs and the needs of others: our family, neighborhood, and the world. For each need we say, "Lord, hear our prayer."

◆ All may add their own prayers here.

Let us pray: **Our Father . . . Amen.**

Good and loving God,
you created the cycles of nature
so that there is a time to plant
and a time to rest.
Help us to honor the gift of time.
We ask this in Jesus' name.

Amen.

✦ All make the Sign of the Cross.

OPENING

St. Ignatius of Antioch was an early Christian bishop of Antioch, which is in modern day Turkey. Today is his memorial. His extensive writings focused on the importance of the Eucharist. In today's reading, religious leaders try to trick Jesus about observing the Sabbath. Listen to how Jesus answers them.

✤ All make the Sign of the Cross.

In the name of the Father, and of the Son, and of the Holy Spirit. Amen.

PSALM

(For a longer psalm, see page xi.) Psalm 145:2–3

I will praise your name for ever, LORD.

I will praise your name for ever, LORD.

Every day I will bless you,
 and praise your name forever and ever.
Great is the LORD, and greatly to be praised;
 his greatness is unsearchable.

I will praise your name for ever, LORD.

◆ All stand and sing **Alleluia.**

GOSPEL

Mark 2:23–28

A reading from the holy Gospel according to Mark.

One sabbath Jesus was going through the cornfields; and as they made their way his disciples began to pluck heads of grain. The Pharisees said to him, "Look, why are they doing what is not lawful on the sabbath?" And Jesus said to them, "Have you never read what David did when he and his companions were hungry and in need of food? He entered the house of God, when Abiathar was high priest, and ate the bread of the Presence, which it is not lawful for any but the priests to eat, and he gave some to his companions." Then he said to them, "The sabbath was made for humankind, and not humankind for the sabbath; so the Son of Man is lord even of the sabbath."

The Gospel of the Lord.

◆ All sit and observe silence.

FOR SILENT REFLECTION

Think about this silently in your heart. What do you think Jesus means when he says that "the Sabbath was made for humankind," that is, for us?

CLOSING PRAYER

Let us pray to God for our needs and the needs of others: our family, neighborhood, and the world. For each need we say, "Lord, hear our prayer."

◆ All may add their own prayers here.

Let us pray: **Our Father . . . Amen.**

Dear God, our lives are very busy.
It is difficult to keep Sundays as days to rest, pray, and enjoy family and friends.
Help us to commit to follow
your commandment
to keep the Sabbath holy.

Amen.

✤ All make the Sign of the Cross.

OPENING

St. Luke the Evangelist, whose feast is today, is known as the author of both the Gospel that bears his name and the Acts of the Apostles. When we receive the Eucharist we remember the last Passover meal that Jesus shared with his disciples. Receiving the Eucharist at Mass on Sunday is an important way to keep the Sabbath holy.

✛ All make the Sign of the Cross.

In the name of the Father, and of the Son, and of the Holy Spirit. Amen.

PSALM (For a longer psalm, see page xi.) Psalm 145:2–3

I will praise your name for ever, LORD.

I will praise your name for ever, LORD.

Every day I will bless you,
  and praise your name forever and ever.
Great is the LORD, and greatly to be praised;
  his greatness is unsearchable.

I will praise your name for ever, LORD.

◆ All stand and sing **Alleluia.**

GOSPEL Mark 14:12–16

A reading from the holy Gospel according to Mark.

On the first day of Unleavened Bread, when the Passover lamb is sacrificed, his disciples said to him, "Where do you want us to go and make the preparations for you to eat the Passover?" So he sent two of his disciples, saying to them, "Go into the city, and a man carrying a jar of water will meet you; follow him, and wherever he enters, say to the owner of the house, "The Teacher asks, 'Where is my guest room where I may eat the Passover with my disciples?' He will show you a large room upstairs, furnished and ready. Make preparations for us there." So the disciples set out and went to the city, and found everything as he had told them; and they prepared the Passover meal.

The Gospel of the Lord.

◆ All sit and observe silence.

FOR SILENT REFLECTION

Think about this silently in your heart. Why is going to Sunday Mass a particularly helpful way to observe the Sabbath?

CLOSING PRAYER

Let us pray to God for our needs and the needs of others: our family, neighborhood, and the world. For each need we say, "Lord, hear our prayer."

◆ All may add their own prayers here.

Let us pray: **Our Father . . . Amen.**

We give you thanks, O God,
for the gift of the Mass.
Each Sunday you invite us
to pray together with the Church
around the world.

Amen.

✛ All make the Sign of the Cross.

OPENING

Today is the memorial of Sts. John Brébeuf and Isaac Jogues, who were early martyrs in America. They worked among the Huron Indians and converted many to the Christian faith. After Jesus was gone, his disciples traveled extensively spreading his teachings to many part of the known world. Today's passage shows that honoring the Sabbath by going to temple was part of St. Paul's regular practice.

✜ All make the Sign of the Cross.

In the name of the Father, and of the Son, and of the Holy Spirit. Amen.

PSALM
(For a longer psalm, see page xi.) Psalm 145:2–3

I will praise your name for ever, LORD.

I will praise your name for ever, LORD.

Every day I will bless you,
    and praise your name forever and ever.
Great is the LORD, and greatly to be praised;
    his greatness is unsearchable.

I will praise your name for ever, LORD.

READING
Acts 17:1–4

A reading from the Acts of the Apostles.

After Paul and Silas had passed through Amphipolis and Apollonia, they came to Thessalonica, where there was a synagogue of the Jews. And Paul went in, as was his custom, and on three sabbath days argued with them from the scriptures, explaining and proving that it was necessary for the Messiah to suffer and to rise from the dead, and saying, "This is the Messiah, Jesus whom I am proclaiming to you." Some of them were persuaded and joined Paul and Silas, as did a great many of the devout Greeks and not a few of the leading women.

The Word of the Lord.

◆ All observe silence.

FOR SILENT REFLECTION

Think about this silently in your heart. What can you do to make this Sunday more restful and prayerful?

CLOSING PRAYER

Let us pray to God for our needs and the needs of others: our family, neighborhood, and the world. For each need we say, "Lord, hear our prayer."

◆ All may add their own prayers here.

Let us pray: **Our Father . . . Amen.**

Thank you, O God,
for the gift of the Sabbath.
We are grateful for a day of rest
and a time to offer you praise.
Help us to honor you by observing
this day which you have given to us.

Amen.

✜ All make the Sign of the Cross.

PRAYER FOR THE WEEK
WITH A READING FROM THE GOSPEL FOR **SUNDAY, OCTOBER 21, 2018**

OPENING

The Apostles James and John were confused about what it meant to follow Jesus. Jesus had to help them understand that being a Christian is not about power, prestige, and glory. It is about service.

✚ All make the Sign of the Cross.

In the name of the Father, and of the Son, and of the Holy Spirit. Amen.

PSALM
(For a longer psalm, see page xii.) Psalm 98:1

The LORD has made known his victory.

The LORD has made known his victory.

O sing to the LORD a new song,
   for he has done marvelous things.
His right hand and his holy arm
   have gotten him victory.

The LORD has made known his victory.

◆ All stand and sing **Alleluia.**

GOSPEL
Mark 10:35–37, 41–42a, 43, 45

A reading from the holy Gospel according to Mark.

James and John, the sons of Zebedee [ZEB-uh-dee], came forward to him and said to him, "Teacher, we want you to do for us whatever we ask of you." And he said to them, "What is it you want me to do for you?" And they said to him, "Grant us to sit, one at your right hand and one at your left, in your glory." When the ten heard this, they began to be angry with James and John. So Jesus called them and said to them, "You know that among the Gentiles those whom they recognize as their rulers lord it over them. But it is not so among you; but whoever wishes to become great among you must be your servant. For the Son of Man came not to be served but to serve, and to give his life a ransom for many."

The Gospel of the Lord.

◆ All sit and observe silence.

FOR SILENT REFLECTION

Think about this silently in your heart. To serve means to help someone. Is there something you can do to be of service to someone today?

CLOSING PRAYER

Let us pray to God for our needs and the needs of others: our family, neighborhood, and the world. For each need we say, "Lord, hear our prayer."

◆ All may add their own prayers here.

Let us pray: **Our Father . . . Amen.**

Loving God,
in the life and teaching of your son, Jesus,
we learn how you want us to live.
Help us to care for others, especially those who are suffering or are in need.

Amen.

✚ All make the Sign of the Cross.

OPENING

Today we remember St. John Paul II, who was pope from 1978 to 2005. He was the first pope to visit a Jewish synagogue since St. Peter, and he appealed to both Jews and Christians to be "a blessing to one another." The focus of our readings this week is prayer. Today we hear the prayer that Jesus taught his followers to say.

✝ All make the Sign of the Cross.

In the name of the Father, and of the Son, and of the Holy Spirit. Amen.

PSALM   (For a longer psalm, see page xii.) Psalm 98:1

The LORD has made known his victory.

The LORD has made known his victory.

O sing to the LORD a new song,
  for he has done marvelous things.
His right hand and his holy arm
  have gotten him victory.

The LORD has made known his victory.

◆ All stand and sing **Alleluia.**

GOSPEL   Matthew 6:7–14a

A reading from the holy Gospel according to Matthew.

"When you are praying, do not heap up empty phrases as the Gentiles do; for they think that they will be heard because of their many words. Do not be like them, for your Father knows what you need before you ask him. Pray then in this way: Our Father in heaven, hallowed be your name. Your kingdom come. Your will be done, on earth as it is in heaven.

Give us this day our daily bread. And forgive us our debts, as we also have forgiven our debtors. And do not bring us to the time of trial, but rescue us from the evil one. For if you forgive others their trespasses, your heavenly Father will also forgive you."

The Gospel of the Lord.

◆ All sit and observe silence.

FOR SILENT REFLECTION

Think about this silently in your heart. Is there a line from the Our Father that speaks deeply to you? Think about that line.

CLOSING PRAYER

Let us pray to God for our needs and the needs of others: our family, neighborhood, and the world. For each need we say, "Lord, hear our prayer."

◆ All may add their own prayers here.

Let us pray: **Our Father . . . Amen.**

We pray that you will help us, O God,
to do your will every day.
We pray in thanksgiving
for Jesus, who taught us to call you Father.

Amen.

✝ All make the Sign of the Cross.

PRAYER FOR
TUESDAY, OCTOBER 23, 2018

OPENING

Today is the memorial of St. John of Capistrano (1386–1456), an Italian Franciscan priest. He was such a great preacher that no church could hold the crowds that came to hear him, so he preached outside. We can tell from today's Gospel reading that Jesus truly believed in the power of prayer.

✛ All make the Sign of the Cross.

In the name of the Father, and of the Son, and of the Holy Spirit. Amen.

PSALM
(For a longer psalm, see page xii.) Psalm 98:1

The Lord has made known his victory.

The Lord has made known his victory.

O sing to the Lord a new song,
    for he has done marvelous things.
His right hand and his holy arm
    have gotten him victory.

The Lord has made known his victory.

◆ All stand and sing **Alleluia.**

GOSPEL
Mark 11:12ac, 13–14a, 20–22, 23e, 24

A reading from the holy Gospel according to Mark.

On the following day, Jesus was hungry. Seeing in the distance a fig tree in leaf, he went to see whether perhaps he would find anything on it. When he came to it, he found nothing but leaves, for it was not the season for figs. He said to it, "May no one ever eat fruit from you again."

In the morning as they passed by, they saw the fig tree withered away to its roots. Then Peter remembered and said to him, "Rabbi, look! The fig tree that you cursed has withered." Jesus answered them, "Have faith in God. Believe that what you say will come to pass. So I tell you, whatever you ask for in prayer, believe that you have received it, and it will be yours."

The Gospel of the Lord.

◆ All sit and observe silence.

FOR SILENT REFLECTION

Think about this silently in your heart. How do you listen to God when you pray?

CLOSING PRAYER

Let us pray to God for our needs and the needs of others: our family, neighborhood, and the world. For each need we say, "Lord, hear our prayer."

◆ All may add their own prayers here.

Let us pray: **Our Father . . . Amen.**

Gracious God,
may we learn to listen to your voice
and to believe that you hear our prayers.

Amen.

✛ All make the Sign of the Cross.

OPENING

Today we remember St. Anthony Mary Claret who lived in Spain in the nineteenth century. He founded the religious order of Claretian priests and brothers who serve in ministries devoted to issues of social justice, peace, and the environment. Jesus prayed and asked his disciples to pray. Listen to today's reading.

✚ All make the Sign of the Cross.

In the name of the Father, and of the Son, and of the Holy Spirit. Amen.

PSALM   (For a longer psalm, see page xii.) Psalm 98:1

The LORD has made known his victory.

The LORD has made known his victory.

O sing to the LORD a new song,
 for he has done marvelous things.
His right hand and his holy arm
 have gotten him victory.

The LORD has made known his victory.

◆ All stand and sing **Alleluia.**

GOSPEL   Mark 14:32, 34–38a, 39

A reading from the holy Gospel according to Mark.

They went to a place called Gethsemane [geth-SEM-uh-nee]; and Jesus said to his disciples, "Sit here while I pray." And he said to them, "I am deeply grieved, even to death; remain here, and keep awake." And going a little farther, he threw himself on the ground and prayed that, if it were possible, the hour might pass from him. He said, "Abba, Father, for you all things are possible; remove this cup from me; yet, not what I want, but what you want." He came and found them sleeping; and he said to Peter, "Simon, are you asleep? Could you not keep awake one hour? Keep awake and pray that you may not come into the time of trial." And again he went away and prayed, saying the same words.

The Gospel of the Lord.

◆ All sit and observe silence.

FOR SILENT REFLECTION

Think about this silently in your heart. Even Jesus prayed in his hour of need.

CLOSING PRAYER

Let us pray to God for our needs and the needs of others: our family, neighborhood, and the world. For each need we say, "Lord, hear our prayer."

◆ All may add their own prayers here.

Let us pray: **Our Father . . . Amen.**

God our Father,
may we turn to you, as Jesus did,
when we are afraid or sad.
May we trust that you hear us.
Help us to hear your voice.
We ask this in Jesus' name.

Amen.

✚ All make the Sign of the Cross.

PRAYER FOR
THURSDAY, OCTOBER 25, 2018

OPENING

Today we hear how the community prayed for Peter when he was arrested for preaching the Gospel. Sometimes praying together in a group or community can help people have strength, wisdom, and courage they didn't think they had. When we pray, we trust, one way or the other, that God is with us.

✛ All make the Sign of the Cross.

In the name of the Father, and of the Son, and of the Holy Spirit. Amen.

PSALM   (For a longer psalm, see page xii.) Psalm 98:1

The LORD has made known his victory.

The LORD has made known his victory.

O sing to the LORD a new song,
   for he has done marvelous things.
His right hand and his holy arm
   have gotten him victory.

The LORD has made known his victory.

READING   Acts 12:3b, 4ab, 5, 7, 8b, 10

A reading from the Acts of the Apostles.

King Herod proceeded to arrest Peter also. When he had seized Peter, Herod put him in prison and handed him over to four squads of soldiers to guard him. While Peter was kept in prison, the church prayed fervently to God for him. Suddenly an angel of the Lord appeared and a light shone in the cell. He tapped Peter on the side and woke him, saying, "Get up quickly." Then the angel said to Peter, "Wrap your cloak around you and follow me." After they had passed the first and the second guard, they came before the iron gate leading into the city. It opened for them of its own accord, and they went outside and walked along a lane, when suddenly the angel left him.

The Word of the Lord.

◆ All observe silence.

FOR SILENT REFLECTION

Think about this silently in your heart. Have you ever felt a sense of peace or courage as you prayed?

CLOSING PRAYER

Let us pray to God for our needs and the needs of others: our family, neighborhood, and the world. For each need we say, "Lord, hear our prayer."

◆ All may add their own prayers here.

Let us pray: **Our Father . . . Amen.**

Loving God,
we trust that you hear our prayers.
As the community prayed for Peter,
we, the Church on earth today,
pray for all who are imprisoned unjustly.
We ask that you send your Spirit
to give them hope, courage, and strength.

Amen.

✛ All make the Sign of the Cross.

OPENING

Praying reminds us of our relationship to God. Praying several times a day helps us to stay connected to God all day long: in the morning, at meal times, in the evening, and at bedtime. People who practice the Muslim religion pray five times a day. St. Paul and his disciples prayed often. Listen to today's reading.

✛ All make the Sign of the Cross.

In the name of the Father, and of the Son, and of the Holy Spirit. Amen.

PSALM (For a longer psalm, see page xii.) Psalm 98:1

The LORD has made known his victory.

The LORD has made known his victory.

O sing to the LORD a new song,
  for he has done marvelous things.
His right hand and his holy arm
  have gotten him victory.

The LORD has made known his victory.

READING Acts 20:36, 37d; 21:2–6

A reading from the Acts of the Apostles.

When Paul had finished speaking, he knelt down with them all and prayed. Then they brought him to the ship. When we found a ship bound for Phoenicia, we went on board and set sail. We came in sight of Cyprus; and leaving it on our left, we sailed to Syria and landed at Tyre, because the ship was to unload its cargo there. We looked up the disciples and stayed there for seven days. Through the Spirit they told Paul not to go on to Jerusalem. When our days there were ended, we left and proceeded on our journey; and all of them, with wives and children, escorted us outside the city. There we knelt down on the beach and prayed and said farewell to one another. Then we went on board the ship, and they returned home.

The Word of the Lord.

◆ All observe silence.

FOR SILENT REFLECTION

Think about this silently in your heart. Are there times in the day that you can say a silent prayer?

CLOSING PRAYER

Let us pray to God for our needs and the needs of others: our family, neighborhood, and the world. For each need we say, "Lord, hear our prayer."

◆ All may add their own prayers here.

Let us pray: **Our Father . . . Amen.**

We thank you, O God, for the gift of prayer.
Help us to remember that you
are with us at all times.
We know that you hear our prayers.
Help us to listen to your voice.

Amen.

✛ All make the Sign of the Cross.

PRAYER FOR THE WEEK

WITH A READING FROM THE GOSPEL FOR **SUNDAY, OCTOBER 28, 2018**

OPENING

Pope Francis says, "The name of God is mercy." To show mercy means to be gentle and forgiving to someone who has done something wrong. It also means showing kindness to those who are suffering or are victims of misfortune.

✚ All make the Sign of the Cross.

In the name of the Father, and of the Son, and of the Holy Spirit. Amen.

PSALM
(For a longer psalm, see page xii.) Psalm 98:1

The LORD has made known his victory.

The LORD has made known his victory.

O sing to the LORD a new song,
  for he has done marvelous things.
His right hand and his holy arm
  have gotten him victory.

The LORD has made known his victory.

◆ All stand and sing **Alleluia.**

GOSPEL
Mark 10:46b–52

A reading from the holy Gospel according to Mark.

A blind beggar was sitting by the roadside. When he heard that it was Jesus of Nazareth, he began to shout out and say, "Jesus, Son of David, have mercy on me!" Many sternly ordered him to be quiet, but he cried out even more loudly, "Son of David, have mercy on me!" Jesus stood still and said, "Call him here." And they called the blind man, saying to him, "Take heart; get up, he is calling you." So throwing off his cloak, he sprang up and came to Jesus. Then Jesus said to him, "What do you want me to do for you?" The blind man said to him, "My teacher, let me see again." Jesus said to him, "Go; your faith has made you well." Immediately he regained his sight and followed him on the way.

The Gospel of the Lord.

◆ All sit and observe silence.

FOR SILENT REFLECTION

Think about this silently in your heart. When have you experienced mercy?

CLOSING PRAYER

Let us pray to God for our needs and the needs of others: our family, neighborhood, and the world. For each need we say, "Lord, hear our prayer."

◆ All may add their own prayers here.

Let us pray: **Our Father . . . Amen.**

Merciful God,
you are quick to forgive.
Help us to be as kind, forgiving, and merciful to others as you are to us.
We ask this in Jesus' name.

Amen.

✚ All make the Sign of the Cross.

OPENING

For the next three weeks we will read the story of Moses, one of the great heroes in the Old Testament. As we read the highlights of Moses' story, listen and use your imagination to visualize all of the events in this man's journey with God. The Israelite people had been living in Egypt peacefully for about four hundred years. Then a new King arose. This is where the reading begins today.

✛ All make the Sign of the Cross.

In the name of the Father, and of the Son, and of the Holy Spirit. Amen.

PSALM
(For a longer psalm, see page xii.) Psalm 98:1

The LORD has made known his victory.

The LORD has made known his victory.

O sing to the LORD a new song,
  for he has done marvelous things.
His right hand and his holy arm
  have gotten him victory.

The LORD has made known his victory.

READING
Exodus 1:8a, 9–11a, 13–14a, 22

A reading from the Book of Exodus.

Now a new king arose over Egypt. He said to his people, "Look, the Israelite people are more numerous and more powerful than we. Come, let us deal shrewdly with them, or they will increase and, in the event of war, join our enemies and fight against us and escape from the land." The Egyptians became ruthless in imposing tasks on the Israelites, and made their lives bitter with hard service in mortar and brick and in every kind of field labor. Then Pharaoh commanded all his people, "Every boy that is born to the Hebrews you shall throw into the Nile, but you shall let every girl live."

The Word of the Lord.

◆ All observe silence.

FOR SILENT REFLECTION

Think about this silently in your heart. Why do you think the King of Egypt was cruel to the Israelites?

CLOSING PRAYER

Let us pray to God for our needs and the needs of others: our family, neighborhood, and the world. For each need we say, "Lord, hear our prayer."

◆ All may add their own prayers here.

Let us pray: **Our Father . . . Amen.**

Faithful God,
there are so many wars in our world today.
Teach us how to live together
in peace and respect.
We need your help.
We ask this in Jesus' name.

Amen.

✛ All make the Sign of the Cross.

OPENING

Today's reading is a familiar part of the story of Moses. Remember what the Pharaoh [FAYR-oh] commanded, "Every boy that is born to the Hebrews you shall throw into the Nile." The Levite people were one of the twelve tribes of Israel. Hebrew is another name for Israelite.

✠ All make the Sign of the Cross.

In the name of the Father, and of the Son, and of the Holy Spirit. Amen.

PSALM   (For a longer psalm, see page xii.) Psalm 98:1

The LORD has made known his victory.

The LORD has made known his victory.

O sing to the LORD a new song,
  for he has done marvelous things.
His right hand and his holy arm
  have gotten him victory.

The LORD has made known his victory.

READING   Exodus 2:2a, 3ab–4a, 5ac, 6ac–8, 9c–10

A reading from the Book of Exodus.

A Levite woman bore a son. When she could hide him no longer she got a papyrus basket for him; she put the child in it and placed it among the reeds on the bank of the river. His sister stood at a distance. The daughter of Pharaoh came down to bathe at the river. She saw the basket among the reeds. When she opened it, she saw the child. "This must be one of the Hebrews' children," she said. Then his sister said to Pharaoh's daughter, "Shall I go and get you a nurse from the Hebrew women to nurse the child for you?" Pharaoh's daughter said to her, "Yes." So the girl went and called the child's mother. So the woman took the child and nursed it. When the child grew up, she brought him to Pharaoh's daughter, and she took him as her son. She named him Moses, "because," she said, "I drew him out of the water."

The Word of the Lord.

◆ All observe silence.

FOR SILENT REFLECTION

Think about this silently in your heart. Pray for all the babies who need someone to care for them.

CLOSING PRAYER

Let us pray to God for our needs and the needs of others: our family, neighborhood, and the world. For each need we say, "Lord, hear our prayer."

◆ All may add their own prayers here.

Let us pray: **Our Father . . . Amen.**

Loving God,
when times are difficult, you are faithful.
As you watched over Moses
when he was a baby,
we ask that you provide good care
for all children who are in need.

Amen.

✠ All make the Sign of the Cross.

OPENING

Although Moses was raised in Pharaoh's court as one of Pharaoh's sons, he knew that he was a Hebrew. When he saw how the Hebrew people were mistreated he was angered. One day he attacked and killed him a man who was beating a Hebrew. This action changed Moses' life forever.

✚ All make the Sign of the Cross.

In the name of the Father, and of the Son, and of the Holy Spirit. Amen.

PSALM
(For a longer psalm, see page xii.) Psalm 98:1

The Lord has made known his victory.

The Lord has made known his victory.

O sing to the Lord a new song,
   for he has done marvelous things.
His right hand and his holy arm
   have gotten him victory.

The Lord has made known his victory.

READING
Exodus 2:11–15b

A reading from the Book of Exodus.

One day, after Moses had grown up, he went out to his people and saw their forced labor. He saw an Egyptian beating a Hebrew, one of his kinsfolk. He looked this way and that, and seeing no one he killed the Egyptian and hid him in the sand. When he went out the next day, he saw two Hebrews fighting; and he said to the one who was in the wrong, "Why do you strike your fellow Hebrew?" He answered, "Who made you a ruler and judge over us? Do you mean to kill me as you killed the Egyptian?"

Then Moses was afraid and thought, "Surely the thing is known." When Pharaoh heard of it, he sought to kill Moses. But Moses fled from Pharaoh. He settled in the land of Midian.

The Word of the Lord.

◆ All observe silence.

FOR SILENT REFLECTION

Think about this silently in your heart. How can we help people who are being mistreated?

CLOSING PRAYER

Let us pray to God for our needs and the needs of others: our family, neighborhood, and the world. For each need we say, "Lord, hear our prayer."

◆ All may add their own prayers here.

Let us pray: **Our Father . . . Amen.**

God of Justice,
create in us an intolerance for injustice.
Give us courage to speak out
when we see someone being mistreated.
We ask this in Jesus' name.

Amen.

✚ All make the Sign of the Cross.

HOME PRAYER
CELEBRATING THE SAINTS, REMEMBERING THE DEAD

Find the reading (1 Thessalonians 4:13–18) in your Bible, ask for a volunteer to read it, and encourage the reader to practice reading it a few times. Then gather the household in one room. You may want to light a candle to create an even more prayerful environment.

LEADER:
Saints live among us today as well as with Christ in heaven. These heroes of our faith persevere in troubled times as they follow the path of Jesus. Their unselfish actions, as well as their talents, skills, and virtuous living inspire us as they pray for us.

✚ All make the Sign of the Cross.

ALL: In the name of the Father, and of the Son, and of the Holy Spirit. Amen.

LEADER: Psalm 112: 1–6
Let us pray the psalm response:
Happy are those who fear the Lord.

ALL: Happy are those who fear the Lord.

LEADER:
Praise the LORD!
   Happy are those who fear the LORD,
      who greatly delight in his commandments.
Their descendants will be mighty in the land;
      the generation of the upright will
            be blessed.

ALL: Happy are those who fear the Lord.

LEADER:
Wealth and riches are in their houses,
      and their righteousness endures forever.
They rise in the darkness as a light for
            the upright;
      they are gracious, merciful, and righteous.

ALL: Happy are those who fear the Lord.

LEADER: 1 Thessalonians 4:13–18
A reading from the First Letter of Paul to the Thessalonians.

◆ Read the Scripture passage from the Bible.

The Word of the Lord.

◆ All observe a brief silence.

LEADER:
And now let us remember family members and friends who have died:

◆ The leader begins, then pauses so others may add names too.

LEADER:
Lord God,
we ask you to bring these and all
those who have gone before us
into your beloved presence.

◆ Leader pauses, then continues.

Jesus, our Savior,
you are the Source of all life.
We are grateful for our leaders in faith,
as well as our family members and friends
who are with you now in heaven.
Their goodness reveals your holy truth.
Help us to honor your Spirit within us in
everything we do.
We ask this in your name.

ALL: Amen.

✚ All make the Sign of the Cross.

OPENING

Today is All Saints, a solemnity when we honor all the holy men and women that the Church recognizes in a special way. We continue to read about Moses, who had to flee for his life to a town called Midian. There he married and lived a quiet life tending sheep. Moses was an ordinary person, but God called him to do something very big.

✛ All make the Sign of the Cross.

In the name of the Father, and of the Son, and of the Holy Spirit. Amen.

PSALM
(For a longer psalm, see page xii.) Psalm 98:1

The LORD has made known his victory.

The LORD has made known his victory.

O sing to the LORD a new song,
    for he has done marvelous things.
His right hand and his holy arm
    have gotten him victory.

The LORD has made known his victory.

READING
Exodus 3:1b–2,4b,6a,7ab,8a,10

A reading from the Book of Exodus.

Moses led his flock beyond the wilderness, and came to Horeb, the mountain of God. There the angel of the LORD appeared to him in a flame of fire out of a bush; he looked, and the bush was blazing, yet it was not consumed. God called to him out of the bush, "Moses, Moses!" And he said, "Here I am." Then the LORD said, "I am the God of your father, the God of Abraham, the God of Isaac, and the God of Jacob. I have observed the misery of my people who are in Egypt; I have heard their cry. And I have come down to deliver them from the Egyptians. So come, I will send you to Pharaoh to bring my people, the Israelites, out of Egypt."

The Word of the Lord.

◆ All observe silence.

FOR SILENT REFLECTION

Think about this silently in your heart. Imagine how Moses must have felt when he saw a bush in flames but not burning and heard his name being called?

CLOSING PRAYER

Let us pray to God for our needs and the needs of others: our family, neighborhood, and the world. For each need we say, "Lord, hear our prayer."

◆ All may add their own prayers here.

Let us pray: **Our Father . . . Amen.**

God of Wisdom,
Moses was an ordinary man
but you chose him to be a great leader.
The world needs great leaders today.
Please guide people who are wise,
compassionate, and courageous
into positions of leadership.

Amen.

✛ All make the Sign of the Cross.

OPENING

God asked Moses to go to the Pharaoh [FAYR-oh] and bring the Hebrew people out of Egypt. Moses was afraid, and asked God what authority he would have to convince the Pharaoh. God used the words "I AM" to describe himself, meaning that he is the Creator that has been present from all time. Today is All Souls' Day, when we remember all those who have died.

✦ All make the Sign of the Cross.

In the name of the Father, and of the Son, and of the Holy Spirit. Amen.

PSALM
(For a longer psalm, see page xii.) Psalm 98:1

The LORD has made known his victory.

The LORD has made known his victory.

O sing to the LORD a new song,
 for he has done marvelous things.
His right hand and his holy arm
 have gotten him victory.

The LORD has made known his victory.

READING
Exodus 3:11–12a, 13–15

A reading from the Book of Exodus.

But Moses said to God, "Who am I that I should go to Pharaoh, and bring the Israelites out of Egypt?" God said, "I will be with you." But Moses said to God, "If I come to the Israelites and say to them, 'The God of your ancestors has sent me to you,' and they ask me, 'What is his name?' what shall I say to them?" God said to Moses, "I AM WHO I AM." He said further, "Thus you shall say to the Israelites, 'I AM has sent me to you.'" God also said to Moses, "Thus you shall say to the Israelites, 'The LORD, the God of your ancestors, the God of Abraham, the God of Isaac, and the God of Jacob, has sent me to you': This is my name forever, and this my title for all generations."

The Word of the Lord.

◆ All observe silence.

FOR SILENT REFLECTION

Think about this silently in your heart. God is always with you and will support you.

CLOSING PRAYER

Let us pray to God for our needs and the needs of others: our family, neighborhood, and the world. For each need we say, "Lord, hear our prayer."

◆ All may add their own prayers here.

Let us pray: **Our Father . . . Amen.**

Dear God, you assured Moses
that you would be with him.
You reminded him who You are:
The Creator who has been present
since the beginning of time.
We give you praise and glory.

Amen.

✦ All make the Sign of the Cross.

PRAYER FOR THE WEEK
WITH A READING FROM THE GOSPEL FOR **SUNDAY, NOVEMBER 4, 2018**

OPENING

In Jesus' time, there were over six hundred religious laws that religious leaders were expected to know. With so many laws people tried to decide which were most important to follow. Listen to Jesus' answer when one of the religious leaders asked him that question.

✦ All make the Sign of the Cross.

> **In the name of the Father, and of the Son, and of the Holy Spirit. Amen.**

PSALM
(For a longer psalm, see page xii.) Psalm 98:1

The LORD has made known his victory.

The LORD has made known his victory.

O sing to the LORD a new song,
   for he has done marvelous things.
His right hand and his holy arm
   have gotten him victory.

The LORD has made known his victory.

✦ All stand and sing **Alleluia.**

GOSPEL
Mark 12:28–31

A reading from the holy Gospel according to Mark.

One of the scribes came near and heard them disputing with one another, and seeing that he answered them well, he asked him, "Which commandment is the first of all?" Jesus answered, "The first is, 'Hear, O Israel: the Lord our God, the Lord is one; you shall love the Lord your God with all your heart, and with all your soul, and with all your mind, and with all your strength.' The second is this, 'You shall love your neighbor as yourself.' There is no other commandment greater than these."

The Gospel of the Lord.

✦ All sit and observe silence.

FOR SILENT REFLECTION

Think about this silently in your heart. How do you show that you love God? How do you show that you love your neighbor?

CLOSING PRAYER

Let us pray to God for our needs and the needs of others: our family, neighborhood, and the world. For each need we say, "Lord, hear our prayer."

✦ All may add their own prayers here.

Let us pray: **Our Father . . . Amen.**

Heavenly Creator,
we praise you and give you glory.
Help us to love you with all our heart,
all our soul, all our mind, and all our strength.
Help us to love our neighbor
as we love ourselves.
We ask this in Jesus' name.

Amen.

✦ All make the Sign of the Cross.

OPENING

Moses took his family and, accompanied by his brother Aaron, went down to Egypt as the Lord had asked him to do. Through the hand of Moses, God sent ten plagues or troubles (such as frogs, disease, swarms of flies, darkness) to force the Pharaoh to let his people go. The Pharaoh continued to refuse until the last plague, which we hear about today.

◆ All make the Sign of the Cross.

In the name of the Father, and of the Son, and of the Holy Spirit. Amen.

PSALM
(For a longer psalm, see page xii.) Psalm 98:1

The LORD has made known his victory.

The LORD has made known his victory.

O sing to the LORD a new song,
    for he has done marvelous things.
His right hand and his holy arm
    have gotten him victory.

The LORD has made known his victory.

READING
Exodus 12:1a, 3a, 6c–7, 11c–12b, 13–14b

A reading from the Book of Exodus.

The LORD said to Moses: Tell the whole congregation of Israel that on the tenth of this month they are to take a lamb for each family and slaughter it at twilight. They shall take some of the blood and put it on the two doorposts and the lintel of the houses in which they eat it. It is the passover of the LORD. For I will pass through the land of Egypt that night, and I will strike down every firstborn in the land of Egypt. The blood shall be a sign for you on the houses where you live: when I see the blood, I will pass over you, and no plague shall destroy you when I strike the land of Egypt. This day shall be a day of remembrance for you. You shall celebrate it as a festival to the LORD; throughout your generations.

The Word of the Lord.

◆ All observe silence.

FOR SILENT REFLECTION

Think about this silently in your heart. Why do you think God protected the Israelites?

CLOSING PRAYER

Let us pray to God for our needs and the needs of others: our family, neighborhood, and the world. For each need we say, "Lord, hear our prayer."

◆ All may add their own prayers here.

Let us pray: **Our Father . . . Amen.**

Faithful God,
you helped the Hebrew people
through hard and difficult times.
Help us to remember that you
are with us when times are difficult.

Amen.

✦ All make the Sign of the Cross.

OPENING

For the Jewish people, Passover is a seven-day feast that is celebrated every year. The first day of Passover begins as a holy day and recalls how the Hebrew people were freed from slavery in Egypt. The final day of Passover observes how Moses led the people safely through the Red Sea. At every Seder Meal, celebrated on the Passover, this story is retold.

✦ All make the Sign of the Cross.

In the name of the Father, and of the Son, and of the Holy Spirit. Amen.

PSALM

(For a longer psalm, see page xii.) Psalm 98:1

The LORD has made known his victory.

The LORD has made known his victory.

O sing to the LORD a new song,
  for he has done marvelous things.
His right hand and his holy arm
  have gotten him victory.

The LORD has made known his victory.

READING

Exodus 12:30–32a, 40–42

A reading from the Book of Exodus.

Pharaoh arose in the night, he and all his officials and all the Egyptians; and there was a loud cry in Egypt, for there was not a house without someone dead. Then he summoned Moses and Aaron in the night, and said, "Rise up, go away from my people, both you and the Israelites! Go, worship the LORD, as you said. Take your flocks and your herds, as you said, and be gone." The time that the Israelites had lived in Egypt was four hundred thirty years.

At the end of four hundred thirty years, on that very day, all the companies of the LORD went out from the land of Egypt. That was for the LORD a night of vigil, to bring them out of the land of Egypt. That same night is a vigil to be kept for the LORD by all the Israelites throughout their generations.

The Word of the Lord.

◆ All observe silence.

FOR SILENT REFLECTION

Think about this silently in your heart. How do you think the Israelites felt when Pharaoh told them to leave?

CLOSING PRAYER

Let us pray to God for our needs and the needs of others: our family, neighborhood, and the world. For each need we say, "Lord, hear our prayer."

◆ All may add their own prayers here.

Let us pray: **Our Father . . . Amen.**

Faithful and loving God,
Please protect us from all
that could harm us, as you protected
your people, the Israelites.

Amen.

✦ All make the Sign of the Cross.

WEDNESDAY, NOVEMBER 7, 2018

OPENING

Even though Pharaoh had agreed to let the people go, very soon he had a change of heart and came after them. Today's story of the crossing of the Red Sea tells us that even when things feel overwhelming and hopeless, with God's help, people can find the strength and courage.

> ✦ All make the Sign of the Cross.

> **In the name of the Father, and of the Son, and of the Holy Spirit. Amen.**

PSALM   (For a longer psalm, see page xii.) Psalm 98:1

The Lord has made known his victory.

The Lord has made known his victory.

O sing to the Lord a new song,
   for he has done marvelous things.
His right hand and his holy arm
   have gotten him victory.

The Lord has made known his victory.

READING   Exodus 14:15a, 16, 21–23a, 26ab, 27a, 28, 30a

A reading from the Book of Exodus.

Then the Lord said to Moses: 'Lift up your staff, and stretch out your hand over the sea and divide it, that the Israelites may go into the sea on dry ground. Then Moses stretched out his hand over the sea. The Lord drove the sea back by a strong east wind all night, and turned the sea into dry land; and the waters were divided. The Israelites went into the sea on dry ground, the waters forming a wall for them on their right and on their left. The Egyptians pursued. Then the Lord said to Moses,

"Stretch out your hand over the sea, so that the water may come back upon the Egyptians." So Moses stretched out his hand over the sea. The waters returned and covered the entire army of Pharaoh; not one of them remained. Thus the Lord saved Israel that day from the Egyptians.

The Word of the Lord.

> ◆ All observe silence.

FOR SILENT REFLECTION

Think about this silently in your heart. Has there been a time when you overcame something that seemed very difficult?

CLOSING PRAYER

Let us pray to God for our needs and the needs of others: our family, neighborhood, and the world. For each need we say, "Lord, hear our prayer."

> ◆ All may add their own prayers here.

Let us pray: **Our Father . . . Amen.**

Faithful God, as you aided the Israelites,
please help us in our times of struggle.
Help us to trust that you
will lead us to what is right and good.

Amen.

> ✦ All make the Sign of the Cross.

OPENING

The Israelites celebrated their escape from the Pharaoh and his army. They were happy for a while, but their journey in the desert was long and hard. Soon they began to complain about the heat and the lack of food.

✦ All make the Sign of the Cross.

In the name of the Father, and of the Son, and of the Holy Spirit. Amen.

PSALM

(For a longer psalm, see page xii.) Psalm 98:1

The Lord has made known his victory.

The Lord has made known his victory.

O sing to the Lord a new song,
   for he has done marvelous things.
His right hand and his holy arm
   have gotten him victory.

The Lord has made known his victory.

READING

Exodus 16:11–14, 15c, 31

A reading from the Book of Exodus.

The Lord spoke to Moses and said, "I have heard the complaining of the Israelites; say to them, 'At twilight you shall eat meat, and in the morning you shall have your fill of bread; then you shall know that I am the Lord your God.'" In the evening quails came up and covered the camp; and in the morning there was a layer of dew around the camp. When the layer of dew lifted, there on the surface of the wilderness was a fine flaky substance, as fine as frost on the ground. Moses said to them, "It is the bread that the Lord has given you to eat." The house of Israel called it manna; it was like coriander seed, white and the taste of it was like wafers made with honey.

The Word of the Lord.

◆ All observe silence.

FOR SILENT REFLECTION

Think about this silently in your heart. God listened to the people's cries and provided food for them. Is there something on your heart that you would like to bring to God today?

CLOSING PRAYER

Let us pray to God for our needs and the needs of others: our family, neighborhood, and the world. For each need we say, "Lord, hear our prayer."

◆ All may add their own prayers here.

Let us pray: **Our Father . . . Amen.**

Good and gracious God,
you provided the manna for the Israelites.
You provide us with the
Bread of Life in the Eucharist.
We give you thanks for your great love.

Amen.

✦ All make the Sign of the Cross.

OPENING

Today the Church throughout the world celebrates a feast in honor of a church in Rome: the Basilica of St. John Lateran, the cathedral of the Pope. In today's reading we hear about how the Israelites suffered from a lack of water in the desert. In the desert, people and animals could live for only a few days without water.

✝ All make the Sign of the Cross.

In the name of the Father, and of the Son, and of the Holy Spirit. Amen.

PSALM
(For a longer psalm, see page xii.) Psalm 98:1

The LORD has made known his victory.

The LORD has made known his victory.

O sing to the LORD a new song,
for he has done marvelous things.
His right hand and his holy arm
have gotten him victory.

The LORD has made known his victory.

READING
Exodus 17:1b, 3b–4a, 5c, 6ab, 7

A reading from the Book of Exodus.

The Israelites camped at Rephidim [REF-ih-dim], but there was no water for the people to drink. The people complained against Moses and said, "Why did you bring us out of Egypt, to kill us and our children and livestock with thirst?" So Moses cried out to the LORD, "What shall I do with this people?" The LORD said to Moses, "Take in your hand the staff with which you struck the Nile, and go. I will be standing there in front of you on the rock at Horeb. Strike the rock, and water will come

out of it, so that the people may drink." Moses did so. He called the place Massah and Meribah, because the Israelites quarreled and tested the LORD, saying, "Is the LORD among us or not?"

The Word of the Lord.

◆ All observe silence.

FOR SILENT REFLECTION

Think about this silently in your heart. The people were angry because their life was difficult. God listened to them. Are you angry about something you would like to tell God about?

CLOSING PRAYER

Let us pray to God for our needs and the needs of others: our family, neighborhood, and the world. For each need we say, "Lord, hear our prayer."

◆ All may add their own prayers here.

Let us pray: **Our Father . . . Amen.**

Loving God, just as you
listened to the cries of the Israelites,
we trust that you hear us when we
are sad or angry or confused.
Help us to listen to you.

Amen.

✝ All make the Sign of the Cross.

OPENING

Jesus had a deep empathy or compassion for the poor. He understood that people who have less are often more generous with what they have than people who have a lot.

✝ All make the Sign of the Cross.

> **In the name of the Father, and of the Son, and of the Holy Spirit. Amen.**

PSALM

(For a longer psalm, see page xii.) Psalm 98:1

The LORD has made known his victory.

The LORD has made known his victory.

O sing to the LORD a new song,
  for he has done marvelous things.
His right hand and his holy arm
  have gotten him victory.

The LORD has made known his victory.

◆ All stand and sing **Alleluia.**

GOSPEL

Mark 12:41–44

A reading from the holy Gospel according to Mark.

Jesus sat down and watched the crowd putting money into the treasury. Many rich people put in large sums. A poor widow came and put in two small copper coins, which are worth a penny. Then he called his disciples and said to them, "Truly I tell you, this poor widow has put in more than all those who are contributing to the treasury. For all of them have contributed out of their abundance; but she out of her poverty has put in everything she had, all she had to live on."

The Gospel of the Lord.

◆ All sit and observe silence.

FOR SILENT REFLECTION

Think about this silently in your heart. What does Jesus mean when he says that the widow has contributed more than those who gave large sums of money?

CLOSING PRAYER

Let us pray to God for our needs and the needs of others: our family, neighborhood, and the world. For each need we say, "Lord, hear our prayer."

◆ All may add their own prayers here.

Let us pray: **Our Father . . . Amen.**

God of love and justice,
Help us to be generous.
Help us to think more about giving
than receiving.
Open our hearts and our eyes
so that we may see and respond
to the needs of others.

Amen.

✝ All make the Sign of the Cross.

OPENING

Today is the memorial of St. Josaphat [JOS-uh-fat], a bishop of Lithuania in the sixteenth century. He worked tirelessly to bring the Orthodox Church into full communion with the Catholic Church. This week we continue the story of Moses. Today's reading tells of the covenant or sacred promise between God and his people.

✚ All make the Sign of the Cross.

In the name of the Father, and of the Son, and of the Holy Spirit. Amen.

PSALM   (For a longer psalm, see page xii.) Psalm 98:1

The LORD has made known his victory.

The LORD has made known his victory.

O sing to the LORD a new song,
    for he has done marvelous things.
His right hand and his holy arm
    have gotten him victory.

The LORD has made known his victory.

READING   Exodus 19:2b–3ac, 4–6a, 7–8

A reading from the Book of Exodus.

The Israelites entered the wilderness of Sinai, and camped there in front of the mountain. Then Moses went up to God; the LORD called to him from the mountain, saying, "Tell the Israelites: You have seen what I did to the Egyptians, and how I bore you on eagles' wings and brought you to myself. Now therefore, if you obey my voice and keep my covenant, you shall be my treasured possession out of all the peoples. Indeed, the whole earth is mine, but

you shall be for me a priestly kingdom and a holy nation." So Moses came, summoned the elders of the people, and set before them all these words that the LORD had commanded him. The people all answered as one: "Everything that the LORD has spoken we will do." Moses reported the words of the people to the LORD.

The Word of the Lord.

◆ All observe silence.

FOR SILENT REFLECTION

Think about this silently in your heart. You are also God's "treasured possession."

CLOSING PRAYER

Let us pray to God for our needs and the needs of others: our family, neighborhood, and the world. For each need we say, "Lord, hear our prayer."

◆ All may add their own prayers here.

Let us pray: **Our Father . . . Amen.**

Almighty God,
open our ears
so that we might listen to you.
Open our hearts
so that we might follow your commandments.

Amen.

✚ All make the Sign of the Cross.

OPENING

Today is the memorial of St. Frances Xavier Cabrini (1850–1917), also known as Mother Cabrini, the first American citizen to be canonized. She founded the Missionary Sisters of the Sacred Heart of Jesus who help immigrants and the poor throughout the world. The Ten Commandments, which Moses received from God, are called "The Gift of the Law."

✚ All make the Sign of the Cross.

In the name of the Father, and of the Son, and of the Holy Spirit. Amen.

PSALM   (For a longer psalm, see page xii.) Psalm 98:1

The LORD has made known his victory.

The LORD has made known his victory.

O sing to the LORD a new song,
   for he has done marvelous things.
His right hand and his holy arm
   have gotten him victory.

The LORD has made known his victory.

READING   Exodus 19:9, 16–18b, 19

A reading from the Book of Exodus.

Then the LORD said to Moses, "I am going to come to you in a dense cloud, in order that the people may hear when I speak with you and so trust you ever after." On the morning of the third day there was thunder and lightning, as well as a thick cloud on the mountain, and a blast of a trumpet so loud that all the people who were in the camp trembled. Moses brought the people out of the camp to meet God. They took their stand at the foot of the mountain. Now Mount Sinai was wrapped in smoke, because the LORD had descended upon it in fire; while the whole mountain shook violently. As the blast of the trumpet grew louder and louder, Moses would speak and God would answer him in thunder.

The Word of the Lord.

◆ All observe silence.

FOR SILENT REFLECTION

Think about this silently in your heart. Try to imagine what it was like for Moses to encounter God.

CLOSING PRAYER

Let us pray to God for our needs and the needs of others: our family, neighborhood, and the world. For each need we say, "Lord, hear our prayer."

◆ All may add their own prayers here.

Let us pray: **Our Father . . . Amen.**

Almighty and powerful God,
you revealed yourself
in your glory and majesty.
We praise you, and we thank you
for making a covenant with us.

Amen.

✚ All make the Sign of the Cross.

PRAYER FOR
WEDNESDAY, NOVEMBER 14, 2018

OPENING

Today's reading describes the first three commandments God gives to Moses on Mount Sinai [SĪ-nī]. These three commandments are about the people's relationship with God. God tells us not to worship false idols. False idols can be things like money or power or possessions. Remember, the Sabbath day for Christians is Sunday.

✦ All make the Sign of the Cross.

In the name of the Father, and of the Son, and of the Holy Spirit. Amen.

PSALM
(For a longer psalm, see page xii.) Psalm 98:1

The LORD has made known his victory.

The LORD has made known his victory.

O sing to the LORD a new song,
  for he has done marvelous things.
His right hand and his holy arm
  have gotten him victory.

The LORD has made known his victory.

READING
Exodus 20:1–2b, 4, 7a, 8–10a, 11

A reading from the Book of Exodus.

Then God spoke: I am the LORD your God, who brought you out of the land of Egypt; you shall have no other gods before me. You shall not make for yourself an idol, whether in the form of anything that is in heaven above, or that is on the earth beneath, or that is in the water under the earth. You shall not make wrongful use of the name of the LORD your God. Remember the sabbath day, and keep it holy. Six days you shall labor and do all your work. But the seventh day is a sabbath to the LORD your God; you shall not do any work. For in six days the LORD made heaven and earth, the sea, and all that is in them, but rested the seventh day; therefore the LORD blessed the sabbath day and consecrated it.

The Word of the Lord.

✦ All observe silence.

FOR SILENT REFLECTION

Think about this silently in your heart. Why is it important to worship God alone?

CLOSING PRAYER

Let us pray to God for our needs and the needs of others: our family, neighborhood, and the world. For each need we say, "Lord, hear our prayer."

✦ All may add their own prayers here.

Let us pray: **Our Father . . . Amen.**

Good and gracious God,
we give you thanks for the gift of the law.
By following your commands,
our lives give you honor and glory.
Help us to obey the commandments.

Amen.

✦ All make the Sign of the Cross.

OPENING

Today we remember St. Albert the Great, who lived in the thirteenth century. He was a Dominican priest. He loved to study and was a great teacher. In our reading, we hear the final seven commandments that God gave to Moses. These are about people's relationships with one another. Adultery is when a married man or woman breaks his or her marriage vows to be faithful to one another. Bearing false witness means telling lies about another person. Covet means not just to want something that someone else has, but to wish they didn't have it.

✦ All make the Sign of the Cross.

In the name of the Father, and of the Son, and of the Holy Spirit. Amen.

PSALM

(For a longer psalm, see page xii.) Psalm 98:1

The Lord has made known his victory.

The Lord has made known his victory.

O sing to the Lord a new song,
   for he has done marvelous things.
His right hand and his holy arm
   have gotten him victory.

The Lord has made known his victory.

READING

Exodus 20:1, 12–17

A reading from the Book of Exodus.

Then God spoke all these words: Honor your father and your mother, so that your days may be long in the land that the Lord your God is giving you. You shall not murder. You shall not commit adultery. You shall not steal. You shall not bear false witness against your neighbor. You shall not covet your neighbor's house; you shall not covet your neighbor's wife, or male or female slave, or ox, or donkey, or anything that belongs to your neighbor.

The Word of the Lord.

✦ All observe silence.

FOR SILENT REFLECTION

Think about this silently in your heart. How does following these commandments help us to live peacefully with others?

CLOSING PRAYER

Let us pray to God for our needs and the needs of others: our family, neighborhood, and the world. For each need we say, "Lord, hear our prayer."

✦ All may add their own prayers here.

Let us pray: **Our Father . . . Amen.**

Loving God,
we thank you for the commandments.
In your wisdom, you provide us with laws
that will help us live in harmony with others.
Help us when we struggle to follow your law.
We ask this in Jesus' name.

Amen.

✦ All make the Sign of the Cross.

OPENING

Today we finish the readings of the story of Moses. Moses is one of the patriarchs [PAY-tree-ahrks] of our faith. He responded to God's call and became a great leader. The Ten Commandments are called the "Gift of the Law" because they were given to help people to live peacefully together and be prosperous. To be prosperous means to live well and be healthy. The sacred promise between God and his people to be faithful to one another is called the covenant.

✝ All make the Sign of the Cross.

In the name of the Father, and of the Son, and of the Holy Spirit. Amen.

PSALM
(For a longer psalm, see page xii.) Psalm 98:1

The LORD has made known his victory.

The LORD has made known his victory.

O sing to the LORD a new song,
    for he has done marvelous things.
His right hand and his holy arm
    have gotten him victory.

The LORD has made known his victory.

READING
Deuteronomy 30:9–10

A reading from the Book of Deuteronomy.

Then God spoke all these words: The LORD your God will make you abundantly prosperous in all your undertakings, in the fruit of your body, in the fruit of your livestock, and in the fruit of your soil. For the LORD will again take delight in prospering you, just as he delighted in prospering your ancestors, when you obey the LORD your God by observing his commandments and decrees that are written in this book of the law, because you turn to the LORD your God with all your heart and with all your soul.

The Word of the Lord.

◆ All observe silence.

FOR SILENT REFLECTION

Think about this silently in your heart. What do you remember most from the story of Moses?

CLOSING PRAYER

Let us pray to God for our needs and the needs of others: our family, neighborhood, and the world. For each need we say, "Lord, hear our prayer."

◆ All may add their own prayers here.

Let us pray: **Our Father . . . Amen.**

Loving God,
through the story of Moses
we have seen how you remain
faithful to your people.
You help them in difficult times.
You give them guidance and great blessings.
With grateful hearts, we sing your praises.

Amen.

✝ All make the Sign of the Cross.

PRAYER FOR THE WEEK

WITH A READING FROM THE GOSPEL FOR **SUNDAY, NOVEMBER 18, 2018**

OPENING

In today's Gospel we hear Jesus describe what we call "the end times." We don't know when Jesus, the Son of Man, will come again, but we believe that he will.

✚ All make the Sign of the Cross.

In the name of the Father, and of the Son, and of the Holy Spirit. Amen.

PSALM
(For a longer psalm, see page xii.) Psalm 98:1

The LORD has made known his victory.

The LORD has made known his victory.

O sing to the LORD a new song,
   for he has done marvelous things.
His right hand and his holy arm
   have gotten him victory.

The LORD has made known his victory.

◆ All stand and sing **Alleluia.**

GOSPEL
Mark 13:24–29, 32

A reading from the holy Gospel according to Mark.

Jesus said, "But in those days, after that suffering, the sun will be darkened, and the moon will not give its light, and the stars will be falling from heaven, and the powers in the heavens will be shaken. Then they will see 'the Son of Man coming in clouds' with great power and glory. Then he will send out the angels, and gather his elect from the four winds, from the ends of the earth to the ends of heaven. From the fig tree learn its lesson: as soon as its branch becomes tender and puts forth its leaves, you know that summer is near. So also, when you see these things taking place, you know that he is near, at the very gates. But about that day or hour no one knows, neither the angels in heaven, nor the Son, but only the Father."

The Gospel of the Lord.

◆ All sit and observe silence.

FOR SILENT REFLECTION

Think about this silently in your heart. The word *Parousia* [pare-oo-SEE-uh] means the time when Jesus will return and God will be all in all.

CLOSING PRAYER

Let us pray to God for our needs and the needs of others: our family, neighborhood, and the world. For each need we say, "Lord, hear our prayer."

◆ All may add their own prayers here.

Let us pray: **Our Father . . . Amen.**

Holy and loving God,
help us to be faithful followers
of your son, Jesus.
Help us to do our part
to bring your Kingdom to earth.

Amen.

✚ All make the Sign of the Cross.

PRAYER FOR
MONDAY, NOVEMBER 19, 2018

OPENING

Names are important because they tell something about who a person is. For example, a last name helps identify what family a person is part of. In the Gospel of Mark, Jesus is called by different names to help people understand who he is. In this Gospel, Jesus is called the "Son of God."

✦ All make the Sign of the Cross.

In the name of the Father, and of the Son, and of the Holy Spirit. Amen.

PSALM
(For a longer psalm, see page xii.) Psalm 98:1

The LORD has made known his victory.

The LORD has made known his victory.

O sing to the LORD a new song,
for he has done marvelous things.
His right hand and his holy arm
have gotten him victory.

The LORD has made known his victory.

◆ All stand and sing **Alleluia.**

GOSPEL
Mark 3:7–11

A reading from the holy Gospel according to Mark.

Jesus departed with his disciples to the sea, and a great multitude from Galilee followed him; hearing all that he was doing, they came to him in great numbers from Judea, Jerusalem, Idumea, beyond the Jordan, and the region around Tyre and Sidon. He told his disciples to have a boat ready for him because of the crowd, so that they would not crush him; for he had cured many, so that all who had diseases pressed upon him to touch him. Whenever the unclean spirits saw him, they fell down before him and shouted, "You are the Son of God!" But he sternly ordered them not to make him known.

The Gospel of the Lord.

◆ All sit and observe silence.

FOR SILENT REFLECTION

Think about this silently in your heart. Why would Jesus not want his identity as the Son of God to be known at this time?

CLOSING PRAYER

Let us pray to God for our needs and the needs of others: our family, neighborhood, and the world. For each need we say, "Lord, hear our prayer."

◆ All may add their own prayers here.

Let us pray: **Our Father . . . Amen.**

Dear God,
in Jesus you came to us in human form.
Jesus showed us how to honor you
by being kind to the sick, the hungry,
and the homeless.
Help us to be thoughtful and generous
so that others might know your goodness
through our actions.
We ask this in Jesus' name.

Amen.

✦ All make the Sign of the Cross.

OPENING

In today's Gospel, Jesus refers to himself as the Son of Man. We know that Jesus was both divine and human. He knew that to fulfill his mission on earth, he would experience suffering. Jesus told his disciples that as his followers they would suffer as well.

✦ All make the Sign of the Cross.

In the name of the Father, and of the Son, and of the Holy Spirit. Amen.

PSALM
(For a longer psalm, see page xii.) Psalm 98:1

The Lord has made known his victory.

The Lord has made known his victory.

O sing to the Lord a new song,
   for he has done marvelous things.
His right hand and his holy arm
   have gotten him victory.

The Lord has made known his victory.

◆ All stand and sing **Alleluia.**

GOSPEL
Mark 8:31–32b, 33bc, 34–35

A reading from the holy Gospel according to Mark.

Then Jesus began to teach the disciples that the Son of Man must undergo great suffering, and be rejected by the elders, the chief priests, and the scribes, and be killed, and after three days rise again. And Peter took him aside and began to rebuke him. Jesus rebuked Peter and said, "Get behind me, Satan! For you are setting your mind not on divine things but on human things." He called the crowd with his disciples, and said to them, "If any want to become my followers, let them deny themselves and take up their cross and follow me. For those who want to save their life will lose it, and those who lose their life for my sake, and for the sake of the gospel, will save it."

The Gospel of the Lord.

◆ All sit and observe silence.

FOR SILENT REFLECTION

Think about this silently in your heart. What cross, or suffering, do you need to take up?

CLOSING PRAYER

Let us pray to God for our needs and the needs of others: our family, neighborhood, and the world. For each need we say, "Lord, hear our prayer."

◆ All may add their own prayers here.

Let us pray: **Our Father . . . Amen.**

God our Father,
you did not spare you son Jesus from suffering.
When we suffer, help us to join
our suffering to his.
Help us to carry our small crosses with love
and to trust in your saving power.

Amen.

✦ All make the Sign of the Cross.

OPENING

Scripture tells of the Presentation of the Lord Jesus in the Temple. But the Blessed Virgin Mary was also presented in the Temple when she was a small girl. Today is the memorial of the Presentation of the Blessed Virgin Mary and we remember that special day when her life was dedicated to God. In today's reading Jesus once again calls himself "The Son of Man." Jewish people would recognize the phrase from the Book of the prophet Daniel where the Son of Man is described as a powerful person from heaven.

✚ All make the Sign of the Cross.

In the name of the Father, and of the Son, and of the Holy Spirit. Amen.

PSALM

(For a longer psalm, see page xii.) Psalm 98:1

The Lord has made known his victory.

The Lord has made known his victory.

O sing to the Lord a new song,
for he has done marvelous things.
His right hand and his holy arm
have gotten him victory.

The Lord has made known his victory.

◆ All stand and sing **Alleluia.**

GOSPEL

Mark 9:9–10, 12ac, 30–31

A reading from the holy Gospel according to Mark.

As they were coming down the mountain, Jesus ordered them to tell no one about what they had seen, until after the Son of Man had risen from the dead. So they kept the matter to themselves, questioning what this rising from the dead could mean. Jesus said to them, "How then is it written about the Son of Man, that he is to go through many sufferings and be treated with contempt?" They went on from there and passed through Galilee. He did not want anyone to know it; for he was teaching his disciples, saying to them, "The Son of Man is to be betrayed into human hands, and they will kill him, and three days after being killed, he will rise again."

The Gospel of the Lord.

◆ All sit and observe silence.

FOR SILENT REFLECTION

Think about this silently in your heart. The prophet Daniel described "The Son of Man" as an awesome and powerful person from heaven. How does the Gospel writer, Mark, describe Jesus?

CLOSING PRAYER

Let us pray to God for our needs and the needs of others: our family, neighborhood, and the world. For each need we say, "Lord, hear our prayer."

◆ All may add their own prayers here.

Let us pray: **Our Father . . . Amen.**

O God, please, hold people who suffer close to you and give them strength.

Amen.

✚ All make the Sign of the Cross.

Find the reading (John 15:12–17) in your Bible, ask for a volunteer to read the Scripture passage, and encourage the reader to practice reading it a few times. If practical, light candles for your Thanksgiving table. You may wish to begin with a simple song of thanksgiving or a favorite "Alleluia." Then an older child or an adult reads the leader parts.

LEADER:

Almighty God,
look at the abundance here before us!
It fills us with joy and gratitude.
Let us begin our prayer with the
      Sign of the Cross.

✚ All make the Sign of the Cross.

In the name of the Father, and of the Son, and of the Holy Spirit. Amen.

◆ All stand and sing **Alleluia.**

READER: John 15:12–17

A reading from the holy Gospel according to John.

◆ Read the Gospel passage from the Bible.

The Gospel of the Lord.

◆ All sit and observe silence.

LEADER:

We come to this table,
grateful for the delicious meal
we're about to share,
as well as the family and friends who
surround us here.
Let us pray:
Heavenly Father,
we thank you for the love and friendship
that envelops us today.
Help us to nurture one another
with your peace and serenity in the
midst of our busy lives.
We thank all those who helped prepare
      this meal.
We are mindful of people in our
      community and
in other regions who may not have enough to
      eat today.
May we appreciate all that you provide for us
      now, and
we look forward to our heavenly banquet
      with you.
We ask this through our Lord Jesus Christ,
your Son, who lives and reigns with you
in the unity of the Holy Spirit, one God,
      for ever and ever.
All: Amen.

✚ All make the Sign of the Cross.

CHILDREN'S DAILY PRAYER 2018–2019 © 2018 Archdiocese of Chicago: Liturgy Training Publications, 3949 South Racine Avenue, Chicago IL 60609. All rights reserved. Orders: 800-933-1800 or www.LTP.org. Scripture excerpts are taken from *The New Revised Standard Version Bible: Catholic Edition*, © 1989, Division of Christian Education of the National Council of the Churches of Christ in the United States of America. Used with permission. All rights reserved.

PRAYER SERVICE
FOR THANKSGIVING

Prepare seven leaders for this service. The fourth leader will need a Bible to read the Gospel passage and may need help finding and practicing the reading. You may want to begin by singing "One Bread, One Body," and end with "Table of Plenty." If the group will sing, prepare a song leader.

FIRST LEADER:

✝ All make the Sign of the Cross.

> **In the name of the Father, and of the Son, and of the Holy Spirit. Amen.**

Let us pray:

Almighty God,
you bless us every day with the
signs and wonders of your creation.
We thank you for the fresh air,
trees, stars, and planets, as well as
all the animals and creatures that live on
      land and in the sea.
We are grateful that you have entrusted us
with care of your environment.

SECOND LEADER: Psalm 136:1–9
Our refrain is: For his steadfast love
endures forever.

ALL: For his steadfast love endures forever.

LEADER: O give thanks to the LORD,
for he is good,

ALL: For his steadfast love endures forever;

LEADER: Who alone does great wonders,

ALL: For his steadfast love endures forever;

LEADER: Who by understanding made
the heavens,

ALL: For his steadfast love endures forever;

CHILDREN'S DAILY PRAYER 2018–2019, © 2018 Archdiocese of Chicago: Liturgy Training Publications. All rights reserved. Orders: 800-933-1800 or www.LTP.org.

LEADER: Who spread out the earth on the waters,

ALL: For his steadfast love endures forever;

LEADER: Who made the great lights,

ALL: For his steadfast love endures forever;

LEADER: The sun to rule over the day,

ALL: For his steadfast love endures forever;

LEADER: The moon and stars to rule over the night,

ALL: For his steadfast love endures forever.

THIRD LEADER:
Creator God,
your presence is with us
today and always.
We are grateful for the
gift of your Son Jesus,
who lived and walked among us,
and whose Spirit fills our hearts
with gratitude and joy.

ALL: Amen.

FOURTH LEADER: 1 John 4:7–16
A reading from the first Letter of John.

◆ Read the Scripture passage from the Bible.

The Word of the Lord

FIFTH LEADER: Psalm 100:1–5
Our refrain is: Make a joyful noise to the Lord.

ALL: Make a joyful noise to the Lord.

LEADER: Make a joyful noise to the Lord,
all the earth,
Worship the Lord with gladness;
Come into his presence with singing.

ALL: Make a joyful noise to the Lord.

LEADER: Know that the Lord is God.
It is he that made us, and we are his;
We are his people, and the sheep of
his pasture.

ALL: Make a joyful noise to the Lord.

LEADER: Enter his gates with thanksgiving,
and his courts with praise.
Give thanks to him, bless his name.

ALL: Make a joyful noise to the Lord.

SIXTH LEADER:
Loving God,
we thank you for all that you
provide for us.
We are grateful for all the loved ones
in our lives now,
and those who have gone before us.
You nurture us in so many ways.
May we always remember to praise you
and love others as you love us.
We ask this through Christ our Lord.

SEVENTH LEADER:
May the love of God,

✝ All make the Sign of the Cross.

Father, Son, and Holy Spirit,

always surround us in faith,
now and forever.

ALL: Amen.

CHILDREN'S DAILY PRAYER 2018–2019, © 2018 Archdiocese of Chicago: Liturgy Training Publications. All rights reserved. Orders: 800-933-1800 or www.LTP.org.

PRAYER FOR THE WEEK

WITH A READING FROM THE GOSPEL FOR **SUNDAY, NOVEMBER 25, 2018**

OPENING

Pope Pius XI (eleventh) instituted the Solemnity of Christ the King in 1925 in response to a world increasingly torn apart by war. Jesus comes to us not as a great conquering military leader who oppresses and abuses the conquered. Rather, he comes as the Prince of Peace, the one whose reign proclaims peace, justice, liberation, and above all, service.

✦ All make the Sign of the Cross.

In the name of the Father, and of the Son, and of the Holy Spirit. Amen.

PSALM
(For a longer psalm, see page xii.) Psalm 98:1

The LORD has made known his victory.

The LORD has made known his victory.

O sing to the LORD a new song,
for he has done marvelous things.
His right hand and his holy arm
have gotten him victory.

The LORD has made known his victory.

✦ All stand and sing **Alleluia.**

GOSPEL
John 18:33b–37

A reading from the holy Gospel according to John.

Then Pilate entered the headquarters again, summoned Jesus, and asked him, "Are you the King of the Jews?" Jesus answered, "Do you ask this on your own, or did others tell you about me?" Pilate replied, "I am not a Jew, am I? Your own nation and the chief priests have handed you over to me. What have you done?"

Jesus answered, "My kingdom is not from this world. If my kingdom were from this world, my followers would be fighting to keep me from being handed over to the Jews. But as it is, my kingdom is not from here." Pilate asked him, "So you are a king?" Jesus answered, "You say that I am a king. For this I was born, and for this I came into the world, to testify to the truth. Everyone who belongs to the truth listens to my voice."

The Gospel of the Lord.

✦ All sit and observe silence.

FOR SILENT REFLECTION

Think about this silently in your heart. What kind of a king is Jesus?

CLOSING PRAYER

Let us pray to God for our needs and the needs of others: our family, neighborhood, and the world. For each need we say, "Lord, hear our prayer."

✦ All may add their own prayers here.

Let us pray: **Our Father . . . Amen.**

O God, we pray for the leaders of the world. May they work for peace and justice for all.

Amen.

✦ All make the Sign of the Cross.

OPENING

Yesterday we celebrated the Solemnity of Christ the King. This week we will see what the Bible tells us of Jesus' kingship. Today's reading gives many beautiful images of the kind of world that God desires. The word "righteous" means to do what is right. Justice means to be fair to everyone. The prophet Isaiah wrote to give people hope during a time when they were being treated badly by the Babylonians.

◆ All make the Sign of the Cross.

In the name of the Father, and of the Son, and of the Holy Spirit. Amen.

PSALM

(For a longer psalm, see page xii.) Psalm 98:1

The LORD has made known his victory.

The LORD has made known his victory.

O sing to the LORD a new song,
  for he has done marvelous things.
His right hand and his holy arm
  have gotten him victory.

The LORD has made known his victory.

READING

Isaiah 32:1, 2ac, 16–18; 33:17

A reading from the Book of the prophet Isaiah.

Then God spoke all these words:

See, a king will reign in righteousness, and princes will rule with justice. Each will be like a hiding place from the wind, alike streams of water in a dry place, like the shade of a great rock in a weary land. Then justice will dwell in the wilderness, and righteousness abide in the fruitful field. The effect of righteousness will be peace, and the result of righteousness, quietness and trust forever. My people will abide in a peaceful habitation, in secure dwellings, and in quiet resting places. Your eyes will see the king in his beauty; they will behold a land that stretches far away.

The Word of the Lord.

◆ All observe silence.

FOR SILENT REFLECTION

Think about this silently in your heart. Imagine what would the world be like if all people acted with righteousness and justice?

CLOSING PRAYER

Let us pray to God for our needs and the needs of others: our family, neighborhood, and the world. For each need we say, "Lord, hear our prayer."

◆ All may add their own prayers here.

Let us pray: **Our Father . . . Amen.**

God of justice and peace,
make us people who work for justice.
Give us courage to do what is right.
We ask this in the name of Christ Jesus.

Amen.

◆ All make the Sign of the Cross.

107

PRAYER FOR
TUESDAY, NOVEMBER 27, 2018

OPENING

Today we hear the prophet Jeremiah compare the leaders of Israel to shepherds. This reference made sense to the people of that time because they were shepherds who tended flocks of sheep. Jeremiah tells them they have been bad shepherds because they have not cared for their people. Jeremiah promises that God will send a shepherd who will care for them. We know that Good Shepherd was Jesus.

✚ All make the Sign of the Cross.

In the name of the Father, and of the Son, and of the Holy Spirit. Amen.

PSALM
(For a longer psalm, see page xii.) Psalm 98:1

The LORD has made known his victory.

The LORD has made known his victory.

O sing to the LORD a new song,
   for he has done marvelous things.
His right hand and his holy arm
   have gotten him victory.

The LORD has made known his victory.

READING
Jeremiah 22:1; 23:1, 2acd, 3ab, 4

A reading from the Book of the prophet Jeremiah.

Thus says the LORD: Go down to the house of the king of Judah, and speak there this word, Woe to the shepherds who destroy and scatter the sheep of my pasture! says the LORD. Therefore thus says the LORD, the God of Israel, concerning the shepherds who shepherd my people: It is you who have scattered my flock, and you have not attended to them. So

I will attend to you for your evil doings, says the LORD. Then I myself will gather the remnant of my flock out of all the lands where I have driven them, and I will bring them back to their fold. I will raise up shepherds over them who will shepherd them, and they shall not fear any longer, or be dismayed, nor shall any be missing, says the LORD.

The Word of the Lord.

◆ All observe silence.

FOR SILENT REFLECTION

Think about this silently in your heart. What qualities would a good shepherd who takes care of his sheep have?

CLOSING PRAYER

Let us pray to God for our needs and the needs of others: our family, neighborhood, and the world. For each need we say, "Lord, hear our prayer."

◆ All may add their own prayers here.

Let us pray: **Our Father . . . Amen.**

O God, we pray for the leaders of our Church: our priests and bishops and the pope.
May they work for peace and justice for all.

Amen.

✚ All make the Sign of the Cross.

OPENING

The prophet Zechariah wrote about 520 BC after the Jews had returned to Jerusalem from their exile in Babylonia. He promoted the work of rebuilding the temple and encouraged the Jewish leaders. Like others prophets, Zechariah had a vision of what the world could look like if the Lord was worshipped above all.

✛ All make the Sign of the Cross.

In the name of the Father, and of the Son, and of the Holy Spirit. Amen.

PSALM
(For a longer psalm, see page xii.) Psalm 98:1

The LORD has made known his victory.

The LORD has made known his victory.

O sing to the LORD a new song,
   for he has done marvelous things.
His right hand and his holy arm
   have gotten him victory.

The LORD has made known his victory.

READING
Zechariah 14:1, 5c, 6–7abd, 9

A reading from the Book of the prophet Zechariah.

See, a day is coming for the LORD, when the plunder taken from you will be divided in your midst. Then the LORD my God will come, and all the holy ones with him. On that day there shall not be either cold or frost. And there shall be continuous day, not day and not night, for at evening time there shall be light. On that day living waters shall flow out from Jerusalem, half of them to the eastern sea and half of them to the western sea; it shall continue in summer as in winter. And the LORD will become king over all the earth; on that day the LORD will be one and his name one.

The Word of the Lord.

◆ All observe silence.

FOR SILENT REFLECTION

Think about this silently in your heart. What images do you remember from today's reading?

CLOSING PRAYER

Let us pray to God for our needs and the needs of others: our family, neighborhood, and the world. For each need we say, "Lord, hear our prayer."

◆ All may add their own prayers here.

Let us pray: **Our Father . . . Amen.**

God of justice and peace,
make us people who work for justice.
Give us courage to do what is right,
so that we can help bring about the day
when there will be peace on earth.
We ask this in the name of Christ Jesus.

Amen.

✛ All make the Sign of the Cross.

OPENING

In today's reading, Pilate asks Jesus if he claims to be the King of the Jews. Pilate was thinking of a king as a great military leader. But Jesus said his kingdom was not of this world. Jesus came to earth to witness to God, the Creator, who is faithful, just, and merciful. God is the Lord and King of all nations.

✦ All make the Sign of the Cross.

In the name of the Father, and of the Son, and of the Holy Spirit. Amen.

PSALM   (For a longer psalm, see page xii.) Psalm 98:1

The LORD has made known his victory.

The LORD has made known his victory.

O sing to the LORD a new song,
   for he has done marvelous things.
His right hand and his holy arm
   have gotten him victory.

The LORD has made known his victory.

✦ All stand and sing **Alleluia.**

GOSPEL   Mark 15:1–2, 8–9, 11–13

A reading from the holy Gospel according to Mark.

As soon as it was morning, the chief priests held a consultation with the elders and scribes and the whole council. They bound Jesus, led him away, and handed him over to Pilate. Pilate asked him, "Are you the King of the Jews?" He answered him, "You say so." So the crowd came and began to ask Pilate to do for them according to his custom. Then he answered them, "Do you want me to release for you the King of the Jews?" But the chief priests stirred up the crowd to have him release Barabbas for them instead. Pilate spoke to them again, "Then what do you wish me to do with the man you call the King of the Jews?" They shouted back, "Crucify him!"

The Gospel of the Lord.

◆ All sit and observe silence.

FOR SILENT REFLECTION

Think about this silently in your heart. Jesus is named: Christ the King and the Prince of Peace. What do these names tell you about Jesus?

CLOSING PRAYER

Let us pray to God for our needs and the needs of others: our family, neighborhood, and the world. For each need we say, "Lord, hear our prayer."

◆ All may add their own prayers here.

Let us pray: **Our Father . . . Amen.**

Dear God, many people are fighting
for power in the world today.
We know that this is not want you want.
We pray for the world and all of creation.
Lord, God, hear our prayer.

Amen.

✦ All make the Sign of the Cross.

OPENING

St. Andrew, whose feast we celebrate today, was one of the Twelve Apostles of Jesus. St. Andrew traveled extensively bringing the gospel of Jesus to many countries. The reading today is a letter that St. Paul wrote Timothy, who was a leader of early Christians community of Ephesus [EF-uh suhs], which is now in the country of Turkey.

✝ All make the Sign of the Cross.

In the name of the Father, and of the Son, and of the Holy Spirit. Amen.

PSALM   (For a longer psalm, see page xii.) Psalm 98:1

The Lord has made known his victory.

The Lord has made known his victory.

O sing to the Lord a new song,
   for he has done marvelous things.
His right hand and his holy arm
   have gotten him victory.

The Lord has made known his victory.

READING   1 Timothy 6:11ac, 12a, 13ac, 14–16

A reading from the First Letter of Paul to Timothy.

But as for you, man of God; pursue righteousness, godliness, faith, love, endurance, gentleness. Fight the good fight of the faith. In the presence of God, who gives life to all things, and of Christ Jesus, I charge you to keep the commandment without spot or blame until the manifestation of our Lord Jesus Christ, which he will bring about at the right time—he who is the blessed and only Sovereign, the King of kings and Lord of lords. It is he alone who has immortality and dwells in unapproachable light, whom no one has ever seen or can see; to him be honor and eternal dominion. Amen.

The Word of the Lord.

◆ All observe silence.

FOR SILENT REFLECTION

Think about this silently in your heart. Why do you think St. Paul calls God the King of kings?

CLOSING PRAYER

Let us pray to God for our needs and the needs of others: our family, neighborhood, and the world. For each need we say, "Lord, hear our prayer."

◆ All may add their own prayers here.

Let us pray: **Our Father . . . Amen.**

Holy God,
you are the King of kings and the Lord of lords.
We praise you. We worship you.
We pray that you will give your guidance
to rulers everywhere so that peace and justice
will reign on earth.

Amen.

✝ All make the Sign of the Cross.

HOME PRAYER
GATHERING AROUND AN ADVENT WREATH FOR PRAYER

Find the reading (John 15:12–17) in your Bible, ask for a volunteer to read the Scripture passage, and encourage the reader to practice reading it a few times. If practical, light candles for your Thanksgiving table. You may wish to begin with a simple song of thanksgiving or a favorite "Alleluia." Then an older child or an adult reads the leader parts.

LEADER:
Almighty God,
look at the abundance here before us!
It fills us with joy and gratitude.
Let us begin our prayer with the
Sign of the Cross.

✝ All make the Sign of the Cross.

In the name of the Father, and of the Son, and of the Holy Spirit. Amen.

◆ All stand and sing **Alleluia.**

READER:　　　　　　　　　　　　John 15:12–17
A reading from the holy Gospel according to John.

◆ Read the Gospel passage from the Bible.

The Gospel of the Lord.

◆ All sit and observe silence.

LEADER:
We come to this table,
grateful for the delicious meal
we're about to share,
as well as the family and friends who
surround us here.
Let us pray:
Heavenly Father,
we thank you for the love and friendship
that envelops us today.
Help us to nurture one another
with your peace and serenity in the
midst of our busy lives.
We thank all those who helped prepare
this meal.
We are mindful of people in our
community and
in other regions who may not have enough to
eat today.
May we appreciate all that you provide for us
now, and
we look forward to our heavenly banquet
with you.
We ask this through our Lord Jesus Christ,
your Son, who lives and reigns with you
in the unity of the Holy Spirit, one God,
for ever and ever.
All: Amen.

✝ All make the Sign of the Cross.

CHILDREN'S DAILY PRAYER 2018–2019, © 2018 Archdiocese of Chicago: Liturgy Training Publications, 3949 South Racine Avenue, Chicago, IL 60609. All rights reserved. Orders: 800-933-1800 or www.LTP.org. Scripture excerpts are taken from *The New Revised Standard Version Bible: Catholic Edition*, copyright © 1989, Division of Christian Education of the National Council of the Churches of Christ in the United States of America. Used with permission. All rights reserved.

ADVENT

SUNDAY, DECEMBER 2 — FRIDAY, DECEMBER 23

ADVENT

THE MEANING OF ADVENT

"A shoot shall come out from the stump of Jesse, and a branch shall grow out of his roots" (Isaiah 11:1).

Jesse was the father of King David, a great leader of the Jewish people. But then Jesse's descendants became weak and scattered. The Jewish people no longer had a strong ruler and they suffered many periods of darkness, misery, and despair. The people of Israel had become like a great tree cut down to its stump. Yet God did not forsake the people. God, Israel's faithful protector, promised to make a new tree sprout from the root of the stump. The people waited and prayed and hoped for many years knowing God would keep this promise. We, too, are a people to whom God has made a solemn promise.

We wait, then, as did our spiritual ancestors, to celebrate the nativity of the Messiah. The Church tells us Advent is our time of waiting in "devout and joyful expectation" (*General Norms for the Liturgical Year*, 39) for the celebration of Christ's Incarnation and also for his Second Coming. We prepare as we wait by baking cookies and thinking about gifts for those we love as well as giving a little more to the poor and taking stock of our souls. The increased generosity and good cheer in people during this time, even in people who are not believers, may be a sign of God's joy breaking into our sometimes sad world. The first Sunday of Advent is also when the Church's begins her new calendar year.

We begin our Advent with a week of Scriptures called the Messianic Prophecies. The prophets foretell where Jesus will be born and who his Mother will be. They also predict Jesus' triumphant entry into Jerusalem on a donkey, his title of Good Shepherd, and that he will suffer. In the second and third week of our waiting we hear encouraging words that the Messiah will be the Light that breaks the darkness of injustice and brings peace. We'll hear the call of John the Baptist to "Prepare the Way of the Lord" (Luke 3:4). Our final week tells the great Infancy Narrative stories of the angel's announcement to Mary and reassurance to Joseph and Mary's visit to Elizabeth with her joyful hymn of praise for God's wonderful work, the Magnificat.

PREPARING TO CELEBRATE ADVENT IN THE CLASSROOM

SACRED SPACE

During Advent create a mood of anticipation in the classroom. Use purples and violets on the bulletin boards instead of red and green since we are an Advent people in the Catholic school. You might place the empty manger from a Christmas Nativity scene on your classroom prayer table. Slowly add elements like straw and animals and, in the last week, the Holy Family and shepherds. You might wait to add the star and the Magi after Christmas vacation, but it is not necessary.

You can also use an Advent wreath that has a circular candleholder usually decorated with pine branches. It has four candles: three violet and one rose-colored. But, you can use all violet or even white. It is the light that matters. When you first introduce the wreath to your class, invite the children to wonder why it's circular, why do we use pine boughs, why four candles? Children will often come up with beautiful answers to these questions: the wreath is round because God's love has no beginning and no end; the pine branches never lose their leaves or color just as God's love for us can never die; and, the four candles represent the four Sundays of Advent, the four points of the compass, the four branches of the cross, the four Gospels, and so on. Explain that each day you will light one candle for each week in Advent; when all the candles are lit, then Christmas will be right around the corner! The children may be curious about the rose-colored candle. Explain that it is the third one that we light, for the third Sunday in Advent, which is called Gaudete [gow-DAY-tay], Latin for "rejoice." We rejoice that our wait is almost over!

MOVEMENT AND GESTURE

Children of all ages love solemn processions. Consider organizing an Advent procession. After sharing some of the material in "The Meaning of Advent" with them explain that Advent has a new color, violet. Suggest to the children that you have a procession to change the color of your prayer table cloth. You will want to speak with the children about processions they have participated in or have seen in church. Explain that a procession is a prayerful way to walk, and stress the importance of silence (or singing along if you plan to sing). You'll need other children to place the Bible, Advent Wreath, and other elements after the cloth is laid and finally, someone to light the first candle. If you are not singing the procession could be accompanied by a wind chime. You might use a procession each week to add elements to the Nativity scene.

FESTIVITY IN SCHOOL AND HOME

There are two wonderful feasts to celebrate in Advent, St. Nicholas (hand out candy canes or "gold" chocolate coins) on December 6, and on December 13, St. Lucy (hand out cookies and hot chocolate). Acquaint the children with their lovely stories and discuss what we might learn from them. Please consider saving your celebration of Christmas until true Christmas Time after December 25. The time of Advent is a great spiritual gift that helps us grow in the beautiful theological virtue of hope. Also, if you wait until you return from Christmas break to celebrate the great Christmas feast of Epiphany, the children will have settled down and may be better able to listen to the glad tidings of great joy that you have to share with them.

In this book you will find special prayer service for Advent, pages 118–119, which could be used at any time in the season in the classroom or with a larger group. A "Home Prayer," has been created for Advent. This can be photocopied and sent home with the students so that their households can pray together at special times: Gathering around an Advent Wreath for Prayer appeared at the end of Ordinary Time in Autumn on page 118 so that you can send it home before the First Sunday of Advent.

SACRED MUSIC

Discover which songs your parish will be singing during Advent. Sometimes the setting for the sung parts of the Mass will change especially for a new liturgical season. Some Advent songs that children love include "The King of Glory Comes," "People Look East," and "O Come, O Come Emmanuel."

PRAYERS FOR ADVENT

A wonderful prayer to become acquainted with during Advent is Mary's prayer of praise, the Magnificat (Luke 1:46–55). All those who pray the Liturgy of the Hours recite this beautiful prayer each evening to remember Mary's joy as she prayed to God, the Mighty One. It has been set to various tunes and may be sung. Two lovely sung versions are the Taizé canon, "Magnificat," and "And Holy Is Your Name." The verses to the Magnificat in St. Luke's Gospel might make a lovely meditation and discussion for older children. The class might create a series of drawings based on the verses that illuminate the song.

A NOTE TO CATECHISTS

Make arrangements with your religious education director to store your Advent wreath somewhere in the classroom during the week so that you don't need to carry it back and forth between school and home. Read the Festivity in School and Home section of the Introduction for ways to celebrate the saints that help us anticipate the celebration of Christmas. Be sure to send home the Home Prayer service for gathering around the Advent Wreath that is found on page 112.

GRACE BEFORE MEALS

ADVENT

LEADER:

Let the clouds rain down the Just One,
and the earth bring forth a Savior.

✚ All make the Sign of the Cross.

In the name of the Father, and of the Son, and of the Holy Spirit. Amen.

LEADER:

Lord God,
you provide for us in so many ways.
You have given us the earth,
full of so much goodness.
You have blessed us with water to drink
and food to nourish our bodies.
As we look forward to your gift of the
Christ child,
we also think about the day
when we will be with you in heaven,
where everyone is filled with the joy
of your glorious presence.
We ask this through Jesus Christ our Lord.

ALL: Amen.

✚ All make the Sign of the Cross.

In the name of the Father, and of the Son, and of the Holy Spirit. Amen.

PRAYER AT DAY'S END

ADVENT

LEADER:

O Wisdom of our God Most High,
guiding creation with power and love,
come to teach us the path of knowledge!

+ All make the Sign of the Cross.

**In the name of the Father, and of the
Son, and of the Holy Spirit. Amen.**

LEADER:

Holy God,
we thank you for this day
with all of its adventures, big and small.
May our days continue to be filled
with the light of your Son, our Lord,
your gift to us,
who shows us the way of
patience and forgiveness and love.
We ask this in his name.

ALL: Amen.

+ All make the Sign of the Cross.

**In the name of the Father, and of the
Son, and of the Holy Spirit. Amen.**

PRAYER SERVICE
FOR ADVENT

Prepare a leader, reader, intercessor, and (if possible) a music leader for the service. Go over the intercessions with the class, and mention they are based on some Old Testament titles for Jesus we call the O Antiphons. Practice singing the refrain to "O Come, O Come Emmanuel" as the response, if possible. Place an Advent wreath on the table with a Bible and a purple cloth. Place the reading into the Bible and mark it with a ribbon or book mark. Review the reading with the reader and note that some verses are omitted. Decide who will light and extinguish the candles on the wreath. You might sing "Soon and Very Soon" at the end of the service.

LEADER:

◆ Gesture for all to stand.

✚ All make the sign of the Cross.

In the name of the Father, and of the Son, and of the Holy Spirit. Amen.

LEADER:
Let us pray:
O God of wonder,
as we are busy preparing for Christmas
help us prepare our hearts for Jesus.
We are grateful for your simple words
     of hope
and the gift of new life in the Christ child.
May we follow the true light of Jesus
that shines for all people
through the darkness of sin and sorrow.
We ask this through Christ our Lord.

ALL: Amen.

◆ Gesture for all to sit. Someone lights the appropriate candles on the Advent wreath. Allow a moment of silence to enjoy the beauty of the lit wreath. (For a discussion of the significance of the Advent wreath see Preparing to Celebrate Advent in the Classroom, the section on Sacred Space on page 114.)

CHILDREN'S DAILY PRAYER 2018–2019, © 2018 Archdiocese of Chicago: Liturgy Training Publications. All rights reserved. Orders: 800-933-1800 or www.LTP.org.

READER: Isaiah 11:1–2, 6–7, 10

A reading from the Book of the Prophet Isaiah.

◆ Proclaim the Scripture passage from the Bible.

The Word of the Lord.

◆ After a moment of silence the intercessor and music leader move forward.

INTERCESSOR:

Let us bring our hopes and needs to God as we sing (pray),

MUSIC LEADER: "Rejoice! Rejoice! Emmanuel shall come to you, O Israel."

ALL: "Rejoice! Rejoice! Emmanuel shall come to you, O Israel."

◆ Intercessions are read, pausing after each for the response.

INTERCESSOR:

O come, Emmanuel, free people who are held captive by racism, prejudice, and bullying. We sing:

ALL: "Rejoice! Rejoice! Emmanuel shall come to you, O Israel."

O come, Wisdom. Teach us how to be good to one another. We sing (say):

O come, Lord. Rule our hearts and minds in goodness. We sing (say):

O come, Shoot of Jesse's Stem. Forgive us our sins. We sing (say):

O come, Key of David. Open heaven for us. We sing (say):

O come, Dayspring. Replace the darkness of sin. We sing (say):

O come, Desire of Nations. Unite all the world's people. We sing (say):

LEADER:

Come quickly, Lord Jesus,
and guide us in God's way
of peace and justice.
Fill us with your gentle love
as we look forward to celebrating Christmas
with our family and friends.
You are our light and joy!

✝ All make the Sign of the Cross,

In the name of the Father, and of the Son and of the Holy Spirit.

◆ After the service someone extinguishes the candles on the Advent wreath.

PRAYER FOR THE WEEK

WITH A READING FROM THE GOSPEL FOR **SUNDAY, DECEMBER 2, 2018**

OPENING

This week we begin our season of Advent, our time of preparing. We prepare to celebrate Jesus' Incarnation, that is, his first coming, this Christmas. And, we prepare for the Parousia [pare-oo-SEE-uh], Jesus' Second Coming at the end of time. Advent gives us time to prepare our hearts and minds for both events. In the Gospel Jesus says to be alert for the signs of his Second Coming.

◆ All make the Sign of the Cross.

In the name of the Father, and of the Son, and of the Holy Spirit. Amen.

PSALM
(For a longer psalm, see page xii.) Psalm 85:8

Restore us again, O God of our salvation!

Restore us again, O God of our salvation!

Let me hear what God the LORD will speak,
   for he will speak peace to his people,
to his faithful, to those who turn to him in
   their hearts.

Restore us again, O God of our salvation!

◆ All stand and sing **Alleluia.**

GOSPEL
Luke 21:25, 27–28, 36

A reading from the holy Gospel according to Luke.

Jesus said, "There will be signs in the sun, the moon, and the stars, and on the earth distress among nations confused by the roaring of the sea and the waves. Then they will see 'the Son of Man coming in a cloud' with power and great glory. Now when these things begin to take place, stand up and raise your heads, because your redemption is drawing near. Be alert at all times, praying that you may have the strength to escape all these things that will take place, and to stand before the Son of Man."

The Gospel of the Lord.

◆ All sit and observe silence.

FOR SILENT REFLECTION

Think about this silently in your heart. How can you be alert to the presence of Jesus in your life?

CLOSING PRAYER

Let us pray to God for our needs and the needs of others: our family, neighborhood, and the world. For each need we say, "Lord, hear our prayer."

◆ All may add their own prayers here.

Let us pray: **Our Father . . . Amen.**

Keep us alert, O God,
to the ways we can prepare
to celebrate Jesus' Incarnation.
Help us make our hearts and minds
ready for Christmas
with prayer and good works.
We ask this in Jesus' name.

Amen.

✛ All make the Sign of the Cross.

OPENING

We begin the first week of Advent, a time to prepare for the Christmas celebration of Jesus' first coming and Jesus' Second Coming at the end of time. We'll hear the Old Testament's messianic [messy-ANN-ic] prophecies that point to Jesus. The Messiah had not yet come to the Hebrew people and the prophets wanted to give them hope. Micah says the Messiah will come from Bethlehem. Today is the memorial of St. Francis Xavier, the patron of missions.

✝ All make the Sign of the Cross.

In the name of the Father, and of the Son, and of the Holy Spirit. Amen.

PSALM

(For a longer psalm, see page xii.) Psalm 85:8

Restore us again, O God of our salvation!

Restore us again, O God of our salvation!

Let me hear what God the LORD will speak,
   for he will speak peace to his people,
to his faithful, to those who turn to him in
   their hearts.

Restore us again, O God of our salvation!

READING

Micah 1:2a; 5:1–2, 4–5a

A reading from the Book of the
prophet Micah.

Hear, you peoples, all of you. Now you are walled around with a wall; siege is laid against us; with a rod they strike the ruler of Israel upon the cheek. But you, O Bethlehem of Ephrathah [EF-ruh-thuh], who are one of the little clans of Judah, from you shall come forth for me one who is to rule in Israel, whose origin is from of old, from ancient days. And he shall stand and feed his flock in the strength of the LORD, in the majesty of the name of the LORD his God. And they shall live secure, for now he shall be great to the ends of the earth; and he shall be the one of peace.

The Word of the Lord.

◆ All observe silence.

FOR SILENT REFLECTION

Think about this silently in your heart. Bethlehem is a "little town." Why do you think Jesus would be born in a small town?

CLOSING PRAYER

Let us pray to God for our needs and the needs of others: our family, neighborhood, and the world. For each need we say, "Lord, hear our prayer."

◆ All may add their own prayers here.

Let us pray: **Our Father . . . Amen.**

Loving, all-powerful God,
you willed that your son Jesus
be born in the town of Bethlehem.
Help us to prepare our hearts
for his coming.

Amen.

✝ All make the Sign of the Cross.

PRAYER FOR
TUESDAY, DECEMBER 4, 2018

OPENING

Isaiah the prophet tells King Ahaz to ask God for a sign that things will go well, but Ahaz won't because he's lost his faith. God is loving and gracious and gives the sign anyway through Isaiah. Isaiah prophesied that the Messiah will be named "Immanuel," one of Jesus' many titles. We often sing the song "O Come, O Come, Emmanuel" in Advent.

✦ All make the Sign of the Cross.

In the name of the Father, and of the Son, and of the Holy Spirit. Amen.

PSALM   (For a longer psalm, see page xii.) Psalm 85:8

Restore us again, O God of our salvation!

Restore us again, O God of our salvation!

Let me hear what God the LORD will speak,
  for he will speak peace to his people,
to his faithful, to those who turn to him in
  their hearts.

Restore us again, O God of our salvation!

READING   Isaiah 7:3a, 4abc, 10–14

A reading from the Book of the prophet Isaiah.

Then the LORD said to Isaiah, Go out to meet Ahaz, and say to him, Take heed, be quiet, do not fear. Again the LORD spoke to Ahaz, saying, Ask a sign of the LORD your God; let it be deep as Sheol or high as heaven. But Ahaz said, I will not ask, and I will not put the LORD to the test. Then Isaiah said: 'Hear then, O house of David! Is it too little for you to weary mortals, that you weary my God also? Therefore the Lord himself will give you a sign. Look, the young woman is with child and shall bear a son, and shall name him Immanuel.'

The Word of the Lord.

◆ All observe silence.

FOR SILENT REFLECTION

Think about this silently in your heart. "Emmanuel" means "God-with-us." How do you know that God is with you?

CLOSING PRAYER

Let us pray to God for our needs and the needs of others: our family, neighborhood, and the world. For each need we say, "Lord, hear our prayer."

◆ All may add their own prayers here.

Let us pray: **Our Father . . . Amen.**

O come, Emmanuel!
We are eager to celebrate your birth.
Help us make our hearts and minds ready for Christmas
with our prayers and good works.
We ask this in Jesus' name.

Amen.

✦ All make the Sign of the Cross.

OPENING

Ezekiel's [ee-ZEE-kee-uhlz] messianic prophesy says God is a good shepherd who rescues the lost sheep, binds up their wounds, and feeds them with justice. What Ezekiel calls "the fat and the strong" refers to people who are unkind and unfair to others. Jesus calls himself the Good Shepherd who knows each of us by name.

✦ All make the Sign of the Cross.

In the name of the Father, and of the Son, and of the Holy Spirit. Amen.

PSALM
(For a longer psalm, see page xii.) Psalm 85:8

Restore us again, O God of our salvation!

Restore us again, O God of our salvation!

Let me hear what God the LORD will speak, for he will speak peace to his people, to his faithful, to those who turn to him in their hearts.

Restore us again, O God of our salvation!

READING
Ezekiel 34:11, 12c, 14–16

A reading from the Book of the prophet Ezekiel.

For thus says the Lord GOD: I myself will search for my sheep, and will seek them out. I will rescue them from all the places to which they have been scattered on a day of clouds and thick darkness. I will feed them with good pasture, and the mountain heights of Israel shall be their pasture; there they shall lie down in good grazing land, and they shall feed on rich pasture on the mountains of Israel. I myself will be the shepherd of my sheep, and I will make them lie down, says the Lord GOD. I will seek the lost, and I will bring back the strayed, and I will bind up the injured, and I will strengthen the weak, but the fat and the strong I will destroy. I will feed them with justice.

The Word of the Lord.

◆ All observe silence.

FOR SILENT REFLECTION

Think about this silently in your heart. Is there someone you can pray for because they are treated unkindly or unjustly?

CLOSING PRAYER

Let us pray to God for our needs and the needs of others: our family, neighborhood, and the world. For each need we say, "Lord, hear our prayer."

◆ All may add their own prayers here.

Let us pray: **Our Father . . . Amen.**

O God, our good shepherd, feed us with your Spirit of justice so we can stand against cruelty and prejudice. We ask this in Jesus' name.

Amen.

✦ All make the Sign of the Cross.

PRAYER FOR
THURSDAY, DECEMBER 6, 2018

OPENING

Today is the feast of St. Nicholas, who was known for his generosity and his love of the Church. In Zechariah's prophecy we hear that the Messiah will be a different kind of king. He'll ride humbly into town on a young donkey instead of a big war horse. This Messiah will show the way to have freedom and peace. Jesus did exactly that!

✛ All make the Sign of the Cross.

In the name of the Father, and of the Son, and of the Holy Spirit. Amen.

PSALM
(For a longer psalm, see page xii.) Psalm 85:8

Restore us again, O God of our salvation!

Restore us again, O God of our salvation!

Let me hear what God the LORD will speak,
   for he will speak peace to his people,
to his faithful, to those who turn to him in
   their hearts.

Restore us again, O God of our salvation!

READING
Zechariah 9:9–10bd, 11, 16–17a

A reading from the Book of the prophet Zechariah.

Rejoice greatly, O daughter Zion! Shout aloud, O daughter Jerusalem! Lo, your king comes to you; triumphant and victorious is he, humble and riding on a donkey, on a colt, the foal of a donkey. The battle-bow shall be cut off, and he shall command peace to the nations; his dominion shall be from sea to sea. As for you also, because of the blood of my covenant with you, I will set your prisoners free from the waterless pit. On that day the LORD their God will save them, for they are the flock of his people; for like the jewels of a crown they shall shine on his land. For what goodness and beauty are his!

The Word of the Lord.

◆ All observe silence.

FOR SILENT REFLECTION

Think about this silently in your heart. On Palm Sunday, Jesus, our Messiah, rode into Jerusalem on a humble donkey. What does that tell us about Jesus?

CLOSING PRAYER

Let us pray to God for our needs and the needs of others: our family, neighborhood, and the world. For each need we say, "Lord, hear our prayer."

◆ All may add their own prayers here.

Let us pray: **Our Father . . . Amen.**

Keep us alert, O God,
to the ways we can be generous
like St. Nicholas.
Help us notice the needs of others
and show us how to help them.
We ask this in Jesus' name.

Amen.

✛ All make the Sign of the Cross.

OPENING

Isaiah prophesied the Messiah would be unjustly punished. That is what happened to Jesus. Today is St. Ambrose's memorial day. Ambrose authored many of the Church's important writings and is called a "wise teacher" and a Doctor of the Church.

✦ All make the Sign of the Cross.

In the name of the Father, and of the Son, and of the Holy Spirit. Amen.

PSALM
(For a longer psalm, see page xii.) Psalm 85:8

Restore us again, O God of our salvation!

Restore us again, O God of our salvation!

Let me hear what God the Lord will speak,
   for he will speak peace to his people,
to his faithful, to those who turn to him in
   their hearts.

Restore us again, O God of our salvation!

READING
Isaiah 52:13a; 53:3ac, 4ac, 5ab, 7ab, 9

A reading from the Book of the prophet Isaiah.

See, my servant shall prosper. He was despised and rejected by others; and we held him of no account. Surely he has borne our infirmities and carried our diseases; yet we accounted him stricken, and afflicted. But he was wounded for our transgressions; upon him was the punishment that made us whole, and by his bruises we are healed. He was oppressed, and he was afflicted, yet he did not open his mouth. They made his grave with the wicked and his tomb with the rich, although he had done no violence, and there was no deceit in his mouth.

The Word of the Lord.

✦ All observe silence.

FOR SILENT REFLECTION

Think about this silently in your heart. How does today's reading from Isaiah remind you of Jesus?

CLOSING PRAYER

Let us pray to God for our needs and the needs of others: our family, neighborhood, and the world. For each need we say, "Lord, hear our prayer."

✦ All may add their own prayers here.

Let us pray: **Our Father . . . Amen.**

We thank you, God, for Jesus,
who suffered so that we might live.
Jesus is the suffering servant.
Help us to learn from his example
and unite our suffering with his.
We ask this in Jesus' name.

Amen.

✦ All make the Sign of the Cross.

OPENING

We begin our second week of waiting and preparing for Christmas. Today we hear how John the Baptist helped to prepare the way for Jesus.

✦ All make the Sign of the Cross.

> **In the name of the Father, and of the Son, and of the Holy Spirit. Amen.**

PSALM

(For a longer psalm, see page xii.) Psalm 85:8

Restore us again, O God of our salvation!

Restore us again, O God of our salvation!

Let me hear what God the LORD will speak,
  for he will speak peace to his people,
to his faithful, to those who turn to him in
  their hearts.

Restore us again, O God of our salvation!

◆ All stand and sing **Alleluia.**

GOSPEL

Luke 3:1ab, 2b–6

A reading from the holy Gospel according to Luke.

In the fifteenth year of the reign of Emperor Tiberius, when Pontius Pilate was governor of Judea, and Herod was ruler of Galilee, the word of God came to John son of Zechariah in the wilderness. He went into all the region around the Jordan, proclaiming a baptism of repentance for the forgiveness of sins, as it is written in the book of the words of the prophet Isaiah, "The voice of one crying out in the wilderness: 'Prepare the way of the Lord, make his paths straight. Every valley shall be filled, and every mountain and hill shall be made low, and the crooked shall be made straight, and the rough ways made smooth; and all flesh shall see the salvation of God.'"

The Gospel of the Lord.

◆ All sit and observe silence.

FOR SILENT REFLECTION

Think about this silently in your heart. How are you preparing the way for Jesus during this Advent season?

CLOSING PRAYER

Let us pray to God for our needs and the needs of others: our family, neighborhood, and the world. For each need we say, "Lord, hear our prayer."

◆ All may add their own prayers here.

Let us pray: **Our Father . . . Amen.**

O God, giver of great gifts,
we wait anxiously to celebrate
your greatest gift, Jesus.
Show us the straight path to goodness.
Help us to make the rough places smooth
so that we might welcome Jesus
into our hearts and our homes.
We ask this in Jesus' name.

Amen.

✦ All make the Sign of the Cross.

OPENING

In our second week of Advent we read from Isaiah the prophet who has many encouraging things to say about the coming of the Messiah. However, Isaiah begins with an image of darkness. In the Northern Hemisphere Advent is associated with longer dark periods in the day, but Isaiah's reference is to a spiritual darkness that is a result of the human sin of injustice.

✠ All make the Sign of the Cross.

In the name of the Father, and of the Son, and of the Holy Spirit. Amen.

PSALM
(For a longer psalm, see page xii.) Psalm 85:8

Restore us again, O God of our salvation!

Restore us again, O God of our salvation!

Let me hear what God the LORD will speak,
   for he will speak peace to his people,
to his faithful, to those who turn to him in
   their hearts.

Restore us again, O God of our salvation!

READING
Isaiah 59:9–12

A reading from the Book of the prophet Isaiah.

Therefore justice is far from us, and righteousness does not reach us; we wait for light, and lo! there is darkness; and for brightness, but we walk in gloom. We grope like the blind along a wall, groping like those who have no eyes; we stumble at noon as in the twilight, among the vigorous as though we were dead. We all growl like bears; like doves we moan mournfully. We wait for justice, but there is

none; for salvation, but it is far from us. For our transgressions before you are many, and our sins testify against us. Our transgressions indeed are with us, and we know our iniquities.

The Word of the Lord.

◆ All observe silence.

FOR SILENT REFLECTION

Think about this silently in your heart. How is Jesus a light in the darkness?

CLOSING PRAYER

Let us pray to God for our needs and the needs of others: our family, neighborhood, and the world. For each need we say, "Lord, hear our prayer."

◆ All may add their own prayers here.

Let us pray: **Our Father . . . Amen.**

Give us your light, O God,
so we may see ourselves clearly.
Help us be your people of justice
so we may bring your light to others.
We ask this in Jesus' name.

Amen.

✠ All make the Sign of the Cross.

PRAYER FOR
TUESDAY, DECEMBER 11, 2018

OPENING

Yesterday, Isaiah described the darkness the sin of injustice can cause among people. Today he assures us that we are God's people and, therefore, people of light. We have the power and the responsibility to share God's light with others by acting justly toward everyone and speaking out against injustice.

✦ All make the Sign of the Cross.

In the name of the Father, and of the Son, and of the Holy Spirit. Amen.

PSALM
(For a longer psalm, see page xii.) Psalm 85:8

Restore us again, O God of our salvation!

Restore us again, O God of our salvation!

Let me hear what God the LORD will speak,
  for he will speak peace to his people,
to his faithful, to those who turn to him in
  their hearts.

Restore us again, O God of our salvation!

READING
Isaiah 60:1–5b

A reading from the Book of the prophet Isaiah.

Arise, shine; for your light has come, and the glory of the LORD has risen upon you. For darkness shall cover the earth, and thick darkness the peoples; but the LORD will arise upon you, and his glory will appear over you. Nations shall come to your light, and kings to the brightness of your dawn. Lift up your eyes and look around; they all gather together, they come to you; your sons shall come from far away, and your daughters shall be carried on their nurses' arms. Then you shall see and be radiant; your heart shall thrill and rejoice.

The Word of the Lord.

◆ All observe silence.

FOR SILENT REFLECTION

Think about this silently in your heart. What do you think "the glory of the Lord" might look like?

CLOSING PRAYER

Let us pray to God for our needs and the needs of others: our family, neighborhood, and the world. For each need we say, "Lord, hear our prayer."

◆ All may add their own prayers here.

Let us pray: **Our Father . . . Amen.**

We pray, O God,
for your light to shine forth
on our broken world.
Shine your light in the dark places of sin
so that we may see what is right,
and your glory may fill all the earth.
We ask this in Jesus' name.

Amen.

✦ All make the Sign of the Cross.

OPENING

Isaiah describes the Messiah's ancestor, Jesse, the father of King David, as tree stump. The Messiah is a new shoot, or branch, that grows from the root and is full of God's wisdom. Jesus is "of the house of David" so he is descended from Jesse. Today is the feast of Our Lady of Guadalupe, Patroness of the Americas. Mary is especially loved under this title by those living in Mexico and Latin America.

✝ All make the Sign of the Cross.

In the name of the Father, and of the Son, and of the Holy Spirit. Amen.

PSALM
(For a longer psalm, see page xii.) Psalm 85:8

Restore us again, O God of our salvation!

Restore us again, O God of our salvation!

Let me hear what God the LORD will speak, for he will speak peace to his people, to his faithful, to those who turn to him in their hearts.

Restore us again, O God of our salvation!

READING
Isaiah 11:1–3a, 5, 10

A reading from the Book of the prophet Isaiah.

A shoot shall come out from the stump of Jesse, and a branch shall grow out of his roots. The spirit of the LORD shall rest on him, the spirit of wisdom and understanding, the spirit of counsel and might, the spirit of knowledge and the fear of the LORD. His delight shall be in the fear of the LORD. Righteousness shall be the belt around his waist, and faithfulness the belt around his loins. On that day the root of Jesse shall stand as a signal to the peoples; the nations shall inquire of him, and his dwelling shall be glorious.

The Word of the Lord.

◆ All observe silence.

FOR SILENT REFLECTION

Think about this silently in your heart. Pray that the Spirit will rest in you.

CLOSING PRAYER

Let us pray to God for our needs and the needs of others: our family, neighborhood, and the world. For each need we say, "Lord, hear our prayer."

◆ All may add their own prayers here.

Let us pray: **Our Father . . . Amen.**

Rest on us, O Spirit of God and
awaken in us the gifts
of knowledge and wisdom.
Help us cling to and grow on
Jesus' branch all our lives.
We ask this in Jesus' name.

Amen.

✝ All make the Sign of the Cross.

OPENING

Today is the memorial of St. Lucy, a brave woman who died a martyr. Her name means "light," making her a perfect saint for Advent. Yesterday Isaiah described the characteristics of the Messiah. Today he describes the peaceful world the Messiah will bring. Sadly, humans don't always follow Jesus' teachings so our world is not this peaceful yet.

✛ All make the Sign of the Cross.

In the name of the Father, and of the Son, and of the Holy Spirit. Amen.

PSALM
(For a longer psalm, see page xii.) Psalm 85:8

Restore us again, O God of our salvation!

Restore us again, O God of our salvation!

Let me hear what God the Lord will speak,
  for he will speak peace to his people,
to his faithful, to those who turn to him in
  their hearts.

Restore us again, O God of our salvation!

READING
Isaiah 11:6–9

A reading from the Book of the prophet Isaiah.

The wolf shall live with the lamb, the leopard shall lie down with the kid, the calf and the lion and the fatling together, and a little child shall lead them. The cow and the bear shall graze, their young shall lie down together; and the lion shall eat straw like the ox. The nursing child shall play over the hole of the asp, and the weaned child shall put its hand on the adder's den. They will not hurt or destroy on all my holy mountain; for the earth will be full of the knowledge of the Lord as the waters cover the sea.

The Word of the Lord.

◆ All observe silence.

FOR SILENT REFLECTION

Think about this silently in your heart. How can you help build a peaceful world in your school this week?

CLOSING PRAYER

Let us pray to God for our needs and the needs of others: our family, neighborhood, and the world. For each need we say, "Lord, hear our prayer."

◆ All may add their own prayers here.

Let us pray: **Our Father . . . Amen.**

We ask for your help, O God,
to build a world of peace.
Jesus showed us the way.
We pray for the courage and strength
to continue his mission.
We pray that peace will come soon.
We ask this in Jesus' name.

Amen.

✛ All make the Sign of the Cross.

OPENING

Isaiah prophesied that when the Messiah is the ruler there will be righteousness everywhere. In the Bible, "righteousness" means people are in right relationship with God and with one another. "Righteousness" is mentioned four times in just seven lines! Where people are righteous there is justice, and where there is justice there is security and peace.

✦ All make the Sign of the Cross.

In the name of the Father, and of the Son, and of the Holy Spirit. Amen.

PSALM

(For a longer psalm, see page xii.) Psalm 85:8

Restore us again, O God of our salvation!

Restore us again, O God of our salvation!

Let me hear what God the LORD will speak,
for he will speak peace to his people,
to his faithful, to those who turn to him in
their hearts.

Restore us again, O God of our salvation!

READING

Isaiah 32:1, 16–18

A reading from the Book of the prophet Isaiah.

See, a king will reign in righteousness, and princes will rule with justice. Then justice will dwell in the wilderness, and righteousness abide in the fruitful field. The effect of righteousness will be peace, and the result of righteousness, quietness and trust forever. My people will abide in a peaceful habitation, in secure dwellings, and in quiet resting places.

The Word of the Lord.

◆ All observe silence.

FOR SILENT REFLECTION

Think about this silently in your heart. What does it mean to be in right relationship with God and with others?

CLOSING PRAYER

Let us pray to God for our needs and the needs of others: our family, neighborhood, and the world. For each need we say, "Lord, hear our prayer."

◆ All may add their own prayers here.

Let us pray: **Our Father . . . Amen.**

Help us become your righteous people, almighty God.
Show us how to be in right relationship with you, so that we may be in right relationship with others.
We ask this in Jesus' name.

Amen.

✦ All make the Sign of the Cross.

OPENING

Today is Gaudete (Gow-DAY-tay) Sunday. Gaudete come from a Latin word that means "rejoice!" In Advent, the priest normally wears violet vestments, but on Gaudete Sunday he may wear rose vestments. The change in color gives us encouragement to continue our spiritual preparation for Christmas. For this same reason, the third candle of the Advent wreath is traditionally rose-colored. In today's Gospel reading, people listen to John the Baptist.

✚ All make the Sign of the Cross.

In the name of the Father, and of the Son, and of the Holy Spirit. Amen.

PSALM   (For a longer psalm, see page xii.) Psalm 85:8

Restore us again, O God of our salvation!

Restore us again, O God of our salvation!

Let me hear what God the LORD will speak,
   for he will speak peace to his people,
to his faithful, to those who turn to him in
   their hearts.

Restore us again, O God of our salvation!

◆ All stand and sing **Alleluia.**

GOSPEL   Luke 3:10–14

A reading from the holy Gospel according to Luke.

And the crowds who came to be baptized asked John the Baptist, "What then should we do?" In reply he said to them, "Whoever has two coats must share with anyone who has none; and whoever has food must do likewise." Even tax-collectors came to be baptized, and they asked him, "Teacher, what should we do?" He said to them, "Collect no more than the amount prescribed for you." Soldiers also asked him, "And we, what should we do?" He said to them, "Do not extort money from anyone by threats or false accusation, and be satisfied with your wages."

The Gospel of the Lord.

◆ All sit and observe silence.

FOR SILENT REFLECTION

Think about this silently in your heart. How can you keep your heart filled with joy for the coming of the Christ at Christmas?

CLOSING PRAYER

Let us pray to God for our needs and the needs of others: our family, neighborhood, and the world. For each need we say, "Lord, hear our prayer."

◆ All may add their own prayers here.

Let us pray: **Our Father . . . Amen.**

O come, Lord Jesus.
Come and fill our hearts with your peace.
Come and fill our hearts with your love.
O come, Lord Jesus.

Amen.

✚ All make the Sign of the Cross.

OPENING

This week the theme is *waiting*—waiting for the birth of the Christ child. In Mexico and Central America, the most popular Advent devotion is Las Posadas. Children dressed as Mary and Joseph knock at the doors of houses, offering each household the opportunity to welcome the Holy Family. On the ninth day they are welcomed in. Las Posadas is a vivid reminder that the Holy Family still seeks a place to stay, and that when we answer yes, Christ is born in us again.

✢ All make the Sign of the Cross.

In the name of the Father, and of the Son, and of the Holy Spirit. Amen.

PSALM
(For a longer psalm, see page xii.) Psalm 85:8

Restore us again, O God of our salvation!

Restore us again, O God of our salvation!

Let me hear what God the LORD will speak,
for he will speak peace to his people,
to his faithful, to those who turn to him in
their hearts.

Restore us again, O God of our salvation!

READING
Isaiah 35:1–2b, 4–6

A reading from the Book of the prophet Isaiah.

The wilderness and the dry land shall be glad, the desert shall rejoice and blossom; like the crocus it shall blossom abundantly, and rejoice with joy and singing. Say to those who are of a fearful heart, "Be strong, do not fear! Here is your God. He will come with vengeance, with terrible recompense. He will come and save you." Then the eyes of the blind shall be opened, and the ears of the deaf unstopped; then the lame shall leap like a deer, and the tongue of the speechless sing for joy. For waters shall break forth in the wilderness, and streams in the desert.

The Word of the Lord.

◆ All observe silence.

FOR SILENT REFLECTION

Think about this silently in your heart. What images do you remember from today's reading?

CLOSING PRAYER

Let us pray to God for our needs and the needs of others: our family, neighborhood, and the world. For each need we say, "Lord, hear our prayer."

◆ All may add their own prayers here.

Let us pray: **Our Father . . . Amen.**

Lord God,
we long for the day
that the prophet Isaiah describes:
when the blind shall see,
and the lame shall walk.
Come quickly, O Lord, we pray.

Amen.

✢ All make the Sign of the Cross.

PRAYER FOR
TUESDAY, DECEMBER 18, 2018

OPENING

Today's words from the prophet Isaiah were written at a joyous time. The Hebrew people were returning to Jerusalem after many years in exile. Isaiah calls for the people to rejoice and reminds them that God, their shepherd, is leading them home. Calling God a shepherd helped them understand God's complete love and care for them. The word Zion refers to Israel as the people of God.

✛ All make the Sign of the Cross.

In the name of the Father, and of the Son, and of the Holy Spirit. Amen.

PSALM   (For a longer psalm, see page xii.) Psalm 85:8

Restore us again, O God of our salvation!

Restore us again, O God of our salvation!

Let me hear what God the LORD will speak,
    for he will speak peace to his people,
to his faithful, to those who turn to him in
    their hearts.

Restore us again, O God of our salvation!

READING   Isaiah 40:9–11

A reading from the Book of the prophet Isaiah.

Get you up to a high mountain, O Zion, herald of good tidings; lift up your voice with strength, O Jerusalem, herald of good tidings, lift it up, do not fear; say to the cities of Judah, "Here is your God!" See, the Lord GOD comes with might, and his arm rules for him; his reward is with him, and his recompense before him. He will feed his flock like a shepherd; he will gather the lambs in his arms, and carry them in his bosom, and gently lead the mother sheep.

The Word of the Lord.

◆ All observe silence.

FOR SILENT REFLECTION

Think about this silently in your heart. If God is the shepherd and we are the lambs, how does God treat us?

CLOSING PRAYER

Let us pray to God for our needs and the needs of others: our family, neighborhood, and the world. For each need we say, "Lord, hear our prayer."

◆ All may add their own prayers here.

Let us pray: **Our Father . . . Amen.**

Lord God,
you are the Shepherd.
We are the flock.
We trust that you will care for us.
We follow you, knowing that you will
lead us in the right direction.
We listen for your voice when we are lost.
We rest like lambs in your arms.

Amen.

✛ All make the Sign of the Cross.

OPENING

In the Philippines, a novena of Masses in honor of the Blessed Virgin Mary is held every day from December 16 to 24 as people wait for the birth of the Christ Child. This Advent devotion is called Simbang Gabi (Mass of the Rooster), as it is traditionally offered a dawn so people can attend before going to work. In today's reading, Isaiah reminds people of the wondrous works of God, who separated the Red Sea so that the Hebrew people could pass on dry land and escape from Egypt.

✦ All make the Sign of the Cross.

In the name of the Father, and of the Son, and of the Holy Spirit. Amen.

PSALM

(For a longer psalm, see page xii.) Psalm 85:8

Restore us again, O God of our salvation!

Restore us again, O God of our salvation!

Let me hear what God the LORD will speak,
    for he will speak peace to his people,
to his faithful, to those who turn to him in
    their hearts.

Restore us again, O God of our salvation!

READING

Isaiah 51:9ab, 10–11

A reading from the Book of the prophet Isaiah.

Awake, awake, put on strength, O arm of the LORD! Awake, as in days of old, the generations of long ago! Was it not you who dried up the sea, the waters of the great deep; who made the depths of the sea a way for the redeemed to cross over? So the ransomed of the LORD shall return, and come to Zion with singing; everlasting joy shall be upon their heads; they shall obtain joy and gladness, and sorrow and sighing shall flee away.

The Word of the Lord.

◆ All observe silence.

FOR SILENT REFLECTION

Think about this silently in your heart. Do you feel joy and gladness about the coming of Jesus?

CLOSING PRAYER

Let us pray to God for our needs and the needs of others: our family, neighborhood, and the world. For each need we say, "Lord, hear our prayer."

◆ All may add their own prayers here.

Let us pray: **Our Father . . . Amen.**

Loving God,
we have been waiting for the birth
 of the Christ Child.
Help us to remember that Christmas
is about welcoming your light into the world.
May your light shine brightly in us.
We ask this in Jesus' name.

Amen.

✦ All make the Sign of the Cross.

OPENING

The manger scene or crèche has been part of the celebration of Christmas for centuries. The custom is traced to St. Francis of Assisi, who created the first manger scene in the Italian village of Greccio on Christmas Eve, 1223. He wanted people to do more than read about the Christmas story: he wanted them to see the stable at Bethlehem and the poverty that surrounded Jesus on the night he was born. In today's reading, the prophet Isaiah says that the Messiah will come and make things right.

✦ All make the Sign of the Cross.

In the name of the Father, and of the Son, and of the Holy Spirit. Amen.

PSALM
(For a longer psalm, see page xii.) Psalm 85:8

Restore us again, O God of our salvation!

Restore us again, O God of our salvation!

Let me hear what God the LORD will speak,
    for he will speak peace to his people,
to his faithful, to those who turn to him in
    their hearts.

Restore us again, O God of our salvation!

READING
Isaiah 40:3–5a

A reading from the Book of the prophet Isaiah.

A voice cries out: "In the wilderness prepare the way of the LORD, make straight in the desert a highway for our God. Every valley shall be lifted up, and every mountain and hill be made low; the uneven ground shall become level, and the rough places a plain. Then the glory of the LORD shall be revealed, and all people shall see it together, for the mouth of the LORD has spoken."

The Word of the Lord.

◆ All observe silence.

FOR SILENT REFLECTION

Think about this silently in your heart. Christmas is getting closer. How are you preparing to welcome the Christ Child?

CLOSING PRAYER

Let us pray to God for our needs and the needs of others: our family, neighborhood, and the world. For each need we say, "Lord, hear our prayer."

◆ All may add their own prayers here.

Let us pray: **Our Father . . . Amen.**

Good and gracious God,
soon we shall see your glory
revealed in the birth of a small child,
your son, Jesus.
We pray that we are ready to welcome him
and give you thanks for this great gift.

Amen.

✦ All make the Sign of the Cross.

OPENING

Today's reading prepares us for Jesus' birth by telling us a story of John the Baptist, who was born to Zechariah [zek-uh-RI-uh)] and Elizabeth, a cousin of Jesus' mother Mary. Later in his life, John the Baptist was a great preacher who baptized people and proclaimed that Jesus was the Messiah.

✛ All make the Sign of the Cross.

In the name of the Father, and of the Son, and of the Holy Spirit. Amen.

PSALM   (For a longer psalm, see page xii.) Psalm 85:8

Restore us again, O God of our salvation!

Restore us again, O God of our salvation!

Let me hear what God the LORD will speak,
    for he will speak peace to his people,
to his faithful, to those who turn to him in
    their hearts.

Restore us again, O God of our salvation!

◆ All stand and sing **Alleluia.**

GOSPEL   Luke 1:5–6a, 7a, 8–9ac, 11a, 12a, 13–15a

A reading from the holy Gospel according to Luke.

In the days of King Herod of Judea, there was a priest named Zechariah, who belonged to the priestly order of Abijah [uh-BĪ-juh]. His wife was a descendant of Aaron, and her name was Elizabeth. Both of them were righteous before God. But they had no children. Once when Zechariah was serving as priest before God and his section was on duty, he was cho-sen to enter the sanctuary of the Lord and offer incense. Then there appeared to him an angel of the Lord. When Zechariah saw him, he was terrified. But the angel said to him, "Do not be afraid, Zechariah, for your prayer has been heard. Your wife Elizabeth will bear you a son, and you will name him John. You will have joy and gladness, and many will rejoice at his birth, for he will be great in the sight of the Lord."

The Gospel of the Lord.

◆ All sit and observe silence.

FOR SILENT REFLECTION

Think about this silently in your heart. The angel said to Zechariah, "Do not be afraid." Do these words, "Do not be afraid" comfort you?

CLOSING PRAYER

Let us pray to God for our needs and the needs of others: our family, neighborhood, and the world. For each need we say, "Lord, hear our prayer."

◆ All may add their own prayers here.

Let us pray: **Our Father . . . Amen.**

Wondrous God,
soon we will celebrate the birth of Jesus.
Thank you for this season of Advent.
We are ready to welcome him once again.

Amen.

✛ All make the Sign of the Cross.

PRAYER FOR THE WEEK
WITH A READING FROM THE GOSPEL FOR **SUNDAY, DECEMBER 23, 2018**

OPENING

Today's Gospel reading is the story of Mary's visit to her cousin Elizabeth to tell her she was pregnant. Elizabeth, in her old age, was also pregnant. Mary's baby was to be Jesus. Elizabeth's baby was to be John the Baptist. In this story, both Elizabeth and the baby in her womb recognized the baby inside Mary's womb as extraordinary and divine.

✛ All make the Sign of the Cross.

In the name of the Father, and of the Son, and of the Holy Spirit. Amen.

PSALM   (For a longer psalm, see page xii.) Psalm 85:8

Restore us again, O God of our salvation!

Restore us again, O God of our salvation!

Let me hear what God the LORD will speak,
   for he will speak peace to his people,
to his faithful, to those who turn to him in
   their hearts.

Restore us again, O God of our salvation!

◆ All stand and sing **Alleluia.**

GOSPEL   Luke 1:39–45

A reading from the holy Gospel according to Luke.

In those days Mary set out and went with haste to a Judean town in the hill country, where she entered the house of Zechariah (zek-uh-RI-uh) and greeted Elizabeth. When Elizabeth heard Mary's greeting, the child leapt in her womb. And Elizabeth was filled with the Holy Spirit and exclaimed with a loud cry, "Blessed are you among women, and blessed is the fruit of your womb. And why has this happened to me, that the mother of my Lord comes to me? For as soon as I heard the sound of your greeting, the child in my womb leapt for joy. And blessed is she who believed that there would be a fulfillment of what was spoken to her by the Lord."

The Gospel of the Lord.

◆ All sit and observe silence.

FOR SILENT REFLECTION

Think about this silently in your heart. Elizabeth recognized the love of God in Mary. Is there a special person who holds the love of God for you?

CLOSING PRAYER

Let us pray to God for our needs and the needs of others: our family, neighborhood, and the world. For each need we say, "Lord, hear our prayer."

◆ All may add their own prayers here.

Let us pray: **Our Father . . . Amen.**

Hail, Mary,
full of grace.
The Lord is with you.
Blessed are you among women,
and blessed is the fruit of your womb, Jesus.

Amen.

✛ All make the Sign of the Cross.

CHRISTMAS TIME

SUNDAY, JANUARY 6 — SUNDAY, JANUARY 13

THE MEANING OF CHRISTMAS

"For a child has been born for us, a son given to us; authority rests upon his shoulders; and he is named Wonderful Counselor, Mighty God, Everlasting Father, Prince of Peace" (Isaiah 9:6).

God keeps the great promise of the gift of Jesus! Of course, God amazes us with other gifts we never could have imagined or asked for. The earth is filled with God's gifts. Think of the solid ground that supports us, gravity that keeps us from floating away, the atmosphere that provides oxygen for breathing and a shield to protect us from the heat of the sun, and water that keeps our cells healthy. We need so many things just to stay alive. And yet the earth contains much more than is necessary to keep us going. Within the earth, precious metals and gems delight us with their shine. Seashells and spider webs amaze us with their geometry. Roses and lilacs fill the air with perfume. Peacocks and pinecones and pecans add to the world's great fascination. And every day our friends and family share new ways to love. What a world we have been given!

But God wants to give us something even more precious: a share in God's very own life. So Emmanuel, God-with-us, came to us in Bethlehem. God, who was there before the universe, who was the Word who spoke the world into existence, gave himself to us as an infant who could do nothing for itself. This gift has changed everything. God's heart is opened for us. In Advent we mentioned the Old Testament prophecy about Israel who was compared to an old tree stump in her defeat. Out of the tree stump of despair, God has brought a flowering branch. We will also celebrate Mary's resounding "Yes!" to God and Joseph's courageous faith in God.

Christmas season Scriptures are full of epiphanies, that is, events that clearly show people realize this Baby Jesus is the promised Messiah. In our homes and churches we, too, will stand in front of the manger in Bethlehem and gaze in wonder with Mary, Joseph, the angels, the shepherds, and the Magi as we realize this holy child, Jesus, is our God.

PREPARING TO CELEBRATE CHRISTMAS IN THE CLASSROOM

SACRED SPACE

Replace the Advent Wreath with a new, white pillar candle and change the purple cloth to a white one. You might add some gold tinsel or a gold piece of cloth, too. Place the star and the Magi in the Nativity scene. As you set up the Nativity scene, involve the children in placing the figures. "Silent Night" and "Away in the Manger" are perfect carols to sing as you gather.

MOVEMENT AND GESTURE

If your students enjoyed the Advent procession, you can have another procession to celebrate Christmas that includes the star and the Magi. If you have congregational candles (thin tapers) older students might light and hold them during the Epiphany Prayer Service. Ask the liturgy coordinator, priest or deacon if the parish has some you can have. Small battery-operated lights also work well in procession and are safe and suitable for children of all ages.

FESTIVITY IN SCHOOL AND HOME

The prayer service for Epiphany on pages 144–145 provides a beautiful and prayerful way to celebrate the arrival of the Magi in Bethlehem.

SACRED MUSIC

Christmas Time is a time of music! There are so many beautiful carols you can sing with the children. Don't forget "Joy to the World," "Angels We Have Heard On High," or "O Come, All Ye Faithful" and "We Three Kings." You may even wish to organize a caroling party and go door to door through your school.

PRAYERS FOR CHRISTMAS

The opening verses of the Gospel according to St. John contain some of the most beautiful poetry in the world:

In the beginning was the Word, and the Word was with God, and the Word was God. He was in the beginning with God. All things came into being through him, and without him not one thing came into being. What has come into being in him was life, and the life was the light of all people. The light shines in the darkness, and the darkness did not overcome it (John 1:1–5).

These verses beautifully express the mystery of the Incarnation, the mystery of God becoming a human being to be close to us. You might want to spend some time during religion class reading this beautiful hymn line by line. Ask the children who St. John means when he speaks about the "Word of God." See what they say when you ask them how "all things came into being" through Christ when we know Jesus was born after the creation of the world. How can one person be the "light of all people"? What kind of light do people need? What do the children think St. John means when he says, "the darkness did not overcome" the Light of the World?

A NOTE TO CATECHISTS

See whether you can share a Christmas Nativity scene with the teacher who shares your classroom. Or bring your students on a "field trip" to the church and let them pray in front of the parish Nativity scene!

Perhaps families could share their Nativity sets, or pieces from them. This is especially wonderful if you have a variety of nationalities and ethnic groups among your children.

GRACE BEFORE MEALS

CHRISTMAS TIME

LEADER:

"For a child has been born for us,"

ALL: "a son given to us."

✚ All make the Sign of the Cross.

In the name of the Father, and of the Son, and of the Holy Spirit. Amen.

LEADER:

Heavenly Father,
may the food we are about to share
help to nourish our bodies and minds,
just as you nurture us always
with the gift of your Son
and your everlasting Spirit.
May we be a living sign of the
presence of Jesus,
who is hope for the world.
We ask this through Christ our Lord.

ALL: Amen.

✚ All make the Sign of the Cross.

In the name of the Father, and of the Son, and of the Holy Spirit. Amen.

PRAYER AT DAY'S END

CHRISTMAS TIME

LEADER:

Sing to the Lord a new song,

ALL: for he has done wondrous deeds!

✛ All make the Sign of the Cross.

In the name of the Father, and of the Son, and of the Holy Spirit. Amen.

LEADER:

Heavenly Father,
the gift of your Son
gives us so much joy!
We thank you for this day,
filled with wonder and small adventures.
May we always remember that you
are the source of all goodness
as we praise the miracle of Jesus,
whom you sent to us
to lead the way back to you.
We ask this through Christ our Lord
and Savior.

ALL: Amen.

✛ All make the Sign of the Cross.

In the name of the Father, and of the Son, and of the Holy Spirit. Amen.

PRAYER SERVICE
FOR EPIPHANY

Prepare six leaders and a song leader for this service. The second and fourth leaders will need Bibles to read the Scripture passages and may need help finding and practicing them. Before you begin, remove the figures of shepherds and the three kings from your Nativity scene. Put the shepherds away until next year. Place the kings a short distance from the Nativity scene. Then gather the class near it. This service calls for two songs. Help the song leader prepare to lead the singing.

SONG LEADER:

Please stand and join in singing our opening song, "We Three Kings."

FIRST LEADER:

✚ All make the Sign of the Cross.

May the light of our Creator guide us in this prayer of praise.

ALL: Amen.

Let us pray:
Almighty God,
You are the light of the world!
Guide us with your radiance
as we reflect your goodness in our lives.
We ask this through Christ our Lord.

ALL: Amen.

◆ Gesture for all to sit.

SECOND LEADER: Isaiah 9:2–7

A reading from the Book of the Prophet Isaiah.

◆ Read the Scripture passage from the Bible.

The Word of the Lord.

◆ All observe silence.

CHILDREN'S DAILY PRAYER 2018–2019, © 2018 Archdiocese of Chicago: Liturgy Training Publications, 3949 South Racine Avenue, Chicago IL 60609. All rights reserved. Orders: 800-933-1800 or www.LTP.org. Scripture excerpts are taken from *The New Revised Standard Version Bible: Catholic Edition*, copyright © 1989, Division of Christian Education of the National Council of the Churches of Christ in the United States of America. Used with permission. All rights reserved.

PRAYER SERVICE
FOR EPIPHANY

THIRD LEADER:　　　　Psalm 148:1–2, 3–4, 9–10, 11–12, 13

Our refrain is: Praise the LORD!

ALL: Praise the LORD!

Praise the LORD from the heavens;
　praise him in the heights!
Praise him, all his angels;
　praise him, all his host!

ALL: Praise the LORD!

Praise him, sun and moon;
　praise him, all you shining stars!
Praise him, you highest heavens,
　and you waters above the heavens!

ALL: Praise the LORD!

Mountains and all hills,
　fruit trees and all cedars!
Wild animals and all cattle,
　creeping things and flying birds!

ALL: Praise the LORD!

Kings of the earth and all peoples,
　princes and all rulers of the earth!
Young men and women alike,
　old and young together!

ALL: Praise the LORD!

◆ All stand and sing Alleluia.

FOURTH LEADER:　　　　Matthew 2:9b–12

A reading from the holy Gospel according to
Matthew.

◆ Read the Scripture passage from a Bible.

The Gospel of the Lord.

◆ All sit and observe silence.

◆ In silence, an adult slowly moves the three figures
of the Wise Men, one at a time, into the stable.

SONG LEADER:

Let us stand and sing, "Joy to the World."

FIFTH LEADER:

Heavenly Father,
you created the sun, planets,
moon, and stars,
and everything that breathes
to give you glory.
You are almighty and powerful,
yet you are as close to us as our breath,
and you live within our hearts.
Inspire us more with your
gentle Spirit and direction
just as you did the wise men
who traveled far to
see your glory in the Christ child.
We ask this through your Son Jesus.

Amen.

Let us pray: **Our Father . . . Amen.**

SIXTH LEADER:

May God's love, found in the Trinity of
Father, Son, and Spirit,
always surround us on our journey.

ALL: Amen.

✚ All make the Sign of the Cross.

CHILDREN'S DAILY PRAYER 2018–2019 © 2018 Archdiocese of Chicago: Liturgy Training Publications, 3949 South Racine Avenue, Chicago IL 60609. All rights reserved. Orders: 800-933-1800 or www.LTP.org. Scripture excerpts are taken from *The New Revised Standard Version Bible: Catholic Edition*, © 1989, Division of Christian Education of the National Council of the Churches of Christ in the United States of America. Used with permission. All rights reserved.

PRAYER FOR THE WEEK
WITH A READING FROM THE GOSPEL FOR **SUNDAY, JANUARY 6, 2019**

OPENING

Today we celebrate the Solemnity of the Epiphany [ih-PIF-uh-nee] of the Lord. The Gospel reading tells the story of the three wise men, or Magi, who saw a star and came in search of the infant Christ. The word "epiphany" is Greek for "showing forth." When the Magi followed the star, they recognized Jesus as the long awaited Messiah and worshiped him.

✛ All make the Sign of the Cross.

In the name of the Father, and of the Son, and of the Holy Spirit. Amen.

PSALM   (For a longer psalm, see page xiii.) Psalm 96:1–2a

Let the heavens be glad and the earth rejoice!

Let the heavens be glad and the earth rejoice!

Sing to the LORD a new song;
   sing to the LORD, all the earth.
Sing to the LORD; bless his name.

Let the heavens be glad and the earth rejoice!

◆ All stand and sing **Alleluia.**

GOSPEL   Matthew 2:1ac, 2, 8a, 9a, 11

A reading from the holy Gospel according to Matthew.

In the time of King Herod, wise men from the East came to Jerusalem, asking, "Where is the child who has been born king of the Jews? For we observed his star at its rising, and have come to pay him homage." Then King Herod sent them to Bethlehem, saying, "Go and search diligently for the child." When they had heard the king, they set out; and there, ahead of them, went the star that they had seen at its rising. When they saw that the star had stopped, they were overwhelmed with joy. On entering the house, they saw the child with Mary his mother; and they knelt down and paid him homage. Then, opening their treasure-chests, they offered him gifts of gold, frankincense, and myrrh.

The Gospel of the Lord.

◆ All sit and observe silence.

FOR SILENT REFLECTION

Think about this silently in your heart. The wise men brought gifts. What gifts can you give to Jesus, the infant King?

CLOSING PRAYER

Let us pray to God for our needs and the needs of others: our family, neighborhood, and the world. For each need we say, "Lord, hear our prayer."

◆ All may add their own prayers here.

Let us pray: **Our Father . . . Amen.**

Glory to you, O God.
Help us to see Jesus in one another as the Magi saw him in the manger.

Amen.

✛ All make the Sign of the Cross.

OPENING

An epiphany [ih-PIF-uh-nee] is a revelation. It can be an event or action that helps us recognize something clearly. This week we will look at some epiphanies in Scripture. Isaiah tells us that a marvelous child will be born and he will have special qualities. This child will bring justice and peace to the world.

✦ All make the Sign of the Cross.

In the name of the Father, and of the Son, and of the Holy Spirit. Amen.

PSALM
(For a longer psalm, see page xiii.) Psalm 96:1–2a

Let the heavens be glad and the earth rejoice!

Let the heavens be glad and the earth rejoice!

Sing to the LORD a new song;
  sing to the LORD, all the earth.
Sing to the LORD; bless his name.

Let the heavens be glad and the earth rejoice!

READING
Isaiah 1a, 2–3ab, 6–7a

A reading from the Book of the prophet Isaiah.

But there will be no gloom for those who were in anguish. The people who walked in darkness have seen a great light; those who lived in a land of deep darkness—on them light has shined. You have multiplied the nation, you have increased its joy; they rejoice before you as with joy at the harvest. For a child has been born for us, a son given to us; authority rests upon his shoulders; and he is named Wonderful Counselor, Mighty God, Everlasting Father, Prince of Peace. His authority shall grow continually, and there shall be endless peace for the throne of David and his kingdom. He will establish and uphold it with justice and with righteousness from this time onwards and for evermore.

The Word of the Lord.

◆ All observe silence.

FOR SILENT REFLECTION

Think about this silently in your heart. Isaiah named Jesus "Prince of Peace." What would a Prince of Peace do?

CLOSING PRAYER

Let us pray to God for our needs and the needs of others: our family, neighborhood, and the world. For each need we say, "Lord, hear our prayer."

◆ All may add their own prayers here.

Let us pray: **Our Father . . . Amen.**

O God, there are many problems in the world today: wars, hunger, and harm to nature.
Sometimes it feels like a time of darkness.
But Jesus is a light for us.
Jesus is the Prince of Peace
who shows us the way to justice and peace.
 Help us to follow his light,

Amen.

✦ All make the Sign of the Cross.

OPENING

The shepherds in the fields around Bethlehem, experienced an epiphany or revelation when angels appeared to them and announced Jesus' birth. This not only surprised them but scared them too. What does the angel say to them? It is interesting that the angels did not announce the birth of the Messiah to wealthy people or religious leaders.

✚ All make the Sign of the Cross.

In the name of the Father, and of the Son, and of the Holy Spirit. Amen.

PSALM   (For a longer psalm, see page xiii.) Psalm 96:1–2a

Let the heavens be glad and the earth rejoice!

Let the heavens be glad and the earth rejoice!

Sing to the LORD a new song;
   sing to the LORD, all the earth.
Sing to the LORD; bless his name.

Let the heavens be glad and the earth rejoice!

◆ All stand and sing **Alleluia.**

GOSPEL   Luke 2:8–14

A reading from the holy Gospel according to Luke.

In that region there were shepherds living in the fields, keeping watch over their flock by night. Then an angel of the Lord stood before them, and the glory of the Lord shone around them, and they were terrified. But the angel said to them, "Do not be afraid; for see—I am bringing you good news of great joy for all the people: to you is born this day in the city of David a Savior, who is the Messiah, the Lord.

This will be a sign for you: you will find a child wrapped in bands of cloth and lying in a manger." And suddenly there was with the angel a multitude of the heavenly host, praising God and saying, "Glory to God in the highest heaven, and on earth peace among those whom he favors!"

The Gospel of the Lord.

◆ All sit and observe silence.

FOR SILENT REFLECTION

Think about this silently in your heart. Why do you think the angels announced the birth of Jesus to poor shepherds?

CLOSING PRAYER

Let us pray to God for our needs and the needs of others: our family, neighborhood, and the world. For each need we say, "Lord, hear our prayer."

◆ All may add their own prayers here.

Let us pray: **Our Father . . . Amen.**

Loving God,
thank you for the gift of Jesus.
Jesus is our guiding light.
With the multitude of angels we sing
your praises.
Glory to you in the highest heaven
and peace on earth.

Amen.

✚ All make the Sign of the Cross.

OPENING

All Jewish people in Jesus' time waited for the coming of the Messiah. "Messiah" means "promised one"—one who will do great things on earth. The angel told the shepherds they would find the Messiah wrapped in bands of cloth and lying in a manger—a baby. Frightened but astonished, they went.

✛ All make the Sign of the Cross.

In the name of the Father, and of the Son, and of the Holy Spirit. Amen.

PSALM   (For a longer psalm, see page xiii.) Psalm 96:1–2a

Let the heavens be glad and the earth rejoice!

Let the heavens be glad and the earth rejoice!

Sing to the LORD a new song;
  sing to the LORD, all the earth.
Sing to the LORD; bless his name.

Let the heavens be glad and the earth rejoice!

◆ All stand and sing **Alleluia.**

GOSPEL   Luke 2:15–20

A reading from the holy Gospel according to Luke.

When the angels had left them and gone into heaven, the shepherds said to one another, "Let us go now to Bethlehem and see this thing that has taken place, which the Lord has made known to us." So they went with haste and found Mary and Joseph, and the child lying in the manger. When they saw this, they made known what had been told them about this child; and all who heard it were amazed at what the shepherds told them. But Mary trea-

sured all these words and pondered them in her heart. The shepherds returned, glorifying and praising God for all they had heard and seen, as it had been told them.

The Gospel of the Lord.

◆ All sit and observe silence.

FOR SILENT REFLECTION

Think about this silently in your heart. The shepherds praised God for the gift of Jesus. What would you like to give thanks for in your life today?

CLOSING PRAYER

Let us pray to God for our needs and the needs of others: our family, neighborhood, and the world. For each need we say, "Lord, hear our prayer."

◆ All may add their own prayers here.

Let us pray: **Our Father . . . Amen.**

Loving and holy God,
fill us with the joy and amazement
that the shepherds felt.
Help us to spread this Christmas joy
throughout the year by the way we live.
We ask this in Jesus' name.

Amen.

✛ All make the Sign of the Cross.

PRAYER FOR
THURSDAY, JANUARY 10, 2019

OPENING

The wise men brought gifts of gold, frankincense, and myrrh to Jesus. Gold, an expensive gift, was often given to kings. Frankincense was incense used in the Temple by the priests. Its smoke drifted upward carrying prayers to God. Myrrh is a beautiful and expensive perfume. People brought myrrh to anoint the body when someone they loved had died.

✝ All make the Sign of the Cross.

In the name of the Father, and of the Son, and of the Holy Spirit. Amen.

PSALM   (For a longer psalm, see page xiii.) Psalm 96:1–2a

Let the heavens be glad and the earth rejoice!

Let the heavens be glad and the earth rejoice!

Sing to the LORD a new song;
  sing to the LORD, all the earth.
Sing to the LORD; bless his name.

Let the heavens be glad and the earth rejoice!

◆ All stand and sing **Alleluia.**

GOSPEL   Matthew 2:1ac, 2, 8a, 9a, 11

A reading from the holy Gospel according to Matthew.

In the time of King Herod, wise men from the East came to Jerusalem, asking, "Where is the child who has been born king of the Jews? For we observed his star at its rising, and have come to pay him homage." Then King Herod sent them to Bethlehem, saying, "Go and search diligently for the child." When they had heard the king, they set out; and there, ahead of them, went the star that they had seen at its rising. When they saw that the star had stopped, they were overwhelmed with joy. On entering the house, they saw the child with Mary his mother; and they knelt down and paid him homage. Then, opening their treasure-chests, they offered him gifts of gold, frankincense, and myrrh.

The Gospel of the Lord.

◆ All sit and observe silence.

FOR SILENT REFLECTION

Think about this silently in your heart. Why were gifts of gold, frankincense and myrrh appropriate to give to Jesus?

CLOSING PRAYER

Let us pray to God for our needs and the needs of others: our family, neighborhood, and the world. For each need we say, "Lord, hear our prayer."

◆ All may add their own prayers here.

Let us pray: **Our Father . . . Amen.**

O God, the wise men brought precious gifts. The most precious gift
we can give to Jesus is our love.
Help us to love.

Amen.

✝ All make the Sign of the Cross.

OPENING

In Scripture, heavenly phenomena, such as angels or stars, often reveal God's messages. This week we have read the stories of the shepherds and the wise men. Today's reading describes an epiphany that Joseph, the husband of Mary and father of Jesus, had in a dream.

✛ All make the Sign of the Cross.

In the name of the Father, and of the Son, and of the Holy Spirit. Amen.

PSALM
(For a longer psalm, see page xiii.) Psalm 96:1–2a

Let the heavens be glad and the earth rejoice!

Let the heavens be glad and the earth rejoice!

Sing to the LORD a new song;
  sing to the LORD, all the earth.
Sing to the LORD; bless his name.

Let the heavens be glad and the earth rejoice!

◆ All stand and sing **Alleluia.**

GOSPEL
Matthew 2:13abd, 14ac, 15a, 19–20ac, 23

A reading from the holy Gospel according to Matthew.

Now after the Magi had left, an angel of the Lord appeared to Joseph in a dream and said, "Get up, take the child and his mother, and flee to Egypt; for Herod is about to search for the child, to destroy him." Then Joseph got up, and went to Egypt, and remained there until the death of Herod. When Herod died, an angel of the Lord suddenly appeared in a dream to Joseph in Egypt and said, "Get up, and go to the land of Israel, for those who were seeking the child's life are dead." There he made his home in a town called Nazareth, so that what had been spoken through the prophets might be fulfilled, "He will be called a Nazorean."

The Gospel of the Lord.

◆ All sit and observe silence.

FOR SILENT REFLECTION

Think about this silently in your heart. Do you ever feel like dreams give you new insights into something you have been thinking or worrying about?

CLOSING PRAYER

Let us pray to God for our needs and the needs of others: our family, neighborhood, and the world. For each need we say, "Lord, hear our prayer."

◆ All may add their own prayers here.

Let us pray: **Our Father . . . Amen.**

O God, keep us open to see signs of you
and to hear your voice every day and night.
You are present everywhere:
in the beauty of nature,
in the kindness of our teachers,
in the love of our family and friends.
Thank you for all of these gifts.

Amen.

✛ All make the Sign of the Cross.

OPENING

Today we celebrate the Solemnity of the Baptism of the Lord. When Jesus was baptized the heavens opened, the Holy Spirit descended like a dove, and a voice from heaven spoke. We are baptized too, and the words that God says to Jesus are true about us.

✛ All make the Sign of the Cross.

In the name of the Father, and of the Son, and of the Holy Spirit. Amen.

PSALM
(For a longer psalm, see page xiii.) Psalm 96:1–2a

Let the heavens be glad and the earth rejoice!

Let the heavens be glad and the earth rejoice!

Sing to the LORD a new song;
  sing to the LORD, all the earth.
Sing to the LORD; bless his name.

Let the heavens be glad and the earth rejoice!

◆ All stand and sing **Alleluia.**

GOSPEL
Luke 3:15–16, 21–22

A reading from the holy Gospel according to Luke.

As the people were filled with expectation, and all were questioning in their hearts concerning John the Baptist, whether he might be the Messiah, John answered all of them by saying, "I baptize you with water; but one who is more powerful than I is coming; I am not worthy to untie the thong of his sandals. He will baptize you with the Holy Spirit and fire." Now when all the people were baptized, and when Jesus also had been baptized and was praying, the heaven was opened, and the Holy Spirit descended upon him in bodily form like a dove. And a voice came from heaven, "You are my Son, the Beloved; with you I am well pleased."

The Gospel of the Lord.

◆ All sit and observe silence.

FOR SILENT REFLECTION

Think about this silently in your heart. You are God's beloved son or daughter in whom God is well pleased. How does that make you feel?

CLOSING PRAYER

Let us pray to God for our needs and the needs of others: our family, neighborhood, and the world. For each need we say, "Lord, hear our prayer."

◆ All may add their own prayers here.

Let us pray: **Our Father . . . Amen.**

Dear God,
help us to trust in your love for us.
Help us to hear your words and believe them:
"You are my Beloved with whom I am
well pleased."
We ask this in Jesus' name.

Amen.

✛ All make the Sign of the Cross.

ORDINARY TIME WINTER

MONDAY, JANUARY 14 — TUESDAY, MARCH 5

WINTER ORDINARY TIME

THE MEANING OF ORDINARY TIME

We've just celebrated the two great seasons of Advent and Christmas and now move back into Ordinary Time. Our seasons celebrate certain aspects of what we call Christ's "Paschal Mystery." For example, during the four weeks of Advent we focused on preparing to celebrate Christ's first coming in the Incarnation and preparing for Christ's second coming at the Parousia [pare-OO-see-uh]. The several weeks of Christmas focus on the wonder and joy of that first reality of God-With-Us in Jesus. Now we move into the beginning of this year's ordered, that is counted, Sundays of Ordinary Time. Winter Ordinary time is usually quite short lasting only a few weeks.

The Prayers for the Week will reflect the Sunday Gospels and week one of Ordinary Time comes after the great celebration of Epiphany Sunday. That Monday we celebrate the Solemnity of the Baptism of the Lord so, in the rest of the week, the Scriptures will lead us to think about what it means to be baptized into God's family. We'll hear about Jesus' early years with the great stories of the Presentation in the Temple (an epiphany for Simeon and Anna), the finding in the Temple and Jesus' baptism. We end the week with Jesus' instruction to the Apostles and to us to go out and proclaim the Gospel, the "good news." Week two focuses on God's abundance and how God calls us to share abundantly with others. The readings in week three explore God's revelation about who God is. We will read stories about the prophets Elijah and Daniel, the apostles Peter, James, and John, and a miracle that Jesus performed. Week four focuses on St. Paul's teaching that the Church is the Body of Christ. Each person has different gifts but the Church needs us all. Each person is necessary and important. Just as a body needs all its part, we all need each other.

PREPARING TO CELEBRATE ORDINARY TIME IN THE CLASSROOM

You will need to replace your white cloth with a green one, now that it is Ordinary Time again. Plan another procession with your students if they respond well to them. Otherwise, you might ask them if they have any ideas about how to change the cloths with care and dignity. You might be surprised at the depth of their suggestions. Don't forget to copy the Home Prayer for Lent and send it before Ash Wednesday.

SACRED SPACE

Place a clear bowl with water in the prayer space for the first week to honor the baptism of Jesus and our own.

A plain vase with a bunch of bare branches would be appropriate or a potted plant. A spider plant or an ivy will withstand long weekends without attention. Give the care and watering over to your students. Make a job chart and allow them to take turns fetching water for the plant. Watching the plant grow will provide a concrete sign of the growth that can take place in our hearts during this liturgical season.

In February consider placing a St. Brigid's cross (February 1) and/or two candles tied with a red ribbon for St. Blase (February 3) in the space.

MOVEMENT AND GESTURE

Integrate the bowl of water into the daily prayer by bringing the bowl to the children or having them go to the bowl to make the sign of the cross. You might get holy water from the parish church but using tap water is fine. Water is intrinsically holy. If the water becomes dirty it should be used to water plants or poured into the earth because it is holy by God's creation and by our use.

See the suggestions for February 2, the Presentation of the Lord, below.

FESTIVITY IN SCHOOL AND HOME

From January 18 through 25, the Church joins with our Protestant brothers and sisters in the Week of Prayer for Christian Unity. A special prayer service, which may be used anytime during the week, is provided on page 163.

On February 2 we celebrate the feast of the Presentation of the Lord, also known as "Candlemas." This is a beautiful feast to celebrate with children. If your school does not attend Mass that day you might use the scriptures from Monday and Tuesday of the first week of Ordinary Time. Before you begin prayer that day, dim the classroom lights and light a candle. Help the student proclaiming the Scripture to practice so that it can be done well, and allow time for the class to ponder the story together. If the children are old enough they might light and hold congregational candles (tapers) during the Gospel. (See more below, under Prayers for Ordinary Time and A Note to Catechists.)

SACRED MUSIC

This would be the perfect time to learn how to sing one of the psalms. Psalm 27 ("The Lord Is My Light and My Salvation") and Psalm 23 ("The Lord Is My Shepherd") are two beautiful psalms that have many different musical settings. Children might also enjoy "This Little Light of Mine" and "I Want to Walk as a Child of the Light"). Invite children to share favorite spiritual songs from their ethnic backgrounds and try singing songs from other countries ("We are Marching in the Light," "Pan de Vida," the round "Shalom Chevarim"). Also, don't forget to sing Alleluia often during these days. When Lent arrives, we will have to wait a long time before Easter when we can sing it again. The best Alleluia to sing is the one your parish uses before the Sunday Gospel.

PRAYERS FOR ORDINARY TIME

Each night before going to bed, Catholic men and women around the world pray the Canticle of Simeon, the prayer of the elderly man who met the Holy Family in the temple of Jerusalem when Mary and Joseph brought Jesus there as a baby. God had promised Simeon he would not die before he saw the Messiah. Simeon took the child Jesus, in his arms and said this prayer:

> "Master, now you are dismissing your servant
> in peace,
> according to your word;
> for my eyes have seen your salvation,
> which you have prepared in the presence
> of all peoples,
> a light for revelation to the Gentiles
> and for glory to your people Israel"
> (Luke 2:29–32).

Introduce this prayer on February 2, the feast of the Presentation of the Lord. You may want to ask the children about certain key words in the prayer. Possible "wondering" questions could include: Why does Simeon call himself God's "servant"? Does the word "servant" recall anything that Mary once said? How did Simeon know that Jesus was a special baby? How is this small baby a "light" and a "glory"?

A NOTE TO CATECHISTS

Sometimes building codes will not allow school teachers or catechists to burn matches or light candles in the classroom. If possible, for February 2, plan a visit to a room where fire is permitted so that your celebration of the feast of the Presentation of the Lord will be set apart from the days surrounding it.

GRACE BEFORE MEALS

ORDINARY TIME • WINTER

LEADER:

Who is this King of glory?

ALL: The Lord, strong and mighty.

+ All make the Sign of the Cross.

> **In the name of the Father, and of the Son, and of the Holy Spirit. Amen.**

LEADER:

Heavenly Father,
we thank you for
the food we are about to share.
The abundance of this meal
reflects your goodness,
and how you provide for us
every day, in so many ways.
We ask this through Christ our Lord.

All: Amen.

+ All make the Sign of the Cross.

> **In the name of the Father, and of the Son, and of the Holy Spirit. Amen.**

PRAYER AT DAY'S END
ORDINARY TIME • WINTER

LEADER:
Your word is a light to my feet,

ALL: and a light to my path.

✚ All make the Sign of the Cross.

In the name of the Father, and of the Son, and of the Holy Spirit. Amen.

LEADER:
Heavenly Father,
thank you for this day of learning.
As we make our way home or
to other activities,
help us turn to you
for guidance in everything we do.
Keep us safe as we respond
to your Word in our hearts
as we meet with family and friends.
We ask this through Christ our Lord.

All: Amen.

✚ All make the Sign of the Cross.

In the name of the Father, and of the Son, and of the Holy Spirit. Amen.

OPENING

In today's reading we meet a holy man named Simeon, who recognized Jesus as the Messiah. According to Jewish law, firstborn sons were presented in the Temple to recognize that the baby was a gift from God. Simeon, who lived at the Temple, had prayed that he would live long enough to see the Messiah.

✚ All make the Sign of the Cross.

In the name of the Father, and of the Son, and of the Holy Spirit. Amen.

PSALM   (For a longer psalm, see page xiii.) Psalm 23:1–3a

I shall dwell in the house of the LORD my whole life long.

I shall dwell in the house of the LORD my whole life long.

The LORD is my shepherd, I shall not want.
   He makes me lie down in green pastures;
he leads me beside still waters;
   he restores my soul.

I shall dwell in the house of the LORD my whole life long.

◆ All stand and sing **Alleluia.**

GOSPEL   Luke 2:21, 22b, 25ab, 26–27b, 28–32

A reading from the holy Gospel according to Luke.

After eight days had passed, Mary and Joseph brought Jesus up to Jerusalem to present him to the Lord. Now there was a man in Jerusalem whose name was Simeon; this man was righteous and devout. It had been revealed to him by the Holy Spirit that he would not see death before he had seen the Lord's Messiah. Guided by the Spirit, Simeon came into the temple; and when the parents brought in the child Jesus, Simeon took him in his arms and praised God, saying, "Master, now you are dismissing your servant in peace, according to your word; for my eyes have seen your salvation, which you have prepared in the presence of all peoples, a light for revelation to the Gentiles and for glory to your people Israel."

The Gospel of the Lord.

◆ All sit and observe silence.

FOR SILENT REFLECTION

Think about this silently in your heart. Why do you think Simeon called Jesus a light?

CLOSING PRAYER

Let us pray to God for our needs and the needs of others: our family, neighborhood, and the world. For each need we say, "Lord, hear our prayer."

◆ All may add their own prayers here.

Let us pray: **Our Father . . . Amen.**

Jesus, Light of the World,
shine on us and in us.

Amen.

✚ All make the Sign of the Cross.

OPENING

Many Jewish people were eagerly awaiting a mighty and magnificent king who would lead them to glorious victory against their enemies. But there were also many good people who were looking for a just and godly Messiah. Today we meet Anna, a prophetess. She lived in the Temple and listened to God's word so she could teach and guide the people of Israel.

✛ All make the Sign of the Cross.

In the name of the Father, and of the Son, and of the Holy Spirit. Amen.

PSALM
(For a longer psalm, see page xiii.) Psalm 23:1–3a

I shall dwell in the house of the LORD my whole life long.

I shall dwell in the house of the LORD my whole life long.

The LORD is my shepherd, I shall not want.
  He makes me lie down in green pastures;
he leads me beside still waters;
  he restores my soul.

I shall dwell in the house of the LORD my whole life long.

◆ All stand and sing **Alleluia.**

GOSPEL
Luke 2:36–38

A reading from the holy Gospel according to Luke.

In the temple, there was also a prophet, Anna the daughter of Phanuel, of the tribe of Asher. She was of a great age, having lived with her husband seven years after her marriage, then as a widow to the age of eighty-four. She never left the temple but worshiped there with fasting and prayer night and day. At that moment she came, and began to praise God and to speak about the child to all who were looking for the redemption of Jerusalem.

The Gospel of the Lord.

◆ All sit and observe silence.

FOR SILENT REFLECTION

Think about this silently in your heart. Anna was a holy and wise woman who taught and guided people. Who is a guide for you?

CLOSING PRAYER

Let us pray to God for our needs and the needs of others: our family, neighborhood, and the world. For each need we say, "Lord, hear our prayer."

◆ All may add their own prayers here.

Let us pray: **Our Father . . . Amen.**

We give thanks for all the holy women
and men who spread your word,
who speak out for justice and peace,
and who guide us in paths of righteousness.

Amen.

✛ All make the Sign of the Cross.

OPENING

As a young boy, Jesus showed that he had a special relationship with God. He journeyed with his parents every year to Jerusalem to celebrate the feast of the Passover. The Temple was located in Jerusalem, the religious capital for the Jewish people.

✛ All make the Sign of the Cross.

In the name of the Father, and of the Son, and of the Holy Spirit. Amen.

PSALM
(For a longer psalm, see page xiii.) Psalm 23:1–3a

I shall dwell in the house of the LORD my
    whole life long.

**I shall dwell in the house of the LORD my
    whole life long.**

The LORD is my shepherd, I shall not want.
  He makes me lie down in green pastures;
he leads me beside still waters;
  he restores my soul.

**I shall dwell in the house of the LORD my
    whole life long.**

◆ All stand and sing **Alleluia.**

GOSPEL
Luke 2:41–47

A reading from the holy Gospel according to Luke.

Now every year Jesus' parents went to Jerusalem for the festival of the Passover. And when he was twelve years old, they went up as usual for the festival. When the festival was ended and they started to return, the boy Jesus stayed behind in Jerusalem, but his parents did not know it. Assuming that he was in the group of travelers, they went a day's journey. Then they started to look for him among their relatives and friends. When they did not find him, they returned to Jerusalem to search for him. After three days they found Jesus in the temple, sitting among the teachers, listening to them and asking them questions. And all who heard him were amazed at his understanding and his answers.

The Gospel of the Lord.

◆ All sit and observe silence.

FOR SILENT REFLECTION

Think about this silently in your heart. Jesus listened to the teachers and asked them questions. What does that tell you about Jesus?

CLOSING PRAYER

Let us pray to God for our needs and the needs of others: our family, neighborhood, and the world. For each need we say, "Lord, hear our prayer."

◆ All may add their own prayers here.

Let us pray: **Our Father . . . Amen.**

Dear God, although we are young,
we can learn about you.
Help us to know and love you as Jesus did.

Amen.

✛ All make the Sign of the Cross.

OPENING

John the Baptist was a great preacher. He baptized people and foretold the coming of the Messiah. When John baptized Jesus, the heavens opened up and the Holy Spirit descended on Jesus in the form of a dove. A voice comes from heaven that announced Jesus as the Son of God.

◆ All make the Sign of the Cross.

In the name of the Father, and of the Son, and of the Holy Spirit. Amen.

PSALM   (For a longer psalm, see page xiii.) Psalm 23:1–3a

I shall dwell in the house of the LORD my
   whole life long.

**I shall dwell in the house of the LORD my
   whole life long.**

The LORD is my shepherd, I shall not want.
   He makes me lie down in green pastures;
he leads me beside still waters;
   he restores my soul.

**I shall dwell in the house of the LORD my
   whole life long.**

◆ All stand and sing **Alleluia.**

GOSPEL   Mark 1:7–11

A reading from the holy Gospel according to Mark.

John the Baptist proclaimed, "The one who is more powerful than I is coming after me; I am not worthy to stoop down and untie the thong of his sandals. I have baptized you with water; but he will baptize you with the Holy Spirit." In those days Jesus came from Nazareth of Galilee and was baptized by John in the Jordan. And just as he was coming up out of the water, he saw the heavens torn apart and the Spirit descending like a dove on him. And a voice came from heaven, "You are my Son, the Beloved; with you I am well pleased."

The Gospel of the Lord.

◆ All sit and observe silence.

FOR SILENT REFLECTION

Think about this silently in your heart. Why do you think a dove, the symbol of peace, descended on Jesus?

CLOSING PRAYER

Let us pray to God for our needs and the needs of others: our family, neighborhood, and the world. For each need we say, "Lord, hear our prayer."

◆ All may add their own prayers here.

Let us pray: **Our Father . . . Amen.**

Almighty God,
you say to us what you said to Jesus,
"You are my Beloved."
Help us to live daughters and sons of God,
pouring kindness and love into the world.
Help us to be builders of peace.

Amen.

✚ All make the Sign of the Cross.

OPENING

Today Catholics and Protestants begin seven days of Prayer for Christian Unity. During this time people from neighborhood churches may get together to pray for unity. In today's reading, Jesus empowers his disciples to go out among the people of the world to preach and baptize. The reference to casting out demons means to overcome the power of sin.

✦ All make the Sign of the Cross.

In the name of the Father, and of the Son, and of the Holy Spirit. Amen.

PSALM   (For a longer psalm, see page xiii.) Psalm 23:1–3a

I shall dwell in the house of the LORD my
    whole life long.

**I shall dwell in the house of the LORD my
    whole life long.**

The LORD is my shepherd, I shall not want.
   He makes me lie down in green pastures;
he leads me beside still waters;
   he restores my soul.

**I shall dwell in the house of the LORD my
    whole life long.**

◆ All stand and sing **Alleluia.**

GOSPEL   Mark 16:14a, 15–16a, 17, 19–20

A reading from the holy Gospel according to Mark.

Later Jesus appeared to the eleven disciples as they were sitting at the table. And he said to them, "Go into all the world and proclaim the good news to the whole creation. The one who believes and is baptized will be saved. And these signs will accompany those who believe: by using my name they will cast out demons; they will speak in new tongues." So then the Lord Jesus, after he had spoken to them, was taken up into heaven and sat down at the right hand of God. And they went out and proclaimed the good news everywhere, while the Lord worked with them and confirmed the message by the signs that accompanied it.

The Gospel of the Lord.

◆ All sit and observe silence.

FOR SILENT REFLECTION

Think about this silently in your heart. How can you proclaim or show the love of God today?

CLOSING PRAYER

Let us pray to God for our needs and the needs of others: our family, neighborhood, and the world. For each need we say, "Lord, hear our prayer."

◆ All may add their own prayers here.

Let us pray: **Our Father . . . Amen.**

Lord God, we are your disciples.
Empower us to proclaim the good news
of your love to the world.

Amen.

✦ All make the Sign of the Cross.

WEEK OF PRAYER FOR CHRISTIAN UNITY

Perhaps you can display pictures of Catholic and Protestant churches in the neighborhood. Prepare the leader, a reader, and an intercessor.

LEADER:

May the peace of Christ,
who unites all God's people
around the world,
be with you,
now and forever.

All: Amen.

LEADER:

Let us pray:
Almighty God, you created us in love
to be one family.
You gave us Jesus,
who proclaimed your love
and called us to be united.
Send your Holy Spirit
to guide us
as we seek your truth,
and help us become closer to one another.
We ask this in the name of your Son, Jesus.

All: Amen.

◆ All sit down.

READER: 1 Cor. 1:10-13a

A reading from St. Paul's First Letter to the Corinthians.

Now I appeal to you, brothers and sisters, by the name of our Lord Jesus Christ, that all of you be in agreement and that there be no divisions among you, but that you be united in the same mind and the same purpose. For it has been reported to me by Chloe's people that there are quarrels among you, my brothers and sisters. What I mean is that each of you says,

"I belong to Paul," or "I belong to Apollos," or "I belong to Cephas," or "I belong to Christ." Has Christ been divided?

The Word of the Lord.

◆ Observe silence and pray for unity among Christians.

◆ All stand.

INTERCESSOR:

"Lord, hear our prayer."

That all Christians may we be true to God's commandment to love one another,
        we pray . . .

That we may be united in doing Jesus' work of peace and justice, we pray . . .

That we may we be united in caring for the
        poor and oppressed, we pray . . .

That we accept our differences with respect and see one another's goodness and holiness, we pray . . .

◆ All offer one another a sign of peace.

✙ All make the Sign of the Cross.

In the name of the Father, and of the Son, and of the Holy Spirit. Amen.

OPENING

Today's reading is a story that some scholars say is the beginning of Jesus' public ministry. At his mother's request, Jesus turns water into fine wine.

✚ All make the Sign of the Cross.

> **In the name of the Father, and of the Son, and of the Holy Spirit. Amen.**

PSALM

(For a longer psalm, see page xiii.) Psalm 23:1–3a

I shall dwell in the house of the LORD my
   whole life long.

**I shall dwell in the house of the LORD my
   whole life long.**

The LORD is my shepherd, I shall not want.
   He makes me lie down in green pastures;
he leads me beside still waters;
   he restores my soul.

**I shall dwell in the house of the LORD my
   whole life long.**

◆ All stand and sing **Alleluia.**

GOSPEL

John 2:1–11

A reading from the holy Gospel according to John.

On the third day there was a wedding in Cana of Galilee. When the wine gave out, the mother of Jesus said to Jesus, "They have no wine." And Jesus said to her, "Woman, what concern is that to you and to me? My hour has not yet come." His mother said to the servants, "Do whatever he tells you." Now standing there were six stone water jars. Jesus said to them, "Fill the jars with water." And they filled them up to the brim. He said to them, "Now draw some out, and take it to the chief steward." So they took it. When the steward tasted the water that had become wine, and did not know where it came from, the steward called the bridegroom and said to him, "Everyone serves the good wine first, and then the inferior wine after the guests have become drunk. But you have kept the good wine until now."

The Gospel of the Lord.

◆ All sit and observe silence.

FOR SILENT REFLECTION

Think about this silently in your heart. How do you imagine the bridegroom felt when he tasted the wine?

CLOSING PRAYER

Let us pray to God for our needs and the needs of others: our family, neighborhood, and the world. For each need we say, "Lord, hear our prayer."

◆ All may add their own prayers here.

Let us pray: **Our Father . . . Amen.**

Dear God, open and hearts and minds
as we listen to stories about Jesus.
Help us to know Jesus more and more.

Amen.

✚ All make the Sign of the Cross.

OPENING

The theme for this week is the abundant ways in which God's love has been present to people throughout history. After the Hebrew people had escaped from Egypt, they spent a long time wandering in the desert. They faced lack of food and water. But God did not forget them.

✝ All make the Sign of the Cross.

> **In the name of the Father, and of the Son, and of the Holy Spirit. Amen.**

PSALM   (For a longer psalm, see page xiii.) Psalm 23:1–3a

I shall dwell in the house of the LORD my
    whole life long.

**I shall dwell in the house of the LORD my
    whole life long.**

The LORD is my shepherd, I shall not want.
    He makes me lie down in green pastures;
he leads me beside still waters;
    he restores my soul.

**I shall dwell in the house of the LORD my
    whole life long.**

READING   Numbers 20:1a, 2a, 3a, 4, 7–8c, 9–11

A reading from the Book of Numbers.

The Israelites came into the wilderness of Zin. Now there was no water for the congregation; so they gathered together against Moses and against Aaron. The people quarreled with Moses and said, "Why have you brought the assembly of the LORD into this wilderness for us and our livestock to die here?" The LORD spoke to Moses, saying: "Take the staff, and assemble the congregation, and command the rock before their eyes to yield its water." So Moses took the staff from before the LORD, as he had commanded him. Moses and Aaron gathered the assembly together before the rock, and he said to them, "Listen, you rebels, shall we bring water for you out of this rock?" Then Moses lifted up his hand and struck the rock twice with his staff; water came out abundantly, and the congregation and their livestock drank.

The Word of the Lord.

◆ All observe silence.

FOR SILENT REFLECTION

Think about this silently in your heart. Pray for guidance about a concern you have today.

CLOSING PRAYER

Let us pray to God for our needs and the needs of others: our family, neighborhood, and the world. For each need we say, "Lord, hear our prayer."

◆ All may add their own prayers here.

Let us pray: **Our Father . . . Amen.**

Faithful God, help us to remember
that you are with us
when we are worried or sad or fearful.

Amen.

✝ All make the Sign of the Cross.

PRAYER SERVICE
DR. MARTIN LUTHER KING JR.

Place an image of Martin Luther King Jr. in the sacred space. Prepare a leader, four readers, and a song leader. If possible, sing the refrain of "We Are Called" or "Let Justice Roll Like a River," or some other suitable song. Be sure to keep some silence where it's indicated. Since the Scriptures are abridged, copy them and put them in the Bible marked with ribbons. Put the MLK quotes in a binder.

LEADER:

◆ Gesture for all to stand.

✝ All make the sign of the Cross.

> **In the name of the Father, and of the Son, and of the Holy Spirit. Amen**

LEADER:
We remember and celebrate
Dr. Martin Luther King,
who worked for the just treatment
of African Americans.
Even though he received many death threats,
he spoke out courageously
and taught us how to make changes
through non-violent protest.

◆ Gesture for all to sit.

READER 1
From Dr. King's "I Have a Dream" Speech.
"I have a dream that my four little
children will one day live in a nation
where they will not be judged
by the color of their skin,
but by the content of their character."

◆ Observe some silence.

READER 2
A quote from Dr. King's book *Strength to Love.*

"Returning hate for hate multiplies hate, adding deeper darkness to a night already devoid of stars. Darkness cannot drive out darkness; only light can do that. Hate cannot drive out hate; only love can do that."

◆ Observe some silence.

READER 3   Colossians 3:12, 14–15a
A reading from St. Paul's Letter to
the Colossians.

As God's chosen ones, holy and beloved, clothe yourselves with compassion, kindness, humility, meekness, and patience. Above all, clothe yourselves with love, which binds everything together in perfect harmony. And let the peace of Christ rule in your hearts.

The Word of the Lord.

◆ Observe some silence.

LEADER:

◆ Gesture for all to stand.

◆ All stand to sing the song.

LEADER:
Let us pray.
O God of justice and love,
give us the courage
to challenge injustice wherever we see it.
Help us be open to all your children
and not let race, religion,
or anything else divide us.
We ask this in Jesus' name.

ALL: Amen

✝ All make the Sign of the Cross.

> **In the name of the Father, and of the Son, and of the Holy Spirit. Amen**

 CHILDREN'S DAILY PRAYER 2018–2019, © 2018 Archdiocese of Chicago: Liturgy Training Publications. All rights reserved. Orders: 800-933-1800 or www.LTP.org.

OPENING

Today's reading from the prophet Isaiah reminds us that God's words are nourishing like good water and good food. God promises an everlasting covenant. The word *covenant* means a special agreement. Today is a Day of Prayer for the Legal Protection of Unborn Children, when we pray that parents of unborn babies will experience delight in them.

✚ All make the Sign of the Cross.

In the name of the Father, and of the Son, and of the Holy Spirit. Amen.

PSALM
(For a longer psalm, see page xiii.) Psalm 23:1–3a

I shall dwell in the house of the LORD my
whole life long.

**I shall dwell in the house of the LORD my
whole life long.**

The LORD is my shepherd, I shall not want.
  He makes me lie down in green pastures;
he leads me beside still waters;
  he restores my soul.

**I shall dwell in the house of the LORD my
whole life long.**

READING
Isaiah 55:1–3c

A reading from the Book of prophet Isaiah.

Ho, everyone who thirsts, come to the waters; and you that have no money, come, buy and eat! Come, buy wine and milk without money and without price. Why do you spend your money for that which is not bread, and your labor for that which does not satisfy? Listen carefully to me, and eat what is good, and delight yourselves in rich food. Incline your ear, and come to me; listen, so that you may live. I will make with you an everlasting covenant, my steadfast, sure love for David.

The Word of the Lord.

◆ All observe silence.

FOR SILENT REFLECTION

Think about this silently in your heart. God promises everlasting love. Everlasting means forever. How does that feel?

CLOSING PRAYER

Let us pray to God for our needs and the needs of others: our family, neighborhood, and the world. For each need we say, "Lord, hear our prayer."

◆ All may add their own prayers here.

Let us pray: **Our Father . . . Amen.**

Loving God,
you call us to listen to your words
which will quench our thirst
and satisfy our hunger.
Help us to remember to turn to you
when life feels difficult.
Comfort us and fill us with your love.
We ask this in Jesus' name.

Amen.

✚ All make the Sign of the Cross.

OPENING

The prophet Isaiah wrote during a time when life was very difficult for the Jewish people. They were exiled from Jerusalem. People felt hopeless, not knowing if they would ever return to their homeland. Isaiah sows seeds of hope by using images of rain and snow that water the earth making it possible for new life to grow.

✦ All make the Sign of the Cross.

In the name of the Father, and of the Son, and of the Holy Spirit. Amen.

PSALM   (For a longer psalm, see page xiii.) Psalm 23:1–3a

I shall dwell in the house of the LORD my
　　whole life long.

**I shall dwell in the house of the LORD my
　　whole life long.**

The LORD is my shepherd, I shall not want.
　He makes me lie down in green pastures;
he leads me beside still waters;
　he restores my soul.

**I shall dwell in the house of the LORD my
　　whole life long.**

READING   Isaiah 55:6, 9–11

A reading from the Book of prophet Isaiah.

Seek the LORD while he may be found, call upon him while he is near. For as the heavens are higher than the earth, so are my ways higher than your ways and my thoughts than your thoughts. For as the rain and the snow come down from heaven, and do not return there until they have watered the earth, making it bring forth and sprout, giving seed to the sower and bread to the eater, so shall my word be that goes out from my mouth; it shall not return to me empty, but it shall accomplish that which I purpose, and succeed in the thing for which I sent it.

The Word of the Lord.

◆ All observe silence.

FOR SILENT REFLECTION

Think about this silently in your heart. How can you sow a seed of kindness today?

CLOSING PRAYER

Let us pray to God for our needs and the needs of others: our family, neighborhood, and the world. For each need we say, "Lord, hear our prayer."

◆ All may add their own prayers here.

Let us pray: **Our Father . . . Amen.**

Faithful God,
you promise that just as the earth
is fruitful, so our lives will be fruitful
if we follow your teachings.
May we hear your word and do your will.

Amen.

✦ All make the Sign of the Cross.

OPENING

Today is the memorial of St. Francis de Sales, who lived from 1567 to 1622. Along with close friends Sts. Vincent de Paul and Louise de Marillac, he transformed the Church in France to focus on service to the poor. In today's reading, the prophet Isaiah proclaims how things will be different when the Messiah comes.

✦ All make the Sign of the Cross.

In the name of the Father, and of the Son, and of the Holy Spirit. Amen.

PSALM
(For a longer psalm, see page xiii.) Psalm 23:1–3a

I shall dwell in the house of the LORD my whole life long.

I shall dwell in the house of the LORD my whole life long.

The LORD is my shepherd, I shall not want.
  He makes me lie down in green pastures;
he leads me beside still waters;
  he restores my soul.

I shall dwell in the house of the LORD my whole life long.

READING
Isaiah 55:5, 12–13

A reading from the Book of prophet Isaiah.

See, you shall call nations that you do not know, and nations that do not know you shall run to you, because of the LORD your God, the Holy One of Israel, for he has glorified you. For you shall go out in joy, and be led back in peace; the mountains and the hills before you shall burst into song, and all the trees of the field shall clap their hands. Instead of the thorn shall come up the cypress; instead of the brier shall come up the myrtle; and it shall be to the LORD for a memorial, for an everlasting sign that shall not be cut off.

The Word of the Lord.

◆ All observe silence.

FOR SILENT REFLECTION

Think about this silently in your heart. What images do you remember from Isaiah words?

CLOSING PRAYER

Let us pray to God for our needs and the needs of others: our family, neighborhood, and the world. For each need we say, "Lord, hear our prayer."

◆ All may add their own prayers here.

Let us pray: **Our Father . . . Amen.**

God of joy and peace,
for you, mountains and hills burst into song.
Trees clap their hands.
Thorns turn into flowers.
We praise you and give you thanks.
Glory to you forever and ever.

Amen.

✦ All make the Sign of the Cross.

PRAYER FOR
FRIDAY, JANUARY 25, 2019

OPENING

Today is the feast of the Conversion of St. Paul the Apostle. Saul of Tarsus persecuted Christians. One day he was blinded by a bright light and heard the voice of Christ saying, "Why do you persecute me?" Saul converted to Christianity, took the name Paul, and traveled the known world preaching the Gospel. Today's reading is a letter that Paul wrote to the people in Corinth, which is now Greece.

✦ All make the Sign of the Cross.

> **In the name of the Father, and of the Son, and of the Holy Spirit. Amen.**

PSALM
(For a longer psalm, see page xiii.) Psalm 23:1–3a

I shall dwell in the house of the LORD my
   whole life long.

**I shall dwell in the house of the LORD my
   whole life long.**

The LORD is my shepherd, I shall not want.
   He makes me lie down in green pastures;
he leads me beside still waters;
   he restores my soul.

**I shall dwell in the house of the LORD my
   whole life long.**

READING
2 Corinthians 9:6–8, 11

A reading from the Second Letter of Paul to the Corinthians [kohr-IN-thee-uhnz].

The point is this: the one who sows sparingly will also reap sparingly, and the one who sows bountifully will also reap bountifully. Each of you must give as you have made up your mind, not reluctantly or under compulsion, for God loves a cheerful giver. And God is able to provide you with every blessing in abundance, so that by always having enough of everything, you may share abundantly in every good work. You will be enriched in every way for your great generosity, which will produce thanksgiving to God through us.

The Word of the Lord.

◆ All observe silence.

FOR SILENT REFLECTION

Think about this silently in your heart. How can you be generous today?

CLOSING PRAYER

Let us pray to God for our needs and the needs of others: our family, neighborhood, and the world. For each need we say, "Lord, hear our prayer."

◆ All may add their own prayers here.

Let us pray: **Our Father . . . Amen.**

God of abundance, help us to be generous. Give us creative minds and loving hearts so we can help people who need help. May we share our talents for the good of others.

Amen.

✦ All make the Sign of the Cross.

PRAYER FOR THE WEEK

WITH A READING FROM THE GOSPEL FOR **SUNDAY, JANUARY 27, 2019**

OPENING

In today's Gospel reading, Jesus reveals who he is in the town where he grew up. He is the one who fulfills the prophecies of Isaiah. And he claims that the mission of the Son of God is to help the poor and oppressed.

✝ All make the Sign of the Cross.

In the name of the Father, and of the Son, and of the Holy Spirit. Amen.

PSALM

(For a longer psalm, see page xiii.) Psalm 23:1–3a

I shall dwell in the house of the LORD my whole life long.

I shall dwell in the house of the LORD my whole life long.

The LORD is my shepherd, I shall not want.
  He makes me lie down in green pastures;
he leads me beside still waters;
  he restores my soul.

I shall dwell in the house of the LORD my whole life long.

◆ All stand and sing **Alleluia.**

GOSPEL

Luke 4:16–21

A reading from the holy Gospel according to Luke.

When Jesus came to Nazareth, where he had been brought up, he went to the synagogue on the sabbath day, as was his custom. He stood up to read, and the scroll of the prophet Isaiah was given to him. He unrolled the scroll and found the place where it was written: "The Spirit of the Lord is upon me, because he has anointed me to bring good news to the poor. He has sent me to proclaim release to the captives and recovery of sight to the blind, to let the oppressed go free, to proclaim the year of the Lord's favor." And he rolled up the scroll, gave it back to the attendant, and sat down. The eyes of all in the synagogue were fixed on him. Then he began to say to them, "Today this scripture has been fulfilled in your hearing."

The Gospel of the Lord.

◆ All sit and observe silence.

FOR SILENT REFLECTION

Think about this silently in your heart. How can you help someone who has less than you?

CLOSING PRAYER

Let us pray to God for our needs and the needs of others: our family, neighborhood, and the world. For each need we say, "Lord, hear our prayer."

◆ All may add their own prayers here.

Let us pray: **Our Father . . . Amen.**

Lord God, you sent your son Jesus
to show us how to live.
Help us to care about fairness and justice.
Help us to be a healing presence in the world.

Amen.

✝ All make the Sign of the Cross.

OPENING

Today is the memorial of St. Thomas Aquinas (1225–1274), who was born in Naples, Italy. This week the readings focus on the revelation of who God is.

✝ All make the Sign of the Cross.

In the name of the Father, and of the Son, and of the Holy Spirit. Amen.

PSALM

(For a longer psalm, see page xiii.) Psalm 23:1–3a

I shall dwell in the house of the LORD my
    whole life long.

**I shall dwell in the house of the LORD my
    whole life long.**

The LORD is my shepherd, I shall not want.
  He makes me lie down in green pastures;
he leads me beside still waters;
  he restores my soul.

**I shall dwell in the house of the LORD my
    whole life long.**

READING

Exodus 3:1c–6

A reading from the Book of Exodus.

Moses led his flock beyond the wilderness, and came to Horeb, the mountain of God. There the angel of the LORD appeared to him in a flame of fire out of a bush; he looked, and the bush was blazing, yet it was not consumed. Then Moses said, "I must turn aside and look at this great sight, and see why the bush is not burned up." When the LORD saw that he had turned aside to see, God called to him out of the bush, "Moses, Moses!" And he said, "Here I am." Then he said, "Come no closer! Remove the sandals from your feet, for the place on which you are standing is holy ground." He said further, "I am the God of your father, the God of Abraham, the God of Isaac, and the God of Jacob." And Moses hid his face, for he was afraid to look at God.

The Word of the Lord.

◆ All observe silence.

FOR SILENT REFLECTION

Think about this silently in your heart. Why do you think Moses was afraid to look at God?

CLOSING PRAYER

Let us pray to God for our needs and the needs of others: our family, neighborhood, and the world. For each need we say, "Lord, hear our prayer."

◆ All may add their own prayers here.

Let us pray: **Our Father . . . Amen.**

Faithful God,
Moses responded, "Here I am,"
when you called his name.
We pray that we may respond
to your call as Moses did.

Amen.

✝ All make the Sign of the Cross.

OPENING

Elijah [ee-LI-juh] was one of the greatest prophets in Jewish history. He lived in the ninth century BC and called for people to turn away from violent, sinful ways of living. Prophets listen closely to the voice of God. Sometimes it is hard to hear God's voice because the world is very busy and loud. Listen to where Elijah hears God's voice.

✦ All make the Sign of the Cross.

In the name of the Father, and of the Son, and of the Holy Spirit. Amen.

PSALM   (For a longer psalm, see page xiii.) Psalm 23:1–3a

I shall dwell in the house of the LORD my
    whole life long.

**I shall dwell in the house of the LORD my
    whole life long.**

The LORD is my shepherd, I shall not want.
    He makes me lie down in green pastures;
he leads me beside still waters;
    he restores my soul.

**I shall dwell in the house of the LORD my
    whole life long.**

READING   1 Kings 19:11–13

A reading from the First Book of Kings.

The angel of the LORD said to Elijah, "Go out and stand on the mountain, for the LORD is about to pass by." Now there was a great wind, so strong that it was splitting mountains and breaking rocks in pieces, but the LORD was not in the wind; and after the wind an earthquake, but the LORD was not in the earthquake; and after the earthquake a fire, but the LORD was not in the fire; and after the fire a sound of sheer silence. When Elijah heard it, he wrapped his face in his mantle and went out and stood at the entrance of the cave. Then there came a voice to him that said, "What are you doing here, Elijah?"

The Word of the Lord.

✦ All observe silence.

FOR SILENT REFLECTION

Think about this silently in your heart. Can you be still and listen for God's voice?

CLOSING PRAYER

Let us pray to God for our needs and the needs of others: our family, neighborhood, and the world. For each need we say, "Lord, hear our prayer."

✦ All may add their own prayers here.

Let us pray: **Our Father . . . Amen.**

Almighty God, although you are great,
you often speak to us in quiet ways.
Help us to listen for your voice.
We ask this in Jesus' name.

Amen.

✦ All make the Sign of the Cross.

OPENING

Daniel, a major prophet of the Old Testament, lived in the sixth century BC during a time the Hebrew people were in exile in Babylonia. In today's reading, Daniel sees God in a vision and God speaks to him.

✚ All make the Sign of the Cross.

In the name of the Father, and of the Son, and of the Holy Spirit. Amen.

PSALM   (For a longer psalm, see page xiii.) Psalm 23:1–3a

I shall dwell in the house of the LORD my
    whole life long.

**I shall dwell in the house of the LORD my
    whole life long.**

The LORD is my shepherd, I shall not want.
  He makes me lie down in green pastures;
he leads me beside still waters;
  he restores my soul.

**I shall dwell in the house of the LORD my
    whole life long.**

READING   Daniel 10:4a, 5a, 6ab, 9c, 11ac, 12

A reading from the Book of prophet Daniel.

On the twenty-fourth day of the first month, I looked up and saw a man clothed in linen. His body was like beryl, his face like lightning, his eyes like flaming torches, his arms and legs like the gleam of burnished bronze. My strength left me. I fell into a trance, face to the ground. He said to me, "Daniel, greatly beloved, pay attention to the words that I am going to speak to you. For I have now been sent to you." He said to me, "Do not fear, Daniel, for from the first day that you set your mind to gain understanding and to humble yourself before your God, your words have been heard, and I have come because of your words."

The Word of the Lord.

◆ All observe silence.

FOR SILENT REFLECTION

Think about this silently in your heart. God heard Daniel and responded to him. Trust that God will hear your voice.

CLOSING PRAYER

Let us pray to God for our needs and the needs of others: our family, neighborhood, and the world. For each need we say, "Lord, hear our prayer."

◆ All may add their own prayers here.

Let us pray: **Our Father . . . Amen.**

Good and loving God,
help us long to know more about you.
Help us to find time to study and pray
so that we may see and feel your presence.
We ask this in Jesus' name.

Amen.

✚ All make the Sign of the Cross.

OPENING

Today is the memorial of St. John Bosco. He lived in the nineteenth century and founded the Salesians, a religious congregation devoted to helping the poor, especially young men. In today's reading Jesus heals a young boy who probably had epilepsy. But in Jesus' time people thought that physical and mental illness were caused by evil spirits.

✚ *All make the Sign of the Cross.*

In the name of the Father, and of the Son, and of the Holy Spirit. Amen.

PSALM   (For a longer psalm, see page xiii.) Psalm 23:1–3a

I shall dwell in the house of the LORD my
    whole life long.

**I shall dwell in the house of the LORD my
    whole life long.**

The LORD is my shepherd, I shall not want.
    He makes me lie down in green pastures;
he leads me beside still waters;
    he restores my soul.

**I shall dwell in the house of the LORD my
    whole life long.**

◆ *All stand and sing* **Alleluia.**

GOSPEL   Luke 9:37–43

A reading from the holy Gospel according to Luke.

On the next day, when Jesus, Peter, John and James had come down from the mountain, a great crowd met him. Just then a man from the crowd shouted, "Teacher, I beg you to look at my son; he is my only child. Suddenly a spirit seizes him, and all at once he shrieks. It convulses him until he foams at the mouth; it mauls him and will scarcely leave him. I begged your disciples to cast it out, but they could not." Jesus answered, "You faithless and perverse generation, how much longer must I be with you and bear with you? Bring your son here." While he was coming, the demon dashed him to the ground in convulsions. But Jesus rebuked the unclean spirit, healed the boy, and gave him back to his father. And all were astounded at the greatness of God.

The Gospel of the Lord.

◆ *All sit and observe silence.*

FOR SILENT REFLECTION

Think about this silently in your heart. What concern do you bring to Jesus today?

CLOSING PRAYER

Let us pray to God for our needs and the needs of others: our family, neighborhood, and the world. For each need we say, "Lord, hear our prayer."

◆ *All may add their own prayers here.*

Let us pray: **Our Father . . . Amen.**

Lord God, we need your healing grace. Help us to have faith in you.

Amen.

✚ *All make the Sign of the Cross.*

OPENING

Today is the feast of St. Brigid of Kildare (c. 451–c. 524) who, along with St. Patrick, is a patron saint of Ireland. Tradition says that she founded twin monasteries, one for men and one for women, and was abbess over both. In today's reading, the true identity of Jesus is revealed to the apostles Peter, James, and John.

✛ All make the Sign of the Cross.

In the name of the Father, and of the Son, and of the Holy Spirit. Amen.

PSALM   (For a longer psalm, see page xiii.) Psalm 23:1–3a

I shall dwell in the house of the LORD my
    whole life long.

**I shall dwell in the house of the LORD my
    whole life long.**

The LORD is my shepherd, I shall not want.
    He makes me lie down in green pastures;
he leads me beside still waters;
    he restores my soul.

**I shall dwell in the house of the LORD my
    whole life long.**

◆ All stand and sing **Alleluia.**

GOSPEL   Luke 9:28–30, 32c–35

A reading from the holy Gospel according to Luke.

Jesus took with him Peter and John and James, and went up on the mountain to pray. And while he was praying, the appearance of his face changed, and his clothes became dazzling white. Suddenly they saw two men, Moses and Elijah, talking to him. They saw his glory and the two men who stood with him. Just as they were leaving him, Peter said to Jesus, "Master, it is good for us to be here; let us make three dwellings, one for you, one for Moses, and one for Elijah"—not knowing what he said. While he was saying this, a cloud came and overshadowed them; and they were terrified as they entered the cloud. Then from the cloud came a voice that said, "This is my Son, my Chosen; listen to him!"

The Gospel of the Lord.

◆ All sit and observe silence.

FOR SILENT REFLECTION

Think about this silently in your heart. Have you ever had a "mountaintop experience" in which you felt close to God?

CLOSING PRAYER

Let us pray to God for our needs and the needs of others: our family, neighborhood, and the world. For each need we say, "Lord, hear our prayer."

◆ All may add their own prayers here.

Let us pray: **Our Father . . . Amen.**

Almighty God, help us to listen for your presence in our lives.

Amen.

✛ All make the Sign of the Cross.

PRAYER FOR THE WEEK

OPENING

Jesus has returned home to Nazareth, where he had grown up. He is in the synagogue, where the Jewish people gathered to celebrate the Sabbath, the Hebrew holy day. Although they are impressed with his knowledge, they do not believe in him.

✝ All make the Sign of the Cross.

In the name of the Father, and of the Son, and of the Holy Spirit. Amen.

PSALM

(For a longer psalm, see page xiii.) Psalm 23:1–3a

I shall dwell in the house of the LORD my
    whole life long.

**I shall dwell in the house of the LORD my
    whole life long.**

The LORD is my shepherd, I shall not want.
  He makes me lie down in green pastures;
he leads me beside still waters;
  he restores my soul.

**I shall dwell in the house of the LORD my
    whole life long.**

◆ All stand and sing **Alleluia.**

GOSPEL

Luke 4:21–23ac, 24, 28–30

A reading from the holy Gospel according to Luke.

Then Jesus began to say to them, "Today this scripture has been fulfilled in your hearing." All spoke well of him and were amazed at the gracious words that came from his mouth. They said, "Is not this Joseph's son?" Jesus said to them, "And you will say, 'Do here also in your home town the things that we have heard you did at Capernaum.'" And he said, "Truly I tell you, no prophet is accepted in the prophet's home town." When they heard this, all in the synagogue were filled with rage. They got up, drove Jesus out of the town, and led him to the brow of the hill on which their town was built, so that they might hurl him off the cliff. But he passed through the midst of them and went on his way.

The Gospel of the Lord.

◆ All sit and observe silence.

FOR SILENT REFLECTION

Think about this silently in your heart. What goodness can you see in somebody you know?

CLOSING PRAYER

Let us pray to God for our needs and the needs of others: our family, neighborhood, and the world. For each need we say, "Lord, hear our prayer."

◆ All may add their own prayers here.

Let us pray: **Our Father . . . Amen.**

Lord, open our eyes so we can see your face. Open our ears so we can hear your voice. Open our hearts so we can love like you.

Amen.

✝ All make the Sign of the Cross.

PRAYER FOR
MONDAY, FEBRUARY 4, 2019

OPENING

After Jesus' death, St. Paul traveled the known world preaching the Gospel. In today's reading he teaches the people in Corinth about who we are as God's Church. We each have different gifts, but the Church needs us all.

✝ All make the Sign of the Cross.

In the name of the Father, and of the Son, and of the Holy Spirit. Amen.

PSALM
(For a longer psalm, see page xiii.) Psalm 23:1–3a

I shall dwell in the house of thc LORD my
    whole life long.

**I shall dwell in the house of the LORD my
    whole life long.**

The LORD is my shepherd, I shall not want.
  He makes me lie down in green pastures;
he leads me beside still waters;
  he restores my soul.

**I shall dwell in the house of the LORD my
    whole life long.**

READING
1 Corinthians 12:12–14, 24b, 25, 27

A reading from the First Letter of Paul to the Corinthians.

For just as the body is one and has many members, and all the members of the body, though many, are one body, so it is with Christ. For in the one Spirit we were all baptized into one body—Jews or Greeks, slaves or free—and we were all made to drink of one Spirit. Indeed, the body does not consist of one member but of many. But God has so arranged the body, that there may be no dissension within the body, but the members may have the same care for one another. Now you are the body of Christ and individually members of it.

The Word of the Lord.

◆ All observe silence.

FOR SILENT REFLECTION

Think about this silently in your heart. What is your gift? How can you use it to help other people?

CLOSING PRAYER

Let us pray to God for our needs and the needs of others: our family, neighborhood, and the world. For each need we say, "Lord, hear our prayer."

◆ All may add their own prayers here.

Let us pray: **Our Father . . . Amen.**

God of all,
in your wisdom you created
a world with people with many different gifts.
You call us to use our unique gifts
for the good of all.
Together we build up the body of Christ,
which glorifies you.

Amen.

✝ All make the Sign of the Cross.

OPENING

St. Agatha, whose memorial is today, was born in Italy, probably around the year 231. She is one of the women mentioned by name in a Eucharistic Prayer that is said at Mass. In today's reading, St. Paul continues his metaphor about the Church as the Body of Christ. Just as a body needs all its part, we all need each other.

✛ All make the Sign of the Cross.

In the name of the Father, and of the Son, and of the Holy Spirit. Amen.

PSALM   (For a longer psalm, see page xiii.) Psalm 23:1–3a

I shall dwell in the house of the LORD my
    whole life long.

**I shall dwell in the house of the LORD my
    whole life long.**

The LORD is my shepherd, I shall not want.
    He makes me lie down in green pastures;
he leads me beside still waters;
    he restores my soul.

**I shall dwell in the house of the LORD my
    whole life long.**

READING   1 Corinthians 12:14, 16–20, 26

A reading from the First Letter of Paul to the Corinthians.

Indeed, the body does not consist of one member but of many. And if the ear were to say, "Because I am not an eye, I do not belong to the body," that would not make it any less a part of the body. If the whole body were an eye, where would the hearing be? If the whole body were hearing, where would the sense of smell be? But as it is, God arranged the members in the body, each one of them, as he chose. If all were a single member, where would the body be? As it is, there are many members, yet one body. If one member suffers, all suffer together with it; if one member is honored, all rejoice together with it.

The Word of the Lord.

◆ All observe silence.

FOR SILENT REFLECTION

Think about this silently in your heart. Can you feel empathy with someone who is suffering? Can you feel joy with someone who is happy?

CLOSING PRAYER

Let us pray to God for our needs and the needs of others: our family, neighborhood, and the world. For each need we say, "Lord, hear our prayer."

◆ All may add their own prayers here.

Let us pray: **Our Father . . . Amen.**

Lord God, help us to remember
that we all belong to your family.
Help us to see your face
in all the people we meet.
We ask this in Jesus' name.

Amen.

✛ All make the Sign of the Cross.

PRAYER FOR
WEDNESDAY, FEBRUARY 6, 2019

OPENING

St. Paul Miki, whose memorial is today, was a Jesuit priest killed by an anti-Christian Japanese government in the sixteenth century. When Christian missionaries returned to Japan in the nineteenth century, they found a secret Christian community that had survived for generations. St. Paul again states that everyone has gifts from the Holy Spirit.

✚ All make the Sign of the Cross.

In the name of the Father, and of the Son, and of the Holy Spirit. Amen.

PSALM

(For a longer psalm, see page xiii.) Psalm 23:1–3a

I shall dwell in the house of the Lord my
    whole life long.

**I shall dwell in the house of the Lord my
    whole life long.**

The Lord is my shepherd, I shall not want.
  He makes me lie down in green pastures;
he leads me beside still waters;
  he restores my soul.

**I shall dwell in the house of the Lord my
    whole life long.**

READING

1 Corinthians 12:4–11

A reading from the First Letter of Paul to the Corinthians.

Now there are varieties of gifts, but the same Spirit; and there are varieties of services, but the same Lord; and there are varieties of activities, but it is the same God who activates all of them in everyone. To each is given the manifestation of the Spirit for the common good. To one is given through the Spirit the utterance of wisdom, and to another the utterance of knowledge according to the same Spirit, to another faith by the same Spirit, to another gifts of healing by the one Spirit, to another the working of miracles, to another prophecy, to another the discernment of spirits, to another various kinds of tongues, to another the interpretation of tongues. All these are activated by one and the same Spirit, who allots to each one individually just as the Spirit chooses.

The Word of the Lord.

◆ All observe silence.

FOR SILENT REFLECTION

Think about this silently in your heart. What gift has God given to you?

CLOSING PRAYER

Let us pray to God for our needs and the needs of others: our family, neighborhood, and the world. For each need we say, "Lord, hear our prayer."

◆ All may add their own prayers here.

Let us pray: **Our Father . . . Amen.**

Dear God, all your gifts are wonderful. We give you thanks and praise.

Amen.

✚ All make the Sign of the Cross.

OPENING

St. Paul continues to talk about our role as members of the Body of Christ. In the previous readings this week, we have heard how we all have different gifts and each is important and necessary. In today's reading, Paul singles out one gift that is most important.

✝ All make the Sign of the Cross.

In the name of the Father, and of the Son, and of the Holy Spirit. Amen.

PSALM   (For a longer psalm, see page xiii.) Psalm 23:1–3a

I shall dwell in the house of the LORD my
    whole life long.

**I shall dwell in the house of the LORD my
    whole life long.**

The LORD is my shepherd, I shall not want.
    He makes me lie down in green pastures;
he leads me beside still waters;
    he restores my soul.

**I shall dwell in the house of the LORD my
    whole life long.**

READING   1 Corinthians 12:1, 31;13:1–3

A reading from the First Letter of Paul to the Corinthians.

Now concerning spiritual gifts, brothers and sisters, I do not want you to be uninformed. But strive for the greater gifts. And I will show you a still more excellent way. If I speak in the tongues of mortals and of angels, but do not have love, I am a noisy gong or a clanging cymbal. And if I have prophetic powers, and understand all mysteries and all knowledge, and if I have all faith, so as to remove mountains, but do not have love, I am nothing. If I give away all my possessions, and if I hand over my body so that I may boast, but do not have love, I gain nothing.

The Word of the Lord.

◆ All observe silence.

FOR SILENT REFLECTION

Think about this silently in your heart. What gift does Paul say is most important? Why do you think he says that?

CLOSING PRAYER

Let us pray to God for our needs and the needs of others: our family, neighborhood, and the world. For each need we say, "Lord, hear our prayer."

◆ All may add their own prayers here.

Let us pray: **Our Father . . . Amen.**

O God, we do not want to be
noisy gongs, boastful and proud.
We want to reflect your kindness
and generosity.
We want to be more loving and peaceful.

Amen.

✝ All make the Sign of the Cross.

OPENING

St. Jerome Emiliani, whose memorial is today, was a good example of St. Paul's teaching about love as the most important spiritual gift. St. Jerome was born in Venice, Italy. The plague and famine of 1518 left many children orphans, and St. Jerome founded orphanages and hospitals that took care of the poor and the sick.

✝ All make the Sign of the Cross.

In the name of the Father, and of the Son, and of the Holy Spirit. Amen.

PSALM   (For a longer psalm, see page xiii.) Psalm 23:1–3a

I shall dwell in the house of the LORD my
   whole life long.

**I shall dwell in the house of the LORD my
   whole life long.**

The LORD is my shepherd, I shall not want.
   He makes me lie down in green pastures;
he leads me beside still waters;
   he restores my soul.

**I shall dwell in the house of the LORD my
   whole life long.**

READING   1 Corinthians 13:4–8a, 13; 14:1a

A reading from the First Letter of Paul to the Corinthians.

Love is patient; love is kind; love is not envious or boastful or arrogant or rude. It does not insist on its own way; it is not irritable or resentful; it does not rejoice in wrongdoing, but rejoices in the truth. It bears all things, believes all things, hopes all things, endures all things. Love never ends. But as for prophecies, they will come to an end; as for tongues, they will cease; as for knowledge, it will come to an end. And now faith, hope, and love abide, these three; and the greatest of these is love. Pursue love and strive for the spiritual gifts.

The Word of the Lord.

◆ All observe silence.

FOR SILENT REFLECTION

Think about this silently in your heart. Who in your life is especially loving? Say a prayer for them.

CLOSING PRAYER

Let us pray to God for our needs and the needs of others: our family, neighborhood, and the world. For each need we say, "Lord, hear our prayer."

◆ All may add their own prayers here.

Let us pray: **Our Father . . . Amen.**

We pray, O God, for qualities of love.
May we be patient and kind.
May we be generous, respectful, and tolerant.
May we be the reflection of your
love in the world.

Amen.

✝ All make the Sign of the Cross.

PRAYER FOR THE WEEK

WITH A READING FROM THE GOSPEL FOR **SUNDAY, FEBRUARY 10, 2019**

OPENING

In the Gospel, Peter calls himself "a sinful man." Jesus knows Peter's heart is good and wants him to be a leader. We all sin, but God still loves us. Jesus wants all of us to take up his mission of teaching people how much God loves them.

✛ All make the Sign of the Cross.

In the name of the Father, and of the Son, and of the Holy Spirit. Amen.

PSALM
(For a longer psalm, see page xiii.) Psalm 23:1–3a

I shall dwell in the house of the LORD my
    whole life long.

**I shall dwell in the house of the LORD my
    whole life long.**

The LORD is my shepherd, I shall not want.
   He makes me lie down in green pastures;
he leads me beside still waters;
   he restores my soul.

**I shall dwell in the house of the LORD my
    whole life long.**

◆ All stand and sing **Alleluia.**

GOSPEL
Luke 5:3a, 4–6, 8, 10b–11

A reading from the holy Gospel according to Luke.

Jesus got into one of the boats and asked Simon to put out a little way from the shore. He said to Simon, "Put out into the deep water and let down your nets for a catch." Simon answered, "Master, we have worked all night long but have caught nothing. Yet if you say so I will let down the nets." When they had done this, they caught so many fish that their nets were beginning to break. But when Simon Peter saw it, he fell down at Jesus' knees, saying, "Go away from me, Lord, for I am a sinful man." Then Jesus said to Simon, "Do not be afraid; from now on you will be catching people." When they had brought their boats to shore, they left everything and followed him.

The Gospel of the Lord.

◆ All sit and observe silence.

FOR SILENT REFLECTION

Think about this silently in your heart. How does Jesus want you to take up his mission today?

CLOSING PRAYER

Let us pray to God for our needs and the needs of others: our family, neighborhood, and the world. For each need we say, "Lord, hear our prayer."

◆ All may add their own prayers here.

Let us pray: **Our Father . . . Amen.**

Loving God,
we pray that we may be like Peter
and follow Jesus wherever he leads.

Amen.

✛ All make the Sign of the Cross.

PRAYER FOR
MONDAY, FEBRUARY 11, 2019

OPENING

We will "walk through the Bible" this week examining the theme of *light*. The writer of the Book of Proverbs asks us to cling to wisdom, which comes from the good teachings of our parents and others. Wisdom is a quality closely associated with God. Wise teachings are like a light on a dark path.

✠ All make the Sign of the Cross.

In the name of the Father, and of the Son, and of the Holy Spirit. Amen.

PSALM   (For a longer psalm, see page xiii.) Psalm 23:1–3a

I shall dwell in the house of the LORD my
    whole life long.

**I shall dwell in the house of the LORD my
    whole life long.**

The LORD is my shepherd, I shall not want.
  He makes me lie down in green pastures;
he leads me beside still waters;
  he restores my soul.

**I shall dwell in the house of the LORD my
    whole life long.**

READING   Proverbs 4:10–13; 6:20–23

A reading from the Book of Proverbs.

Hear, my child, and accept my words, that the years of your life may be many. I have taught you the way of wisdom; I have led you in the paths of uprightness. When you walk, your step will not be hampered; and if you run, you will not stumble. Keep hold of instruction; do not let go; guard wisdom, for she is your life. My child, keep your father's commandment, and do not forsake your mother's teaching.

Bind them upon your heart always; tie them around your neck. When you walk, they will lead you; when you lie down, they will watch over you; and when you awake, they will talk with you. For the commandment is a lamp and the teaching a light, and the reproofs of discipline are the way of life.

The Word of the Lord.

◆ All observe silence.

FOR SILENT REFLECTION

Think about this silently in your heart. Can you think of some wise teachings from your parents or teachers?

CLOSING PRAYER

Let us pray to God for our needs and the needs of others: our family, neighborhood, and the world. For each need we say, "Lord, hear our prayer."

◆ All may add their own prayers here.

Let us pray: **Our Father . . . Amen.**

O God, our holy Wisdom,
be our light.
We ask this in Jesus' name.

Amen.

✠ All make the Sign of the Cross.

OPENING

Jesus uses the metaphor of a lamp to talk about the importance of letting a light shine brightly.

✛ All make the Sign of the Cross.

In the name of the Father, and of the Son, and of the Holy Spirit. Amen.

PSALM   (For a longer psalm, see page xiii.) Psalm 23:1–3a

I shall dwell in the house of the LORD my
   whole life long.

**I shall dwell in the house of the LORD my
   whole life long.**

The LORD is my shepherd, I shall not want.
   He makes me lie down in green pastures;
he leads me beside still waters;
   he restores my soul.

**I shall dwell in the house of the LORD my
   whole life long.**

◆ All stand and sing **Alleluia.**

GOSPEL   Luke 8:1–3ab, 4, 16–17

A reading from the holy Gospel according to Luke.

Soon afterwards Jesus went on through cities and villages, proclaiming and bringing the good news of the kingdom of God. The twelve were with him, as well as some women who had been cured of evil spirits and infirmities: Mary, called Magdalene, from whom seven demons had gone out, and Joanna, the wife of Herod's steward Chuza, and Susanna, and many others. When a great crowd gathered and people from town after town came to him, Jesus said in a parable: "No one after lighting a lamp hides it under a jar, or puts it under a bed, but puts it on a lampstand, so that those who enter may see the light. For nothing is hidden that will not be disclosed, nor is anything secret that will not become known and come to light."

The Gospel of the Lord.

◆ All sit and observe silence.

FOR SILENT REFLECTION

Think about this silently in your heart. How can you let your light shine?

CLOSING PRAYER

Let us pray to God for our needs and the needs of others: our family, neighborhood, and the world. For each need we say, "Lord, hear our prayer."

◆ All may add their own prayers here.

Let us pray: **Our Father . . . Amen.**

Most holy God,
may we proclaim the light of Jesus
by our words and our actions
to everyone we meet.
We ask this in Jesus' name.

Amen.

✛ All make the Sign of the Cross.

OPENING

St. Paul uses a light metaphor to teach about love. He says to put on "the armor of light" that will protect us against the darkness of forgetting to love our neighbor. That armor is Jesus and his teachings. It was given to us at Baptism.

✝ *All make the Sign of the Cross.*

In the name of the Father, and of the Son, and of the Holy Spirit. Amen.

PSALM   (For a longer psalm, see page xiii.) Psalm 23:1–3a

I shall dwell in the house of the LORD my
  whole life long.

**I shall dwell in the house of the LORD my
  whole life long.**

The LORD is my shepherd, I shall not want.
  He makes me lie down in green pastures;
he leads me beside still waters;
  he restores my soul.

**I shall dwell in the house of the LORD my
  whole life long.**

READING   Romans 13:8–9ad, 10–13ad, 14a

A reading from the Letter of Paul to the Romans.

Owe no one anything except to love one another; for the one who loves another has fulfilled the law. The commandments are summed up in this word, "Love your neighbor as yourself." Love does no wrong to a neighbor; therefore, love is fulfilling of the law. Besides this, you know what time it is, how it is now the moment for you to wake from sleep. For salvation is nearer to us now than when we became believers; the night is far gone, the day is near. Let us then lay aside the works of darkness and put on the armor of light; let us live honorably as in the day, not in quarreling and jealousy. Instead, put on the Lord Jesus Christ.

The Word of the Lord.

◆ *All observe silence.*

FOR SILENT REFLECTION

Think about this silently in your heart. What does it mean to "put on the armor of light"?

CLOSING PRAYER

Let us pray to God for our needs and the needs of others: our family, neighborhood, and the world. For each need we say, "Lord, hear our prayer."

◆ *All may add their own prayers here.*

Let us pray: **Our Father . . . Amen.**

O God, armor us with your light
so we can share Jesus' teachings
of love and justice.
We ask this in Jesus' name.

Amen.

✝ *All make the Sign of the Cross.*

OPENING

God is light, and we show God's light through our loving actions. On this date we celebrate Valentine's Day, a day that we let others know that we love them.

✝ All make the Sign of the Cross.

In the name of the Father, and of the Son, and of the Holy Spirit. Amen.

PSALM

(For a longer psalm, see page xiii.) Psalm 23:1–3a

I shall dwell in the house of the LORD my
    whole life long.

**I shall dwell in the house of the LORD my
    whole life long.**

The LORD is my shepherd, I shall not want.
    He makes me lie down in green pastures;
he leads me beside still waters;
    he restores my soul.

**I shall dwell in the house of the LORD my
    whole life long.**

READING

Ephesians 5:8–11, 13–15a, 17a, 18c, 20

A reading from the Letter of Paul to the Ephesians.

For once you were darkness, but now in the Lord you are light. Live as children of light— for the fruit of the light is found in all that is good and right and true. Try to find out what is pleasing to the Lord. Take no part in the unfruitful works of darkness, but instead expose them. But everything exposed by the light becomes visible, for everything that becomes visible is light. Therefore it says, "Sleeper, awake! Rise from the dead, and Christ will shine on you." Be careful then how you live. So do not be foolish, but be filled with the Spirit, giving thanks to God the Father at all times and for everything in the name of our Lord Jesus Christ.

The Word of the Lord.

◆ All observe silence.

FOR SILENT REFLECTION

Think about this silently in your heart. How can you live as a child of the light?

CLOSING PRAYER

Let us pray to God for our needs and the needs of others: our family, neighborhood, and the world. For each need we say, "Lord, hear our prayer."

◆ All may add their own prayers here.

Let us pray: **Our Father . . . Amen.**

Keep us in your light, holy God.
Help us be people who choose
what is "good and right and true."
We ask this in Jesus' name.

Amen.

✝ All make the Sign of the Cross.

OPENING

Jesus is the brightest of all lights. The darkness Jesus overcomes with his great light is sin and death. Jesus is a light for everyone. He is a light for the world.

✚ All make the Sign of the Cross.

In the name of the Father, and of the Son, and of the Holy Spirit. Amen.

PSALM
(For a longer psalm, see page xiii.) Psalm 23:1–3a

I shall dwell in the house of the Lord my
    whole life long.

I shall dwell in the house of the Lord my
    whole life long.

The Lord is my shepherd, I shall not want.
  He makes me lie down in green pastures;
he leads me beside still waters;
  he restores my soul.

I shall dwell in the house of the Lord my
    whole life long.

◆ All stand and sing **Alleluia.**

GOSPEL
John 1:1–9

A reading from the holy Gospel according to John.

In the beginning was the Word, and the Word was with God, and the Word was God. He was in the beginning with God. All things came into being through him, and without him not one thing came into being. What has come into being in him was life, and the life was the light of all people. The light shines in the darkness, and the darkness did not overcome it. There was a man sent from God, whose name was John.

He came as a witness to testify to the light, so that all might believe through him. John himself was not the light, but he came to testify to the light. The true light, which enlightens everyone, was coming into the world.

The Gospel of the Lord.

◆ All sit and observe silence.

FOR SILENT REFLECTION

Think about this silently in your heart. Why is Jesus the light that no darkness can overcome?

CLOSING PRAYER

Let us pray to God for our needs and the needs of others: our family, neighborhood, and the world. For each need we say, "Lord, hear our prayer."

◆ All may add their own prayers here.

Let us pray: **Our Father . . . Amen.**

Fill our minds and hearts
with the light of Jesus.
When we experience the darkness of sin,
help us to turn to him.
Teach us to walk in the light.
We ask this in Jesus' name.

Amen.

✚ All make the Sign of the Cross.

OPENING

Jesus preaches that those who are poor or suffering will experience the Kingdom of Heaven.

✝ All make the Sign of the Cross.

In the name of the Father, and of the Son, and of the Holy Spirit. Amen.

PSALM

(For a longer psalm, see page xiii.) Psalm 23:1–3a

I shall dwell in the house of the LORD my
    whole life long.

**I shall dwell in the house of the LORD my
    whole life long.**

The LORD is my shepherd, I shall not want.
    He makes me lie down in green pastures;
he leads me beside still waters;
    he restores my soul.

**I shall dwell in the house of the LORD my
    whole life long.**

◆ All stand and sing **Alleluia.**

GOSPEL

Luke 6:20–26

A reading from the holy Gospel according to Luke.

Jesus looked up at his disciples and said: "Blessed are you who are poor, for yours is the kingdom of God. Blessed are you who are hungry now, for you will be filled. Blessed are you who weep now, for you will laugh. Blessed are you when people hate you, and when they exclude you, revile you, and defame you on account of the Son of Man. Rejoice in that day and leap for joy, for surely your reward is great in heaven; for that is what their ancestors did to the prophets. But woe to you who are rich, for you have received your consolation. Woe to you who are full now, for you will be hungry. Woe to you who are laughing now, for you will mourn and weep. Woe to you when all speak well of you, for that is what their ancestors did to the false prophets."

The Gospel of the Lord.

◆ All sit and observe silence.

FOR SILENT REFLECTION

Think about this silently in your heart. Pray for those who are poor, or hungry, or sad.

CLOSING PRAYER

Let us pray to God for our needs and the needs of others: our family, neighborhood, and the world. For each need we say, "Lord, hear our prayer."

◆ All may add their own prayers here.

Let us pray: **Our Father . . . Amen.**

O God, we want to be counted
among the "Blessed."
When we feel sad or excluded,
help us to remember that you are with us.

Amen.

✝ All make the Sign of the Cross.

OPENING

This week we will hear Bible passages about people who are healed. Today we hear about King Naaman who follows the prophet Elisha's [ee-Lī-shuh] command and is healed.

✚ All make the Sign of the Cross.

In the name of the Father, and of the Son, and of the Holy Spirit. Amen.

PSALM   (For a longer psalm, see page xiii.) Psalm 23:1–3a

I shall dwell in the house of the LORD my
　　whole life long.

**I shall dwell in the house of the LORD my
　　whole life long.**

The LORD is my shepherd, I shall not want.
　He makes me lie down in green pastures;
he leads me beside still waters;
　he restores my soul.

**I shall dwell in the house of the LORD my
　　whole life long.**

READING   2 Kings 5:1ad, 9–11b, 13–14

A reading from the Second Book of Kings.

Naaman, commander of the army of the king of Aram, suffered from leprosy. Naaman came with his horses and chariots to the land of Israel, and halted at the entrance of Elisha's house. Elisha sent a messenger to him, saying, "Go, wash in the Jordan seven times, and your flesh shall be restored and you shall be clean." But Naaman became angry and went away, saying, "I thought that for me he would surely come out." But his servants said, "Father, if the prophet had commanded you to do something difficult, would you not have done it? How much more, when all he said to you was, 'Wash, and be clean'?" So Naaman went down and immersed himself seven times in the Jordan, according to the word of the man of God; his flesh was restored like the flesh of a young boy, and he was clean.

The Word of the Lord.

◆ All observe silence.

FOR SILENT REFLECTION

Think about this silently in your heart. Pray for all who need healing.

CLOSING PRAYER

Let us pray to God for our needs and the needs of others: our family, neighborhood, and the world. For each need we say, "Lord, hear our prayer."

◆ All may add their own prayers here.

Let us pray: **Our Father . . . Amen.**

O merciful God, help us remember
that in sickness and trouble,
you are with us and will support us.
We ask this in Jesus' name.

Amen.

✚ All make the Sign of the Cross.

OPENING

Healing is a mystery. Not even doctors always know how and why it happens. The Bible tells us that Jesus was a great healer. Today we hear how Jesus heals a child people thought was dead, but Jesus said she was sleeping.

✛ All make the Sign of the Cross.

In the name of the Father, and of the Son, and of the Holy Spirit. Amen.

PSALM
(For a longer psalm, see page xiii.) Psalm 23:1–3a

I shall dwell in the house of the LORD my
    whole life long.

**I shall dwell in the house of the LORD my
    whole life long.**

The LORD is my shepherd, I shall not want.
    He makes me lie down in green pastures;
he leads me beside still waters;
    he restores my soul.

**I shall dwell in the house of the LORD my
    whole life long.**

◆ All stand and sing **Alleluia.**

GOSPEL
Luke 8:41–42, 49, 52–56a

A reading from the holy Gospel according to Luke.

A man came to Jesus named Jairus, a leader of the synagogue. He fell at Jesus' feet and begged him to come to his house, for he had an only daughter, about twelve years old, who was dying. While he was still speaking, someone came from the leader's house to say, "Your daughter is dead; do not trouble the teacher any longer." When Jesus came to the house, they were all weeping and wailing for her; but he said, "Do not weep; for she is not dead but sleeping." And they laughed at him, knowing that she was dead. But he took her by the hand and called out, "Child, get up!" Her spirit returned, and she got up at once. Then he directed them to give her something to eat. Her parents were astounded.

The Gospel of the Lord.

◆ All sit and observe silence.

FOR SILENT REFLECTION

Think about this silently in your heart. Pray for all children who are sick and dying.

CLOSING PRAYER

Let us pray to God for our needs and the needs of others: our family, neighborhood, and the world. For each need we say, "Lord, hear our prayer."

◆ All may add their own prayers here.

Let us pray: **Our Father . . . Amen.**

Loving God,
Jesus' miracles of healing
reveal your love.
Please be with all who are sick and dying today.
We ask this in the name of Jesus.

Amen.

✛ All make the Sign of the Cross.

PRAYER FOR
WEDNESDAY, FEBRUARY 20, 2019

OPENING

Today we understand that people who are described in the Gospel as suffering from demons may have suffered from mental disorders. Healing can be needed for the mind and emotions. As a Church family, it is important to pray for and anoint the sick.

✝ All make the Sign of the Cross.

In the name of the Father, and of the Son, and of the Holy Spirit. Amen.

PSALM (For a longer psalm, see page xiii.) Psalm 23:1–3a

I shall dwell in the house of the LORD my
   whole life long.

**I shall dwell in the house of the LORD my
   whole life long.**

The LORD is my shepherd, I shall not want.
   He makes me lie down in green pastures;
he leads me beside still waters;
   he restores my soul.

**I shall dwell in the house of the LORD my
   whole life long.**

◆ All stand and sing **Alleluia.**

GOSPEL Luke 4:38–41

A reading from the holy Gospel according to Luke.

After leaving the synagogue Jesus entered Simon's house. Now Simon's mother-in-law was suffering from a high fever, and they asked him about her. Then he stood over her and rebuked the fever, and it left her. Immediately she got up and began to serve them. As the sun was setting, all those who had any who were sick with various kinds of diseases brought them to him; and he laid his hands on each of them and cured them. Demons also came out of many, shouting, "You are the Son of God!" But he rebuked them and would not allow them to speak, because they knew that he was the Messiah.

The Gospel of the Lord.

◆ All sit and observe silence.

FOR SILENT REFLECTION

Think about this silently in your heart. How do you think a person felt when Jesus laid his hands on them?

CLOSING PRAYER

Let us pray to God for our needs and the needs of others: our family, neighborhood, and the world. For each need we say, "Lord, hear our prayer."

◆ All may add their own prayers here.

Let us pray: **Our Father . . . Amen.**

Holy, all powerful God,
we thank you for the gift of healing.
We thank you for doctors, nurses,
and all who care for those who are ill.
Bless them with your healing grace.

Amen.

✝ All make the Sign of the Cross.

OPENING

The reading today tells us that Peter and the Apostles carried on Jesus' ministry of healing.

✦ All make the Sign of the Cross.

In the name of the Father, and of the Son, and of the Holy Spirit. Amen.

PSALM

(For a longer psalm, see page xiii.) Psalm 23:1–3a

I shall dwell in the house of the LORD my
  whole life long.

**I shall dwell in the house of the LORD my
  whole life long.**

The LORD is my shepherd, I shall not want.
  He makes me lie down in green pastures;
he leads me beside still waters;
  he restores my soul.

**I shall dwell in the house of the LORD my
  whole life long.**

READING

Acts 5:12–16

A reading from the Acts of the Apostles.

Now many signs and wonders were done among the people through the apostles. And they were all together in Solomon's Portico. None of the rest dared to join them, but the people held them in high esteem. Yet more than ever believers were added to the Lord, great numbers of both men and women, so that they even carried out the sick into the streets, and laid them on cots and mats, in order that Peter's shadow might fall on some of them as he came by. A great number of people would also gather from the towns around Jerusalem, bring-ing the sick and those tormented by unclean spirits, and they were all cured.

The Word of the Lord.

◆ All observe silence.

FOR SILENT REFLECTION

Think about this silently in your heart. Why are miracles of healing a sign of God's kingdom?

CLOSING PRAYER

Let us pray to God for our needs and the needs of others: our family, neighborhood, and the world. For each need we say, "Lord, hear our prayer."

◆ All may add their own prayers here.

Let us pray: **Our Father . . . Amen.**

Dear God,
give wisdom and strength
to all who care for the sick.
Help them to know that all healing
comes from you and is a sign of your love.
We ask this in Jesus' name.

Amen.

✦ All make the Sign of the Cross.

PRAYER FOR
FRIDAY, FEBRUARY 22, 2019

OPENING

Today is the feast of the Chair of St. Peter, Apostle, who was Bishop of Rome. His chair is called by its Latin name *cathedra*. This is why a bishop's church is called a "cathedral." Each bishop has a special chair only he sits in. The chair of Peter represents an unbroken line from St. Peter to our present Pope.

✚ All make the Sign of the Cross.

In the name of the Father, and of the Son, and of the Holy Spirit. Amen.

PSALM
(For a longer psalm, see page xiii.) Psalm 23:1–3a

I shall dwell in the house of the LORD my
    whole life long.

**I shall dwell in the house of the LORD my
    whole life long.**

The LORD is my shepherd, I shall not want.
    He makes me lie down in green pastures;
he leads me beside still waters;
    he restores my soul.

**I shall dwell in the house of the LORD my
    whole life long.**

READING
Acts 9:36ab, 36d–37a, 38b–39c, 40–42

A reading from the Acts of the Apostles.

Now in Joppa there was a disciple whose name was Tabitha. She was devoted to good works and acts of charity. At that time she became ill and died. The disciples, who heard that Peter was near, sent two men to him with the request, "Please come to us without delay." So Peter got up and went with them; and when he arrived, they took him to the room upstairs. All the widows stood beside him, weeping. Peter put all of them outside, and then he knelt down and prayed. He turned to the body and said, "Tabitha, get up." Then she opened her eyes, and seeing Peter, she sat up. He gave her his hand and helped her up. Then calling the saints and widows, he showed her to be alive. This became known throughout Joppa and many believed in the Lord.

The Word of the Lord.

◆ All observe silence.

FOR SILENT REFLECTION

Think about this silently in your heart. How do you think Tabitha felt when she opened her eyes?

CLOSING PRAYER

Let us pray to God for our needs and the needs of others: our family, neighborhood, and the world. For each need we say, "Lord, hear our prayer."

◆ All may add their own prayers here.

Let us pray: **Our Father . . . Amen.**

May we always believe
in your healing presence, O God.
We ask this in Jesus' name.

Amen.

✚ All make the Sign of the Cross.

PRAYER FOR THE WEEK

WITH A READING FROM THE GOSPEL FOR **SUNDAY, FEBRUARY 24, 2019**

OPENING

Jesus shocks the disciples when he teaches them to love their enemies. In those days it was believed that one should hate enemies and curse those who cursed you. Jesus insists God wants us to be merciful as God is merciful.

✦ All make the Sign of the Cross.

In the name of the Father, and of the Son, and of the Holy Spirit. Amen.

PSALM (For a longer psalm, see page xiii.) Psalm 23:1–3a

I shall dwell in the house of the LORD my
   whole life long.

**I shall dwell in the house of the LORD my
   whole life long.**

The LORD is my shepherd, I shall not want.
   He makes me lie down in green pastures;
he leads me beside still waters;
   he restores my soul.

**I shall dwell in the house of the LORD my
   whole life long.**

◆ All stand and sing **Alleluia.**

GOSPEL Luke 6:27–28, 32–33, 35–36

A reading from the holy Gospel according to Luke.

Jesus said to his disciples, "I say to you that listen, Love your enemies, do good to those who hate you, bless those who curse you, pray for those who abuse you. If you love those who love you, what credit is that to you? For even sinners love those who love them. If you do good to those who do good to you, what credit is that to you? For even sinners do the same.

But love your enemies, do good, expecting nothing in return. Your reward will be great, and you will be children of the Most High; for he is kind to the ungrateful and the wicked. Be merciful, just as your Father is merciful."

The Gospel of the Lord.

◆ All sit and observe silence.

FOR SILENT REFLECTION

Think about this silently in your heart. How can you love your enemy?

CLOSING PRAYER

Let us pray to God for our needs and the needs of others: our family, neighborhood, and the world. For each need we say, "Lord, hear our prayer."

◆ All may add their own prayers here.

Let us pray: **Our Father . . . Amen.**

God of love,
show us how to follow Jesus' teaching.
Take away our anger and hate
and help us be merciful and loving.
We ask this in Jesus' name.

Amen.

✦ All make the Sign of the Cross.

OPENING

This week we will look at sacramental signs in the Old Testament and how they connect with the sacraments. The ancient Hebrews believed that God's love for them was revealed in signs like water flowing in the desert.

✢ All make the Sign of the Cross.

In the name of the Father, and of the Son, and of the Holy Spirit. Amen.

PSALM   (For a longer psalm, see page xiii.) Psalm 23:1–3a

I shall dwell in the house of the LORD my
   whole life long.

**I shall dwell in the house of the LORD my
   whole life long.**

The LORD is my shepherd, I shall not want.
   He makes me lie down in green pastures;
he leads me beside still waters;
   he restores my soul.

**I shall dwell in the house of the LORD my
   whole life long.**

READING   Isaiah 41:8ab, 10abcde, 17abc, 18, 20acd

A reading from the Book of prophet Isaiah.

But you, Israel, my servant, Jacob, whom I have chosen; the offspring of Abraham, my friend; do not fear, for I am with you, do not be afraid, for I am your God; I will strengthen you, I will help you. When the poor and needy seek water, and there is none, and their tongue is parched with thirst, I the LORD will answer them. I will open rivers on the bare heights, and fountains in the midst of the valleys; I will make the wilderness a pool of water, and the dry land springs of water so that all may see

and know that the hand of the LORD has done this, the Holy One of Israel has created it.

The Word of the Lord.

◆ All observe silence.

FOR SILENT REFLECTION

Think about this silently in your heart. In what ways is the water used in Baptism a sign of God's goodness?

CLOSING PRAYER

Let us pray to God for our needs and the needs of others: our family, neighborhood, and the world. For each need we say, "Lord, hear our prayer."

◆ All may add their own prayers here.

Let us pray: **Our Father . . . Amen.**

We praise you and thank you,
Creator God, for water.
Water is essential for all life on earth.
By the waters of Baptism we are given new life.
We praise and thank you,
Creator God, for water.

Amen.

✢ All make the Sign of the Cross.

OPENING

Fire can be a powerful element. In the Scripture we hear how God guides the Hebrews out of Egypt with a pillar of fire, so they can see at night and know God is near. Fire, or a flame, is a sacramental sign of God, the Holy Spirit, in Confirmation.

✝ All make the Sign of the Cross.

In the name of the Father, and of the Son, and of the Holy Spirit. Amen.

PSALM   (For a longer psalm, see page xiii.) Psalm 23:1–3a

I shall dwell in the house of the LORD my
    whole life long.

**I shall dwell in the house of the LORD my
    whole life long.**

The LORD is my shepherd, I shall not want.
    He makes me lie down in green pastures;
he leads me beside still waters;
    he restores my soul.

**I shall dwell in the house of the LORD my
    whole life long.**

READING   Exodus 13:17abc, 18, 21–22

A reading from the Book of Exodus.

When Pharaoh let the people go, God did not lead them by way of the land of the Philistines, although that was nearer. So God led the people by the roundabout way of the wilderness toward the Red Sea. The Israelites went up out of the land of Egypt prepared for battle. The LORD went in front of them in a pillar of cloud by day, to lead them along the way, and in a pillar of fire by night, to give them light, so that they might travel by day and by night. Neither the pillar of cloud by day nor the pillar of fire by night left its place in front of the people.

The Word of the Lord.

◆ All observe silence.

FOR SILENT REFLECTION

Think about this silently in your heart. Think about times that we use candles in Church. The lit candles are a sign of God's presence with us.

CLOSING PRAYER

Let us pray to God for our needs and the needs of others: our family, neighborhood, and the world. For each need we say, "Lord, hear our prayer."

◆ All may add their own prayers here.

Let us pray: **Our Father . . . Amen.**

Thank you, God,
for the flame of the Holy Spirit
that guides our minds and hearts.
As the Israelites followed the pillar of fire,
may we follow the guidance of the Holy Spirit.
We ask this in Jesus' name.

Amen.

✝ All make the Sign of the Cross.

PRAYER FOR
WEDNESDAY, FEBRUARY 27, 2019

OPENING

We use the sign of oil in Baptism, Confirmation, Holy Orders, and Anointing of the Sick. As the Scripture indicates, the tradition of using oil to mark people as holy and dedicated to God is an ancient sacramental sign. Myrrh and cinnamon made the oil smell lovely. A *hin* measures about one and a half gallons of oil.

✚ All make the Sign of the Cross.

In the name of the Father, and of the Son, and of the Holy Spirit. Amen.

PSALM   (For a longer psalm, see page xiii.) Psalm 23:1–3a

I shall dwell in the house of the LORD my
　　whole life long.

**I shall dwell in the house of the LORD my
　　whole life long.**

The LORD is my shepherd, I shall not want.
　　He makes me lie down in green pastures;
he leads me beside still waters;
　　he restores my soul.

**I shall dwell in the house of the LORD my
　　whole life long.**

READING   Exodus 30:22–23ac, 24a, 25b, 26a, 27c, 29–31

A reading from the Book of Exodus.

The LORD spoke to Moses: Take the finest spices: of liquid myrrh five hundred shekels, and of sweet-smelling cinnamon half as much, and a hin of olive oil; and you shall make of these a sacred anointing oil—blended as by the perfumer. With it you shall anoint the tent of meeting and the ark of the covenant, and the altar of incense. You shall consecrate them, so that they may be most holy; whatever touches them will become holy. You shall anoint Aaron and his sons, and consecrate them, in order that they may serve me as priests. You shall say to the Israelites, "This shall be my holy anointing oil throughout your generations."

The Word of the Lord.

◆ All observe silence.

FOR SILENT REFLECTION

Think about this silently in your heart. What does it mean that we are anointed with oil at Baptism and Confirmation?

CLOSING PRAYER

Let us pray to God for our needs and the needs of others: our family, neighborhood, and the world. For each need we say, "Lord, hear our prayer."

◆ All may add their own prayers here.

Let us pray: **Our Father . . . Amen.**

May the mark of oil we received
at Baptism and Confirmation be a
sign that we belong to you, O God.

Amen.

✚ All make the Sign of the Cross.

OPENING

Ancient people made sacrifices to their gods. The Hebrews offered wine and bread. God asks for a hin of wine and an ephah [EE-fah] of bread flour. An *ephah* measures three fifths of a bushel. Bread and wine are the central sacramental signs of our Eucharist.

✝ All make the Sign of the Cross.

In the name of the Father, and of the Son, and of the Holy Spirit. Amen.

PSALM

(For a longer psalm, see page xiii.) Psalm 23:1–3a

I shall dwell in the house of the LORD my whole life long.

I shall dwell in the house of the LORD my whole life long.

The LORD is my shepherd, I shall not want.
  He makes me lie down in green pastures;
he leads me beside still waters;
  he restores my soul.

I shall dwell in the house of the LORD my whole life long.

READING

Numbers 15:1–5

A reading from the Book of Numbers.

The LORD spoke to Moses, saying: Speak to the Israelites and say to them: When you come into the land you are to inhabit, which I am giving you, and you make an offering by fire to the LORD from the herd or from the flock— whether a burnt offering or a sacrifice, to fulfill a vow or as a freewill offering or at your appointed festivals—to make a pleasing odor for the LORD, then whoever presents such an offering to the LORD shall present also a grain offering, one-tenth of an ephah of choice flour, mixed with one-fourth of a hin of oil. Moreover, you shall offer one-fourth of a hin of wine as a drink offering with the burnt offering or the sacrifice, for each lamb.

The Word of the Lord.

◆ All observe silence.

FOR SILENT REFLECTION

Think about this silently in your heart. What can you offer to God to show your love for him?

CLOSING PRAYER

Let us pray to God for our needs and the needs of others: our family, neighborhood, and the world. For each need we say, "Lord, hear our prayer."

◆ All may add their own prayers here.

Let us pray: **Our Father . . . Amen.**

Help us, O God,
to offer you praise and glory
by our words and actions.
We ask this in Jesus' name.

Amen.

✝ All make the Sign of the Cross.

PRAYER FOR
FRIDAY, MARCH 1, 2019

OPENING

Almost every human culture has a bread like staple in their diet because it is nourishing and filling. In the Mass, the bread becomes the Body of Christ, which nourishes us.

✚ All make the Sign of the Cross.

> **In the name of the Father, and of the Son, and of the Holy Spirit. Amen.**

PSALM
(For a longer psalm, see page xiii.) Psalm 23:1–3a

I shall dwell in the house of the LORD my
    whole life long.

**I shall dwell in the house of the LORD my
    whole life long.**

The LORD is my shepherd, I shall not want.
    He makes me lie down in green pastures;
he leads me beside still waters;
    he restores my soul.

**I shall dwell in the house of the LORD my
    whole life long.**

READING
Leviticus 23:9–10a, 17acd, 18–20ab

A reading from the Book of Leviticus.

The LORD spoke to Moses: Speak to the people of Israel and say to them: You shall bring from your settlements two loaves of bread as an elevation-offering; they shall be of choice flour, baked with leaven, as first fruits to the LORD. You shall present with the bread seven lambs a year old without blemish, one young bull, and two rams; they shall be a burnt-offering to the LORD, along with their grain-offering and their drink-offerings, an offering by fire of pleasing odor to the LORD. You shall also offer one male goat for a sin-offering, and two male

lambs a year old as a sacrifice of well-being. The priest shall raise them with the bread of the first fruits as an elevation-offering before the LORD, together with the two lambs.

The Word of the Lord.

◆ All observe silence.

FOR SILENT REFLECTION

Think about this silently in your heart. Give thanks for the gift of Jesus in the Eucharist.

CLOSING PRAYER

Let us pray to God for our needs and the needs of others: our family, neighborhood, and the world. For each need we say, "Lord, hear our prayer."

◆ All may add their own prayers here.

Let us pray: **Our Father . . . Amen.**

Gracious God,
we offer you praise and thanksgiving.
We praise you for your great goodness.
We thank you for the gift of Jesus
who strengthens and nourishes us.

Amen.

✚ All make the Sign of the Cross.

OPENING

Today's Gospel challenges us in two ways. It reminds us that we need to be careful of criticizing others; rather, we need to look at our own actions and habits first. The Gospel also reminds us that if we seek to do God's will, then our actions will be good.

✚ All make the Sign of the Cross.

In the name of the Father, and of the Son, and of the Holy Spirit. Amen.

PSALM

(For a longer psalm, see page xiii.) Psalm 23:1–3a

I shall dwell in the house of the LORD my
      whole life long.

**I shall dwell in the house of the LORD my
      whole life long.**

The LORD is my shepherd, I shall not want.
   He makes me lie down in green pastures;
he leads me beside still waters;
   he restores my soul.

**I shall dwell in the house of the LORD my
      whole life long.**

◆ All stand and sing **Alleluia.**

GOSPEL

Luke 6:39–42a; 43–44a

A reading from the holy Gospel according to Luke.

Jesus told them a parable: "Can a blind person guide a blind person? Will not both fall into a pit? A disciple is not above the teacher. Why do you see the speck in your neighbor's eye, but do not notice the log in your own eye? Or how can you say to your neighbor, 'Friend, let me take out the speck in your eye,' when you yourself do not see the log in your own eye? No good tree bears bad fruit, nor again does a bad tree bear good fruit; for each tree is known by its own fruit. Figs are not gathered from thorns, nor are grapes picked from a bramble bush. The good person out of the good treasure of the heart produces good."

The Gospel of the Lord.

◆ All sit and observe silence.

FOR SILENT REFLECTION

Think about this silently in your heart. Why is it important to look at our own faults rather than criticizing someone else?

CLOSING PRAYER

Let us pray to God for our needs and the needs of others: our family, neighborhood, and the world. For each need we say, "Lord, hear our prayer."

◆ All may add their own prayers here.

Let us pray: **Our Father . . . Amen.**

Loving God,
your Son Jesus taught us how to live
in harmony with one another.
We pray that we have good hearts,
so that our lives may be good and holy.

Amen.

✚ All make the Sign of the Cross.

OPENING

On Wednesday we will enter the season of Lent. During Lent we practice almsgiving, fasting and praying. Today and tomorrow we will see what the Old Testament says about *alms*, an ancient word meaning "compassion and mercy." The Scripture says it is not the amount of alms we give, but the act of giving that is important.

✝ All make the Sign of the Cross.

In the name of the Father, and of the Son, and of the Holy Spirit. Amen.

PSALM   (For a longer psalm, see page xiii.) Psalm 23:1–3a

I shall dwell in the house of the LORD my
　　whole life long.

**I shall dwell in the house of the LORD my
　　whole life long.**

The LORD is my shepherd, I shall not want.
　He makes me lie down in green pastures;
he leads me beside still waters;
　he restores my soul.

**I shall dwell in the house of the LORD my
　　whole life long.**

READING   Tobit 4:5ab, 7acd, 8, 11, 19af

A reading from the Book of Tobit.

"Revere the Lord all your days, my son, and refuse to sin or to transgress his commandments. Give alms from your possessions. Do not turn your face from anyone who is poor, and the face of God will not be turned away from you. If you have many possessions, make your gift from them in proportion; if few, do not be afraid to give according to the little you

have. Indeed, almsgiving, for all who practice it, is an excellent offering in the presence of the Most High. At all times bless the Lord, and ask him that your ways may be made straight and that all your paths and plans may prosper. So now, my child, remember these commandments and do not let them be erased from your heart."

The Word of the Lord.

◆ All observe silence.

FOR SILENT REFLECTION

Think about this silently in your heart. What alms can you give?

CLOSING PRAYER

Let us pray to God for our needs and the needs of others: our family, neighborhood, and the world. For each need we say, "Lord, hear our prayer."

◆ All may add their own prayers here.

Let us pray: **Our Father . . . Amen.**

Make us a generous people,
dear God, who always notice
those in needs of our help.
We ask this in Jesus' name.

Amen.

✝ All make the Sign of the Cross.

OPENING

Sirach tells us our almsgiving is like a signet [SIG-net] ring from God. In the old days a ruler gave this kind of ring to someone to indicate they had the ruler's authority. God gave the care of the whole earth to us. Our almsgiving shows God that we understand our responsibility of care to our neighbor.

✚ All make the Sign of the Cross.

In the name of the Father, and of the Son, and of the Holy Spirit. Amen.

PSALM   (For a longer psalm, see page xiii.) Psalm 23:1–3a

I shall dwell in the house of the LORD my
    whole life long.

**I shall dwell in the house of the LORD my
    whole life long.**

The LORD is my shepherd, I shall not want.
    He makes me lie down in green pastures;
he leads me beside still waters;
    he restores my soul.

**I shall dwell in the house of the LORD my
    whole life long.**

READING   Sirach 17:1a, 2, 7, 10, 12, 14, 22

A reading from the Book of Sirach [SEER-ak].

The Lord created human beings out of earth. He gave them a fixed number of days but granted them authority over everything on earth. He filled them with knowledge and understanding, and showed them good and evil. And they will praise his holy name. He established with them an eternal covenant, and revealed to them his decrees. He said to them, "Beware of all evil." And he gave com-mandment to each of them concerning a neighbor. All their works are as clear as the sun before him, and his eyes are ever upon their ways. One's almsgiving is like a signet ring with the Lord, and he will keep a person's kindness like the apple of his eye.

The Word of the Lord.

◆ All observe silence.

FOR SILENT REFLECTION

Think about this silently in your heart. Why is being kind a way of giving alms?

CLOSING PRAYER

Let us pray to God for our needs and the needs of others: our family, neighborhood, and the world. For each need we say, "Lord, hear our prayer."

◆ All may add their own prayers here.

Let us pray: **Our Father . . . Amen.**

We praise and thank you, O God.
Show us how we can use our gifts
to help others.
We ask this in Jesus' name.

Amen.

✚ All make the Sign of the Cross.

PRAYER SERVICE
KEEPING LENT

Before you begin, place a candle, an empty bowl, and a jar with a slit cut into the lid (for coins to give to the poor) where the household will gather in prayer. Find the reading (Matthew 7:7–12) in your Bible, ask for a volunteer to read it and encourage him/her to practice reading it a few times. You may wish to begin with a simple song, such as "Jesus, Remember Me," or "Amen" (but not "Alleluia" during Lent). An older child or adult reads the leader parts.

LEADER:

Lent is a time of reflection
and of turning our hearts to God.
We turn our attention to
growing spiritually
so that we can fully cherish the joy of Easter.
Lent helps us to listen more and pray,
just as Jesus did in the desert.

◆ All make the Sign of the Cross.

In the name of the Father, and of the Son, and of the Holy Spirit. Amen.

LEADER: Psalm 37:5a, 3–4, 23–24, 27–28, 30–31
Let us repeat the Psalm Response:
Commit your way to the LORD.

ALL: Commit your way to the LORD.

Trust in the LORD, and do good;
   so you will live in the land, and enjoy
      security.
Take delight in the LORD,
   and he will give you the desires of your
      heart.

ALL: Commit your way to the LORD.

Our steps are made firm by the LORD,
   when he delights in our way;
though we stumble, we shall not fall headlong,
   for the LORD holds us by the hand.

ALL: Commit your way to the LORD.

◆ All stand and sing **Praise to you, Lord Jesus Christ** . . .

LEADER: Matthew 7:7–12
A reading from the holy Gospel according to Matthew

◆ Read the Gospel passage from the Bible.

The Gospel of the Lord.

◆ All sit and observe silence. An adult lights the candle.

LEADER:
Heavenly Father,
you sent your Son to us
to light the way back to you.
Guide us in this season of Lent
so that we can focus on you
and on others who may need our help.
We ask this through our Lord Jesus Christ,
your Son, who lives and reigns with you
in the unity of the Holy Spirit, one God,
forever and ever.

ALL: Amen.

LEADER:
Let us pray as Jesus taught us:
Our Father . . . Amen.

✚ All make the Sign of the Cross.

CHILDREN'S DAILY PRAYER 2018–2019, © 2018 Archdiocese of Chicago: Liturgy Training Publications, 3949 South Racine Avenue, Chicago IL 60609. All rights reserved. Orders: 800-933-1800 or www.LTP.org. Scripture excerpts are taken from *The New Revised Standard Version Bible: Catholic Edition*, copyright © 1989, Division of Christian Education of the National Council of the Churches of Christ in the United States of America. Used with permission. All rights reserved.

LENT

WEDNESDAY, MARCH 6 — WEDNESDAY, APRIL 17

LENT

THE MEANING OF LENT

On Ash Wednesday the Church enters into her great retreat time called Lent. It is a time to reflect on how we are with God, with our neighbor and with ourselves, and make some changes in our attitudes or speech or actions if we need to. We should do this often throughout the year, but we do it more consciously in Lent to prepare for the celebration of Easter when some people will be baptized into our Church and the rest of us will renew our Baptismal promises.

We have six weeks to concentrate on a "conversion of heart," a turning back to or moving closer to God. In fact, the word *conversion* comes from a Latin word that means "turning around." During this time we might ask ourselves a seemingly simple question: "What do I need to stop doing or start doing to be the very good person God made me?" We can ask that question in relation to God, in relation to our family, friends and classmates, and in relation to ourselves. If we find we have some bad habits or have hurt someone (even ourselves) or have neglected to do something we should, we can repent, that is, express our sincere regret and willingness to change, in the celebration of the Sacrament of Reconciliation.

The three Lenten disciplines of praying, fasting, and giving alms can help us. A discipline is a training or study and we'll use these disciplines to train our hearts in love. We often do them throughout the year but again, in Lent, we are more consciously intent about them. We pray more regularly and perhaps for longer periods of time. Praying is a conversation with God and a way to be closer to God.

We also fast to remind ourselves that there is nothing—no food, no activity, no desire—more important than God and the needs of God's people. Perhaps we give up a certain food and give the money we save to the poor. We might give up playing video games and use the time to read to a younger sibling or help around the house. Part of fasting is abstaining from meat on Fridays of Lent so we eat simply and sparingly as poor people must. Perhaps we can also abstain from junk food and desserts.

The third discipline is almsgiving. The word *alms* comes from a Greek word meaning "compassion" and is associated with giving food or money or clothing to the poor. The money we save by giving up a favorite food or activity might be used this way.

We may have a toy or game we no longer use very often that we could give to someone else. Maybe our family can sort through clothes to see what could be given away.

During Lent you may have seen people called catechumens [kat-i-KYOO-muhnz] at Mass. They are preparing to be baptized, confirmed, and come to their First Communion at the Easter Vigil on Holy Saturday. Since they do not yet come to Communion they usually leave Mass after the homily to do more reflection on the Scriptures. In the last few weeks of Lent we do some special prayers with and for them at Mass. Our catechumens are a reminder of how God lovingly seeks us out and calls us to him.

Lent's purpose—to prepare us to celebrate Easter—becomes more focused as we celebrate Palm Sunday of the Lord's Passion and enter into Holy Week. Lent ends Thursday evening with the Mass of the Lord's Supper, and the Triduum [TRID-oo-um]), the three holiest days of the Church year, begins. *Triduum* means "three days." These days, like Sunday, are counted in the Jewish way, from sunset to sunset. So the first day of the Triduum begins on Holy Thursday evening and concludes Good Friday evening. The second day runs from Good Friday evening through Holy Saturday evening. And the third day runs from Holy Saturday evening through Easter Sunday evening.

In our Scriptures in the week of Ash Wednesday, we will hear Jesus' own instructions on the Lenten disciplines and learn from Isaiah about the right kind of fast God wants. Week one of Lent "walks us through the Bible" with the great theme of God's mercy and forgiveness. In week two St. Luke assures us that God wants us back in Jesus' three parables of the lost sheep, coin and sons. Week three invites us to reflect on Jesus' teachings about the good we must do if we are his true followers. In week four we'll reflect on how Jesus's work is now our work. In weeks five and six we sadly follow Jesus from betrayal to burial.

PREPARING TO CELEBRATE LENT IN THE CLASSROOM

SACRED SPACE

Remember that you'll need to change your prayer cloth from green to purple. If you have a plant in the prayer space remove it. Ask the children to bring in their family's dried palms from last year and put them in a simple vase. It is the old palms that are burned for ashes. A clear bowl full of ashes (available through local religious goods stores) would be appropriate. Use the same bowl to hold water in Easter Season.

MOVEMENT AND GESTURE

You may want to use some incense during some of the prayers. Ask the parish priest or deacon for some charcoal and incense. You'll also need a pot full of sand to place the charcoal in. An altar server can help you light the charcoal about ten minutes before the prayer. Then the leader can place a small amount of incense on the charcoal before the Scripture is proclaimed. Be sure to have an open window and let other teachers know you are using the incense. Ask the children with allergies and asthma to stand in the back of the space in case the smoke bothers them. At the end of the prayer cover the charcoal with sand to stop it from smoking.

FESTIVITY IN SCHOOL AND HOME

You will find the Home Prayer: Keeping Lent page to copy and send home for family prayer (page 204). The Prayer Service for Ash Wednesday (pages 210-211) can be used for the classroom or for a larger group. There is also a Home Prayer for Holy Thursday (page 253) and Good Friday (page 254) to send home toward the end of Lent.

SACRED MUSIC

Children love to sing "Jesus, Remember Me," and "What Wondrous Love Is This?" Other songs for Lent are "Amazing Grace," the African American spiritual "Somebody's Knockin' at Your Door," and the Latin hymn "Ubi Caritas." We don't sing "Alleluia" during Lent. Tell the children we are saving all our Alleluia joy for Easter. For the Prayer for the Week, and during the week where there is a Gospel, we sing an acclamation, such as "Praise to you, Lord Jesus Christ" to whatever tune the parish is using.

PRAYERS FOR LENT

Lent is the perfect time to learn or to review the Act of Contrition. Psalm 51 is also a beautiful prayer for this season of penance and conversion.

A NOTE TO CATECHISTS

If any children in your group are preparing to celebrate the sacraments of initiation at the Easter Vigil, gather them to read the following three great accounts from the Gospel of John: 1) Jesus teaches the Woman at the Well who finally understands Jesus is the Messiah (John 4:5–15, 19b–26, 39a, 40–42); 2) Jesus cures the Man Born Blind of physical blindness and the man "sees" and follow him (John 9:1, 6–9, 13–17, 34–38); and 3) Jesus raises Lazarus from the dead (John 11:3–7, 17, 20–27, 33b–45). These are long passages and may require some time to read and discuss with your students, but fight the temptation to rush through them!

GRACE BEFORE MEALS

LENT

LEADER:

We adore you, O Christ, and we praise you

ALL: because by your holy Cross you have redeemed the world.

✛ All make the Sign of the Cross.

> **In the name of the Father, and of the Son, and of the Holy Spirit. Amen.**

LEADER:

God of compassion,
we thank you for this meal
and for those who prepared it.
May we be nourished by this food
and by the love and friendship we share.
Help us to be mindful of people
in our community and other regions
who will remain hungry today.
May we become your true food for others
through gifts of your Spirit and our works
     of charity.
We ask this through Christ our Lord.

All: Amen.

✛ All make the Sign of the Cross.

> **In the name of the Father, and of the Son, and of the Holy Spirit. Amen.**

PRAYER AT DAY'S END

LEADER:
Blessed be the Lord,

ALL: for he has heard the sound of my pleadings.

✚ All make the Sign of the Cross.

In the name of the Father, and of the Son, and of the Holy Spirit. Amen.

LEADER:
Merciful Lord,
sometimes we fail in what
we say or do.
As our school day ends,
help us to remember that
your mercy and love
are never-ending.
Guide us as we renew our
commitment
to deepen our relationship with you
throughout this season of Lent.
We ask this in your name.

All: Amen.

✚ All make the Sign of the Cross.

In the name of the Father, and of the Son, and of the Holy Spirit. Amen.

PRAYER SERVICE
ASH WEDNESDAY

Prepare two leaders, a reader, a song leader (if the group will sing), and a thurifer (someone who handles incense) for this service. See "Movement and Gesture" in the Introduction for Lent, page 206–207 for some instruction about incense. Add a pot with lit charcoal to the sacred space. Notice the Scripture is abridged. You may wish to type it out for the reader, and mark it with a ribbon.

If ashes are distributed, prepare the students to respond "Amen" to the minister.

Prepare the environment by hanging a long piece of butcher-block paper with the word "Alleluia" written on it in block letters. Color in the first two letters, "a-l," but leave the other letters uncolored. Hang the banner where it will be visible and accessible. Plan to color in five of the letters, "l-e-l-u-i" one at a time on the Fridays of Lent—perhaps when you do the Prayer at Day's End for Lent found on page 209. The final letter, "-a," can be filled in the first day school resumes after vacation. Remember to do this silently as we do not say or sing Alleluia during Lent.

You may wish to begin by singing "From Ashes to the Living Font" and end with "Soon and Very Soon."

LEADER I:

Today the whole Church begins our Lenten retreat. The sign of this journey is the mark of a cross with ashes. This cross goes on our forehead, where we were marked for God by holy oil at Baptism. We will pray more, give more to the poor, and fast to strengthen our hearts in love for God and one another.

LEADER II:

◆ All make the sign of the Cross.

In the name of the Father, and of the Son, and of the Holy Spirit. Amen.

Let us pray:
Loving and merciful God,
you love us without condition.
Help us make your will our priority
in word and deed.
We ask this through Jesus Christ our Lord.

◆ All stand and sing **Praise to you, Lord Jesus Christ** . . .

◆ The thurifer and lector go to the table, and the thurifer adds a few grains of incense to the charcoal. When it is smoking the thurifer picks up the incense pot and the lector picks up the Bible and hold it up as he thurifer raised the incense over it three times. The thurifer holds the pot as the lector proclaims and places it back on the table when the Scripture is finished.

READER: Matthew 6:1–6, 16–18

A reading from the holy Gospel according to Matthew.

Beware of practicing your piety before others in order to be seen by them; for then you have now reward from your Father in heaven.

So when you give alms, do not sound a trumpet before you, as the hypocrites do in the synagogues and in the streets, so that they may be praised by others. Truly I tell you, they have received their reward. But when you give alms, do not let your left hand know what your right hand is doing, so that your alms may be done in secret; and your Father who sees in secret will reward you.

And whenever you pray, do not be like the hypocrites; for they love to stand and pray in the synagogues and at the street corners, so that they may e seen by others. Truly I tell you, they have received their reward. But whenever you go to pray, go into your room and shut the door and pray to your Father who is in secret; and your Father who sees in secret will reward you.

And whenever you fast, do not look dismal, like the hypocrites, for they disfigure their faces so as to show that they are fasting. Truly I tell you, they have received their reward. But when you fast, put oil on your head and wash your face, so that your fasting may be seen not by others but by your Father who is in secret; and your Father who sees in secret will reward you.

The Gospel of the Lord.

◆ All remain standing and observe silence.

◆ Ashes may be distributed.

LEADER II:

Let us pray as Jesus taught us:

ALL: Our Father . . . Amen.

Let us offer one another a sign of Christ's peace:

◆ All offer one another a sign of peace.

And may God bless us all,

✚ All make the sign of the Cross.

Give us strength throughout our Lenten season and bring us to everlasting life.

All: Amen.

PRAYER FOR
WEDNESDAY, MARCH 6, 2019

OPENING

Ash Wednesday begins our Lenten season. During Lent, we prepare for Easter through prayer, fasting and almsgiving. We fast from foods or activities to remind us that nothing is more important than God or the needs of God's people. Almsgiving means giving money, time, or possessions to people in need. In today's Gospel, Jesus tells us to do these things with humility.

✛ All make the Sign of the Cross.

In the name of the Father, and of the Son, and of the Holy Spirit. Amen.

PSALM   (For a longer psalm, see page xiv.) Psalm 34:4–5

The LORD saves the crushed in spirit.

The LORD saves the crushed in spirit.

I sought the LORD, and he answered me,
  and delivered me from all my fears.
Look to him, and be radiant;
  so your faces shall never be ashamed.

The LORD saves the crushed in spirit.

◆ All stand and sing **Praise to you, Lord Jesus Christ . . .**

GOSPEL   Matthew 6:2–3, 5–6

A reading from the holy Gospel according to Matthew.

Jesus said, "So whenever you give alms, do not sound a trumpet before you, as the hypocrites do in the synagogues and in the streets, so that they may be praised by others. Truly I tell you, they have received their reward. But when you give alms, do not let your left hand know what your right hand is doing. And whenever you pray, do not be like the hypocrites; for they love to stand and pray in the synagogues and at the street corners, so that they may be seen by others. Truly I tell you, they have received their reward. But whenever you pray, go into your room and shut the door and pray to your Father who is in secret; and your Father who sees in secret will reward you."

The Gospel of the Lord.

◆ All sit and observe silence.

FOR SILENT REFLECTION

Think about this silently in your heart. How will you pray, fast, and help others this Lent?

CLOSING PRAYER

Let us pray to God for our needs and the needs of others: our family, neighborhood, and the world. For each need we say, "Lord, hear our prayer."

◆ All may add their own prayers here.

Let us pray: **Our Father . . . Amen.**

O God, during this holy season
help us to fast from all
that separates us from you.
Help us to be generous and to pray always.

Amen.

✛ All make the Sign of the Cross.

212

OPENING

In today's Gospel, Jesus talks about our attitude when we pray, fast, and give alms. He asks us to think about whether we do things, like giving up a favorite TV show or time on our cell phone, and then brag about how good we are for doing it. We do these things for the love of God and the good of others rather than to get praise.

✦ All make the Sign of the Cross.

In the name of the Father, and of the Son, and of the Holy Spirit. Amen.

PSALM   (For a longer psalm, see page xiv.) Psalm 34:4–5

The Lord saves the crushed in spirit.

The Lord saves the crushed in spirit.

I sought the Lord, and he answered me,
   and delivered me from all my fears.
Look to him, and be radiant;
   so your faces shall never be ashamed.

The Lord saves the crushed in spirit.

◆ All stand and sing **Praise to you, Lord Jesus Christ . . .**

GOSPEL   Matthew 6:1, 7, 16–18

A reading from the holy Gospel according to Matthew.

Jesus said, "Beware of practicing your piety before others in order to be seen by them; for then you have no reward from your Father in heaven. When you are praying, do not heap up empty phrases as the Gentiles do; for they think that they will be heard because of their many words. And whenever you fast, do not look dismal, like the hypocrites, for they disfigure their faces so as to show others that they are fasting. Truly I tell you, they have received their reward. But when you fast, put oil on your head and wash your face, so that your fasting may be seen not by others but by your Father who is in secret; and your Father who sees in secret will reward you."

The Gospel of the Lord.

◆ All sit and observe silence.

FOR SILENT REFLECTION

Think about this silently in your heart. Can you do a kindness for someone today without expecting praise for it?

CLOSING PRAYER

Let us pray to God for our needs and the needs of others: our family, neighborhood, and the world. For each need we say, "Lord, hear our prayer."

◆ All may add their own prayers here.

Let us pray: **Our Father . . . Amen.**

Holy God, our Father,
May all that we do be for your glory.
We ask this in the name of Jesus Christ.

Amen.

✦ All make the Sign of the Cross.

PRAYER FOR
FRIDAY, MARCH 8, 2019

OPENING

Isaiah speaks of the type of fast that God really wants: to break the bonds of injustice. Injustice means that things are not fair. Certain people are not treated with dignity and respect. It means that some people are very, very poor and others are extremely wealthy. God says working for justice makes our own light shine more brightly.

✝ All make the Sign of the Cross.

In the name of the Father, and of the Son, and of the Holy Spirit. Amen.

PSALM   (For a longer psalm, see page xiv.) Psalm 34:4–5

The LORD saves the crushed in spirit.

The LORD saves the crushed in spirit.

I sought the LORD, and he answered me,
    and delivered me from all my fears.
Look to him, and be radiant;
    so your faces shall never be ashamed.

The LORD saves the crushed in spirit.

READING   Isaiah 50:1a; 58:6a, 7–8, 9bc, 10

A reading from the Book of the prophet Isaiah.

Thus says the LORD: Is not this the fast that I choose: to loose the bonds of injustice? Is it not to share your bread with the hungry, and bring the homeless poor into your house; when you see the naked, to cover them, and not to hide yourself from your own kin? Then your light shall break forth like the dawn, and your healing shall spring up quickly; your vindicator shall go before you, the glory of the LORD shall be your rear guard. If you remove the yoke from among you, the pointing of the finger, the speaking of evil, if you offer your food to the hungry and satisfy the needs of the afflicted, then your light shall rise in the darkness and your gloom be like the noonday.

The Word of the Lord.

◆ All observe silence.

FOR SILENT REFLECTION

Think about this silently in your heart. Can you fast from talking unkindly about someone today?

CLOSING PRAYER

Let us pray to God for our needs and the needs of others: our family, neighborhood, and the world. For each need we say, "Lord, hear our prayer."

◆ All may add their own prayers here.

Let us pray: **Our Father . . . Amen.**

Loving God, over and over again
you call us to be fair and just,
loving and generous.
This Lent, help us to be more mindful
of our words and actions.
May the light of your love shine forth in us.
We ask this in the name of Jesus Christ.

Amen.

✝ All make the Sign of the Cross.

PRAYER FOR THE WEEK
WITH A READING FROM THE GOSPEL FOR **SUNDAY, MARCH 10, 2019**

OPENING

After Jesus was baptized, he chose to spend time fasting and praying in the desert. Jesus stayed in the wilderness for forty days listening to the word of God. Lent is forty days long. It is a time for us to pray, reflect on our lives, and think about how we can better serve God and others.

✦ All make the Sign of the Cross.

In the name of the Father, and of the Son, and of the Holy Spirit. Amen.

PSALM   (For a longer psalm, see page xiv.) Psalm 34:4–5

The LORD saves the crushed in spirit.

The LORD saves the crushed in spirit.

I sought the LORD, and he answered me,
 and delivered me from all my fears.
Look to him, and be radiant;
 so your faces shall never be ashamed.

The LORD saves the crushed in spirit.

◆ All stand and sing **Praise to you, Lord Jesus Christ . . .**

GOSPEL   Luke 4:1ac, 2, 3ac, 4, 9abd, 10, 12–13

A reading from the holy Gospel according to Luke.

Jesus returned from the Jordan and was led by the Spirit in the wilderness, where for forty days he was tempted by the devil. He ate nothing at all during those days, and when they were over, he was famished. The devil said to him, "command this stone to become a loaf of bread." Jesus answered him, "It is written, 'One does not live by bread alone.'" Then the devil took him to Jerusalem, and placed him on the pinnacle of the temple, saying to him, "Throw yourself down from here, for it is written, 'God will command his angels concerning you, to protect you.'" Jesus answered him, "It is said, 'Do not put the Lord your God to the test.'" When the devil had finished every test, he departed from Jesus until an opportune time.

The Gospel of the Lord.

◆ All sit and observe silence.

FOR SILENT REFLECTION

Think about this silently in your heart. Praying helps you to say "no" when you feel tempted to do things you know you shouldn't do.

CLOSING PRAYER

Let us pray to God for our needs and the needs of others: our family, neighborhood, and the world. For each need we say, "Lord, hear our prayer."

◆ All may add their own prayers here.

Let us pray: **Our Father . . . Amen.**

Almighty God,
give us the strength
we need to do the work
you entrust to us.
We ask this in the name of Jesus Christ.

Amen.

✦ All make the Sign of the Cross.

PRAYER FOR
MONDAY, MARCH 11, 2019

OPENING

This week the Scriptures will teach us about forgiveness. The prophet Nehemiah [nee-huh-MI-uh] called the people to fast and pray to show they were sorry for their sins. Sackcloth was a garment made out of a very rough, uncomfortable material. Ezra [EZ-ruh] was another Jewish prophet. Nehemiah and Ezra lived around 450 years before the birth of Jesus.

✚ All make the Sign of the Cross.

In the name of the Father, and of the Son, and of the Holy Spirit. Amen.

PSALM
(For a longer psalm, see page xiv.) Psalm 34:4–5

The LORD saves the crushed in spirit.

The LORD saves the crushed in spirit.

I sought the LORD, and he answered me,
   and delivered me from all my fears.
Look to him, and be radiant;
   so your faces shall never be ashamed.

The LORD saves the crushed in spirit.

READING
Nehemiah 9:1a, 3, 6ab, 9, 17c

A reading from the Book of Nehemiah.

Now on the twenty-fourth day of this month the people of Israel were assembled with fasting and in sackcloth. They stood up in their place and read from the book of the law of the LORD their God for a fourth part of the day, and for another fourth they made confession and worshiped the LORD their God. And Ezra said: "You are the LORD, you alone. And you saw the distress of our ancestors in Egypt and heard their cry at the Red Sea. But they and our ancestors acted presumptuously and stiffened

their necks and did not obey your commandments. But you are a God ready to forgive, gracious and merciful, slow to anger and abounding in steadfast love, and you did not forsake our ancestors."

The Word of the Lord.

◆ All observe silence.

FOR SILENT REFLECTION

Think about this silently in your heart. Is there something you would like to ask forgiveness for?

CLOSING PRAYER

Let us pray to God for our needs and the needs of others: our family, neighborhood, and the world. For each need we say, "Lord, hear our prayer."

◆ All may add their own prayers here.

Let us pray: **Our Father . . . Amen.**

We are grateful for your faithful love, O God.
Help us to forgive each other graciously
as you forgive us.
We ask this in the name of Jesus Christ.

Amen.

✚ All make the Sign of the Cross.

OPENING

The prophet Daniel lived during the Babylonian exile, about six hundred years before the birth of Jesus. The Jewish people thought their captivity and exile to Babylonia, an evil and wicked city, was punishment for their own sinful ways. Daniel taught the people to be sorry for their sins, ask forgiveness, and trust in God's mercy to lead them one day back home to their homeland.

✦ All make the Sign of the Cross.

In the name of the Father, and of the Son, and of the Holy Spirit. Amen.

PSALM   (For a longer psalm, see page xiv.) Psalm 34:4–5

The LORD saves the crushed in spirit.

The LORD saves the crushed in spirit.

I sought the LORD, and he answered me,
　　and delivered me from all my fears.
Look to him, and be radiant;
　　so your faces shall never be ashamed.

The LORD saves the crushed in spirit.

READING   Daniel 9:3–4ab, 5, 17ab, 18ac, 19abc

A reading from the Book of the prophet Daniel.

Then I, Daniel, turned to the Lord God, to seek an answer by prayer and supplication with fasting and sackcloth and ashes. I prayed to the LORD my God and made confession saying, "Ah, Lord, great and awesome God, we have sinned and done wrong, acted wickedly and rebelled, turning aside from your commandments and ordinances. Now, therefore, O our God, listen to the prayer of your servant and to his supplication. Incline your ear, O my God, and hear. We do not present our supplication before you on the ground of our righteousness, but on the ground of your great mercies. O Lord, hear; O Lord, forgive; O Lord, listen and act and do not delay!

The Word of the Lord.

◆ All observe silence.

FOR SILENT REFLECTION

Think about this silently in your heart. Would you like to ask for God's mercy for something you have done or said?

CLOSING PRAYER

Let us pray to God for our needs and the needs of others: our family, neighborhood, and the world. For each need we say, "Lord, hear our prayer."

◆ All may add their own prayers here.

Let us pray: **Our Father . . . Amen.**

Merciful and forgiving God,
help us to see where we need to change.
Give us the courage to make those changes.
We ask this in the name of Jesus Christ.

Amen.

✦ All make the Sign of the Cross.

PRAYER FOR
WEDNESDAY, MARCH 13, 2019

OPENING

Jesus said he was "The Son of Man," which means he was truly human. In this Gospel, Jesus proves he had God's authority to forgive sins by healing the paralyzed man. In Jesus' time it was thought physical ailments were a result of sin. Now we understand there are medical reasons. As we listen to the Gospel today, think about how your heart and mind and soul need healing.

✝ All make the Sign of the Cross.

In the name of the Father, and of the Son, and of the Holy Spirit. Amen.

PSALM   (For a longer psalm, see page xiv.) Psalm 34:4–5

The LORD saves the crushed in spirit.

The LORD saves the crushed in spirit.

I sought the LORD, and he answered me,
    and delivered me from all my fears.
Look to him, and be radiant;
    so your faces shall never be ashamed.

The LORD saves the crushed in spirit.

◆ All stand and sing **Praise to you, Lord Jesus Christ . . .**

GOSPEL   Luke 5:17ad, 18ab, 20–22ab, 24–25ac

A reading from the holy Gospel according to Luke.

One day, while Jesus was teaching, the power of the Lord was with him to heal. Just then some men came, carrying a paralyzed man on a bed. When he saw their faith, he said, "Friend, your sins are forgiven you." Then the scribes and the Pharisees began to question,

"Who is this who is speaking blasphemies? Who can forgive sins but God alone?" When Jesus perceived their questionings, he answered them, "But so that you may know that the Son of Man has authority on earth to forgive sins"—he said to the one who was paralyzed—"I say to you, stand up and take your bed and go to your home." Immediately he stood up before them, and went to his home, glorifying God.

The Gospel of the Lord.

◆ All sit and observe silence.

FOR SILENT REFLECTION

Think about this silently in your heart. Is there someone you need to forgive?

CLOSING PRAYER

Let us pray to God for our needs and the needs of others: our family, neighborhood, and the world. For each need we say, "Lord, hear our prayer."

◆ All may add their own prayers here.

Let us pray: **Our Father . . . Amen.**

Loving God, we thank you
for all the times
you have shown your
kindness and mercy to us.
Help us to reflect this tenderness to
one another.

Amen.

✝ All make the Sign of the Cross.

218

OPENING

St. Peter was a fisherman whose original name was Simon. When he became a disciple of Jesus, Jesus changed his name to Peter, which means "rock." Jesus told Peter and the other disciples that they would be "fishers of men." In today's Gospel, Peter calls people to follow Jesus' teachings by seeking forgiveness for sins and trying to live peacefully with one another.

✠ All make the Sign of the Cross.

In the name of the Father, and of the Son, and of the Holy Spirit. Amen.

PSALM
(For a longer psalm, see page xiv.) Psalm 34:4–5

The LORD saves the crushed in spirit.

The LORD saves the crushed in spirit.

I sought the LORD, and he answered me,
  and delivered me from all my fears.
Look to him, and be radiant;
  so your faces shall never be ashamed.

The LORD saves the crushed in spirit.

READING
Acts 10:34a, 36–37a, 38–39a, 42–43

A reading from the Acts of the Apostles.

Then Peter began to speak to them: "You know the message God sent to the people of Israel, preaching peace by Jesus Christ—he is Lord of all. That message spread throughout Judea, how God anointed Jesus of Nazareth with the Holy Spirit and with power; how he went about doing good and healing all who were oppressed by the devil, for God was with him. We are witnesses to all that he did both in Judea and in Jerusalem. He commanded us to preach to the people and to testify that he is the one ordained by God as judge of the living and the dead. All the prophets testify about him that everyone who believes in him receives forgiveness of sins through his name."

The Word of the Lord.

◆ All observe silence.

FOR SILENT REFLECTION

Think about this silently in your heart. Say a prayer of thanksgiving for the people who love you.

CLOSING PRAYER

Let us pray to God for our needs and the needs of others: our family, neighborhood, and the world. For each need we say, "Lord, hear our prayer."

◆ All may add their own prayers here.

Let us pray: **Our Father . . . Amen.**

Dear God,
we give thanks for all the people
who love us unconditionally.
Help us to be more thoughtful
in our words and actions.
We ask this in the name of Jesus Christ.

Amen.

✠ All make the Sign of the Cross.

PRAYER FOR
FRIDAY, MARCH 15, 2019

OPENING

John was one of the Twelve Apostles. He is thought to have lived to the age of 94, longer than all the other Apostles. In today's reading, John is writing to an early Christian community that is divided into two hostile groups. Each group thinks they are without sin and the other group is with sin. John reminds them that God is the light, and those who follow God's teaching shine with that light.

✦ All make the Sign of the Cross.

In the name of the Father, and of the Son, and of the Holy Spirit. Amen.

PSALM
(For a longer psalm, see page xiv.) Psalm 34:4–5

The LORD saves the crushed in spirit.

The LORD saves the crushed in spirit.

I sought the LORD, and he answered me,
and delivered me from all my fears.
Look to him, and be radiant;
so your faces shall never be ashamed.

The LORD saves the crushed in spirit.

READING
1 John 1:1a, 5–7, 9

A reading from the First Letter of John.

We declare to you what we have seen and heard so that you may have fellowship with us. This is the message we have heard from Jesus and proclaim to you, that God is light and in God there is no darkness at all. If we say that we have fellowship with God while we are walking in darkness, we lie and do not do what is true; but if we walk in the light as he himself is in the light, we have fellowship with one another, and the blood of Jesus his Son cleanses us from all sin. If we confess our sins, God who is faithful and just will forgive us our sins and cleanse us from all unrighteousness.

The Word of the Lord.

◆ All observe silence.

FOR SILENT REFLECTION

Think about this silently in your heart. How does God's light shine through you?

CLOSING PRAYER

Let us pray to God for our needs and the needs of others: our family, neighborhood, and the world. For each need we say, "Lord, hear our prayer."

◆ All may add their own prayers here.

Let us pray: **Our Father . . . Amen.**

Make us one holy people, O God.
Give us open hearts to accept others
and open hands to help others.
Help us to welcome people
who are from different countries or
different backgrounds from us.
We ask this in the name of Jesus Christ.

Amen.

✦ All make the Sign of the Cross.

Prepare six leaders for this service. The third reader will need a Bible for the Gospel passage and may need help finding it and practicing. After the story of St. Patrick, you may wish to begin by singing "Lord of All Hopefulness," and end with "Christ Be Beside Me" (to the tune of "Morning Has Broken") or "The Summons." If there will be singing, prepare a song leader.

◆ All make the Sign of the Cross.

In the name of the Father, and of the Son, and of the Holy Spirit. Amen.

FIRST LEADER:
Praise be to God,
who in every age sends great missionaries
    like St. Patrick
to preach the Good News of Jesus Christ!

ALL: Amen.

Listen now to the story of St. Patrick, who lived in the fifth century: As a teen, St. Patrick was kidnapped from Scotland and sold as a slave in Ireland. Several years later, with God's help, he escaped to Britain, where he studied to become a priest and later was ordained a bishop. Then he went back to Ireland and brought the faith of Jesus to all the Irish people. He helped them believe that God didn't live in the trees of the forest, but in the hearts of all people.

SONG LEADER:
Please join in singing our opening song.

PRAYER SERVICE
MEMORIAL OF ST. PATRICK

SECOND LEADER:

Let us pray:
Holy Trinity, one God in three persons,
we thank you for sending us holy men
     and women
who help people to understand you.
May we always look for guides who will
     give us a deeper knowledge of your
     mysteries.
We ask this through Christ our Lord.

ALL: Amen.

◆ All stand and sing **Praise to you,
Lord Jesus Christ . . .**

THIRD LEADER: Matthew 28: 18–20

A reading from the holy Gospel according
to Matthew.

◆ Read the Gospel passage from the Bible.

The Gospel of the Lord.

◆ All observe silence.

FOURTH LEADER:

Let us bring our hopes and needs to God as
we pray, "Lord, hear our prayer."

For all the children of the world, may we
find good guides and models of faith. May
we develop our talents and use them wisely,
we pray to the Lord.

For our Irish ancestors and all those who
came before us. May we live the faith they
passed on to us and treasure the heritage they
have given us, we pray to the Lord.

For the homeless, the hungry, for those who
are sick or suffering in any way, and for those
who have died, we pray to the Lord.

FIFTH LEADER:

Let us pray as Jesus taught us:
Our Father . . . Amen.

◆ Pause, and then say:

Let us offer one another a sign of
Christ's peace.

◆ All offer one another a sign of peace.

SIXTH LEADER:

Let us pray:
God of our ancestors,
give us the strength and courage
     of St. Patrick
so that we may bring the love and joy
     of your Kingdom
to all the world.
We ask this through Christ our Lord.

ALL: Amen.

✚ All make the Sign of the Cross.

**In the name of the Father, and of the
Son, and of the Holy Spirit. Amen.**

CHILDREN'S DAILY PRAYER 2018–2019, © 2018 Archdiocese of Chicago: Liturgy Training Publications. All rights reserved. Orders: 800-933-1800 or www.LTP.org.

PRAYER FOR THE WEEK
WITH A READING FROM THE GOSPEL FOR **SUNDAY, MARCH 17, 2019**

OPENING

Today's Gospel is the Apostle Luke's account of the moment that God revealed Jesus' true nature to the disciples Peter, John, and James. Moses and Elijah [ee-LI-juh] were both prophets and leaders in Jewish history, revered by all Jewish people.

✚ All make the Sign of the Cross.

In the name of the Father, and of the Son, and of the Holy Spirit. Amen.

PSALM
(For a longer psalm, see page xiv.) Psalm 34:4–5

The Lord saves the crushed in spirit.

The Lord saves the crushed in spirit.

I sought the Lord, and he answered me,
    and delivered me from all my fears.
Look to him, and be radiant;
    so your faces shall never be ashamed.

The Lord saves the crushed in spirit.

◆ All stand and sing **Praise to you, Lord Jesus Christ . . .**

GOSPEL
Luke 9:28b–30, 32c–35

A reading from the holy Gospel according to Luke.

Jesus took with him Peter and John and James, and went up on the mountain to pray. And while he was praying, the appearance of his face changed, and his clothes became dazzling white. Suddenly they saw two men, Moses and Elijah (ee-LI-juh), talking to him. Now Peter and his companions saw his glory and the two men who stood with him. Just as they were leaving him, Peter said to Jesus, "Master, it is good for us to be here; let us make three dwellings, one for you, one for Moses, and one for Elijah"—not knowing what he said. While he was saying this, a cloud came and overshadowed them; and they were terrified as they entered the cloud. Then from the cloud came a voice that said, "This is my Son, my Chosen; listen to him!"

The Gospel of the Lord.

◆ All sit and observe silence.

FOR SILENT REFLECTION

Think about this silently in your heart. The disciples saw and heard amazing things in this reading. Can you remember any of the images?

CLOSING PRAYER

Let us pray to God for our needs and the needs of others: our family, neighborhood, and the world. For each need we say, "Lord, hear our prayer."

◆ All may add their own prayers here.

Let us pray: **Our Father . . . Amen.**

Lord Jesus,
you are God's beloved son.
Help us to listen to your words.
Help us to follow your teachings.
In your name we pray.

Amen.

✚ All make the Sign of the Cross.

223

PRAYER FOR
MONDAY, MARCH 18, 2019

OPENING

The theme for this week is how God continually calls us back. In Jesus' time, tax collectors were considered unclean because they handled money and sometime took unfair advantage of people.

✝ All make the Sign of the Cross.

In the name of the Father, and of the Son, and of the Holy Spirit. Amen.

PSALM

(For a longer psalm, see page xiv.) Psalm 34:4–5

The LORD saves the crushed in spirit.

The LORD saves the crushed in spirit.

I sought the LORD, and he answered me,
    and delivered me from all my fears.
Look to him, and be radiant;
    so your faces shall never be ashamed.

The LORD saves the crushed in spirit.

◆ All stand and sing **Praise to you, Lord Jesus Christ . . .**

GOSPEL

Luke 15:1–7

A reading from the holy Gospel according to Luke.

Tax collectors and sinners were coming near to listen to Jesus. And the Pharisees and the scribes were grumbling and saying, "This fellow welcomes sinners and eats with them." So Jesus told them this parable: "Which one of you, having a hundred sheep and losing one of them, does not leave the ninety-nine in the wilderness and go after the one that is lost until he finds it? When he has found it, he lays it on his shoulders and rejoices. And when he comes home, he calls together his friends and neighbors, saying to them, 'Rejoice with me, for I have found my sheep that was lost.' Just so, I tell you, there will be more joy in heaven over one sinner who repents than over ninety-nine righteous persons who need no repentance."

The Gospel of the Lord.

◆ All sit and observe silence.

FOR SILENT REFLECTION

Think about this silently in your heart. Is there someone I need to welcome back as my friend?

CLOSING PRAYER

Let us pray to God for our needs and the needs of others: our family, neighborhood, and the world. For each need we say, "Lord, hear our prayer."

◆ All may add their own prayers here.

Let us pray: **Our Father . . . Amen.**

Gracious God,
you search for us and
bring us home.
As you rejoice in us
let us rejoice in you.
For this we give thanks and praise.

Amen.

✝ All make the Sign of the Cross.

OPENING

The Pharisees, or religious leaders, were always criticizing Jesus for befriending people who were considered unworthy. In today's Gospel, Luke tells a story about how God welcomes back anyone who has been lost.

✝ All make the Sign of the Cross.

In the name of the Father, and of the Son, and of the Holy Spirit. Amen.

PSALM   (For a longer psalm, see page xiv.) Psalm 34:4–5

The LORD saves the crushed in spirit.

The LORD saves the crushed in spirit.

I sought the LORD, and he answered me,
    and delivered me from all my fears.
Look to him, and be radiant;
    so your faces shall never be ashamed.

The LORD saves the crushed in spirit.

◆ All stand and sing **Praise to you, Lord Jesus Christ . . .**

GOSPEL   Luke 15:1–3, 8–10

A reading from the holy Gospel according to Luke.

Now all the tax collectors and sinners were coming near to listen to him. And the Pharisees and the scribes were grumbling and saying, "This fellow welcomes sinners and eats with them." So he told them this parable: "What woman having ten silver coins, if she loses one of them, does not light a lamp, sweep the house, and search carefully until she finds it? When she has found it, she calls together her friends and neighbors, saying, 'Rejoice with me, for I have found the coin that I had lost.' Just so, I tell you, there is joy in the presence of the angels of God over one sinner who repents."

The Gospel of the Lord.

◆ All sit and observe silence.

FOR SILENT REFLECTION

Think about this silently in your heart. How do you feel when a relationship with a family member or a friend has been repaired?

CLOSING PRAYER

Let us pray to God for our needs and the needs of others: our family, neighborhood, and the world. For each need we say, "Lord, hear our prayer."

◆ All may add their own prayers here.

Let us pray: **Our Father . . . Amen.**

Kind and loving God,
you do not divide people
 into worthy and unworthy.
You see everyone for the goodness
that is within them.
Help us to see the goodness in others
and rejoice in it.

Amen.

✝ All make the Sign of the Cross.

PRAYER SERVICE
SOLEMNITY OF ST. JOSEPH

Prepare six leaders for this service. The third leader will need a Bible for the passage from Matthew. Take time to help the third leader practice the readings. You may wish to sing "You Are the Light of the World," "Blest Are They," or "We Are Called," as opening or closing songs. If the group will sing, prepare someone to lead.

FIRST LEADER:

Today we remember Joseph, the husband of Mary and the foster father of Jesus here on earth. At several key times in his life, Joseph listened and followed special messengers that God directed to this humble carpenter. Joseph's faith led him to marry his fiancée, even though she became pregnant in a divinely inspired way. He courageously took them to Egypt to escape Herod's wrath. And Joseph raised Jesus as his own son, guiding his growth.

✚ All make the Sign of the Cross.

In the name of the Father, and of the Son, and of the Holy Spirit. Amen.

Let us remember Joseph as we begin by singing the opening song.

SONG LEADER:

◆ Gesture for all to stand, and lead the first few verses of the song.

SECOND LEADER:

Let us pray:
Almighty Father,
may we look to Joseph as our guide
as he responded to your call to be
a devoted husband and father.

CHILDREN'S DAILY PRAYER 2018–2019, © 2018 Archdiocese of Chicago: Liturgy Training Publications. All rights reserved. Orders: 800-933-1800 or www.LTP.org.

We pray with him to your Son Jesus,
our Lord and Savior,
in union with the Holy Spirit.

Amen.

◆ Remain standing and sing **Praise to you,
Lord Jesus Christ** . . .

THIRD LEADER: Matthew 2:13–15
A reading from the holy Gospel according
to Matthew.

◆ Read the Gospel passage from the Bible.

The Gospel of the Lord.

◆ All remain standing and observe silence.

FOURTH LEADER:
Let us bring our hopes and needs to God as
we pray, Lord, hear our prayer.
For the courage to live our faith
through word and action
as Joseph did throughout his days,
we pray to the Lord.

For all who are struggling with
tough decisions in life,
may they look to Joseph as
a brave friend on their journey,
we pray to the Lord.

For all married couples,
may they continue to be an example
of the love and devotion that
Joseph and Mary shared,
we pray to the Lord.

For all fathers
and those who nurture others.
Help us to respect and protect life
from conception until natural death.
We pray to the Lord.

May we have the conviction
to lead the way as Joseph did
to hope and the promise
of new life through Jesus.
We pray to the Lord.

FIFTH LEADER:
Let us pray as Jesus taught us:

Our Father . . . Amen.

◆ Pause, and then say:

Let us offer one another the sign of
Christ's peace.

◆ All offer one another a sign of peace.

SIXTH LEADER:
Let us pray:
Heavenly Father,
your servant Joseph
was a man of great faith.
He listened to you in prayer
and to angels whom you sent
in dreams.
He is a symbol for courage
in following God's will.
May we look to him
in times of trouble or doubt.
We ask this through Christ our Lord.

All: Amen.

✦ All make the Sign of the Cross.

OPENING

Today we begin the story of the prodigal son and the forgiving father. Listen to what the younger son did with the money that his father gave him.

✦ All make the Sign of the Cross.

In the name of the Father, and of the Son, and of the Holy Spirit. Amen.

PSALM
(For a longer psalm, see page xiv.) Psalm 34:4–5

The Lᴏʀᴅ saves the crushed in spirit.

The Lᴏʀᴅ saves the crushed in spirit.

I sought the Lᴏʀᴅ, and he answered me,
   and delivered me from all my fears.
Look to him, and be radiant;
   so your faces shall never be ashamed.

The Lᴏʀᴅ saves the crushed in spirit.

◆ All stand and sing **Praise to you, Lord Jesus Christ . . .**

GOSPEL
Luke 15:11–13a, 14a,c, 15–17a,18–19

A reading from the holy Gospel according to Luke.

Jesus said, "There was a man who had two sons. The younger one said to his father, 'Father, give me the share of the property that will belong to me.' So the father divided his property between them. A few days later the younger son gathered all he had and traveled to a distant country. When he had spent everything, he began to be in need. So he went and hired himself out to one of the citizens of that country, who sent him to his fields to feed the pigs. He would gladly have filled himself with the pods that the pigs were eating; and no one gave him anything. But when he came to himself he said, 'I will get up and go to my father, and I will say to him, "Father, I have sinned against heaven and before you; I am no longer worthy to be called your son; treat me like one of your hired hands."'"

The Gospel of the Lord.

◆ All sit and observe silence.

FOR SILENT REFLECTION

Think about this silently in your heart. How did the son feel about what he had done?

CLOSING PRAYER

Let us pray to God for our needs and the needs of others: our family, neighborhood, and the world. For each need we say, "Lord, hear our prayer."

◆ All may add their own prayers here.

Let us pray: **Our Father . . . Amen.**

Forgiving God, we make mistakes.
Sometimes we treat others with disrespect.
Sometimes we feel that what we have done is unforgiveable.
Thank you for teaching us that we can always be forgiven if we ask for forgiveness.

Amen.

✦ All make the Sign of the Cross.

OPENING

In yesterday's reading, Jesus told a story in which a son had lost the inheritance that his father gave him. The son realized the foolishness of what he had done, felt sorry, and returned home to apologize to his father. Listen to how the story continues today.

✚ All make the Sign of the Cross.

In the name of the Father, and of the Son, and of the Holy Spirit. Amen.

PSALM   (For a longer psalm, see page xiv.) Psalm 34:4–5

The LORD saves the crushed in spirit.

The LORD saves the crushed in spirit.

I sought the LORD, and he answered me,
 and delivered me from all my fears.
Look to him, and be radiant;
 so your faces shall never be ashamed.

The LORD saves the crushed in spirit.

◆ All stand and sing **Praise to you, Lord Jesus Christ . . .**

GOSPEL   Luke 15:20–24

A reading from the holy Gospel according to Luke.

Jesus said, "The son set off and went to his father. But while he was still far off, his father saw him and was filled with compassion; he ran and put his arms around his son and kissed him. Then the son said to him, 'Father, I have sinned against heaven and before you; I am no longer worthy to be called your son.' But the father said to his slaves, 'Quickly, bring out a robe—the best one—and put it on him; put a ring on his finger and sandals on his feet. And get the fatted calf and kill it, and let us eat and celebrate; for this son of mine was dead and is alive again; he was lost and is found!' And they began to celebrate."

The Gospel of the Lord.

◆ All sit and observe silence.

FOR SILENT REFLECTION

Think about this silently in your heart. How do you think the son felt by his father's greeting?

CLOSING PRAYER

Let us pray to God for our needs and the needs of others: our family, neighborhood, and the world. For each need we say, "Lord, hear our prayer."

◆ All may add their own prayers here.

Let us pray: **Our Father . . . Amen.**

Loving God,
help us to have the courage
to repair broken relationships.
Help us to feel sorry
when we have harmed or hurt someone.
Help us to apologize. Remind us to celebrate
when friendship is restored.

Amen.

✚ All make the Sign of the Cross.

PRAYER FOR
FRIDAY, MARCH 22, 2019

OPENING

Today we continue the story of the prodigal son and the forgiving father. There was also an older son in the family. Today's story is about him.

✚ All make the Sign of the Cross.

In the name of the Father, and of the Son, and of the Holy Spirit. Amen.

PSALM
(For a longer psalm, see page xiv.) Psalm 34:4–5

The Lord saves the crushed in spirit.

The Lord saves the crushed in spirit.

I sought the Lord, and he answered me,
and delivered me from all my fears.
Look to him, and be radiant;
so your faces shall never be ashamed.

The Lord saves the crushed in spirit.

◆ All stand and sing **Praise to you, Lord Jesus Christ . . .**

GOSPEL
Luke 15:26–32

A reading from the holy Gospel according to Luke.

"The elder son called one of the slaves and asked what was going on. The slave replied, 'Your brother has come, and your father has killed the fatted calf, because he has got him back safe and sound.' Then the older brother became angry and refused to go in. His father came out and began to plead with him. But he answered his father, 'Listen! For all these years I have been working like a slave for you, and I have never disobeyed your command; yet you have never given me even a young goat so that I might celebrate with my friends. But when this son of yours came back, who has devoured your property, you killed the fatted calf for him!' Then the father said to him, 'Son, you are always with me, and all that is mine is yours. But we had to celebrate and rejoice, because this brother of yours was dead and has come to life; he was lost and has been found.'"

The Gospel of the Lord.

◆ All sit and observe silence.

FOR SILENT REFLECTION

Think about this silently in your heart. What do you think about the older son's response?

CLOSING PRAYER

Let us pray to God for our needs and the needs of others: our family, neighborhood, and the world. For each need we say, "Lord, hear our prayer."

◆ All may add their own prayers here.

Let us pray: **Our Father . . . Amen.**

Dear God, your love is abundant.
Help us to celebrate the good fortune of others
and to see and appreciate
the blessings in our own lives.
We ask this in the name of Jesus Christ.

Amen.

✚ All make the Sign of the Cross.

PRAYER FOR THE WEEK

WITH A READING FROM THE GOSPEL FOR **SUNDAY, MARCH 24, 2019**

OPENING

In today's Gospel, Jesus uses a parable about gardening to teach us about God's kindness and patience. A fig tree produces a small pear-shaped fruit that was very common in Jesus' time.

✛ All make the Sign of the Cross.

In the name of the Father, and of the Son, and of the Holy Spirit. Amen.

PSALM
(For a longer psalm, see page xiv.) Psalm 34:4–5

The LORD saves the crushed in spirit.

The LORD saves the crushed in spirit.

I sought the LORD, and he answered me,
  and delivered me from all my fears.
Look to him, and be radiant;
  so your faces shall never be ashamed.

The LORD saves the crushed in spirit.

◆ All stand and sing **Praise to you,
Lord Jesus Christ . . .**

GOSPEL
Luke 13:1–3, 6ab, 8–9

A reading from the holy Gospel according to Luke.

Then Jesus told this parable: "A man had a fig tree planted in his vineyard; and he came looking for fruit on it and found none. So he said to the gardener, 'See here! For three years I have come looking for fruit on this fig tree, and still I find none. Cut it down! Why should it be wasting the soil?' He replied, 'Sir, let it alone for one more year, until I dig around it and put manure on it. If it bears fruit next year, well and good; but if not, you can cut it down.'"

The Gospel of the Lord.

◆ All sit and observe silence.

FOR SILENT REFLECTION

Think about this silently in your heart. What is the good fruit that you produce?

CLOSING PRAYER

Let us pray to God for our needs and the needs of others: our family, neighborhood, and the world. For each need we say, "Lord, hear our prayer."

◆ All may add their own prayers here.

Let us pray: **Our Father . . . Amen.**

Dear God,
thank you for giving us a good home
and a good community to grow up in.
Our family, our teachers, and our priests
 help us to stay healthy in body, mind,
and spirit
 so that we can bear good fruit
 and help make our world
 a better place for all.

Amen.

✛ All make the Sign of the Cross.

PRAYER FOR
MONDAY, MARCH 25, 2019

OPENING

Today we celebrate the Solemnity of the Annunciation of the Lord, when the angel appeared to Mary and asked her to be the mother of Jesus. In today's Gospel, Jesus reminds us that in caring for others, we are serving him.

✦ All make the Sign of the Cross.

In the name of the Father, and of the Son, and of the Holy Spirit. Amen.

PSALM
(For a longer psalm, see page xiv.) Psalm 34:4–5

The Lord saves the crushed in spirit.

The Lord saves the crushed in spirit.

I sought the Lord, and he answered me,
    and delivered me from all my fears.
Look to him, and be radiant;
    so your faces shall never be ashamed.

The Lord saves the crushed in spirit.

◆ All stand and sing **Praise to you, Lord Jesus Christ . . .**

GOSPEL
Matthew 25:34ab, 35–37ab, 40

A reading from the holy Gospel according to Matthew.

Jesus said, "Then the king will say to those at his right hand, 'Come, you that are blessed by my Father; for I was hungry and you gave me food, I was thirsty and you gave me something to drink, I was a stranger and you welcomed me, I was naked and you gave me clothing, I was sick and you took care of me, I was in prison and you visited me.' Then the righteous will answer him, 'Lord, when was it that we saw you hungry and gave you food? And the king will answer them, 'Truly I tell you, just as you did it to one of the least of these who are members of my family, you did it to me.'"

The Gospel of the Lord.

◆ All sit and observe silence.

FOR SILENT REFLECTION

Think about this silently in your heart. We are the hands, feet, and voice of Jesus in the world today.

CLOSING PRAYER

Let us pray to God for our needs and the needs of others: our family, neighborhood, and the world. For each need we say, "Lord, hear our prayer."

◆ All may add their own prayers here.

Let us pray: **Our Father . . . Amen.**

Jesus, there are many ways
 in which we can be your hands,
feet, and voice in the world.
Even though we are young,
we can do our part to make the world better.

Amen.

✦ All make the Sign of the Cross.

OPENING

Jesus' message is not always easy. Mercy even goes beyond forgiveness. It means being kind and forgiving even when it seems like a person doesn't deserve it. Today's Gospel message challenges our idea of fairness.

✝ All make the Sign of the Cross.

In the name of the Father, and of the Son, and of the Holy Spirit. Amen.

PSALM   (For a longer psalm, see page xiv.) Psalm 34:4–5

The LORD saves the crushed in spirit.

The LORD saves the crushed in spirit.

I sought the LORD, and he answered me,
   and delivered me from all my fears.
Look to him, and be radiant;
   so your faces shall never be ashamed.

The LORD saves the crushed in spirit.

◆ All stand and sing **Praise to you, Lord Jesus Christ . . .**

GOSPEL   Luke 6:27–30, 31–32, 35abc, 36

A reading from the holy Gospel according to Luke.

"But I say to you that listen, Love your enemies, do good to those who hate you, bless those who curse you, pray for those who abuse you. If anyone strikes you on the cheek, offer the other also; and from anyone who takes away your coat do not withhold even your shirt. Do to others as you would have them do to you. If you love those who love you, what credit is that to you? For even sinners love those who love them. But love your enemies, do good, and lend, expecting nothing in return. Your reward will be great, and you will be children of the Most High. Be merciful, just as your Father is merciful."

The Gospel of the Lord.

◆ All sit and observe silence.

FOR SILENT REFLECTION

Think about this silently in your heart. How would the world be different if people followed the message in the reading?

CLOSING PRAYER

Let us pray to God for our needs and the needs of others: our family, neighborhood, and the world. For each need we say, "Lord, hear our prayer."

◆ All may add their own prayers here.

Let us pray: **Our Father . . . Amen.**

Lord Jesus, to be your disciple is not
always easy.
You challenge us to be the best we can be.
You call us to give more
than we think we can give.
You are an excellent teacher.
For this, we give you thanks and praise.

Amen.

✝ All make the Sign of the Cross.

OPENING

There is a famous saying: "You reap what you sow." This means that what you put out is what you will get back. People often blame other people for how they are being treated without looking at their own actions.

✚ All make the Sign of the Cross.

In the name of the Father, and of the Son, and of the Holy Spirit. Amen.

PSALM   (For a longer psalm, see page xiv.) Psalm 34:4–5

The LORD saves the crushed in spirit.

The LORD saves the crushed in spirit.

I sought the LORD, and he answered me,
   and delivered me from all my fears.
Look to him, and be radiant;
   so your faces shall never be ashamed.

The LORD saves the crushed in spirit.

◆ All stand and sing **Praise to you, Lord Jesus Christ . . .**

GOSPEL   Luke 6:37–38a, 39a, 43–46

A reading from the holy Gospel according to Luke.

Jesus said, "Do not judge, and you will not be judged; do not condemn, and you will not be condemned. Forgive, and you will be forgiven; give, and it will be given to you." He also told them a parable: "No good tree bears bad fruit, nor again does a bad tree bear good fruit; for each tree is known by its own fruit. Figs are not gathered from thorns, nor are grapes picked from a bramble bush. The good person out of the good treasure of the heart produces good, and the evil person out of evil treasure produces evil; for it is out of the abundance of the heart that the mouth speaks."

The Gospel of the Lord.

◆ All sit and observe silence.

FOR SILENT REFLECTION

Think about this silently in your heart. How have you experienced the truth of today's Gospel?

CLOSING PRAYER

Let us pray to God for our needs and the needs of others: our family, neighborhood, and the world. For each need we say, "Lord, hear our prayer."

◆ All may add their own prayers here.

Let us pray: **Our Father . . . Amen.**

Dear God,
help us to act and speak
out of the goodness of our hearts.
Help us to be the person who acts and speaks
with respect for others.
We ask this in the name of Jesus Christ.

Amen.

✚ All make the Sign of the Cross.

OPENING

Jesus uses the image of a vine to describe our relationship to him and to God. A vine has many branches and every branch has many green leaves. A good vine grower takes excellent care of the vine, cutting away dead leaves so that the vine can produce healthy leaves and fruit. The word *abide* means to remain.

✦ All make the Sign of the Cross.

In the name of the Father, and of the Son, and of the Holy Spirit. Amen.

PSALM

(For a longer psalm, see page xiv.) Psalm 34:4–5

The LORD saves the crushed in spirit.

The LORD saves the crushed in spirit.

I sought the LORD, and he answered me,
    and delivered me from all my fears.
Look to him, and be radiant;
    so your faces shall never be ashamed.

The LORD saves the crushed in spirit.

✦ All stand and sing **Praise to you, Lord Jesus Christ . . .**

GOSPEL

John 15:1–6a

A reading from the holy Gospel according to John.

Jesus said, "I am the true vine, and my Father is the vine grower. He removes every branch in me that bears no fruit. Every branch that bears fruit he prunes to make it bear more fruit. You have already been cleansed by the word that I have spoken to you. Abide in me as I abide in you. Just as the branch cannot bear fruit by itself unless it abides in the vine, neither can you unless you abide in me. I am the vine, you are the branches. Those who abide in me and I in them bear much fruit, because apart from me you can do nothing. Whoever does not abide in me is thrown away like a branch and withers."

The Gospel of the Lord.

✦ All sit and observe silence.

FOR SILENT REFLECTION

Think about this silently in your heart. What helps us to stay closely connected to Jesus?

CLOSING PRAYER

Let us pray to God for our needs and the needs of others: our family, neighborhood, and the world. For each need we say, "Lord, hear our prayer."

✦ All may add their own prayers here.

Let us pray: **Our Father . . . Amen.**

Lord Jesus,
you are always present in our lives.
You abide in us.
May we do everything that helps us to abide in you.

Amen.

✦ All make the Sign of the Cross.

PRAYER FOR
FRIDAY, MARCH 29, 2019

OPENING

James was an Apostle of Jesus. After Jesus' death, James traveled and preached to the early Christian communities. In today's reading, he was helping people understand that the way they acted toward one another, not just their words, is what showed they were followers of Jesus.

✝ All make the Sign of the Cross.

In the name of the Father, and of the Son, and of the Holy Spirit. Amen.

PSALM
(For a longer psalm, see page xiv.) Psalm 34:4–5

The LORD saves the crushed in spirit.

The LORD saves the crushed in spirit.

I sought the LORD, and he answered me,
 and delivered me from all my fears.
Look to him, and be radiant;
 so your faces shall never be ashamed.

The LORD saves the crushed in spirit.

READING
James 2:14abc, 15–18c, 24, 26

A reading from the Letter of the James.

What good is it, my brothers and sisters, if you say you have faith but do not have works? If a brother or sister is naked and lacks daily food, and one of you says to them, "Go in peace; keep warm and eat your fill," and yet you do not supply their bodily needs, what is the good of that? So faith by itself, if it has no works, is dead. I by my works will show you my faith. You see that a person is justified by works and not by faith alone. For just as the body without the spirit is dead, so faith without works is also dead.

The Word of the Lord.

◆ All observe silence.

FOR SILENT REFLECTION

Think about this silently in your heart. Do you believe that actions speak louder than words?

CLOSING PRAYER

Let us pray to God for our needs and the needs of others: our family, neighborhood, and the world. For each need we say, "Lord, hear our prayer."

◆ All may add their own prayers here.

Let us pray: **Our Father . . . Amen.**

Lord Jesus,
thank you for challenging us
to think about how our actions match
our words.
Help us to show our faith through our actions.
Help us to act with compassion, fairness,
and generosity.
We ask this in your name.

Amen.

✝ All make the Sign of the Cross.

PRAYER FOR THE WEEK

WITH A READING FROM THE GOSPEL FOR **SUNDAY, MARCH 31, 2019**

OPENING

Today's Gospel is about a father's love and forgiveness. What does the younger son do with the money his father gives him? Do you think he is wise or foolish? How does the father greet him when he returns?

✝ All make the Sign of the Cross.

In the name of the Father, and of the Son, and of the Holy Spirit. Amen.

PSALM

(For a longer psalm, see page xiv.) Psalm 34:4–5

The LORD saves the crushed in spirit.

The LORD saves the crushed in spirit.

I sought the LORD, and he answered me,
    and delivered me from all my fears.
Look to him, and be radiant;
    so your faces shall never be ashamed.

The LORD saves the crushed in spirit.

◆ All stand and sing **Praise to you, Lord Jesus Christ . . .**

GOSPEL

Luke 15:11–13, 14c, 17ab, 20bd

A reading from the holy Gospel according to Luke.

Then Jesus said, "There was a man who had two sons. The younger of them said to his father, 'Father, give me the share of the property that will belong to me.' So the father divided his property between the sons. A few days later the younger son gathered all he had and traveled to a distant country, and there he squandered his property in dissolute living. He began to be in need. But when he came to himself he said, 'How many of my father's hired hands have bread enough and to spare. I will get up and go to my father, and I will say to him, "Father, I have sinned against heaven and before you."' But while he was still far off, his father ran and put his arms around him and kissed him."

The Gospel of the Lord.

◆ All sit and observe silence.

FOR SILENT REFLECTION

Think about this silently in your heart. Were you surprised the father ran to greet his son and kissed him after what the son had done?

CLOSING PRAYER

Let us pray to God for our needs and the needs of others: our family, neighborhood, and the world. For each need we say, "Lord, hear our prayer."

◆ All may add their own prayers here.

Let us pray: **Our Father . . . Amen.**

Dear God,
no matter how far we stray from you,
you are always willing to welcome us home.
We thank you for your faithful love.

Amen.

✝ All make the Sign of the Cross.

PRAYER FOR
MONDAY, APRIL 1, 2019

OPENING

In Jesus' time, Jewish people and Samaritan people were bitter enemies. Neither Jews nor Samaritans would stop to help the other or do a kindness for the other. Jesus was different. Jesus' message that he is the Messiah (the one sent by God to bring light to the world) is for all peoples.

✜ All make the Sign of the Cross.

In the name of the Father, and of the Son, and of the Holy Spirit. Amen.

PSALM   (For a longer psalm, see page xiv.) Psalm 34:4–5

The LORD saves the crushed in spirit.

The LORD saves the crushed in spirit.

I sought the LORD, and he answered me,
  and delivered me from all my fears.
Look to him, and be radiant;
  so your faces shall never be ashamed.

The LORD saves the crushed in spirit.

◆ All stand and sing **Praise to you, Lord Jesus Christ . . .**

GOSPEL   John 4:7–10, 11c, 14b, 15, 19, 25bc, 26

A reading from the holy Gospel according to John.

A Samaritan woman came to draw water, and Jesus said to her, "Give me a drink." The Samaritan woman said to him, "How is it that you, a Jew, ask a drink of me, a woman of Samaria?" Jesus answered her, "If you knew the gift of God, and who it is that is saying to you, 'Give me a drink,' you would have asked him, and he would have given you living water." The woman said to him, "Where do you get that living water?" Jesus said to her, "The water that I will give will become in them a spring of water gushing up to eternal life." The woman said to him, "Sir, I see that you are a prophet. I know that Messiah is coming" (who is called Christ). "When he comes, he will proclaim all things to us." Jesus said to her, "I am he, the one who is speaking to you."

The Gospel of the Lord.

◆ All sit and observe silence.

FOR SILENT REFLECTION

Think about this silently in your heart. Where do you see the face of Jesus in your life?

CLOSING PRAYER

Let us pray to God for our needs and the needs of others: our family, neighborhood, and the world. For each need we say, "Lord, hear our prayer."

◆ All may add their own prayers here.

Let us pray: **Our Father . . . Amen.**

Dear God,
open our eyes so that we recognize Jesus
in the faces of all people.
We ask this in the name of Jesus Christ.

Amen.

✜ All make the Sign of the Cross.

OPENING

Today's Gospel tells about Jesus restoring the sight of a blind man. In Scripture, blindness does not mean only physical blindness but a lack of awareness or understanding about God.

✚ All make the Sign of the Cross.

In the name of the Father, and of the Son, and of the Holy Spirit. Amen.

PSALM
(For a longer psalm, see page xiv.) Psalm 34:4–5

The LORD saves the crushed in spirit.

The LORD saves the crushed in spirit.

I sought the LORD, and he answered me,
    and delivered me from all my fears.
Look to him, and be radiant;
    so your faces shall never be ashamed.

The LORD saves the crushed in spirit.

◆ All stand and sing **Praise to you, Lord Jesus Christ . . .**

GOSPEL
John 9:1–2, 5–6b, 7abd, 35b, 38

A reading from the holy Gospel according to John.

As Jesus walked along, he saw a man blind from birth. His disciples asked him, "Rabbi, who sinned, this man or his parents, that he was born blind?" Jesus answered, "Neither this man nor his parents sinned; he was born blind so that God's works might be revealed in him. As long as I am in the world, I am the light of the world." He spat on the ground and made mud with the saliva and spread the mud on the man's eyes saying to him, "Go, wash in the pool of Siloam." Then the man went and washed and came back able to see. Jesus said, "Do you believe in the Son of Man?" He said, "Lord, I believe." And he worshiped him.

The Gospel of the Lord.

◆ All sit and observe silence.

FOR SILENT REFLECTION

Think about this silently in your heart. How are you blind at times?

CLOSING PRAYER

Let us pray to God for our needs and the needs of others: our family, neighborhood, and the world. For each need we say, "Lord, hear our prayer."

◆ All may add their own prayers here.

Let us pray: **Our Father . . . Amen.**

Lord Jesus,
help us to recognize our blindness.
Open our eyes.
Help us to see the needs of world around us.
Help us to see the goodness in others.
Lord, cure our "blindness."

Amen.

✚ All make the Sign of the Cross.

PRAYER FOR
WEDNESDAY, APRIL 3, 2019

OPENING

Martha and her brother Lazarus were Jesus' good friends. When Lazarus becomes ill and dies, Martha calls for Jesus to come. Before Jesus raises Lazarus from the dead, he asks Martha if she believes that he is "the resurrection and the life." In faith, Martha declares that Jesus is the Messiah.

✠ All make the Sign of the Cross.

In the name of the Father, and of the Son, and of the Holy Spirit. Amen.

PSALM   (For a longer psalm, see page xiv.) Psalm 34:4–5

The LORD saves the crushed in spirit.

The LORD saves the crushed in spirit.

I sought the LORD, and he answered me,
    and delivered me from all my fears.
Look to him, and be radiant;
    so your faces shall never be ashamed.

The LORD saves the crushed in spirit.

◆ All stand and sing **Praise to you, Lord Jesus Christ . . .**

GOSPEL   John 11:17, 20ab, 21, 23–25, 38ac, 43bc, 44

A reading from the holy Gospel according to John.

When Jesus arrived, he found that Lazarus had already been in the tomb four days. When Martha heard that Jesus was coming, she went and met him. Martha said to Jesus, "Lord, if you had been here, my brother would not have died. Jesus said to her, "Your brother will rise again." Martha said to him, "I know that he will rise again in the resurrection on the last day." Jesus said to her, "I am the resurrection and the life. Those who believe in me, even though they die, will live." Then Jesus came to the tomb. Jesus cried with a loud voice, "Lazarus, come out!" The dead man came out, his hands and feet bound with strips of cloth, and his face wrapped in a cloth. Jesus said to them, "Unbind him, and let him go."

The Gospel of the Lord.

◆ All sit and observe silence.

FOR SILENT REFLECTION

Think about this silently in your heart. Why does Jesus say that he is "the resurrection and the life"?

CLOSING PRAYER

Let us pray to God for our needs and the needs of others: our family, neighborhood, and the world. For each need we say, "Lord, hear our prayer."

◆ All may add their own prayers here.

Let us pray: **Our Father . . . Amen.**

Lord Jesus,
help all who grieve the loss
of someone they love.
In your name, we pray.

Amen.

✠ All make the Sign of the Cross.

OPENING

People in the early Church faced challenges because Christianity was not popular with the Roman authorities and many Jewish people. The Apostle John wrote letters of encouragement. In today's reading, he reminds people of God's love for them, and their responsibility to follow God's commandments.

✝ All make the Sign of the Cross.

In the name of the Father, and of the Son, and of the Holy Spirit. Amen.

PSALM
(For a longer psalm, see page xiv.) Psalm 34:4–5

The LORD saves the crushed in spirit.

The LORD saves the crushed in spirit.

I sought the LORD, and he answered me,
    and delivered me from all my fears.
Look to him, and be radiant;
    so your faces shall never be ashamed.

The LORD saves the crushed in spirit.

READING
1 John 2:1–5

A reading from the First Letter of John.

My little children, I am writing these things to you so that you may not sin. But if anyone does sin, we have an advocate with the Father, Jesus Christ the righteous; and he is the atoning sacrifice for our sins, and not for ours only but also for the sins of the whole world. Now by this we may be sure that we know him, if we obey his commandments. Whoever says, "I have come to know him," but does not obey his commandments, is a liar, and in such a person the truth does not exist; but whoever obeys his word, truly in this person the love of God has reached perfection. By this we may be sure that we are in him: whoever says, "I abide in him," ought to walk just as he walked.

The Word of the Lord.

◆ All observe silence.

FOR SILENT REFLECTION

Think about this silently in your heart. What is something you can do today that would be like something Jesus would do?

CLOSING PRAYER

Let us pray to God for our needs and the needs of others: our family, neighborhood, and the world. For each need we say, "Lord, hear our prayer."

◆ All may add their own prayers here.

Let us pray: **Our Father . . . Amen.**

Loving God,
help us to follow your commands.
We give thanks for our Church
and all the people in our lives
who help us to know and follow Jesus.

Amen.

✝ All make the Sign of the Cross.

OPENING

This week we have heard stories about works that Jesus did. God sent us Jesus to show us how to live. To imitate means "to follow someone else's example." Sometimes it is difficult to imitate or follow Jesus. Hopefully, our Lenten practices are helping us grow stronger and more able to act like a follower of Jesus.

✜ All make the Sign of the Cross.

In the name of the Father, and of the Son, and of the Holy Spirit. Amen.

PSALM   (For a longer psalm, see page xiv.) Psalm 34:4–5

The LORD saves the crushed in spirit.

The LORD saves the crushed in spirit.

I sought the LORD, and he answered me,
  and delivered me from all my fears.
Look to him, and be radiant;
  so your faces shall never be ashamed.

The LORD saves the crushed in spirit.

READING   Ephesians 4:25b–26, 28–29, 32; 5:1–2ab

A reading from the Letter of Paul to Ephesians [ee-FEE-zhuhns].

Let all of us speak the truth to our neighbors, for we are members of one another. Be angry but do not sin; do not let the sun go down on your anger. Thieves must give up stealing; rather let them labor and work honestly with their own hands, so as to have something to share with the needy. Let no evil talk come out of your mouths, but only what is useful for building up, as there is need, so that your words may give grace to those who hear. And be kind to one another, tenderhearted, forgiving one another, as God in Christ has forgiven you. Therefore be imitators of God, as beloved children, and live in love, as Christ loved us and gave himself up for us.

The Word of the Lord.

◆ All observe silence.

FOR SILENT REFLECTION

Think about this silently in your heart. What Lenten practice is helping you grow stronger in your faith?

CLOSING PRAYER

Let us pray to God for our needs and the needs of others: our family, neighborhood, and the world. For each need we say, "Lord, hear our prayer."

◆ All may add their own prayers here.

Let us pray: **Our Father . . . Amen.**

Loving God,
help us to speak kindly and truthfully.
Help us to respect others.
Help us to forgive as you forgive us.
We ask this in the name of Jesus Christ.

Amen.

✜ All make the Sign of the Cross.

PRAYER FOR THE WEEK

WITH A READING FROM THE GOSPEL FOR **SUNDAY, APRIL 7, 2019**

OPENING

Jesus acted differently than many religious leaders of his time. In the Gospel today we hear how Jesus refuses to let people punish a woman accused of breaking a religious law. Jesus doesn't condemn her, but asks her to change her actions. Jesus accepted sinners and showed God's mercy to them.

✝ All make the Sign of the Cross.

In the name of the Father, and of the Son, and of the Holy Spirit. Amen.

PSALM

(For a longer psalm, see page xiv.) Psalm 34:4–5

The LORD saves the crushed in spirit.

The LORD saves the crushed in spirit.

I sought the LORD, and he answered me,
and delivered me from all my fears.
Look to him, and be radiant;
so your faces shall never be ashamed.

The LORD saves the crushed in spirit.

◆ All stand and sing **Praise to you, Lord Jesus Christ . . .**

GOSPEL

John 8:3a, 4–5, 6c–7, 9abe, 10abd, 11ab

A reading from the holy Gospel according to John.

The scribes and the Pharisees brought a woman who had been caught in adultery. They said to Jesus, "Teacher, this woman was caught in the very act of committing adultery. Now in the law Moses commanded us to stone such women. Now what do you say?" Jesus bent down and wrote with his finger on the ground. When they kept on questioning him, he straightened up and said to them, "Let anyone among you who is without sin be the first to throw a stone at her." When they heard it, they went away and Jesus was left alone with the woman standing before him. Jesus straightened up and said to her, "Woman, has no one condemned you?" She said, "No one, sir." And Jesus said, "Neither do I condemn you."

The Gospel of the Lord.

◆ All sit and observe silence.

FOR SILENT REFLECTION

Think about this silently in your heart. How do you think the woman felt when Jesus protected her?

CLOSING PRAYER

Let us pray to God for our needs and the needs of others: our family, neighborhood, and the world. For each need we say, "Lord, hear our prayer."

◆ All may add their own prayers here.

Let us pray: **Our Father . . . Amen.**

Merciful God,
when we do something wrong,
you do not condemn us.
You ask us to change our ways.
For this, we humbly give you thanks
and praise.

Amen.

✝ All make the Sign of the Cross.

PRAYER FOR
MONDAY, APRIL 8, 2019

OPENING

We are now in the fifth week of Lent. This week we follow Jesus through his passion and death. The word *passion* comes for the Latin word that means "to suffer." Judas is the disciple of Jesus who betrayed him for a bag of money.

✚ All make the Sign of the Cross.

In the name of the Father, and of the Son, and of the Holy Spirit. Amen.

PSALM   (For a longer psalm, see page xiv.) Psalm 34:4–5

The LORD saves the crushed in spirit.

The LORD saves the crushed in spirit.

I sought the LORD, and he answered me,
    and delivered me from all my fears.
Look to him, and be radiant;
    so your faces shall never be ashamed.

The LORD saves the crushed in spirit.

◆ All stand and sing **Praise to you, Lord Jesus Christ . . .**

GOSPEL   Luke 22:1–8

A reading from the holy Gospel according to Luke.

Now the festival of Unleavened Bread, which is called the Passover, was near. The chief priests and the scribes were looking for a way to put Jesus to death, for they were afraid of the people. Then Satan entered into Judas called Iscariot, who was one of the twelve; he went away and conferred with the chief priests and officers of the temple police about how he might betray Jesus to them. They were greatly pleased and agreed to give him money. So he consented and began to look for an opportunity to betray Jesus to them when no crowd was present. Then came the day of Unleavened Bread, on which the Passover lamb had to be sacrificed. So Jesus sent Peter and John, saying, "Go and prepare the Passover meal for us that we may eat it."

The Gospel of the Lord.

◆ All sit and observe silence.

FOR SILENT REFLECTION

Think about this silently in your heart. It is hard when a friend betrays you. If that happens, it is helpful to pray about how to respond.

CLOSING PRAYER

Let us pray to God for our needs and the needs of others: our family, neighborhood, and the world. For each need we say, "Lord, hear our prayer."

◆ All may add their own prayers here.

Let us pray: **Our Father . . . Amen.**

Holy Spirit God,
help us to be faithful to our friends.
Help us to see Christ in one another.

Amen.

✚ All make the Sign of the Cross.

OPENING

Passover is one of the most important religious festivals in the Jewish calendar. Passover commemorates the liberation of the Jewish people from slavery in Egypt. Jews have celebrated Passover since about 1300 BC. At the Passover celebration before Jesus was arrested, he did something he had never done before.

✚ All make the Sign of the Cross.

In the name of the Father, and of the Son, and of the Holy Spirit. Amen.

PSALM
(For a longer psalm, see page xiv.) Psalm 34:4–5

The LORD saves the crushed in spirit.

The LORD saves the crushed in spirit.

I sought the LORD, and he answered me,
and delivered me from all my fears.
Look to him, and be radiant;
so your faces shall never be ashamed.

The LORD saves the crushed in spirit.

◆ All stand and sing **Praise to you, Lord Jesus Christ . . .**

GOSPEL
Luke 22:14–15, 17–20

A reading from the holy Gospel according to Luke.

When the hour came, Jesus took his place at the table, and the apostles with him. He said to them, "I have eagerly desired to eat this Passover with you before I suffer." Then he took a cup, and after giving thanks he said, "Take this and divide it among yourselves; for I tell you that from now on I will not drink of the fruit of the vine until the kingdom of God comes." Then he took a loaf of bread, and when he had given thanks, he broke it and gave it to them, saying, "This is my body, which is given for you. Do this in remembrance of me." And he did the same with the cup after supper, saying, "This cup that is poured out for you is the new covenant in my blood."

The Gospel of the Lord.

◆ All sit and observe silence.

FOR SILENT REFLECTION

Think about this silently in your heart. Where do you hear the words that Jesus said at the Passover meal?

CLOSING PRAYER

Let us pray to God for our needs and the needs of others: our family, neighborhood, and the world. For each need we say, "Lord, hear our prayer."

◆ All may add their own prayers here.

Let us pray: **Our Father . . . Amen.**

Lord God, at every Mass, we recall the Last Supper that Jesus had with his disciples.
He promised to be with them and with us forever. We are happy and grateful to receive Jesus
every time we receive Holy Communion.

Amen.

✚ All make the Sign of the Cross.

OPENING

After the Passover meal, Jesus goes to the Mount of Olives to pray. Jesus knows that what lies ahead for him will be difficult, but he accepts God's will.

✝ All make the Sign of the Cross.

In the name of the Father, and of the Son, and of the Holy Spirit. Amen.

PSALM (For a longer psalm, see page xiv.) Psalm 34:4–5

The LORD saves the crushed in spirit.

The LORD saves the crushed in spirit.

I sought the LORD, and he answered me,
 and delivered me from all my fears.
Look to him, and be radiant;
 so your faces shall never be ashamed.

The LORD saves the crushed in spirit.

◆ All stand and sing **Praise to you, Lord Jesus Christ . . .**

GOSPEL Luke 22:39–44

A reading from the holy Gospel according to Luke.

Jesus came out and went, as was his custom, to the Mount of Olives; and the disciples followed him. When he reached the place, he said to them, "Pray that you may not come into the time of trial." Then he withdrew from them about a stone's throw, knelt down, and prayed, "Father, if you are willing, remove this cup from me; yet, not my will but yours be done." Then an angel from heaven appeared to him and gave him strength. In his anguish he prayed more earnestly, and his sweat became like great drops of blood falling down on the ground.

The Gospel of the Lord.

◆ All sit and observe silence.

FOR SILENT REFLECTION

Think about this silently in your heart. Have you had times when you felt alone and afraid? Even in those times, God is with you.

CLOSING PRAYER

Let us pray to God for our needs and the needs of others: our family, neighborhood, and the world. For each need we say, "Lord, hear our prayer."

◆ All may add their own prayers here.

Let us pray: **Our Father . . . Amen.**

Dear God, help us to turn to you in prayer when we are afraid or worried.
Praying to you can give us strength and calm our fears.
We know that you love us and want the best for us.
Help us to always trust in you.

Amen.

✝ All make the Sign of the Cross.

OPENING

Today is the feast of St. Stanislaus, who is the patron saint of Poland. He lived in the eleventh century and was known for his compassionate concern for the poor. In today's reading, Judas betrays Jesus with a kiss.

✚ All make the Sign of the Cross.

In the name of the Father, and of the Son, and of the Holy Spirit. Amen.

PSALM   (For a longer psalm, see page xiv.) Psalm 34:4–5

The LORD saves the crushed in spirit.

The LORD saves the crushed in spirit.

I sought the LORD, and he answered me,
  and delivered me from all my fears.
Look to him, and be radiant;
  so your faces shall never be ashamed.

The LORD saves the crushed in spirit.

◆ All stand and sing **Praise to you, Lord Jesus Christ . . .**

GOSPEL   Luke 22:47bcef, 48–52abcd, 54

A reading from the holy Gospel according to Luke.

Suddenly a crowd came, and the one called Judas was leading them. He approached Jesus to kiss him; but Jesus said to him, "Judas, is it with a kiss that you are betraying the Son of Man?" When those who were around him saw what was coming, they asked, "Lord, should we strike with the sword?" Then one of them struck the slave of the high priest and cut off his right ear. But Jesus said, "No more of this!" And he touched his ear and healed him. Then Jesus said to the chief priests, the officers of the temple police, and the elders who had come for him, "Have you come out with swords and clubs as if I were a bandit?" Then they seized Jesus and led him away, bringing him into the high priest's house.

The Gospel of the Lord.

◆ All sit and observe silence.

FOR SILENT REFLECTION

Think about this silently in your heart. How did Jesus respond to the violence of his followers?

CLOSING PRAYER

Let us pray to God for our needs and the needs of others: our family, neighborhood, and the world. For each need we say, "Lord, hear our prayer."

◆ All may add their own prayers here.

Let us pray: **Our Father . . . Amen.**

Lord God,
Help us to follow the example of Jesus.
Help us find a nonviolent way to react
to stressful events and violence.
We ask this in the name of Jesus Christ.

Amen.

✚ All make the Sign of the Cross.

PRAYER FOR
FRIDAY, APRIL 12, 2019

OPENING

Peter was the leader of Jesus' Apostles. After he saw what Judas had done, Peter pledged to Jesus that he would never betray him. Today's reading tells the story of what happened when Peter was put to the test.

✛ All make the Sign of the Cross.

In the name of the Father, and of the Son, and of the Holy Spirit. Amen.

PSALM
(For a longer psalm, see page xiv.) Psalm 34:4–5

The LORD saves the crushed in spirit.

The LORD saves the crushed in spirit.

I sought the LORD, and he answered me,
    and delivered me from all my fears.
Look to him, and be radiant;
    so your faces shall never be ashamed.

The LORD saves the crushed in spirit.

◆ All stand and sing **Praise to you, Lord Jesus Christ . . .**

GOSPEL
Luke 22:55–56acd, 57a, 58acd, 59ac, 61–62

A reading from the holy Gospel according to Luke.

Peter was following at a distance. When they had kindled a fire in the middle of the courtyard and sat down together, Peter sat among them. Then a servant-girl, stared at him and said, "This man also was with Jesus." But Peter denied it. A little later someone else said, "You also are one of them." But Peter said, "Man, I am not!" Then about an hour later still another kept insisting, "Surely this man also was with him." But Peter said, "Man, I do not know what you are talking about!" At that moment, the cock crowed. The Lord turned and looked at Peter. Then Peter remembered the word of the Lord, "Before the cock crows today, you will deny me three times." And he went out and wept bitterly.

The Gospel of the Lord.

◆ All sit and observe silence.

FOR SILENT REFLECTION

Think about this silently in your heart. Have you ever failed to defend a friend because you were afraid?

CLOSING PRAYER

Let us pray to God for our needs and the needs of others: our family, neighborhood, and the world. For each need we say, "Lord, hear our prayer."

◆ All may add their own prayers here.

Let us pray: **Our Father . . . Amen.**

Lord God, being a follower of Jesus
is not always easy.
Give us strength to be good Christians
and to speak up and stand up for what is right.
We ask this in the name of Jesus Christ.

Amen.

✛ All make the Sign of the Cross.

OPENING

Today is Palm Sunday. During this week, we will remember Jesus' Last Supper with his disciples, and his passion and death. On Palm Sunday, we celebrate Jesus' entrance into the city of Jerusalem, the holy city where Jews came from all over Israel to celebrate the Passover with their families and friends.

✚ All make the Sign of the Cross.

In the name of the Father, and of the Son, and of the Holy Spirit. Amen.

PSALM   (For a longer psalm, see page xiv.) Psalm 34:4–5

The LORD saves the crushed in spirit.

The LORD saves the crushed in spirit.

I sought the LORD, and he answered me,
   and delivered me from all my fears.
Look to him, and be radiant;
   so your faces shall never be ashamed.

The LORD saves the crushed in spirit.

◆ All stand and sing **Praise to you, Lord Jesus Christ . . .**

GOSPEL   Luke 19:28b–29a, 29d–30, 35–36, 37–38a

A reading from the holy Gospel according to Luke.

Jesus went on ahead, going up to Jerusalem. When he had come near Bethpage and Bethany, he sent two of the disciples, saying, "Go into the village ahead of you, and as you enter it you will find tied there a colt that has never been ridden. Untie it and bring it here." Then they brought it to Jesus; and after throwing their cloaks on the colt, they set Jesus on it. As he rode along, people kept spreading their cloaks on the road. As he was now approaching the path down from the Mount of Olives, the whole multitude of the disciples began to praise God joyfully with a loud voice for all the deeds of power that they had seen, saying, "Blessed is the king who comes in the name of the Lord!"

The Gospel of the Lord.

◆ All sit and observe silence.

FOR SILENT REFLECTION

Think about this silently in your heart. How can we welcome Jesus into our hearts today?

CLOSING PRAYER

Let us pray to God for our needs and the needs of others: our family, neighborhood, and the world. For each need we say, "Lord, hear our prayer."

◆ All may add their own prayers here.

Let us pray: **Our Father . . . Amen.**

Lord Jesus, we give praise and thanks
for your teachings.
Help us follow your way of love and sacrifice.
We ask this in your name.

Amen.

✚ All make the Sign of the Cross.

PRAYER FOR
MONDAY, APRIL 15, 2019

OPENING

Today we begin to hear of the trials of Jesus. The religious leaders felt threatened because Jesus was gaining so many followers. They take Jesus to the Roman governor, Pilate, and accuse him of religious crimes. Pilate won't declare Jesus guilty but sends him to the Jewish King Herod.

✚ All make the Sign of the Cross.

In the name of the Father, and of the Son, and of the Holy Spirit. Amen.

PSALM   (For a longer psalm, see page xiv.) Psalm 34:4–5

The LORD saves the crushed in spirit.

The LORD saves the crushed in spirit.

I sought the LORD, and he answered me,
    and delivered me from all my fears.
Look to him, and be radiant;
    so your faces shall never be ashamed.

The LORD saves the crushed in spirit.

◆ All stand and sing **Praise to you, Lord Jesus Christ . . .**

GOSPEL   Luke 23:1–2abd, 4, 7b, 8abd, 9a, 11ac, 12a

A reading from the holy Gospel according to Luke.

Then the assembly rose as a body and brought Jesus before Pilate. They began to accuse him, saying, "We found this man perverting our nation, and saying that he himself is the Messiah, a king." Then Pilate asked him, "Are you the king of the Jews?" Jesus answered, "You say so." Then Pilate said to the chief priests and the crowds, "I find no basis for an accusation against this man." Pilate sent him off to Herod. When Herod saw Jesus, he was very glad, because he had heard about him and was hoping to see him perform some sign. He questioned him at some length. Even Herod with his soldiers treated him with contempt and mocked him and sent him back to Pilate. That same day Herod and Pilate became friends with each other.

The Gospel of the Lord.

◆ All sit and observe silence.

FOR SILENT REFLECTION

Think about this silently in your heart. Even though Pilate and Herod did not believe Jesus was guilty of any crime, they refused to defend him. Why?

CLOSING PRAYER

Let us pray to God for our needs and the needs of others: our family, neighborhood, and the world. For each need we say, "Lord, hear our prayer."

◆ All may add their own prayers here.

Let us pray: **Our Father . . . Amen.**

Lord God, our world needs leaders who will stand up for the rights of the innocent. Send your Spirit to guide our leaders. We ask this in the name of Jesus Christ.

Amen.

✚ All make the Sign of the Cross.

OPENING

Pilate knew Jesus was not guilty of any crimes and tried again to satisfy the crowd by having him whipped. But others insisted Jesus be crucified. Crucifixion was a terrible Roman punishment used for people who were rebels or had committed other very serious crimes.

✦ All make the Sign of the Cross.

In the name of the Father, and of the Son, and of the Holy Spirit. Amen.

PSALM   (For a longer psalm, see page xiv.) Psalm 34:4–5

The Lord saves the crushed in spirit.

The Lord saves the crushed in spirit.

I sought the Lord, and he answered me,
    and delivered me from all my fears.
Look to him, and be radiant;
    so your faces shall never be ashamed.

The Lord saves the crushed in spirit.

◆ All stand and sing **Praise to you, Lord Jesus Christ . . .**

GOSPEL   Luke 23:13ac, 14–16, 22ab, 23–24

A reading from the holy Gospel according to Luke.

Pilate then called together the chief priests and the people, and said to them, "You brought me this man as one who was perverting the people; and here I have examined him in your presence and have not found this man guilty of any of your charges against him. Neither has Herod, for he sent him back to us. Indeed, he has done nothing to deserve death. I will therefore have him flogged and release him." But they kept shouting, "Crucify, crucify him!" He said to them, "Why, what evil has he done?" But they kept urgently demanding with loud shouts that Jesus should be crucified; and their voices prevailed. So Pilate gave his verdict that their demand should be granted.

The Gospel of the Lord.

◆ All sit and observe silence.

FOR SILENT REFLECTION

Think about this silently in your heart. Do you have the courage to speak up for what is right?

CLOSING PRAYER

Let us pray to God for our needs and the needs of others: our family, neighborhood, and the world. For each need we say, "Lord, hear our prayer."

◆ All may add their own prayers here.

Let us pray: **Our Father . . . Amen.**

Lord God, give us the courage
to speak out when we see injustice.
Help us to stand up
when we see people treated badly.
We ask this in the name of Jesus Christ.

Amen.

✦ All make the Sign of the Cross.

PRAYER FOR
WEDNESDAY, APRIL 17, 2019

OPENING

Crucifixion was a humiliating, painful way to die. Jesus was whipped and made to carry his cross to the place where he would be crucified. The Roman guards were afraid Jesus was too weak to make it, so they called a man to help him. Even with all that was done to him, Jesus still said, "Father, forgive them."

✦ All make the Sign of the Cross.

In the name of the Father, and of the Son, and of the Holy Spirit. Amen.

PSALM   (For a longer psalm, see page xiv.) Psalm 34:4–5

The Lord saves the crushed in spirit.

The Lord saves the crushed in spirit.

I sought the Lord, and he answered me,
   and delivered me from all my fears.
Look to him, and be radiant;
   so your faces shall never be ashamed.

The Lord saves the crushed in spirit.

◆ All stand and sing **Praise to you, Lord Jesus Christ . . .**

GOSPEL   Luke 23:26abcef, 32-34ab, 35ab, 36–38

A reading from the holy Gospel according to Luke.

As they led Jesus away, they seized a man, Simon of Cyrene, and they laid the cross on him, and made him carry it behind Jesus. Two others also, who were criminals, were led away to be put to death with him. When they came to the place that is called The Skull, they crucified Jesus there with the criminals, one on his right and one on his left. Then Jesus said, "Father, forgive them." And the people stood by, watching; but the leaders scoffed at him. The soldiers also mocked him, coming up and offering him sour wine, and saying, "If you are the King of the Jews, save yourself!" There was also an inscription over him, "This is the King of the Jews."

The Gospel of the Lord.

◆ All sit and observe silence.

FOR SILENT REFLECTION

Think about this silently in your heart. Say a prayer for someone who has hurt you.

CLOSING PRAYER

Let us pray to God for our needs and the needs of others: our family, neighborhood, and the world. For each need we say, "Lord, hear our prayer."

◆ All may add their own prayers here.

Let us pray: **Our Father . . . Amen.**

To be followers of Jesus,
we must stand up for what is unfair and unjust.
Please give us courage.
We ask this in the name of Jesus Christ.

Amen.

✦ All make the Sign of the Cross.

Before you begin, find the reading (John 13:3–5) in your Bible, ask for a volunteer to read it, and help the reader to practice reading it a few times. You could begin with a simple song, such as "Jesus, Remember Me," or "Amen." (We don't sing "Alleluia" until the Easter Vigil.) An older child or adult reads the leader parts.

LEADER

Today is Holy Thursday, and this evening we will remember two important things that Jesus did for his disciples and for us. On this night of the Last Supper, Jesus offered himself in the form of bread and wine and said, "This is my Body. . . . This is my Blood. Do this in memory of me." Later, he washed the feet of his followers, teaching them by example of how we must be a servant for all.

✝ All make the Sign of the Cross.

In the name of the Father, and of the Son, and of the Holy Spirit. Amen.

LEADER: Psalm 27:1, 4, 5, 11, 13–14

Let us repeat the Psalm Response:
Teach me your way, O LORD.

ALL: Teach me your way, O LORD.

The LORD is my light and my salvation;
  whom shall I fear?
The LORD is the stronghold of my life;
  of whom shall I be afraid?

ALL: Teach me your way, O LORD.

One thing I asked of the LORD,
  that will I seek after:
to live in the house of the LORD
  all the days of my life,
to behold the beauty of the LORD,
  and to inquire in his temple.

ALL: Teach me your way, O LORD.

I believe that I shall see the goodness
    of the LORD
  in the land of the living.
Wait for the LORD;
  be strong, and let your heart take courage;
  wait for the LORD!

ALL: Teach me your way, O LORD.

◆ All stand and sing **Praise to you, Lord Jesus Christ** . . .

LEADER: John 13:3–5
A reading from the holy Gospel according to John.

◆ Read the Gospel passage from the Bible.

The Gospel of the Lord.

◆ All sit and observe silence.

FOR SILENT REFLECTION
Why did Jesus, the disciples' leader, wish to be their servant?

LEADER:
Let us pray as Jesus taught us:

Our Father . . . Amen.

LEADER:
Almighty God,
we remember Jesus's
act of service of washing his friends' feet.
May we honor you with
our acts of love today and always.
We ask this through Christ our Lord.

ALL: Amen.

✝ All make the Sign of the Cross.

CHILDREN'S DAILY PRAYER 2018–2019 © 2018 Archdiocese of Chicago: Liturgy Training Publications, 3949 South Racine Avenue, Chicago IL 60609. All rights reserved. Orders: 800-933-1800 or www.LTP.org. Scripture excerpts are taken from The New Revised Standard Version Bible: Catholic Edition, © 1989, Division of Christian Education of the National Council of the Churches of Christ in the United States of America. Used with permission. All rights reserved.

HOME PRAYER
GOOD FRIDAY

Before you begin, find the reading (John 18:33–37) in your Bible, ask for a volunteer to read it, and help the reader to practice it a few times. You could begin with a simple song, such as "Jesus, Remember Me," or "Amen." (We don't sing "Alleluia" until the Easter Vigil.) An older child or adult reads the leader parts.

LEADER:

Today we remember Jesus' anguish and Death on the Cross. It is a sad time we don't understand. But Good Friday is also a day that we recall the goodness of God's Son who chose to die so that he could save us from sin and death. This day gives us so much hope because of the promise of new life!

✚ All make the Sign of the Cross.

In the name of the Father, and of the Son, and of the Holy Spirit. Amen.

LEADER: Psalm 31:1, 2, 5a, 14–16, 21

Let us repeat the Psalm Response:
Into your hand I commit my spirit.

ALL: Into your hand I commit my spirit.

In you, O LORD, I seek refuge;
   do not let me ever be put to shame;
   in your righteousness deliver me.
Incline your ear to me;
   rescue me speedily.
Be a rock of refuge for me,
   a strong fortress to save me.

ALL: Into your hand I commit my spirit.

Blessed be the LORD,
   for he has wondrously shown his steadfast
      love to me
when I was beset as a city under siege.

ALL: Into your hand I commit my spirit.

◆ All stand and sing **Praise to you, Lord Jesus Christ . . .**

LEADER: John 18:33–37

A reading from the holy Gospel according to John

◆ Read the Gospel passage from the Bible.

The Gospel of the Lord.

◆ All sit and observe silence.

LEADER:

As I reflect on Jesus' love for me, how can I thank him?

LEADER:

Let us pray as Jesus taught us:

Our Father . . . Amen.

LEADER:

Today we remember Jesus' great love. Help us to honor him with our lives. We ask this in the name of the Father, the Son, and the Holy Spirit.

ALL: Amen.

CHILDREN'S DAILY PRAYER 2018–2019 © 2018 Archdiocese of Chicago: Liturgy Training Publications, 3949 South Racine Avenue, Chicago IL 60609. All rights reserved. Orders: 800-933-1800 or www.LTP.org. Scripture excerpts are taken from *The New Revised Standard Version Bible: Catholic Edition*, © 1989, Division of Christian Education of the National Council of the Churches of Christ in the United States of America. Used with permission. All rights reserved.

EASTER TIME

SUNDAY, APRIL 21 — SUNDAY, JUNE 9

EASTER

THE MEANING OF EASTER

The heart of Easter lies in the word "covenant." A covenant is an agreement or contract between two parties. The History of Salvation is the story of God's Covenant with his people. God promised to provide and care for humankind, and humankind's response was to return God's love and follow God's teachings to care for one another and all creation. In the Old Testament, God made covenants with Noah, Abraham and Moses. In the New Testament, Jesus is the new covenant: "Whoever believes in me will never be thirsty" (John 6:35). With Jesus' Resurrection, God promises that the covenant of love will extend to all peoples for all time.

The Prayer for the Week will reflect the Sunday Gospels, but during the week we will again "walk through the Bible." Scripture stories tell us of people throughout history from King David and the Israelites, to the people of Jesus' time, to St. Paul and the early Christians who believed that faith and trust in God helped them to live joyfully in spite of difficulties. As we read the stories of Jesus' appearances to his disciples after the Resurrection, we can reflect on how Jesus is always present in our lives. We will read stories of St. Paul and the early Christians who carried Jesus' teachings to people in many lands.

The Easter Season ends with the wonderful celebration of Pentecost. After Jesus died, his disciples were filled with fear and confusion. Jesus promised that he would send the Spirit to strengthen them. On Pentecost, we celebrate the Holy Spirit who strengthened the disciples. This same Spirit fills us with wisdom, knowledge, courage, and love. These gifts make our lives and the world a better place for all God's creation.

PREPARING TO CELEBRATE EASTER IN THE CLASSROOM

SACRED SPACE

The liturgical color for Easter Time is white, so your prayer tablecloth will need to change once more. You may want to add a vase of fresh daisies or lilies and a small glass bowl with a little water in it to your prayer table. When you introduce the water to your students you may say, "Jesus said, 'Let anyone who is thirsty come to me, and let the one who believes in me drink'" (John 7:37b–38a). Have children process in single file to the prayer table, carrying and placing the white cloth, a white pillar candle, the flowers, the bowl of water and the Bible. If possible, dim the lights before you begin. Then, after all the objects have been placed on the prayer table, light the white pillar and chant (one note is fine) the following phrase and response three times:

LEADER: The Light of Christ!

ALL: Thanks be to God!

Perhaps one of your students, or someone they know, celebrated the Sacrament of Baptism at the Holy Saturday celebration of the Easter Vigil. If so, while standing before the water, you could explain that the water of Baptism recalls the great flood that Noah had to pass through to reach God's promise of peace; the Red Sea that Moses and the Israelites had to pass through to reach freedom; and the death that Jesus had to pass through to the Resurrection that saved us. When we pass through (are baptized with) the water in the baptismal font, we enter into that same new life of the resurrected Christ.

Easter Time ends with the Solemnity of Pentecost. When you celebrate Pentecost as a group, make sure you exchange your white prayer table-cloth with a red one for the fiery color of the Spirit.

MOVEMENT AND GESTURE

Children love this expanded form of the Easter Procession. After you have changed the prayer cloth, carried in the white pillar candle and Bible, placed the objects on the prayer table and lit the candle, sing "The Light of Christ / Thanks be to God" on one note. When you are finished singing, read a Gospel account of the Resurrection (John 20:11–18, for example). Sing "Alleluia!" and then announce: "Jesus has risen from the dead; Jesus, the Light of the World, has destroyed death. The light of the Risen Christ will never go out, for he shares his light and life with each of us. Not only that, but his light can spread and grow. Jesus shares his new life with each of us." Then call each child by name, one at a time, inviting them to come forward. For each child, light a small votive candle or congregational candle from the large pillar. As you give it to the child, say, "The Risen Christ shares his light with you, N.___." The child will then put the votive candle on the prayer table and sit down. Don't rush. Wait until the child is seated before you call the next child's name. If you are worried about fire, allow each child to hold his or her votive holder briefly, then you can place the candle on the table beside the lit pillar. Make sure you light a votive for yourself. When all the small candles are lit, sit in silence with the children and enjoy the beauty of the light. End your celebration by singing all the Alleluias that you know!

FESTIVITY IN SCHOOL AND HOME

You might want to engage some of the older children in making an Easter candle like the one that stands beside the altar in church. Use a tall white pillar candle. There are many different designs that you can find on the Internet. Most today share three symbols: (1) a central cross identifies it as the Christ candle; (2) its flame burns despite the death Christ endured; (3) the letters alpha and omega, which begin and end the Greek alphabet, signify that God is the beginning and the ending of all things. The current year indicates that God is present not just at the beginning and the end of time, but throughout history and among those gathered here and now around the candle. You can stand this candle on a medium tall candleholder beside the table in your prayer corner at school or at home.

In this book you will find special prayer services that may be used in the classroom or with a larger group: the prayer service for Easter, pages 260–261; and the service for the Ascension, pages 300–301. There is also a special prayer service to honor May as the month of Mary, pages 272–273. In May, you might like to add pictures of Mary and fresh spring flowers to your prayer table. For children who know the Rosary, this is an appropriate time to say a decade of the Rosary as part of your daily prayer.

SACRED MUSIC

Here are some Easter songs that children love: "Jesus Christ Is Risen Today," "What Wondrous Love Is This," "Alleluia, Sing to Jesus," "Come Down, O Love Divine," and "O Sons and Daughters." For Pentecost you might enjoy singing "Come, Holy Ghost" or "Veni Sancte Spiritus," or "Spirit of the Living God."

PRAYERS FOR EASTER

The following prayer is a beautiful psalm from the Easter Vigil:

Psalm 42:1–2, 43:3–4

As a deer longs for flowing streams,
    so my soul longs for you, O God.
My soul thirsts for God
    for the living God.
When shall I come and behold
    the face of God?
O send out your light and your truth;
    let them lead me;
let them bring me to your holy hill
    and to your dwelling.
Then I will go to the altar of God
to God my exceeding joy; and I will praise you with the harp, O God, my God.

A NOTE TO CATECHISTS

You may wish to study the prayers of Baptism with your students. The prayer of Blessing the Waters of Baptism is particularly rich in symbolism. You can recall with the children baptisms they remember seeing as well as stories and pictures of their own baptisms. You can find the Baptismal Rite on the Internet or ask your parish priest for a copy.

GRACE BEFORE MEALS

EASTER TIME

LEADER:
Jesus Christ is risen! He is truly risen!

ALL: Alleluia! Alleluia!

✚ All make the Sign of the Cross.

In the name of the Father, and of the Son, and of the Holy Spirit. Amen.

LEADER:
God, our Creator,
we are thankful for the
air we breathe and the
nourishment you offer
in our every moment on earth.
We are grateful for the meal
we are about to share,
for its nutrients sustain us and
give us energy for
working and playing for the glory
of Christ our Savior.
We ask this in his name.

ALL: Amen.

✚ All make the Sign of the Cross.

In the name of the Father, and of the Son, and of the Holy Spirit. Amen.

PRAYER AT DAY'S END

EASTER TIME

LEADER:
All the ends of the earth have seen

ALL: the victory of our God.

> ✚ All make the Sign of the Cross.
>
> **In the name of the Father, and of the Son, and of the Holy Spirit. Amen.**

LEADER:
Heavenly Father,
we are grateful for
what we've learned today.
We thank you for our
teachers, assistants, coaches,
and friends who guide us
along our path.
Help us through the remainder of this day
as we are renewed by your Spirit
and the promise of an
eternal Easter.
We ask this through Christ our Lord.

ALL: Amen.

> ✚ All make the Sign of the Cross.
>
> **In the name of the Father, and of the Son, and of the Holy Spirit. Amen.**

PRAYER SERVICE

EASTER

Prepare a leader, an intercessor, and a reader. The reader will need a Bible with the Scripture passage marked with a ribbon or bookmark. Prepare two processors for an Easter procession to place a large white candle and a large bowl of water in the sacred space. The procession can be accompanied by someone with wind chimes or bells ringing, or singing. If there is singing, prepare a song leader. Sing a familiar song with Alleluias like "Alleluia, Sing to Jesus" or "Jesus Christ Is Risen Today." If you have the Alleluia banner from Lent, fill in the final letter before the service. Prepare the class for the gesture of coming to the bowl of water and signing themselves.

◆ All are standing. **The bowl of water and candle are placed on the table:**

LEADER:

Our Easter joy in Jesus' Resurrection is celebrated for fifty days!
Jesus is the Light of the World and Living Water for us. We know we will rise to new life after death, too.
Let us come to the water and sign ourselves with the Sign of the Cross, the sign of Jesus' triumph over sin and death.

✦ All come to the bowl, place their hand in the water and make the Sign of the Cross.

In the name of the Father, and of the Son, and of the Holy Spirit. Amen.

◆ A refrain from a song may be sung or the wind chimes or bell played during the gesture.

CHILDREN'S DAILY PRAYER 2018–2019, © 2018 Archdiocese of Chicago: Liturgy Training Publications. All rights reserved. Orders: 800-933-1800 or www.LTP.org.

When all have signed themselves:

LEADER:
Let us pray.
God of our rejoicing, our hearts are filled with thanks and praise.
Jesus is risen!
May we follow Jesus by loving and serving your people every day.

We ask this in the name of Jesus Christ,
    our Lord.

◆ All sing Alleluia.

READER: John 21:9–17
A reading from the holy Gospel according to John.

◆ Read the passage from the Bible.

The Gospel of the Lord.

LEADER:
Let's observe some silence and think about the many ways we can do as Christ asks and feed Christ's sheep.

◆ All sit and observe silence.

INTERCESSOR:
Let us stand and pray our Litany of Joy. Our response is, "We thank you and praise you!"

◆ All stand.

For your unlimited love and mercy,
    O God . . .

For Jesus, whose sacrifice saved
    all people . . .

For Jesus, who taught us to love
    and serve . . .

For Jesus, the Good Shepherd . . .

For Jesus, the Light of the World . . .

For Jesus, the Living Water . . .

For Jesus, our Brother and Teacher . . .

For the beauty of our earth . . .

For the love of family and friends . . .

For the joy of the Resurrection and this
    Easter season . . .

LEADER:
Let us pray as Jesus taught us.

ALL: Our Father . . . Amen.

LEADER:
Jesus often gave his peace to the disciples. Let us offer that peace to one another.

◆ All offer one another a sign of Christ's peace.

LEADER:
Let us go forth with the peace and joy of the Resurrection. Alleluia! Alleluia!

PRAYER FOR THE WEEK

WITH A READING FROM THE GOSPEL FOR **SUNDAY, APRIL 21, 2019**

OPENING

How blessed we are! Jesus has risen from the dead. Mary Magdalene is distressed to think someone robbed Jesus' tomb. When they see the neatly folded wrappings Jesus left, they realize he had risen as he said!

✚ All make the Sign of the Cross.

In the name of the Father, and of the Son, and of the Holy Spirit. Amen.

PSALM   (For a longer psalm, see page xiv.) Psalm 105:1–2

Let the hearts of those who seek
　　the Lord rejoice.

**Let the hearts of those who seek
　　the Lord rejoice.**

O give thanks to the Lord, call on his name,
　make known his deeds among the peoples.
Sing to him, sing praises to him;
　tell of all his wonderful works.

**Let the hearts of those who seek
　　the Lord rejoice.**

◆ All stand and sing **Alleluia.**

GOSPEL   John 20:1ac, 2acde, 3, 4b, 6acd, 7–8acd

A reading from the holy Gospel according to John.

Early on the first day of the week, Mary Magdalene came to the tomb and saw that the stone had been removed from the tomb. So she ran and went to Simon Peter and the other disciple, and said to them, "They have taken the Lord out of the tomb, and we do not know where they have laid him." Then Peter and the other disciple set out and went toward the tomb. The other disciple outran Peter and reached the tomb first. Then Simon Peter came, and went into the tomb. He saw the linen wrappings lying there, and the cloth that had been on Jesus' head, not lying with the linen wrappings but rolled up in a place by itself. Then the other disciple also went in, and he saw and believed.

The Gospel of the Lord.

◆ All sit and observe silence.

FOR SILENT REFLECTION

Think about this silently in your heart. Imagine how the disciples felt to see the tomb empty.

CLOSING PRAYER

Let us pray to God for our needs and the needs of others: our family, neighborhood, and the world. For each need we say, "Lord, hear our prayer."

◆ All may add their own prayers here.

Let us pray: **Our Father . . . Amen.**

Alleluia! Alleluia! Jesus is risen!
We give you thanks, O God,
for this wondrous feast.
We rejoice in Jesus' Resurrection,
and again we sing, Alleluia!

Amen.

✚ All make the Sign of the Cross.

OPENING

This week is the Octave of Easter, part of a special eight-day time when we rejoice because our God saved us. In today's reading we hear King David's poem of praise and thanksgiving for God, who listened to him and saved him from violence and distress. David uses the wonderful images of fortress, shield and, especially, rock for God.

✚ All make the Sign of the Cross.

In the name of the Father, and of the Son, and of the Holy Spirit. Amen.

PSALM

(For a longer psalm, see page xiv.) Psalm 105:1–2

Let the hearts of those who seek
the LORD rejoice.

**Let the hearts of those who seek
the LORD rejoice.**

O give thanks to the LORD, call on his name,
make known his deeds among the peoples.
Sing to him, sing praises to him;
tell of all his wonderful works.

**Let the hearts of those who seek
the LORD rejoice.**

READING

2 Samuel 22:2–3, 4a, 7abd, 31ac, 32, 47bcd

A reading from the Second Book of Samuel.

David said: The LORD is my rock, my fortress, and my deliverer, my God, my rock, in whom I take refuge, my shield and the horn of my salvation, my stronghold and my refuge, my savior; you save me from violence. I call upon the LORD. In my distress I called upon the LORD; to my God I called. And my cry came to his ears. This God—his way is perfect; he is a shield for all who take refuge in him. For who is God, but the LORD? And who is a rock, except our God? Blessed be my rock, and exalted be my God, the rock of my salvation.

The Word of the Lord.

◆ All observe silence.

FOR SILENT REFLECTION

Think about this silently in your heart. Why is a large rock a good image of God's saving power?

CLOSING PRAYER

Let us pray to God for our needs and the needs of others: our family, neighborhood, and the world. For each need we say, "Lord, hear our prayer."

◆ All may add their own prayers here.

Let us pray: **Our Father . . . Amen.**

We praise you and give you glory,
O God, for your saving work through Jesus.
May we trust in your love for us
and cling to you like a rock that saves us.
We ask this in Jesus' name.
Alleluia! Alleluia!

Amen.

✚ All make the Sign of the Cross.

OPENING

Isaiah, the prophet, assures the Jewish people that God has redeemed them. In today's reading we hear that God has called Israel by name, that he loves and honors them.

✦ All make the Sign of the Cross.

In the name of the Father, and of the Son, and of the Holy Spirit. Amen.

PSALM   (For a longer psalm, see page xiv.) Psalm 105:1–2

Let the hearts of those who seek
    the LORD rejoice.

**Let the hearts of those who seek
    the LORD rejoice.**

O give thanks to the LORD, call on his name,
    make known his deeds among the peoples.
Sing to him, sing praises to him;
    tell of all his wonderful works.

**Let the hearts of those who seek
    the LORD rejoice.**

READING   Isaiah 43:1–3a, 4ab, 5a, 10abc, 11–12ac

A reading from the Book of the prophet Isaiah.

But now thus says the LORD, he who created you, O Jacob, God who formed you, O Israel: Do not fear, for I have redeemed you; I have called you by name, you are mine. For I am the LORD your God, the Holy One of Israel, your Savior. Because you are precious in my sight, and honored, and I love you, I give people in return for you, nations in exchange for your life. Do not fear, for I am with you; You are my witnesses, says the LORD, and my servant whom I have chosen, so that you may know and believe me and understand that I am he. I, I am the LORD, and besides me there is no savior. I declared and saved and proclaimed; and you are my witnesses, says the LORD.

The Word of the Lord.

◆ All observe silence.

FOR SILENT REFLECTION

Think about this silently in your heart. Why is it important to be called by your name?

CLOSING PRAYER

Let us pray to God for our needs and the needs of others: our family, neighborhood, and the world. For each need we say, "Lord, hear our prayer."

◆ All may add their own prayers here.

Let us pray: **Our Father . . . Amen.**

Alleluia! Alleluia!
From the beginning of time
you have loved us, O God.
You have called each of us by name.
Through your son Jesus
you have saved us.
Alleluia! Alleluia!

Amen.

✦ All make the Sign of the Cross.

OPENING

Today is the fourth day in the Octave of Easter that began on Easter Sunday. We will hear of Jesus' encounter with a woman from Samaria. The Jews and Samaritans were enemies, but both believed God would send the Messiah. The woman at the well believes Jesus is the Messiah, and through her testimony, many others come to believe as well.

✦ All make the Sign of the Cross.

In the name of the Father, and of the Son, and of the Holy Spirit. Amen.

PSALM   (For a longer psalm, see page xiv.) Psalm 105:1–2

Let the hearts of those who seek
    the Lord rejoice.

**Let the hearts of those who seek
    the Lord rejoice.**

O give thanks to the Lord, call on his name,
    make known his deeds among the peoples.
Sing to him, sing praises to him;
    tell of all his wonderful works.

**Let the hearts of those who seek
    the Lord rejoice.**

◆ All stand and sing **Alleluia.**

GOSPEL   John 4:25ab, 26, 28–30, 39a, 40–42ad

A reading from the holy Gospel according to John.

The woman said to Jesus, "I know that Messiah is coming" (who is called Christ). Jesus said to her, "I am he, the one who is speaking to you." Then the woman left her water jar and went back to the city. She said to the people, "Come and see a man who told me everything I have ever done! He cannot be the Messiah, can he?" They left the city and were on their way to him. Many Samaritans from that city believed in him because of the woman's testimony. So when the Samaritans came to him, they asked him to stay with them; and he stayed there two days. And many more believed because of his word. They said to the woman, "We know that this is truly the Savior of the world."

The Gospel of the Lord.

◆ All sit and observe silence.

FOR SILENT REFLECTION

Think about this silently in your heart. How do you think the Samaritan woman felt when Jesus told her everything she had ever done?

CLOSING PRAYER

Let us pray to God for our needs and the needs of others: our family, neighborhood, and the world. For each need we say, "Lord, hear our prayer."

◆ All may add their own prayers here.

Let us pray: **Our Father . . . Amen.**

Alleluia! Alleluia! Jesus is risen.
May we, like the woman from Samaria,
believe in him and listen closely to his word.
Alleluia! Alleluia!

Amen.

✦ All make the Sign of the Cross.

PRAYER FOR
THURSDAY, APRIL 25, 2019

OPENING

St. Paul urges Timothy, a young Church leader, to train himself and others in "godliness"; that is, in devotion to God. Paul tells Timothy not to mind that people think he's too young. Timothy can still be an example of godliness with his words and actions.

✛ All make the Sign of the Cross.

In the name of the Father, and of the Son, and of the Holy Spirit. Amen.

PSALM   (For a longer psalm, see page xiv.) Psalm 105:1–2

Let the hearts of those who seek
    the LORD rejoice.

**Let the hearts of those who seek
    the LORD rejoice.**

O give thanks to the LORD, call on his name,
    make known his deeds among the peoples.
Sing to him, sing praises to him;
    tell of all his wonderful works.

**Let the hearts of those who seek
    the LORD rejoice.**

READING   1 Timothy 4:6, 7b–8, 10–12

A reading from the First Letter of Paul to Timothy.

If you put these instructions before the brothers and sisters, you will be a good servant of Christ Jesus, nourished on the words of the faith and of the sound teaching that you have followed. Train yourself in godliness, for, while physical training is of some value, godliness is valuable in every way, holding promise for both the present life and the life to come.

For to this end we toil and struggle, because we have our hope set on the living God, who is the Savior of all people, especially of those who believe. These are the things you must insist on and teach. Let no one despise your youth, but set the believers an example in speech and conduct, in love, in faith, in purity.

The Word of the Lord.

◆ All observe silence.

FOR SILENT REFLECTION

Think about this silently in your heart. What does it mean to "train in godliness"?

CLOSING PRAYER

Let us pray to God for our needs and the needs of others: our family, neighborhood, and the world. For each need we say, "Lord, hear our prayer."

◆ All may add their own prayers here.

Let us pray: **Our Father . . . Amen.**

Alleluia! Alleluia!
We praise you
and give you glory, O God.
May we be good servants of Christ Jesus by training ourselves in godliness.
We ask this in Jesus' name.
Alleluia! Alleluia!

Amen.

✛ All make the Sign of the Cross.

OPENING

On this sixth day of the Easter Octave, we hear a beautiful assertion that the way we can show our gratitude for God's love is to love one another. When we love others we make a home for God in our hearts.

✚ All make the Sign of the Cross.

In the name of the Father, and of the Son, and of the Holy Spirit. Amen.

PSALM   (For a longer psalm, see page xiv.) Psalm 105:1–2

Let the hearts of those who seek
    the LORD rejoice.

**Let the hearts of those who seek
    the LORD rejoice.**

O give thanks to the LORD, call on his name,
    make known his deeds among the peoples.
Sing to him, sing praises to him;
    tell of all his wonderful works.

**Let the hearts of those who seek
    the LORD rejoice.**

READING   1 John 4:7, 9, 11–14, 16bcd

A reading from the First Letter of John.

Beloved, let us love one another, because love is from God; everyone who loves is born of God and knows God. God's love was revealed among us in this way: God sent his only Son into the world so that we might live through him. Beloved, since God loved us so much, we also ought to love one another. No one has ever seen God; if we love one another, God lives in us, and his love is perfected in us. By this we know that we abide in him and he in us, because he has given us of his Spirit. God is love, and those who abide in love abide in God, and God abides in them.

The Word of the Lord.

◆ All observe silence.

FOR SILENT REFLECTION

Think about this silently in your heart. Why do you think love is so important?

CLOSING PRAYER

Let us pray to God for our needs and the needs of others: our family, neighborhood, and the world. For each need we say, "Lord, hear our prayer."

◆ All may add their own prayers here.

Let us pray: **Our Father . . . Amen.**

Alleluia! Alleluia!
Gracious and loving God,
Help us love you more and more each day.
Help us love all we meet today
We ask this in Jesus' name.
Alleluia! Alleluia!

Amen.

✚ All make the Sign of the Cross.

PRAYER FOR THE WEEK

OPENING

Our second week of Easter rejoicing begins with Divine Mercy Sunday! After the Resurrection, Jesus appeared to the disciples to comfort and encourage them. He sends the Holy Spirit to guide and help them follow Jesus. The disciples feared the Jewish authorities who had crucified Jesus.

✛ All make the Sign of the Cross.

In the name of the Father, and of the Son, and of the Holy Spirit. Amen.

PSALM   (For a longer psalm, see page xiv.) Psalm 105:1–2

Let the hearts of those who seek
the Lord rejoice.

**Let the hearts of those who seek
the Lord rejoice.**

O give thanks to the Lord, call on his name,
make known his deeds among the peoples.
Sing to him, sing praises to him;
tell of all his wonderful works.

**Let the hearts of those who seek
the Lord rejoice.**

◆ All stand and sing **Alleluia.**

GOSPEL   John 20:19–22

A reading from the holy Gospel according to John.

When it was evening on that day, the first day of the week, and the doors of the house where the disciples had met were locked for fear of the Jews, Jesus came and stood among them and said, "Peace be with you." After he said this, he showed them his hands and his side.

Then the disciples rejoiced when they saw the Lord. Jesus said to them again, "Peace be with you. As the Father has sent me, so I send you." When he had said this, he breathed on them and said to them, "Receive the Holy Spirit."

The Gospel of the Lord.

◆ All sit and observe silence.

FOR SILENT REFLECTION

Think about this silently in your heart. Imagine how it would feel to see Jesus in person. What would you say to him?

CLOSING PRAYER

Let us pray to God for our needs and the needs of others: our family, neighborhood, and the world. For each need we say, "Lord, hear our prayer."

◆ All may add their own prayers here.

Let us pray: **Our Father . . . Amen.**

Most holy God,
As Jesus gave the Apostles the gift of peace,
we ask that you give us peace and courage.
Help us to be your faithful disciples.
We ask this in Jesus' name.

Amen.

✛ All make the Sign of the Cross.

OPENING

In this second week of Easter rejoicing we will hear what happened after Jesus' Resurrection. Two men (maybe angels) at the tomb remind the women that Jesus said he would rise on the third day. Today is the memorial of St. Catherine of Siena.

✦ All make the Sign of the Cross.

In the name of the Father, and of the Son, and of the Holy Spirit. Amen.

PSALM
(For a longer psalm, see page xiv.) Psalm 105:1–2

Let the hearts of those who seek
the LORD rejoice.

**Let the hearts of those who seek
the LORD rejoice.**

O give thanks to the LORD, call on his name,
make known his deeds among the peoples.
Sing to him, sing praises to him;
tell of all his wonderful works.

**Let the hearts of those who seek
the LORD rejoice.**

◆ All stand and sing **Alleluia.**

GOSPEL
Luke 24:1b–3, 4b–6b, 7–12

A reading from the holy Gospel according to Luke.

At early dawn, the women came to the tomb, taking the spices that they had prepared. They found the stone rolled away from the tomb, but when they went in, they did not find the body. Suddenly two men in dazzling clothes stood beside them. The women were terrified and bowed their faces to the ground, but the men said to them, "Why do you look for the living among the dead? He is not here, but has risen. Remember how he told you that the Son of Man must be handed over to sinners, and be crucified, and on the third day rise again." Then they remembered his words, and returning from the tomb, they told all this to the eleven and to all the rest. Now it was Mary Magdalene, Joanna, Mary the mother of James, and the other women with them who told this to the apostles.

The Gospel of the Lord.

◆ All sit and observe silence.

FOR SILENT REFLECTION

Think about this silently in your heart. What different emotions did the women at the tomb feel?

CLOSING PRAYER

Let us pray to God for our needs and the needs of others: our family, neighborhood, and the world. For each need we say, "Lord, hear our prayer."

◆ All may add their own prayers here.

Let us pray: **Our Father . . . Amen.**

Dear God, we praise you
and thank you for the new life
that comes through Jesus' Resurrection.
Help us make a new start
in being kind, fair, and honest with others.
We ask this in Jesus' name.
Amen.

✦ All make the Sign of the Cross.

PRAYER FOR
TUESDAY, APRIL 30, 2019

OPENING

Today and tomorrow we will hear about Cleopas [KLEE-oh-puhs] and another disciple on the road to Emmaus. They were very sad about the death of their beloved leader. Jesus appeared to them, but he was so changed they didn't recognize him!

✛ All make the Sign of the Cross.

In the name of the Father, and of the Son, and of the Holy Spirit. Amen.

PSALM   (For a longer psalm, see page xiv.) Psalm 105:1–2

Let the hearts of those who seek
 the LORD rejoice.

**Let the hearts of those who seek
 the LORD rejoice.**

O give thanks to the LORD, call on his name,
 make known his deeds among the peoples.
Sing to him, sing praises to him;
 tell of all his wonderful works.

**Let the hearts of those who seek
 the LORD rejoice.**

◆ All stand and sing **Alleluia.**

GOSPEL   Luke 24:13, 15b–17b, 18,19c–20, 22b–23

A reading from the holy Gospel according to Luke.

Two of Jesus' disciples were going to a village called Emmaus about seven miles from Jerusalem. Jesus himself came near and went with them, but their eyes were kept from recognizing him. Jesus said to them, "What are you discussing with each other?" Then one of them, whose name was Cleopas, answered him, "Are you the only stranger in Jerusalem who does not know the things that have taken place there in these days? The things about Jesus of Nazareth, who was a prophet mighty in deed and word before God and all the people, and how our chief priests and leaders handed him over to be condemned to death and crucified him. Some women of our group were at the tomb early this morning, and when they did not find his body there, they came back and told us that they had indeed seen a vision of angels who said that he was alive."

The Gospel of the Lord.

◆ All sit and observe silence.

FOR SILENT REFLECTION

Think about this silently in your heart. How do you think Jesus was changed after the Resurrection?

CLOSING PRAYER

Let us pray to God for our needs and the needs of others: our family, neighborhood, and the world. For each need we say, "Lord, hear our prayer."

◆ All may add their own prayers here.

Let us pray: **Our Father . . . Amen.**

Almighty and loving God,
Help us to see the face of Jesus
in the people we meet.
We ask this in Jesus' name.
Amen.

✛ All make the Sign of the Cross.

OPENING

Cleopas and the other disciple were very kind to offer Jesus, whom they didn't recognize. But when Jesus broke the bread and gave it to them, they saw him clearly. That's one way Jesus appears to us too: at Mass in the Breaking of the Bread.

✛ All make the Sign of the Cross.

In the name of the Father, and of the Son, and of the Holy Spirit. Amen.

PSALM   (For a longer psalm, see page xiv.) Psalm 105:1–2

Let the hearts of those who seek
    the LORD rejoice.

Let the hearts of those who seek
    the LORD rejoice.

O give thanks to the LORD, call on his name,
    make known his deeds among the peoples.
Sing to him, sing praises to him;
    tell of all his wonderful works.

Let the hearts of those who seek
    the LORD rejoice.

◆ All stand and sing **Alleluia.**

GOSPEL   Luke 24:28–31, 33–34

A reading from the holy Gospel according to Luke.

As they came near the village to which they were going, Jesus walked ahead as if he were going on. But they urged him strongly, saying, "Stay with us, because it is almost evening." So he went in to stay with them. When he was at the table with them, he took bread, blessed and broke it, and gave it to them. Then their eyes were opened, and they recognized him; and he vanished from their sight. They said to each other, "Were not our hearts burning within us while he was talking to us on the road, while he was opening the scriptures to us?" That same hour they got up and returned to Jerusalem; and they found the eleven and their companions gathered together. Then they told what had happened on the road, and how Jesus had been made known to them in the breaking of the bread.

The Gospel of the Lord.

◆ All sit and observe silence.

FOR SILENT REFLECTION

Think about this silently in your heart. What are ways Jesus appears to us today?

CLOSING PRAYER

Let us pray to God for our needs and the needs of others: our family, neighborhood, and the world. For each need we say, "Lord, hear our prayer."

◆ All may add their own prayers here.

Let us pray: **Our Father . . . Amen.**

Loving and almighty God,
make our hearts burn with love for you.
We thank you for the gift of Jesus in the Eucharist.
We thank you for the gift of the Scriptures, which help us to know you.
Amen.

✛ All make the Sign of the Cross.

PRAYER SERVICE
TO HONOR MARY IN MAY

Add an image or statue of Mary to the sacred space. Place some flowers and two candles on a side table for the processors. Prepare the leader, reader, three (or more) processors, intercessor, and song leader (if the group will sing). Mark the Scripture passage in the Bible. You may wish to sing "Sing of Mary" or "Hail Mary, Gentle Woman."

LEADER:

We honor Mary, the Mother of God, and remember she was chosen by God for that important role. Mary taught Jesus his prayers and was his first disciple. Most importantly, we remember that Mary is a model for us because she trusted God and said "Yes!" to God.

SONG LEADER:

◆ Gesture for all to stand and lead the song.

LEADER:

◆ All make the sign of the Cross.

In the name of the Father, and of the Son, and of the Holy Spirit. Amen.

Let us pray.
Holy God,
we praise and thank you for Mary
        our Mother.
We honor her for her trust in you
and her courage to say "yes"
to your request that she
be the mother of Jesus, our Savior.
Help us follow her model of trust
        and courage
as we try to do your will.
We ask this through Christ our Lord.

◆ Remain standing and sing Alleluia.

CHILDREN'S DAILY PRAYER 2018–2019, © 2018 Archdiocese of Chicago: Liturgy Training Publications. All rights reserved. Orders: 800-933-1800 or www.LTP.org.

READER: Luke 1:26–38

A reading from the holy Gospel according to Luke.

- ◆ Read the passage from the Bible.
- ◆ All observe some silence.

PROCESSION

- ◆ The processors place candles and flowers around the image of Mary. A song refrain may be sung. A crown can be placed on the image of Mary or next to it.

INTERCESSOR:

Let us pray a litany to Mary. Our response is "Watch over us."

Mary, who said "yes" to God, we pray . . .

Helper of your cousin Elizabeth, we pray . . .

Mary, faithful spouse of Joseph, we pray . . .

Loving mother of Jesus, we pray . . .

Teacher of Jesus, we pray . . .

First disciple of Jesus, we pray . . .

Mary weeping at the foot of the Cross, we pray . . .

Filled with the Holy Spirit on Pentecost, we pray . . .

Mary, Mother of God, we pray . . .

Mary, assumed into heaven, we pray . . .

Queen of Heaven, we pray . . .

LEADER:

Together let us all pray the "Hail Mary"

ALL: Hail Mary, full of grace . . .

- ✚ All make the Sign of the Cross.

  In the name of the Father, and of the Son, and of the Holy Spirit. Amen.

PRAYER FOR
THURSDAY, MAY 2, 2019

OPENING

Jesus appears to his beloved disciples after his death. At first, they feared that they were seeing a ghost. He reassures them by letting them touch him, and then, by eating some fish. The disciples are overjoyed. Our long Easter season is all about rejoicing.

✚ All make the Sign of the Cross.

In the name of the Father, and of the Son, and of the Holy Spirit. Amen.

PSALM   (For a longer psalm, see page xiv.) Psalm 105:1–2

Let the hearts of those who seek
the LORD rejoice.

**Let the hearts of those who seek
the LORD rejoice.**

O give thanks to the LORD, call on his name,
make known his deeds among the peoples.
Sing to him, sing praises to him;
tell of all his wonderful works.

**Let the hearts of those who seek
the LORD rejoice.**

◆ All stand and sing **Alleluia.**

GOSPEL   Luke 24:36–43

A reading from the holy Gospel according to Luke.

While the disciples were talking about Jesus' death and disappearance from the tomb, Jesus himself stood among them and said to them, "Peace be with you." They were startled and terrified, and thought that they were seeing a ghost. He said to them, "Why are you frightened, and why do doubts arise in your hearts?

Look at my hands and my feet; see that it is I myself. Touch me and see; for a ghost does not have flesh and bones as you see that I have." And when he had said this, he showed them his hands and his feet. While in their joy they were disbelieving and still wondering, he said to them, "Have you anything here to eat?" They gave him a piece of broiled fish, and he took it and ate in their presence.

The Gospel of the Lord.

◆ All sit and observe silence.

FOR SILENT REFLECTION

Think about this silently in your heart. Have you noticed how often Jesus greets the disciples with "Peace be with you"?

CLOSING PRAYER

Let us pray to God for our needs and the needs of others: our family, neighborhood, and the world. For each need we say, "Lord, hear our prayer."

◆ All may add their own prayers here.

Let us pray: **Our Father . . . Amen.**

Gracious and loving God,
as Jesus offered peace to his disciples,
so he offers peace to us.
May we know the peace of Christ today
and each day of our lives.

Amen.

✚ All make the Sign of the Cross.

OPENING

Today is the feast of Sts. Philip and James, two of Jesus' Twelve Apostles. St. Paul lists all of Jesus' appearances after the Resurrection, including the one to him. Two apostles are mentioned by name, Cephas [SEE-phus], who is Peter, and James. Both became important leaders of the early Church and helped the Church grow by welcoming non-Jews.

✚ All make the Sign of the Cross.

In the name of the Father, and of the Son, and of the Holy Spirit. Amen.

PSALM

(For a longer psalm, see page xiv.) Psalm 105:1–2

Let the hearts of those who seek
    the LORD rejoice.

**Let the hearts of those who seek
    the LORD rejoice.**

O give thanks to the LORD, call on his name,
    make known his deeds among the peoples.
Sing to him, sing praises to him;
    tell of all his wonderful works.

**Let the hearts of those who seek
    the LORD rejoice.**

READING

1 Corinthians 15:1ab, 3b–8

A reading from the First Letter of Paul to the Corinthians.

Now I would remind you, brothers and sisters, of the good news that I proclaimed to you: that Christ died for our sins in accordance with the scriptures, and that he was buried, and that he was raised on the third day in accordance with the scriptures, and that he appeared to Cephas, then to the twelve. Then he appeared to more than five hundred brothers and sisters at one time, most of whom are still alive, though some have died. Then he appeared to James, then to all the apostles. Last of all, as to one untimely born, he appeared also to me.

The Word of the Lord.

◆ All observe silence.

FOR SILENT REFLECTION

Think about this silently in your heart. Pray this week for our Church leaders, our pope, our bishops, and our pastors.

CLOSING PRAYER

Let us pray to God for our needs and the needs of others: our family, neighborhood, and the world. For each need we say, "Lord, hear our prayer."

◆ All may add their own prayers here.

Let us pray: **Our Father . . . Amen.**

Holy and gracious God,
Help us to believe in Jesus' presence among us.
We ask this in Jesus name.

Amen.

✚ All make the Sign of the Cross.

PRAYER FOR THE WEEK

WITH A READING FROM THE GOSPEL FOR **SUNDAY, MAY 5, 2019**

OPENING

Our third week of Easter begins with Jesus' third appearance to the disciples. He grills fish for the disciples' breakfast. Fish were a sign of God's loving abundance to early Christians because of the miracle of the loaves and fish.

✚ All make the Sign of the Cross.

In the name of the Father, and of the Son, and of the Holy Spirit. Amen.

PSALM   (For a longer psalm, see page xiv.) Psalm 105:1–2

Let the hearts of those who seek
      the LORD rejoice.

Let the hearts of those who seek
      the LORD rejoice.

O give thanks to the LORD, call on his name,
   make known his deeds among the peoples.
Sing to him, sing praises to him;
   tell of all his wonderful works.

Let the hearts of those who seek
      the LORD rejoice.

◆ All stand and sing **Alleluia.**

GOSPEL   John 21:1a, 2–3d, 9–10, 12a, 13–14

A reading from the holy Gospel according to John.

After these things Jesus showed himself again to the disciples by the Sea of Tiberias. Gathered there together were Simon Peter, Thomas called the Twin, Nathanael of Cana in Galilee, the sons of Zebedee, and two others of his disciples. Simon Peter said to them, "I am going fishing." They said to him, "We will go with you." When they had gone ashore, they saw a charcoal fire there, with fish on it, and bread. Jesus said to them, "Bring some of the fish that you have just caught." Jesus said to them, "Come and have breakfast." Jesus came and took the bread and gave it to them, and did the same with the fish. This was now the third time that Jesus appeared to the disciples after he was raised from the dead.

The Gospel of the Lord.

◆ All sit and observe silence.

FOR SILENT REFLECTION

Think about this silently in your heart. What can you learn about Jesus from today's Gospel?

CLOSING PRAYER

Let us pray to God for our needs and the needs of others: our family, neighborhood, and the world. For each need we say, "Lord, hear our prayer."

◆ All may add their own prayers here.

Let us pray: **Our Father . . . Amen.**

We praise you and thank you, Creator God.
In Jesus we see your love revealed.
In Jesus we see how we should treat one another.
May we follow his example each day.
We ask this in Jesus' name.

Amen.

✚ All make the Sign of the Cross.

276

OPENING

Early Christians were called "Followers of the Way." In this third week of Easter we will hear how the Followers discovered what it meant to be a community that followed Jesus. Today we hear how the disciples preached and called many people to believe in Jesus.

✛ All make the Sign of the Cross.

In the name of the Father, and of the Son, and of the Holy Spirit. Amen.

PSALM   (For a longer psalm, see page xiv.) Psalm 105:1–2

Let the hearts of those who seek
   the LORD rejoice.

Let the hearts of those who seek
   the LORD rejoice.

O give thanks to the LORD, call on his name,
   make known his deeds among the peoples.
Sing to him, sing praises to him;
   tell of all his wonderful works.

Let the hearts of those who seek
   the LORD rejoice.

READING   Acts 2:6, 14ac, 22c, 23ac, 32, 37b–38b, 41

A reading from the Acts of the Apostles.

At the sound the crowd gathered and was bewildered, because they heard the disciples speaking in the native language of each. But Peter raised his voice and addressed them, "Jesus of Nazareth, a man attested to you by God with deeds of power, wonders, and signs, this man, you crucified and killed by the hands of those outside the law. This Jesus God raised up, and of that all of us are witnesses." They were cut to the heart and said to Peter and to the other apostles, "Brothers, what should we do?" Peter said to them, "Repent, and be baptized every one of you in the name of Jesus Christ so that your sins may be forgiven." So those who welcomed his message were baptized, and that day about three thousand persons were added.

The Word of the Lord.

◆ All observe silence.

FOR SILENT REFLECTION

Think about this silently in your heart. Is there anything for which you need to repent?

CLOSING PRAYER

Let us pray to God for our needs and the needs of others: our family, neighborhood, and the world. For each need we say, "Lord, hear our prayer."

◆ All may add their own prayers here.

Let us pray: **Our Father . . . Amen.**

Dear God, may your Holy Spirit
help us be close followers of Jesus
like the early Christians.
May we love you and love
one another as they did.
We ask this in Jesus' name.

Amen.

✛ All make the Sign of the Cross.

PRAYER FOR
TUESDAY, MAY 7, 2019

OPENING

The Followers of the Way were very close to one another. They met each week to share the "Breaking of the Bread," which we call Eucharist or Mass. They also shared their money so that even the very poor had food, clothing, and shelter. The Scripture says this gave them "glad and generous hearts."

✛ All make the Sign of the Cross.

In the name of the Father, and of the Son, and of the Holy Spirit. Amen.

PSALM   (For a longer psalm, see page xiv.) Psalm 105:1–2

Let the hearts of those who seek
    the LORD rejoice.

**Let the hearts of those who seek
    the LORD rejoice.**

O give thanks to the LORD, call on his name,
    make known his deeds among the peoples.
Sing to him, sing praises to him;
    tell of all his wonderful works.

**Let the hearts of those who seek
    the LORD rejoice.**

READING   Acts 2:43–47

A reading from the Acts of the Apostles.

They devoted themselves to the apostles' teaching and fellowship, to the breaking of bread and the prayers. Awe came upon everyone, because many wonders and signs were being done by the apostles. All who believed were together and had all things in common; they would sell their possessions and goods and distribute the proceeds to all, as any had need.

Day by day, as they spent much time together in the temple, they broke bread at home and ate their food with glad and generous hearts, praising God and having the goodwill of all the people. And day by day the Lord added to their number those who were being saved.

The Word of the Lord.

◆ All observe silence.

FOR SILENT REFLECTION

Think about this silently in your heart. What gives you a "glad and generous heart"?

CLOSING PRAYER

Let us pray to God for our needs and the needs of others: our family, neighborhood, and the world. For each need we say, "Lord, hear our prayer."

◆ All may add their own prayers here.

Let us pray: **Our Father . . . Amen.**

Holy God,
grant us hearts that are generous.
Make us glad to know, love, and serve you.
We ask this in Jesus' name.

Amen.

✛ All make the Sign of the Cross.

OPENING

The early Christians did extraordinary sharing in the name of Jesus. Groups of families may have lived together in communities the way religious men and women do today. The word "community" comes from the word "common." They owned everything together or "in common." Our parishes are a form of "Christian Communities."

✝ All make the Sign of the Cross.

In the name of the Father, and of the Son, and of the Holy Spirit. Amen.

PSALM
(For a longer psalm, see page xiv.) Psalm 105:1–2

Let the hearts of those who seek
    the LORD rejoice.

**Let the hearts of those who seek
    the LORD rejoice.**

O give thanks to the LORD, call on his name,
    make known his deeds among the peoples.
Sing to him, sing praises to him;
    tell of all his wonderful works.

**Let the hearts of those who seek
    the LORD rejoice.**

READING
Acts 4:32–36acd, 37

A reading from the Acts of the Apostles.

Now the whole group of those who believed were of one heart and soul, and no one claimed private ownership of any possessions, but everything they owned was held in common. With great power the apostles gave their testimony to the resurrection of the Lord Jesus, and great grace was upon them all. There was not a needy person among them, for as many as owned lands or houses sold them and brought the proceeds of what was sold. They laid it at the apostles' feet, and it was distributed to each as any had need. There was a Levite, Joseph, to whom the apostles gave the name Barnabas. He sold a field that belonged to him, then brought the money, and laid it at the apostles' feet.

The Word of the Lord.

◆ All observe silence.

FOR SILENT REFLECTION

Think about this silently in your heart. How well do you share what you have with others?

CLOSING PRAYER

Let us pray to God for our needs and the needs of others: our family, neighborhood, and the world. For each need we say, "Lord, hear our prayer."

◆ All may add their own prayers here.

Let us pray: **Our Father . . . Amen.**

Generous God,
as the early Christians cared
for the needs of one another
we pray that we may follow their example.
Help us to practice charity with kindness.
We ask this in Jesus' name.

Amen.

✝ All make the Sign of the Cross.

PRAYER FOR
THURSDAY, MAY 9, 2019

OPENING

Following Jesus is often hard. Today we hear how some of the Jewish authorities have accused the Apostles of taking people away from being Jewish. The authorities jailed the Apostles and threatened to kill them if they didn't stop teaching about Jesus. The Apostles were strong in their faith and would not stop.

✚ All make the Sign of the Cross.

In the name of the Father, and of the Son, and of the Holy Spirit. Amen.

PSALM
(For a longer psalm, see page xiv.) Psalm 105:1–2

Let the hearts of those who seek
    the LORD rejoice.

**Let the hearts of those who seek
    the LORD rejoice.**

O give thanks to the LORD, call on his name,
    make known his deeds among the peoples.
Sing to him, sing praises to him;
    tell of all his wonderful works.

**Let the hearts of those who seek
    the LORD rejoice.**

READING
Acts 5:17bd, 18, 27c, 28a, 29a, 33b, 40b–42

A reading from the Acts of the Apostles.

The high priest and all who were with him being filled with jealousy, arrested Peter and the apostles and put them in the public prison. The high priest questioned them, saying, "We gave you strict orders not to teach in this name." But Peter and the apostles answered, "We must obey God rather than any human authority." They were enraged and wanted to kill them. They had them flogged. Then they ordered them not to speak in the name of Jesus, and let them go. As they left the council, the apostles rejoiced that they were considered worthy to suffer dishonor for the sake of the name. And every day in the temple and at home they did not cease to teach and proclaim Jesus as the Messiah.

The Word of the Lord.

◆ All observe silence.

FOR SILENT REFLECTION

Think about this silently in your heart. Pray today for people who are mocked or hurt by others because of their religion.

CLOSING PRAYER

Let us pray to God for our needs and the needs of others: our family, neighborhood, and the world. For each need we say, "Lord, hear our prayer."

◆ All may add their own prayers here.

Let us pray: **Our Father . . . Amen.**

Dear God,
We pray for people of all faith traditions.
May we respect everyone who is searching for you and seeking to build a better world.
We ask this in Jesus' name.

Amen.

✚ All make the Sign of the Cross.

OPENING

The Followers of the Way of Jesus Christ are given the name "Christian" in Antioch. St. Barnabas and St. Paul helped teach the Hellenists (or "Greeks") Jesus' message to love God by loving one another. Everywhere the Apostles went, they found new believers.

✠ All make the Sign of the Cross.

> **In the name of the Father, and of the Son, and of the Holy Spirit. Amen.**

PSALM   (For a longer psalm, see page xiv.) Psalm 105:1–2

Let the hearts of those who seek
    the LORD rejoice.

**Let the hearts of those who seek
    the LORD rejoice.**

O give thanks to the LORD, call on his name,
    make known his deeds among the peoples.
Sing to him, sing praises to him;
    tell of all his wonderful works.

**Let the hearts of those who seek
    the LORD rejoice.**

READING   Acts 11:20acd, 22–23, 24b, 26

A reading from the Acts of the Apostles.

But among them were some men of Cyprus [SĪ-pruhs] and Cyrene [sī-REE-nee] who spoke to the Hellenists also proclaiming the Lord Jesus. News of this came to the ears of the church in Jerusalem, and they sent Barnabas to Antioch. When he came and saw the grace of God, he rejoiced, and he exhorted them all to remain faithful to the Lord with steadfast devotion. And a great many people were brought to the Lord. Then Barnabas went to Tarsus to look for Saul, and when he had found him, he brought him to Antioch. So it was that for an entire year they met with the church and taught a great many people, and it was in Antioch that the disciples were first called "Christians."

The Word of the Lord.

◆ All observe silence.

FOR SILENT REFLECTION

Think about this silently in your heart. How can you teach Jesus' message to love God by loving one another?

CLOSING PRAYER

Let us pray to God for our needs and the needs of others: our family, neighborhood, and the world. For each need we say, "Lord, hear our prayer."

◆ All may add their own prayers here.

Let us pray: **Our Father . . . Amen.**

We give you thanks and praise, O God,
for the gift of our Christian faith.
You desire that we show our love for you
by caring for one another.
Help us to be good Christians.

Amen.

✠ All make the Sign of the Cross.

PRAYER FOR THE WEEK

WITH A READING FROM THE GOSPEL FOR **SUNDAY, MAY 12, 2019**

OPENING

We begin this fourth week of Easter by remembering that Jesus is our Good Shepherd. The Good Shepherd knows each of his sheep, and the sheep know the sound of his voice. We follow Jesus by listening to his word.

✝ All make the Sign of the Cross.

In the name of the Father, and of the Son, and of the Holy Spirit. Amen.

PSALM   (For a longer psalm, see page xv.) Psalm 118:1–2, 4

The stone that the builders rejected
    has become the chief cornerstone.

**The stone that the builders rejected
    has become the chief cornerstone.**

O give thanks to the LORD, for he is good;
  his steadfast love endures forever!
Let Israel say,
  "His steadfast love endures forever."
Let those who fear the LORD say,
  "His steadfast love endures forever."

**The stone that the builders rejected
    has become the chief cornerstone.**

◆ All stand and sing **Alleluia.**

GOSPEL   John 10:23a, 24ac, 25a, 27–30

A reading from the holy Gospel according to John.

Jesus was walking in the temple in the portico of Solomon. So the Jews gathered around him and said to him, "If you are the Messiah, tell us plainly." Jesus answered, "My sheep hear my voice. I know them, and they follow me. I give them eternal life, and they will never per-ish. No one will snatch them out of my hand. What my Father has given me is greater than all else, and no one can snatch it out of the Father's hand. The Father and I are one."

The Gospel of the Lord.

◆ All sit and observe silence.

FOR SILENT REFLECTION

Think about this silently in your heart. How can you listen to the voice of the Good Shepherd?

CLOSING PRAYER

Let us pray to God for our needs and the needs of others: our family, neighborhood, and the world. For each need we say, "Lord, hear our prayer."

◆ All may add their own prayers here.

Let us pray: **Our Father . . . Amen.**

Most loving God,
as a shepherd cares for the sheep,
you care for us.
Thank you for Jesus, our Good Shepherd.
Thank you for his great care and love.
May we always listen for his voice.

Amen.

✝ All make the Sign of the Cross.

OPENING

Some sources list fifty titles, or names, for Jesus. This week we will examine a few of them. Our first title is from the Old Testament. King Ahaz is afraid and has lost faith in God's protection. Isaiah says God will give the people a sign of his faithfulness. Immanuel, which means "God-with-us," will come.

✚ All make the Sign of the Cross.

In the name of the Father, and of the Son, and of the Holy Spirit. Amen.

PSALM   (For a longer psalm, see page xv.) Psalm 118:1–2, 4

The stone that the builders rejected
　　has become the chief cornerstone.

**The stone that the builders rejected
　　has become the chief cornerstone.**

O give thanks to the LORD, for he is good;
　his steadfast love endures forever!
Let Israel say,
　"His steadfast love endures forever."
Let those who fear the LORD say,
　"His steadfast love endures forever."

**The stone that the builders rejected
　　has become the chief cornerstone.**

READING   Isaiah 7:2–3ab, 4ab, 10–11a, 12–14

A reading from the Book of the prophet Isaiah.

When the house of David heard that Aram had allied itself with Ephraim, the heart of Ahaz and the heart of his people shook as the trees of the forest shake before the wind. Then the LORD said to Isaiah, Go out to meet Ahaz and say to him, Take heed, be quiet, do not fear. Again the LORD spoke to Ahaz, saying, Ask a sign of the LORD your God. But Ahaz said, I will not ask, and I will not put the LORD to the test. Then Isaiah said: "Hear then, O house of David! Is it too little for you to weary mortals, that you weary my God also? Therefore the Lord himself will give you a sign. Look, the young woman is with child and shall bear a son, and shall name him Immanuel."

The Word of the Lord.

◆ All observe silence.

FOR SILENT REFLECTION

Think about this silently in your heart. What title would you give Jesus?

CLOSING PRAYER

Let us pray to God for our needs and the needs of others: our family, neighborhood, and the world. For each need we say, "Lord, hear our prayer."

◆ All may add their own prayers here.

Let us pray: **Our Father . . . Amen.**

God, thank you for Jesus, our Immanuel.
Help us to recognize Jesus' presence
in our lives.
Help us to see him in all who we meet.

Amen.

✚ All make the Sign of the Cross.

PRAYER FOR
TUESDAY, MAY 14, 2019

OPENING

Today is St. Matthias' feast day. He was chosen to replace Judas. Matthias was a follower of Jesus from the time of Jesus' baptism. He may have heard Jesus say, "I am the light of the world." The "light of the world" is a title for Jesus.

✚ All make the Sign of the Cross.

In the name of the Father, and of the Son, and of the Holy Spirit. Amen.

PSALM   (For a longer psalm, see page xv.) Psalm 118:1–2, 4

The stone that the builders rejected
    has become the chief cornerstone.

**The stone that the builders rejected
    has become the chief cornerstone.**

O give thanks to the LORD, for he is good;
   his steadfast love endures forever!
Let Israel say,
  "His steadfast love endures forever."
Let those who fear the LORD say,
  "His steadfast love endures forever."

**The stone that the builders rejected
    has become the chief cornerstone.**

◆ All stand and sing **Alleluia.**

GOSPEL   John 8:12–14, 18–19

A reading from the holy Gospel according to John.

Again Jesus spoke to them, saying, "I am the light of the world. Whoever follows me will never walk in darkness but will have the light of life." Then the Pharisees said to him, "You are testifying on your own behalf; your testi-mony is not valid." Jesus answered, "Even if I testify on my own behalf, my testimony is valid because I know where I have come from and where I am going, but you do not know where I come from or where I am going. I testify on my own behalf, and the Father who sent me testifies on my behalf." Then they said to him, "Where is your Father?" Jesus answered, "You know neither me nor my Father. If you knew me, you would know my Father also."

The Gospel of the Lord.

◆ All sit and observe silence.

FOR SILENT REFLECTION

Think about this silently in your heart. What kind of darkness does Jesus overcome with his Light?

CLOSING PRAYER

Let us pray to God for our needs and the needs of others: our family, neighborhood, and the world. For each need we say, "Lord, hear our prayer."

◆ All may add their own prayers here.

Let us pray: **Our Father . . . Amen.**

God, thank you for Jesus,
the Light of the World.
May we follow his light every day.

Amen.

✚ All make the Sign of the Cross.

OPENING

God appoints, or gives, Jesus the title of "High Priest." The role of a high priest is to "deal gently" with people when they sin. The Scripture reminds us that Jesus is fully human and sympathizes with our struggles and pains.

✛ All make the Sign of the Cross.

In the name of the Father, and of the Son, and of the Holy Spirit. Amen.

PSALM
(For a longer psalm, see page xv.) Psalm 118:1–2, 4

The stone that the builders rejected
     has become the chief cornerstone.

**The stone that the builders rejected
     has become the chief cornerstone.**

O give thanks to the LORD, for he is good;
  his steadfast love endures forever!
Let Israel say,
  "His steadfast love endures forever."
Let those who fear the LORD say,
  "His steadfast love endures forever."

**The stone that the builders rejected
     has become the chief cornerstone.**

READING
Hebrews 5:1–5

A reading from the Letter to the Hebrews.

Every high priest chosen from among mortals is put in charge of things pertaining to God on their behalf, to offer gifts and sacrifices for sins. He is able to deal gently with the ignorant and wayward, since he himself is subject to weakness; and because of this he must offer sacrifice for his own sins as well as for those of the people. And one does not presume to take this honor, but takes it only when called by God, just as Aaron was. So also Christ did not glorify himself in becoming a high priest, but was appointed by the one who said to him, "You are my Son, today I have begotten you."

The Word of the Lord.

◆ All observe silence.

FOR SILENT REFLECTION

Think about this silently in your heart. Ask Jesus to encourage you to follow him.

CLOSING PRAYER

Let us pray to God for our needs and the needs of others: our family, neighborhood, and the world. For each need we say, "Lord, hear our prayer."

◆ All may add their own prayers here.

Let us pray: **Our Father . . . Amen.**

God, thank you for Jesus, our High Priest.
May his gentle encouragement
help us ask for forgiveness for our sins.
We ask this in Jesus' name.

Amen.

✛ All make the Sign of the Cross.

PRAYER FOR
THURSDAY, MAY 16, 2019

OPENING

Peter and the Apostles say God gave Jesus the title "Leader and Savior," so the people would know that God loves them and forgives sin. This is very good news.

✦ All make the Sign of the Cross.

In the name of the Father, and of the Son, and of the Holy Spirit. Amen.

PSALM   (For a longer psalm, see page xv.) Psalm 118:1–2, 4

The stone that the builders rejected
    has become the chief cornerstone.

**The stone that the builders rejected
    has become the chief cornerstone.**

O give thanks to the LORD, for he is good;
   his steadfast love endures forever!
Let Israel say,
   "His steadfast love endures forever."
Let those who fear the LORD say,
   "His steadfast love endures forever."

**The stone that the builders rejected
    has become the chief cornerstone.**

READING   Acts 5:17b, 27b–31

A reading from the Acts of the Apostles.

The high priest and all who were with him arrested the apostles and put them in public prison. They had them stand before the council. The high priest questioned them, saying, "We gave you strict orders not to teach in Jesus' name, yet here you have filled Jerusalem with your teaching and you are determined to bring this Jesus' blood on us." But Peter and the apostles answered, "We must obey God rather than any human authority. The God of our ancestors raised up Jesus, whom you had killed by hanging him on a tree. God exalted Jesus at his right hand as Leader and Savior that he might give repentance to Israel and forgiveness of sins."

The Word of the Lord.

◆ All observe silence.

FOR SILENT REFLECTION

Think about this silently in your heart. How does it feel to be forgiven when we've done or said something wrong?

CLOSING PRAYER

Let us pray to God for our needs and the needs of others: our family, neighborhood, and the world. For each need we say, "Lord, hear our prayer."

◆ All may add their own prayers here.

Let us pray: **Our Father . . . Amen.**

God, thank you for Jesus,
our Leader and Savior.
May we follow his lead
and be confident in your forgiveness.

Amen.

✦ All make the Sign of the Cross.

OPENING

In the last book of the Bible we hear that the "home of God is among mortals"; that is, God himself lives with human beings, with us. Monday's title, "Immanuel," said the same thing! Today's title is fitting for Friday. The one on the throne calls himself "Alpha and Omega." The Greek words mean "beginning and end."

✠ All make the Sign of the Cross.

In the name of the Father, and of the Son, and of the Holy Spirit. Amen.

PSALM   (For a longer psalm, see page xv.) Psalm 118:1–2, 4

The stone that the builders rejected
 has become the chief cornerstone.

**The stone that the builders rejected
 has become the chief cornerstone.**

O give thanks to the LORD, for he is good;
  his steadfast love endures forever!
Let Israel say,
  "His steadfast love endures forever."
Let those who fear the LORD say,
  "His steadfast love endures forever."

**The stone that the builders rejected
 has become the chief cornerstone.**

READING   Revelation 20:11a; 21:1ab, 2abc, 3abcd, 5ab, 6abc

A reading from the Book of Revelation.

Then I saw a great white throne and the one who sat on it. Then I saw a new heaven and a new earth; for the first heaven and the first earth had passed away. And I saw the holy city, the new Jerusalem, coming down out of heaven from God. And I heard a loud voice from the throne saying, "See, the home of God is among mortals. He will dwell with them as their God; they will be his peoples. And the one who was seated on the throne said, "See, I am making all things new." Then he said to me, "It is done! I am the Alpha and the Omega, the beginning and the end."

The Word of the Lord.

◆ All observe silence.

FOR SILENT REFLECTION

Think about this silently in your heart. In what way is Jesus "the beginning and the end"?

CLOSING PRAYER

Let us pray to God for our needs and the needs of others: our family, neighborhood, and the world. For each need we say, "Lord, hear our prayer."

◆ All may add their own prayers here.

Let us pray: **Our Father . . . Amen.**

Christ, the Alpha and the Omega,
the beginning and end of all creation.
We worship and praise you, O Lord.

Amen.

✠ All make the Sign of the Cross.

OPENING

In the parable of the vine Jesus encourages us to abide in him. The word "abide" means "to stay in one place." He wants us to stay close to him so we can produce good fruit, just as the branches of a grape vine produce sweet grapes.

✛ All make the Sign of the Cross.

In the name of the Father, and of the Son, and of the Holy Spirit. Amen.

PSALM   (For a longer psalm, see page xv.) Psalm 118:1–2, 4

The stone that the builders rejected
     has become the chief cornerstone.

**The stone that the builders rejected
     has become the chief cornerstone.**

O give thanks to the LORD, for he is good;
   his steadfast love endures forever!
Let Israel say,
   "His steadfast love endures forever."
Let those who fear the LORD say,
   "His steadfast love endures forever."

**The stone that the builders rejected
     has become the chief cornerstone.**

◆ All stand and sing **Alleluia.**

GOSPEL   John 15:1, 2b, 4–5, 7–8

A reading from the holy Gospel according to John.

Jesus said, "I am the true vine, and my Father is the vinegrower. Every branch that bears fruit he prunes to make it bear more fruit. Abide in me as I abide in you. Just as the branch cannot bear fruit by itself unless it abides in the vine, neither can you unless you abide in me. I am the vine, you are the branches. Those who abide in me and I in them bear much fruit, because apart from me you can do nothing. If you abide in me, and my words abide in you, ask for whatever you wish, and it will be done for you. My Father is glorified in this, that you bear much fruit and become my disciples."

The Gospel of the Lord.

◆ All sit and observe silence.

FOR SILENT REFLECTION

Think about this silently in your heart. What kind of good fruit can our words and actions produce?

CLOSING PRAYER

Let us pray to God for our needs and the needs of others: our family, neighborhood, and the world. For each need we say, "Lord, hear our prayer."

◆ All may add their own prayers here.

Let us pray: **Our Father . . . Amen.**

Help us abide in you, O God.
Help us to remain on the vine of your love and to bear good fruit.
We ask this in Jesus' name.

Amen.

✛ All make the Sign of the Cross.

OPENING

In this fifth week of Easter we will hear how Jesus shows us the way to God the Father. Jesus calls himself the "gate," through which we must go in order to know God and be saved.

✦ All make the Sign of the Cross.

In the name of the Father, and of the Son, and of the Holy Spirit. Amen.

PSALM   (For a longer psalm, see page xv.) Psalm 118:1–2, 4

The stone that the builders rejected
    has become the chief cornerstone.

**The stone that the builders rejected
    has become the chief cornerstone.**

O give thanks to the LORD, for he is good;
    his steadfast love endures forever!
Let Israel say,
    "His steadfast love endures forever."
Let those who fear the LORD say,
    "His steadfast love endures forever."

**The stone that the builders rejected
    has become the chief cornerstone.**

◆ All stand and sing **Alleluia.**

GOSPEL   John 10:9–15a

A reading from the holy Gospel according to John.

Jesus said, "I am the gate. Whoever enters by me will be saved, and will come in and go out and find pasture. The thief comes only to steal and kill and destroy. I came that they may have life, and have it abundantly. I am the good shepherd. The good shepherd lays down his life for the sheep. The hired hand, who is not the shepherd and does not own the sheep, sees the wolf coming and leaves the sheep and runs away—and the wolf snatches them and scatters them. The hired hand runs away because a hired hand does not care for the sheep. I am the good shepherd. I know my own and my own know me, just as the Father knows me and I know the Father."

The Gospel of the Lord.

◆ All sit and observe silence.

FOR SILENT REFLECTION

Think about this silently in your heart. In what way is Jesus a "gate"?

CLOSING PRAYER

Let us pray to God for our needs and the needs of others: our family, neighborhood, and the world. For each need we say, "Lord, hear our prayer."

◆ All may add their own prayers here.

Let us pray: **Our Father . . . Amen.**

We want to know you better,
God, our loving Father.
Help us follow Jesus faithfully
until we join you in heaven.
We ask this in Jesus' name.

Amen.

✦ All make the Sign of the Cross.

OPENING

Jesus reminds us that by keeping the commandments we will experience joy. Jesus wants our joy to be complete. He sums up all Ten Commandments into one commandment of love.

✚ All make the Sign of the Cross.

In the name of the Father, and of the Son, and of the Holy Spirit. Amen.

PSALM   (For a longer psalm, see page xv.) Psalm 118:1–2, 4

The stone that the builders rejected
      has become the chief cornerstone.

**The stone that the builders rejected
      has become the chief cornerstone.**

O give thanks to the LORD, for he is good;
   his steadfast love endures forever!
Let Israel say,
   "His steadfast love endures forever."
Let those who fear the LORD say,
   "His steadfast love endures forever."

**The stone that the builders rejected
      has become the chief cornerstone.**

◆ All stand and sing **Alleluia.**

GOSPEL   John 15:9–12

A reading from the holy Gospel according to John.

Jesus said, "As the Father has loved me, so I have loved you; abide in my love. If you keep my commandments, you will abide in my love, just as I have kept my Father's commandments and abide in his love. I have said these things to you so that my joy may be in you, and that your joy may be complete. This is my commandment, that you love one another as I have loved you."

The Gospel of the Lord.

◆ All sit and observe silence.

FOR SILENT REFLECTION

Think about this silently in your heart. Jesus' commandment sounds simple, but is truly loving one another ever simple?

CLOSING PRAYER

Let us pray to God for our needs and the needs of others: our family, neighborhood, and the world. For each need we say, "Lord, hear our prayer."

◆ All may add their own prayers here.

Let us pray: **Our Father . . . Amen.**

God, our Father,
we thank you for Jesus,
who teaches us about your great love.
We pray that we may follow
your commandment
and know the joy that Jesus promises.

Amen.

✚ All make the Sign of the Cross.

OPENING

Jesus calls himself the "way" to God the Father. He says if we know him, we know God. How fortunate the disciples were to be so close to Jesus. They don't seem to realize it, however.

✠ All make the Sign of the Cross.

In the name of the Father, and of the Son, and of the Holy Spirit. Amen.

PSALM

(For a longer psalm, see page xv.) Psalm 118:1–2, 4

The stone that the builders rejected
    has become the chief cornerstone.

**The stone that the builders rejected
    has become the chief cornerstone.**

O give thanks to the LORD, for he is good;
  his steadfast love endures forever!
Let Israel say,
  "His steadfast love endures forever."
Let those who fear the LORD say,
  "His steadfast love endures forever."

**The stone that the builders rejected
    has become the chief cornerstone.**

◆ All stand and sing **Alleluia.**

GOSPEL

John 14:6–7a, 8–9b, 10bc, 11

A reading from the holy Gospel according to John.

Jesus said to him, "I am the way, and the truth, and the life. No one comes to the Father except through me. If you know me, you will know my Father also." Philip said to him, "Lord, show us the Father, and we will be satisfied." Jesus said to him, "Have I been with you all this time, Philip, and you still do not know me?

Whoever has seen me has seen the Father. The words that I say to you I do not speak on my own; but the Father who dwells in me does his works. Believe me that I am in the Father and the Father is in me; but if you do not, then believe me because of the words themselves."

The Gospel of the Lord.

◆ All sit and observe silence.

FOR SILENT REFLECTION

Think about this silently in your heart. Where and when do you feel close to God?

CLOSING PRAYER

Let us pray to God for our needs and the needs of others: our family, neighborhood, and the world. For each need we say, "Lord, hear our prayer."

◆ All may add their own prayers here.

Let us pray: **Our Father . . . Amen.**

We want to know you better, God,
our loving Father.
Help us follow Jesus faithfully
until we join you heaven.
We ask this in Jesus' name.

Amen.

✠ All make the Sign of the Cross.

OPENING

Jesus says the way to love God the Father is to follow his teachings. As he often does, Jesus again offers his disciples the gift of his peace. He promises to send the Holy Spirit, who will continue to guide them.

✚ All make the Sign of the Cross.

In the name of the Father, and of the Son, and of the Holy Spirit. Amen.

PSALM   (For a longer psalm, see page xv.) Psalm 118:1–2, 4

The stone that the builders rejected
    has become the chief cornerstone.

**The stone that the builders rejected
    has become the chief cornerstone.**

O give thanks to the LORD, for he is good;
    his steadfast love endures forever!
Let Israel say,
    "His steadfast love endures forever."
Let those who fear the LORD say,
    "His steadfast love endures forever."

**The stone that the builders rejected
    has become the chief cornerstone.**

◆ All stand and sing **Alleluia.**

GOSPEL   John 14:23–27

A reading from the holy Gospel according to John.

Jesus answered him, "Those who love me will keep my word, and my Father will love them, and we will come to them and make our home with them. Whoever does not love me does not keep my words; and the word that you hear is not mine, but is from the Father who sent me.

I have said these things to you while I am still with you. But the Advocate, the Holy Spirit, whom the Father will send in my name, will teach you everything, and remind you of all that I have said to you. Peace I leave with you; my peace I give to you. I do not give to you as the world gives. Do not let your hearts be troubled, and do not let them be afraid."

The Gospel of the Lord.

◆ All sit and observe silence.

FOR SILENT REFLECTION

Think about this silently in your heart. Tell Jesus what troubles your heart or makes you afraid.

CLOSING PRAYER

Let us pray to God for our needs and the needs of others: our family, neighborhood, and the world. For each need we say, "Lord, hear our prayer."

◆ All may add their own prayers here.

Let us pray: **Our Father . . . Amen.**

We give you thanks, O God,
for the many ways you care for us.
Thank you for the gift of peace.

Amen.

✚ All make the Sign of the Cross.

OPENING

Jesus is the "light in the world," who shows us the way to God the Father. Jesus' light takes away the darkness of knowing God. Jesus says God wants us to have eternal life; that is, life with God in heaven.

✚ All make the Sign of the Cross.

In the name of the Father, and of the Son, and of the Holy Spirit. Amen.

PSALM

(For a longer psalm, see page xv.) Psalm 118:1–2, 4

The stone that the builders rejected
    has become the chief cornerstone.

**The stone that the builders rejected
    has become the chief cornerstone.**

O give thanks to the LORD, for he is good;
  his steadfast love endures forever!
Let Israel say,
  "His steadfast love endures forever."
Let those who fear the LORD say,
  "His steadfast love endures forever."

**The stone that the builders rejected
    has become the chief cornerstone.**

◆ All stand and sing **Alleluia.**

GOSPEL

John 12:44–46, 49–50

A reading from the holy Gospel according to John.

Then Jesus cried aloud: "Whoever believes in me believes not in me but in him who sent me. And whoever sees me sees him who sent me. I have come as light into the world, so that everyone who believes in me should not remain in the darkness. For I have not spoken on my own, but the Father who sent me has himself given me a commandment about what to say and what to speak. And I know that his commandment is eternal life. What I speak, therefore, I speak just as the Father has told me."

The Gospel of the Lord.

◆ All sit and observe silence.

FOR SILENT REFLECTION

Think about this silently in your heart. In what way is Jesus a light for you?

CLOSING PRAYER

Let us pray to God for our needs and the needs of others: our family, neighborhood, and the world. For each need we say, "Lord, hear our prayer."

◆ All may add their own prayers here.

Let us pray: **Our Father . . . Amen.**

Good and holy God,
We thank you for sending Jesus
to show us the way to you.
He is a light for a path.
He is a light in the darkness.
May we live as children of the light.

Amen.

✚ All make the Sign of the Cross.

PRAYER FOR THE WEEK

WITH A READING FROM THE GOSPEL FOR **SUNDAY, MAY 26, 2019**

OPENING

In this sixth week of Easter we hear how Jesus reassures the disciples that they will always have God's help, even when Jesus is gone. The Holy Spirit will remind them of all Jesus taught.

✝ All make the Sign of the Cross.

In the name of the Father, and of the Son, and of the Holy Spirit. Amen.

PSALM

(For a longer psalm, see page xv.) Psalm 118:1–2, 4

The stone that the builders rejected
    has become the chief cornerstone.

**The stone that the builders rejected
    has become the chief cornerstone.**

O give thanks to the LORD, for he is good;
  his steadfast love endures forever!
Let Israel say,
  "His steadfast love endures forever."
Let those who fear the LORD say,
  "His steadfast love endures forever."

**The stone that the builders rejected
    has become the chief cornerstone.**

◆ All stand and sing **Alleluia.**

GOSPEL

John 14:23–24a, 25–27c, 28a, 29

A reading from the holy Gospel according to John.

Jesus said, "Those who love me will keep my word, and my Father will love them, and we will come to them and make our home with them. Whoever does not love me does not keep my words. I have said these things to you while I am still with you. But the Advocate, the Holy Spirit, whom the Father will send in my name, will teach you everything, and remind you of all that I have said to you. Peace I leave with you; my peace I give to you. I do not give to you as the world gives. You heard me say to you, 'I am going away, and I am coming to you.' And now I have told you this before it occurs, so that when it does occur, you may believe."

The Gospel of the Lord.

◆ All sit and observe silence.

FOR SILENT REFLECTION

Think about this silently in your heart. Say a prayer to the Holy Spirit for strength and guidance.

CLOSING PRAYER

Let us pray to God for our needs and the needs of others: our family, neighborhood, and the world. For each need we say, "Lord, hear our prayer."

◆ All may add their own prayers here.

Let us pray: **Our Father . . . Amen.**

O come, Holy Spirit of God.
Help us keep Jesus' words by
giving us your Wisdom and Counsel.
We ask this in Jesus' name.

Amen.

✝ All make the Sign of the Cross.

OPENING

This week we will learn more about St. Paul, who was called Saul. In the Scripture we hear today, we learn that Saul watches the stoning of the Church's first deacon, St. Stephen. This event occurs before Saul's conversion and he takes the name of Paul.

✦ All make the Sign of the Cross.

In the name of the Father, and of the Son, and of the Holy Spirit. Amen.

PSALM

(For a longer psalm, see page xv.) Psalm 118:1–2, 4

The stone that the builders rejected
   has become the chief cornerstone.

**The stone that the builders rejected
   has become the chief cornerstone.**

O give thanks to the LORD, for he is good;
  his steadfast love endures forever!
Let Israel say,
  "His steadfast love endures forever."
Let those who fear the LORD say,
  "His steadfast love endures forever."

**The stone that the builders rejected
   has become the chief cornerstone.**

READING

Acts 6:8ac, 9ac, 10, 13; 7:54, 58–59, 60c; 8:1a

A reading from the Acts of the Apostles.

Stephen did great wonders and signs among the people. Then some of those who belonged to the synagogue of the Freedmen stood up and argued with Stephen. But they could not withstand the wisdom and the Spirit with which he spoke. They set up false witnesses who said,

"This man never stops saying things against this holy place and the law." When the Council heard these things, they became enraged and ground their teeth at Stephen. Then they dragged him out of the city and began to stone him; and the witnesses laid their coats at the feet of a young man named Saul. While they were stoning Stephen, he prayed, "Lord Jesus, receive my spirit." When he had said this, he died. And Saul approved of their killing him.

The Word of the Lord.

◆ All observe silence.

FOR SILENT REFLECTION

Think about this silently in your heart. In what ways is St. Stephen like Jesus?

CLOSING PRAYER

Let us pray to God for our needs and the needs of others: our family, neighborhood, and the world. For each need we say, "Lord, hear our prayer."

◆ All may add their own prayers here.

Let us pray: **Our Father . . . Amen.**

May we spread the Good News about Jesus as St. Stephen did.
We ask this in Jesus' name.

Amen.

✦ All make the Sign of the Cross.

PRARER FOR
TUESDAY, MAY 28, 2019

OPENING

We continue the story of St. Paul. Even as Saul continues his fierce persecution of Christians, St. Philip the Apostle bravely continues to tell the story of Jesus in Samaria.

✛ All make the Sign of the Cross.

In the name of the Father, and of the Son, and of the Holy Spirit. Amen.

PSALM   (For a longer psalm, see page xv.) Psalm 118:1–2, 4

The stone that the builders rejected
  has become the chief cornerstone.

**The stone that the builders rejected
  has become the chief cornerstone.**

O give thanks to the LORD, for he is good;
 his steadfast love endures forever!
Let Israel say,
 "His steadfast love endures forever."
Let those who fear the LORD say,
 "His steadfast love endures forever."

**The stone that the builders rejected
  has become the chief cornerstone.**

READING   Acts 8:1b–8

A reading from the Acts of the Apostles.

That day a severe persecution began against the church in Jerusalem, and all except the apostles were scattered throughout the countryside of Judea and Samaria. Devout men buried Stephen and made loud lamentation over him. But Saul was ravaging the church by entering house after house; dragging off both men and women, he committed them to prison.

Now those who were scattered went from place to place, proclaiming the word. Philip went down to the city of Samaria and proclaimed the Messiah to them. The crowds with one accord listened eagerly to what was said by Philip, hearing and seeing the signs that he did, for unclean spirits, crying with loud shrieks, came out of many who were possessed; and many others who were paralyzed or lame were cured. So there was great joy in that city.

The Word of the Lord.

◆ All observe silence.

FOR SILENT REFLECTION

Think about this silently in your heart. In what ways does St. Philip continue Jesus' ministry?

CLOSING PRAYER

Let us pray to God for our needs and the needs of others: our family, neighborhood, and the world. For each need we say, "Lord, hear our prayer."

◆ All may add their own prayers here.

Let us pray: **Our Father . . . Amen.**

May we act
with the courage of St. Philip.
We ask this in Jesus' name.
Amen.

✛ All make the Sign of the Cross.

OPENING

Today we hear of events that will lead to Saul's conversion. Listen to what he experiences.

✚ All make the Sign of the Cross.

In the name of the Father, and of the Son, and of the Holy Spirit. Amen.

PSALM

(For a longer psalm, see page xv.) Psalm 118:1–2, 4

The stone that the builders rejected
    has become the chief cornerstone.

**The stone that the builders rejected
    has become the chief cornerstone.**

O give thanks to the LORD, for he is good;
    his steadfast love endures forever!
Let Israel say,
    "His steadfast love endures forever."
Let those who fear the LORD say,
    "His steadfast love endures forever."

**The stone that the builders rejected
    has become the chief cornerstone.**

READING

Acts 9:1bc, 2bd, 3–6, 8–9

A reading from the Acts of the Apostles.

Meanwhile Saul, went to the high priest so that if he found any who belonged to the Way, he might bring them bound to Jerusalem. Now as he was going along and approaching Damascus, suddenly a light from heaven flashed around him. He fell to the ground and heard a voice saying to him, "Saul, Saul, why do you persecute me?" He asked, "Who are you, Lord?" The reply came, "I am Jesus, whom you are persecuting. But get up and enter the city, and you will be told what you are to do." Saul got up from the ground, and though his eyes were open, he could see nothing; so they led him by the hand and brought him into Damascus. For three days he was without sight, and neither ate nor drank.

The Word of the Lord.

◆ All observe silence.

FOR SILENT REFLECTION

Think about this silently in your heart. Why do you think Jesus would appear to Saul?

CLOSING PRAYER

Let us pray to God for our needs and the needs of others: our family, neighborhood, and the world. For each need we say, "Lord, hear our prayer."

◆ All may add their own prayers here.

Let us pray: **Our Father . . . Amen.**

Change the hearts, O God,
of all who persecute others
because of their beliefs.
Give hope and courage to those
who suffer because of their faith or religion.
We ask this in Jesus' name.
Amen.

✚ All make the Sign of the Cross.

OPENING

Finally Saul's conversion, or change, is complete. He becomes a great teacher and disciple of Jesus and worked to spread the Christian message through his epistles or letters to early Christian communities. Today is Ascension Thursday in some places. Most of us will celebrate it next Sunday.

✛ All make the Sign of the Cross.

In the name of the Father, and of the Son, and of the Holy Spirit. Amen.

PSALM (For a longer psalm, see page xv.) Psalm 118:1–2, 4

The stone that the builders rejected
    has become the chief cornerstone.

**The stone that the builders rejected
    has become the chief cornerstone.**

O give thanks to the LORD, for he is good;
    his steadfast love endures forever!
Let Israel say,
    "His steadfast love endures forever."
Let those who fear the LORD say,
    "His steadfast love endures forever."

**The stone that the builders rejected
    has become the chief cornerstone.**

READING Acts 9:10a, 11–12, 17abce, 18

A reading from the Acts of the Apostles.

Now there was a disciple in Damascus named Ananias [an-uh-NAHY-us]. The Lord said to him, "Get up and go to the street called Straight, and at the house of Judas look for a man of Tarsus named Saul. At this moment he is praying, and he has seen in a vision a man named Ananias come in and lay his hands on him so that he might regain his sight." So Ananias went and entered the house. He laid his hands on Saul and said, "Brother Saul, the Lord Jesus, has sent me so that you may regain your sight and be filled with the Holy Spirit." And immediately something like scales fell from his eyes, and his sight was restored.

The Word of the Lord.

◆ All observe silence.

FOR SILENT REFLECTION

Think about this silently in your heart. What do you need to see more clearly?

CLOSING PRAYER

Let us pray to God for our needs and the needs of others: our family, neighborhood, and the world. For each need we say, "Lord, hear our prayer."

◆ All may add their own prayers here.

Let us pray: **Our Father . . . Amen.**

Change our hearts, O God,
as you changed St. Paul's.
Help us to follow you as he did.
Amen.

✛ All make the Sign of the Cross.

OPENING

Saul, or Paul, was a powerful speaker who convinced many people to follow Jesus. Sadly, the Jewish authorities became jealous of his success. Today is the feast of the Visitation of the Blessed Virgin Mary to her relative, Elizabeth.

✛ All make the Sign of the Cross.

In the name of the Father, and of the Son, and of the Holy Spirit. Amen.

PSALM   (For a longer psalm, see page xv.) Psalm 118:1–2, 4

The stone that the builders rejected
     has become the chief cornerstone.

**The stone that the builders rejected
     has become the chief cornerstone.**

O give thanks to the LORD, for he is good;
     his steadfast love endures forever!
Let Israel say,
     "His steadfast love endures forever."
Let those who fear the LORD say,
     "His steadfast love endures forever."

**The stone that the builders rejected
     has become the chief cornerstone.**

READING   Acts 9:18c–21a, 22–23, 24b–25

A reading from the Acts of the Apostles.

Then Saul got up and was baptized, and after taking some food, he regained his strength. For several days he was with the disciples in Damascus, and immediately he began to proclaim Jesus in the synagogues, saying, "He is the Son of God." All who heard him were amazed and said, "Is not this the man who made havoc in Jerusalem among those who invoked this name?" Saul became increasingly more powerful and confounded the Jews who lived in Damascus by proving that Jesus was the Messiah. After some time had passed, the Jews plotted to kill him. They were watching the gates day and night so that they might kill him; but his disciples took him by night and let him down through an opening in the wall, lowering him in a basket.

The Word of the Lord.

◆ All observe silence.

FOR SILENT REFLECTION

Think about this silently in your heart. Say a prayer for those who are persecuted for their beliefs.

CLOSING PRAYER

Let us pray to God for our needs and the needs of others: our family, neighborhood, and the world. For each need we say, "Lord, hear our prayer."

◆ All may add their own prayers here.

Let us pray: **Our Father . . . Amen.**

Change our hearts, O God,
as you changed St. Paul's.
Help us to be bearers of the
Good News.
Amen.

✛ All make the Sign of the Cross.

PRAYER SERVICE
FOR ASCENSION

Prepare a leader, a reader, sprinkler, and song leader. Prepare a bowl with water and sturdy branch for a Sprinkling rite. You may wish to begin by singing "All Will Be Well" or other familiar hymn, or you might sing just the refrain to a familiar song.

SONG LEADER:

Please stand and join in singing our opening song.

LEADER:

We celebrate the Ascension of the Lord because we believe Jesus Christ rose from the dead and, after promising to be with us always, ascended into heaven where he sits at the right hand of the Father.

✛ All make the sign of the Cross.

> **In the name of the Father, and of the Son, and of the Holy spirit. Amen.**

We now use this water to remind us of our Baptism into Christ's Resurrection.

◆ Sprinkler uses the water and branch to sprinkle the participants.

LEADER:

Let us pray:
Holy God, we praise you and thank you for Jesus Christ, who redeemed the world and revealed to us of your unending love. We are grateful for the presence the Holy Spirit, who guides our hearts. Help us listen and act according to your will so we will one day enter your Kingdom. We ask this through Jesus Christ, Our Lord.

ALL: Amen.

◆ Gesture for all to sit.

300 CHILDREN'S DAILY PRAYER 2018–2019, © 2018 Archdiocese of Chicago: Liturgy Training Publications, 3949 South Racine Avenue, Chicago, IL 60609. All rights reserved. Orders: 800-933-1800 or www.LTP.org. Scripture excerpts are taken from *The New Revised Standard Version Bible: Catholic Edition*, copyright © 1989, Division of Christian Education of the National Council of the Churches of Christ in the United States of America. Used with permission. All rights reserved.

READER:

Acts 1:6–11

A reading from the Acts of the Apostles.

So when they had come together, they asked him, "Lord, is this the time when you will restore the kingdom to Israel"? He replied, "It is not for you to know the times or periods that the Father has set by his own authority. But you will receive power when the Holy Spirit has come upon you; and you will be my witnesses in Jerusalem, in all Judea and Samaria, and to the ends of the earth." When he had said this, as they were watching, he was lifted up, and a cloud took him out of their sight. When he was going and they were gazing up toward heaven, suddenly two men in white robes stood before them. They said, "Men of Galilee, why do you stand looking up toward heaven? This Jesus, who has been taken up from you into heaven, will come in the same way as you saw him go into heaven."

The Word of the Lord.

◆ All observe silence.

INTERCESSOR:

Let us stand and praise God with our litany. Our response is "Christ is risen, Alleluia!"

God of life, we give you praise and glory . . .

Jesus is victorious over death . . .

Jesus has ascended to heaven . . .

Jesus sends the Spirit to guide our lives . . .

Jesus will come again in glory . . .

Let us say the prayer Jesus taught:

Our Father . . . **Amen.**

LEADER:

May God protect us.
May Jesus watch over us.
May the Holy Spirit inspire us.
We ask this in Jesus' name.

ALL: Amen.

✝ All make the Sign of the Cross.

Let us pray: **Our Father . . . Amen.**

SONG LEADER:

Please join in the closing song.

CHILDREN'S DAILY PRAYER 2018–2019 © 2018 Archdiocese of Chicago: Liturgy Training Publications, 3949 South Racine Avenue, Chicago IL 60609. All rights reserved. Orders: 800-933-1800 or www.LTP.org. Scripture excerpts are taken from *The New Revised Standard Version Bible: Catholic Edition*, © 1989, Division of Christian Education of the National Council of the Churches of Christ in the United States of America. Used with permission. All rights reserved.

PRAYER FOR THE WEEK

OPENING

The Gospel today reflects the disciple's joy in Jesus' Resurrection and Ascension. Jesus tells them to continue his work once he's gone. He will send the Holy Spirit to guide them.

✛ All make the Sign of the Cross.

In the name of the Father, and of the Son, and of the Holy Spirit. Amen.

PSALM   (For a longer psalm, see page xv.) Psalm 118:1–2, 4

The stone that the builders rejected
   has become the chief cornerstone.

**The stone that the builders rejected
   has become the chief cornerstone.**

O give thanks to the Lord, for he is good;
   his steadfast love endures forever!
Let Israel say,
   "His steadfast love endures forever."
Let those who fear the Lord say,
   "His steadfast love endures forever."

**The stone that the builders rejected
   has become the chief cornerstone.**

◆ All stand and sing **Alleluia.**

GOSPEL   Luke 24:46–53

A reading from the holy Gospel according to Luke.

Jesus said to the disciples, "Thus it is written, that the Messiah is to suffer and to rise from the dead on the third day, and that repentance and forgiveness of sins is to be proclaimed in his name to all nations, beginning from Jerusalem. You are witnesses of these things. And see, I am sending upon you what my Father promised; so stay here in the city until you have been clothed with power from on high." Then he led them out as far as Bethany, and, lifting up his hands, he blessed them. While he was blessing them, he withdrew from them and was carried up into heaven. And they worshiped him, and returned to Jerusalem with great joy; and they were continually in the temple blessing God.

The Gospel of the Lord.

◆ All sit and observe silence.

FOR SILENT REFLECTION

Think about this silently in your heart. Do you worship God with great joy?

CLOSING PRAYER

Let us pray to God for our needs and the needs of others: our family, neighborhood, and the world. For each need we say, "Lord, hear our prayer."

◆ All may add their own prayers here.

Let us pray: **Our Father . . . Amen.**

Help us know your presence in us,
Holy Spirit of God.
Give us joy as we continue Jesus' work.

Amen.

✛ All make the Sign of the Cross.

OPENING

In our final week of Easter we will hear more about Jesus' appearances after his Resurrection. Today is the memorial day of St. Charles Lwanga, who was martyred in 1886 in Uganda, Africa.

✛ *All make the Sign of the Cross.*

In the name of the Father, and of the Son, and of the Holy Spirit. Amen.

PSALM

(For a longer psalm, see page xv.) Psalm 118:1–2, 4

The stone that the builders rejected
has become the chief cornerstone.

The stone that the builders rejected
has become the chief cornerstone.

O give thanks to the LORD, for he is good;
his steadfast love endures forever!
Let Israel say,
"His steadfast love endures forever."
Let those who fear the LORD say,
"His steadfast love endures forever."

The stone that the builders rejected
has become the chief cornerstone.

◆ *All stand and sing* **Alleluia.**

GOSPEL

Luke 24:36–42

A reading from the holy Gospel according to Luke.

While they were talking about this, Jesus himself stood among them and said to them, "Peace be with you." They were startled and terrified, and thought that they were seeing a ghost. He said to them, "Why are you frightened, and why do doubts arise in your hearts? Look at my hands and my feet; see that it is I myself. Touch me and see; for a ghost does not have flesh and bones as you see that I have." And when he had said this, he showed them his hands and his feet. While in their joy they were disbelieving and still wondering, he said to them, "Have you anything here to eat?" They gave him a piece of broiled fish, and he took it and ate in their presence.

The Gospel of the Lord.

◆ *All sit and observe silence.*

FOR SILENT REFLECTION

Think about this silently in your heart. How do you imagine the disciples felt when Jesus appeared to them?

CLOSING PRAYER

Let us pray to God for our needs and the needs of others: our family, neighborhood, and the world. For each need we say, "Lord, hear our prayer."

◆ *All may add their own prayers here.*

Let us pray: **Our Father . . . Amen.**

Help us follow and witness to Jesus faithfully. Help us to see him in unexpected places. May we know the peace that he brings.

Amen.

✛ *All make the Sign of the Cross.*

OPENING

"Doubting Thomas" doesn't believe the disciples saw Jesus. Jesus returns, and again he invites the disciples to touch him. We are the blessed ones who haven't seen Jesus' earthly body, but believe in him.

✛ All make the Sign of the Cross.

In the name of the Father, and of the Son, and of the Holy Spirit. Amen.

PSALM   (For a longer psalm, see page xv.) Psalm 118:1–2, 4

The stone that the builders rejected
      has become the chief cornerstone.

**The stone that the builders rejected
      has become the chief cornerstone.**

O give thanks to the LORD, for he is good;
   his steadfast love endures forever!
Let Israel say,
   "His steadfast love endures forever."
Let those who fear the LORD say,
   "His steadfast love endures forever."

**The stone that the builders rejected
      has become the chief cornerstone.**

◆ All stand and sing **Alleluia.**

GOSPEL   John 20:24acd, 25–27abd, 28–29ac

A reading from the holy Gospel according to John.

But Thomas, one of the twelve, was not with them when Jesus came. So the other disciples told him, "We have seen the Lord." But Thomas said to them, "Unless I see the mark of the nails in his hands, and put my finger in the mark of the nails and my hand in his side, I will not believe." A week later his disciples were again in the house, and Thomas was with them. Although the doors were shut, Jesus came and stood among them and said, "Peace be with you." Then he said to Thomas, "Put your finger here and see my hands. Do not doubt but believe." Thomas answered him, "My Lord and my God!" Jesus said to him, "Blessed are those who have not seen and yet have come to believe."

The Gospel of the Lord.

◆ All sit and observe silence.

FOR SILENT REFLECTION

Think about this silently in your heart. Do you think you would be like Thomas and doubt that Jesus had appeared to the disciples?

CLOSING PRAYER

Let us pray to God for our needs and the needs of others: our family, neighborhood, and the world. For each need we say, "Lord, hear our prayer."

◆ All may add their own prayers here.

Let us pray: **Our Father . . . Amen.**

We thank you for the gift of faith, O God.
We believe that Jesus died and rose,
and that he will come again.

Amen.

✛ All make the Sign of the Cross.

OPENING

Today the Gospel records St. Matthew's description of the Ascension, when Jesus tells the disciples they must spread Jesus' teaching throughout the world.

✚ All make the Sign of the Cross.

In the name of the Father, and of the Son, and of the Holy Spirit. Amen.

PSALM

(For a longer psalm, see page xv.) Psalm 118:1–2, 4

The stone that the builders rejected
   has become the chief cornerstone.

**The stone that the builders rejected
   has become the chief cornerstone.**

O give thanks to the LORD, for he is good;
   his steadfast love endures forever!
Let Israel say,
   "His steadfast love endures forever."
Let those who fear the LORD say,
   "His steadfast love endures forever."

**The stone that the builders rejected
   has become the chief cornerstone.**

◆ All stand and sing **Alleluia.**

GOSPEL

Matthew 28:9–10, 16–20

A reading from the holy Gospel according to Matthew.

Suddenly Jesus met them and said, "Greetings!" And they came to him, took hold of his feet, and worshiped him. Then Jesus said to them, "Do not be afraid; go and tell my brothers to go to Galilee; there they will see me." Now the eleven disciples went to Galilee, to the mountain to which Jesus had directed them. When they saw Jesus, they worshiped him; but some doubted. And Jesus came and said to them, "All authority in heaven and on earth has been given to me. Go therefore and make disciples of all nations, baptizing them in the name of the Father and of the Son and of the Holy Spirit, and teaching them to obey everything that I have commanded you. And remember, I am with you always, to the end of the age."

The Gospel of the Lord.

◆ All sit and observe silence.

FOR SILENT REFLECTION

Think about this silently in your heart. Jesus is "with you always, to the end of the age."

CLOSING PRAYER

Let us pray to God for our needs and the needs of others: our family, neighborhood, and the world. For each need we say, "Lord, hear our prayer."

◆ All may add their own prayers here.

Let us pray: **Our Father . . . Amen.**

We praise and thank you, O God,
for Jesus, who is present with us
as we live our daily lives.

Amen.

✚ All make the Sign of the Cross.

PRAYER FOR
THURSDAY, JUNE 6, 2019

OPENING

The Gospel reflects the disciple's joy in seeing Jesus after the Resurrection. Jesus tells them he will send the Holy Spirit to help them continue his work.

✛ All make the Sign of the Cross.

In the name of the Father, and of the Son, and of the Holy Spirit. Amen.

PSALM

(For a longer psalm, see page xv.) Psalm 118:1–2, 4

The stone that the builders rejected
    has become the chief cornerstone.

**The stone that the builders rejected
    has become the chief cornerstone.**

O give thanks to the LORD, for he is good;
    his steadfast love endures forever!
Let Israel say,
    "His steadfast love endures forever."
Let those who fear the LORD say,
    "His steadfast love endures forever."

**The stone that the builders rejected
    has become the chief cornerstone.**

◆ All stand and sing **Alleluia.**

GOSPEL

Luke 24:45–53

A reading from the holy Gospel according to Luke.

Then Jesus opened their minds to understand the scriptures, and he said to them, "Thus it is written, that the Messiah is to suffer and to rise from the dead on the third day, and that repentance and forgiveness of sins is to be proclaimed in his name to all nations, beginning from Jerusalem. You are witnesses of these things. And see, I am sending upon you what my Father promised; so stay here in the city until you have been clothed with power from on high." Then he led them out as far as Bethany, and, lifting up his hands, he blessed them. While he was blessing them, he withdrew from them and was carried up into heaven. And they worshiped him, and returned to Jerusalem with great joy; and they were continually in the temple blessing God.

The Gospel of the Lord.

◆ All sit and observe silence.

FOR SILENT REFLECTION

Think about this silently in your heart. Do you worship God with joy?

CLOSING PRAYER

Let us pray to God for our needs and the needs of others: our family, neighborhood, and the world. For each need we say, "Lord, hear our prayer."

◆ All may add their own prayers here.

Let us pray: **Our Father . . . Amen.**

Help us follow and witness to Jesus faithfully, O God.
May it bring us joy!
We ask in Jesus' name.

Amen.

✛ All make the Sign of the Cross.

OPENING

Today we hear that Jesus did so many good works that the world could not contain all the books that would be needed to record them!

✚ All make the Sign of the Cross.

In the name of the Father, and of the Son, and of the Holy Spirit. Amen.

PSALM

(For a longer psalm, see page xv.) Psalm 118:1–2, 4

The stone that the builders rejected
> has become the chief cornerstone.

**The stone that the builders rejected
> has become the chief cornerstone.**

O give thanks to the LORD, for he is good;
> his steadfast love endures forever!
Let Israel say,
> "His steadfast love endures forever."
Let those who fear the LORD say,
> "His steadfast love endures forever."

**The stone that the builders rejected
> has become the chief cornerstone.**

◆ All stand and sing **Alleluia.**

GOSPEL

John 20:30–31; 21:24–25

A reading from the holy Gospel according to John.

Now Jesus did many other signs in the presence of his disciples, which are not written in this book. But these are written so that you may come to believe that Jesus is the Messiah, the Son of God, and that through believing you may have life in his name. This is the disciple who is testifying to these things and has written them, and we know that his testimony is true. But there are also many other things that Jesus did; if every one of them were written down, I suppose that the world itself could not contain the books that would be written.

The Gospel of the Lord.

◆ All sit and observe silence.

FOR SILENT REFLECTION

Think about this silently in your heart. Offer a prayer of praise for Jesus, our Lord and Savior.

CLOSING PRAYER

Let us pray to God for our needs and the needs of others: our family, neighborhood, and the world. For each need we say, "Lord, hear our prayer."

◆ All may add their own prayers here.

Let us pray: **Our Father . . . Amen.**

We praise and thank you, O God
for the gift of your son, Jesus our Lord.
While he was on earth he revealed your great love.
Even today, through the Holy Spirit,
he continues to show us the way to you.

Amen.

✚ All make the Sign of the Cross.

PRAYER FOR THE WEEK

WITH A READING FROM THE GOSPEL FOR **SUNDAY, JUNE 9, 2019**

OPENING

Today is Pentecost, the fiftieth day after Easter. The Gospel tells about one of the most famous of Jesus' appearances before his Ascension. Pentecost is considered the birth of the Church.

✚ All make the Sign of the Cross.

> **In the name of the Father, and of the Son, and of the Holy Spirit. Amen.**

PSALM   (For a longer psalm, see page xv.) Psalm 118:1–2, 4

The stone that the builders rejected
     has become the chief cornerstone.

**The stone that the builders rejected
     has become the chief cornerstone.**

O give thanks to the LORD, for he is good;
  his steadfast love endures forever!
Let Israel say,
  "His steadfast love endures forever."
Let those who fear the LORD say,
  "His steadfast love endures forever."

**The stone that the builders rejected
     has become the chief cornerstone.**

◆ All stand and sing **Alleluia.**

GOSPEL   John 20:19–23

A reading from the holy Gospel according to John.

When it was evening on that day, the first day of the week, and the doors of the house where the disciples had met were locked for fear of the Jews, Jesus came and stood among them and said, "Peace be with you." After he said this, he showed them his hands and his side. Then the disciples rejoiced when they saw the Lord. Jesus said to them again, "Peace be with you. As the Father has sent me, so I send you." When he had said this, he breathed on them and said to them, "Receive the Holy Spirit. If you forgive the sins of any, they are forgiven them; if you retain the sins of any, they are retained."

The Gospel of the Lord.

◆ All sit and observe silence.

FOR SILENT REFLECTION

Think about this silently in your heart. To whom can you offer the peace of Jesus today?

CLOSING PRAYER

Let us pray to God for our needs and the needs of others: our family, neighborhood, and the world. For each need we say, "Lord, hear our prayer."

◆ All may add their own prayers here.

Let us pray: **Our Father . . . Amen.**

Holy God, we thank you for the gifts
of the Holy Spirit.
Help us to be peacemakers.
Help us to forgive others.
We ask this in Jesus' name.
Amen.

✚ All make the Sign of the Cross.

ORDINARY TIME
SUMMER

MONDAY, JUNE 10 — FRIDAY, JUNE 21

SUMMER ORDINARY TIME

THE MEANING OF ORDINARY TIME

We just celebrated the great feasts of Easter and Pentecost and now move back to Ordinary Time. The Prayers for the Week will reflect the Sunday Gospels, but during the week we will again "walk through the Bible."

On Pentecost, the Spirit descended upon Jesus' disciples strengthening them with wisdom and courage. St. Paul wrote letters to the early Christian communities telling them how this same Spirit guides and strengthens them. Paul names the Fruits of the Spirit: love, joy, peace, patience, gentles, and self-control. Paul assures Jesus followers that the Spirit intercedes for them when they are too weak to pray. Finally, this week we see that the Spirit flows through Peter giving him special ability to heal.

As we end this school year our focus is Mission. The scripture passages tell us that Jesus told his disciples to go out and proclaim the Kingdom of God, and that they did. We read the letters of Paul to Jews and Gentiles (non-Jews) living in Antioch and Corinth. We see that in the early Christian communities many of the leaders were women. As we prepare for summer vacation, it is a good time to remind ourselves that we are Christ's disciples and that our mission is also to proclaim God's love through our words and our actions.

During these weeks of Ordinary Time, we celebrate the solemnity of the Most Holy Trinity. A solemnity is a very high celebration in the church calendar.

PREPARING TO CELEBRATE ORDINARY TIME IN THE CLASSROOM

This will be your last time changing the prayer table-cloth this year. Even if you haven't had a procession each time the cloth changes, try to have one now. As the school year winds down, it is good to bring the students' focus squarely on the prayer life of your classroom community. You may wish to invite the students to choose something to carry in the procession, something that helped their spiritual growth this year. Clear an area near the prayer table, spread it with a green cloth, and let the children place their objects there. As a final project, ask them to write a short essay or poem about the significance of the object they chose. Suggest that they illustrate their work. Invite them to share their writings aloud during one of your final prayer times together. (Some students might feel uncomfortable sharing private thoughts in front of a group. Don't force them to participate in this aspect of your celebration.) You might even consider collecting all the papers into a booklet, which you can photocopy for each student to keep as a memento of the year.

SACRED SPACE

Bring your potted plant back to the prayer table. You may want to discuss how it might be different from how it looked when you first placed it on the prayer table. Some plants, such as spider plants, send out shoots with new plants on them. If your spider plant is sufficiently mature, you may even have enough "spider babies" to clip and give to each of your students in a paper cup with a little soil in it. Or you may like to keep the table adorned with fresh flowers from a spring garden. Children love to bring flowers from their parents' or grandparents' gardens.

MOVEMENT AND GESTURE

Children love to sing this song by David Haas and add movement.

PRAYER FOR PEACE

"Peace before us, peace behind us, peace under our feet. Peace within us, peace over us, let all around us be peace.

Love before us, love behind us, love under our feet. Love within us, love over us, let all around us be love.

Light before us, light behind us, light under our feet. Light within us, light over us, let all around us be light.

Christ before us, Christ behind us, Christ under our feet. Christ within us, Christ over us, let all around us be Christ."

Movement: peace before us (extend arms in front body), peace behind us (extend arms behind body), peace under our feet (bend down and extend arms toward feet), peace within us (stand up and fold hands over heart), peace over us (extend arms over head and open them), let all around us be peace (extend arms in a semicircle in front of body). Repeat movement with each stanza.

SACRED MUSIC

If you have been singing with your students all year, they will probably be quite comfortable with at least one or two of their favorite hymns. Consider scheduling a visit to one of the other classrooms to offer a small concert or sing-along (an older classroom could visit a younger grade; smaller children could sing for the "big kids"). If your students are particularly confident, you may even suggest that they volunteer to sing for an all-school Mass or end-of-the-year prayer service. If you invite parents to the class for one of your final sessions, don't be shy about including them in your prayer. And by all means, sing for them! Some songs that work well in this season are "Christ for the World We Sing," "Lord, I Want to Be a Christian," and "Spirit of the Living God."

PRAYERS FOR ORDINARY TIME

There are only a few precious places in the Gospel where we have the chance to listen to Jesus as he prays to his Father in heaven. In these moments, we can see clearly what it is Jesus wants for the world. The following prayer, taken from the Gospel according to John, shows how much Jesus wants us to abide in his love and to live with each other in the love and peace shared by the Father, Son, and Holy Spirit.

"As you, Father, are in me and I am in you, may my followers also be in us, so that the world may believe that you have sent me. The glory that you have given me I have given them, so that they may be one, as we are one, I in them and you in me, that they may become completely one, so that the world may know that you have sent me and have loved them even as you have loved me" (John 17:21b–23).

A NOTE TO CATECHISTS

You may wish to write the names of your students into your personal calendar during the summer months, so that you will remember to pray for them even when your group is no longer meeting. Prayer is the most useful and effective way we have to be of service to those about whom we care.

GRACE BEFORE MEALS
ORDINARY TIME • SUMMER

LEADER:

O give thanks to the Lord, for he is good;

ALL: for his steadfast love endures forever.

✚ All make the Sign of the Cross.

In the name of the Father, and of the Son, and of the Holy Spirit. Amen.

LEADER:

God of abundance,
your grace fills the hearts of
all those who call you Lord,
and even those who may not
know you yet.
Thank you for the gift of this meal
and the nourishment it will provide.
We are grateful for this time to
share it with each other.
May we work together to fill the plates
of those in our community and around the
world who may experience
extreme hunger or thirst today.
We ask this through Christ our Lord.

ALL: Amen.

✚ All make the Sign of the Cross.

In the name of the Father, and of the Son, and of the Holy Spirit. Amen.

PRAYER AT DAY'S END
ORDINARY TIME • SUMMER

LEADER:

See what love the Father has given us,

ALL: that we should be called children of God.

✝ All make the Sign of the Cross.

In the name of the Father, and of the Son, and of the Holy Spirit. Amen.

LEADER:

Almighty Father,
you created us in your image
of goodness and light.
Grant that we may offer you
all that we are in thanksgiving,
here at the end of our school day,
and this night, when we close our eyes
for restful sleep.
May the peace of Christ remain with us
now and forever.
We ask this in Jesus' name.

ALL: Amen.

✝ All make the Sign of the Cross.

In the name of the Father, and of the Son, and of the Holy Spirit. Amen.

PRAYER FOR
MONDAY, JUNE 10, 2019

OPENING

This week we continue our Pentecost celebration of the Holy Spirit. Our Scripture describes how it looked and felt when the Holy Spirit filled the disciples with the gifts they needed to teach.

✣ All make the Sign of the Cross.

In the name of the Father, and of the Son, and of the Holy Spirit. Amen.

PSALM   (For a longer psalm, see page xv.) Psalm 85:8–9

The Lord speaks of peace to his people.

The Lord speaks of peace to his people.

Let me hear what God the Lord will speak,
     for he will speak peace to his people,
     to his faithful, to those who turn to him in
          their hearts.
Surely his salvation is at hand for those who
          fear him,
     that his glory may dwell in our land.

The Lord speaks of peace to his people.

READING   Acts 2:1–6a, 7–8, 11b–12

A reading from the Acts of the Apostles.

When the day of Pentecost had come, they were all together in one place. And suddenly from heaven there came a sound like the rush of a violent wind, and it filled the entire house where they were sitting. Divided tongues, as of fire, appeared among them, and a tongue rested on each of them. All of them were filled with the Holy Spirit and began to speak in other languages, as the Spirit gave them ability. Now there were devout Jews from every nation under heaven living in Jerusalem. And at this

sound the crowd gathered. Amazed and astonished, they asked, "Are not all these who are speaking Galileans? And how is it that we hear, each of us, in our own native language? In our own languages we hear them speaking about God's deeds of power." All were amazed and perplexed, saying to one another, "What does this mean?"

The Word of the Lord.

◆ All observe silence.

FOR SILENT REFLECTION

Think about this silently in your heart. What symbols or signs of the Holy Spirit did you hear in the reading?

CLOSING PRAYER

Let us pray to God for our needs and the needs of others: our family, neighborhood, and the world. For each need we say, "Lord, hear our prayer."

◆ All may add their own prayers here.

Let us pray: **Our Father . . . Amen.**

Come, Holy Spirit,
fill our hearts with the fire of your love!
We ask this in Jesus' name.
Amen.

✣ All make the Sign of the Cross.

OPENING

Today is the feast of St. Barnabas who, with St. Paul, was a missionary to the Gentiles; that is, to people who were not Jews. St. Paul says we must avoid competing with and envying one another; rather, we must live by the Holy Spirit's guidance. If we do, we will share many good fruits.

✚ All make the Sign of the Cross.

In the name of the Father, and of the Son, and of the Holy Spirit. Amen.

PSALM   (For a longer psalm, see page xv.) Psalm 85:8–9

The LORD speaks of peace to his people.

The LORD speaks of peace to his people.

Let me hear what God the LORD will speak,
    for he will speak peace to his people,
        to his faithful, to those who turn to him in
            their hearts.
Surely his salvation is at hand for those who
            fear him,
    that his glory may dwell in our land.

The LORD speaks of peace to his people.

READING   Galatians 5:13–14, 22–23b, 25–26

A reading from the Letter of Paul to the Galatians [guh-LAY-shuhnz].

For you were called to freedom, brothers and sisters; only do not use your freedom as an opportunity for self-indulgence, but through love become slaves to one another. For the whole law is summed up in a single commandment, 'You shall love your neighbor as yourself.' The fruit of the Spirit is love, joy, peace, patience, kindness, generosity, faithfulness, gentleness, and self-control. If we live by the Spirit, let us also be guided by the Spirit. Let us not become conceited, competing against one another, envying one another.

The Word of the Lord.

◆ All observe silence.

FOR SILENT REFLECTION

Think about this silently in your heart. The fruits of the Spirit are love, joy, peace, patience, kindness, generosity, faithfulness, gentleness, and self-control. Which one do you need the most right now?

CLOSING PRAYER

Let us pray to God for our needs and the needs of others: our family, neighborhood, and the world. For each need we say, "Lord, hear our prayer."

◆ All may add their own prayers here.

Let us pray: **Our Father . . . Amen.**

Come, Holy Spirit,
fill our hearts with the fire of your love!
Help us bear the fruits of your Spirit.
We ask this in Jesus' name.
Amen.

✚ All make the Sign of the Cross.

OPENING

St. Paul wrote yesterday that God's law is summed up in one commandment: love your neighbor as yourself. He explains a little more about what that means. Loving our neighbor is how we love God, and it is the Holy Spirit who helps us do it. Our neighbor is anyone we meet.

✚ All make the Sign of the Cross.

In the name of the Father, and of the Son, and of the Holy Spirit. Amen.

PSALM
(For a longer psalm, see page xv.) Psalm 85:8–9

The Lord speaks of peace to his people.

The Lord speaks of peace to his people.

Let me hear what God the Lord will speak,
   for he will speak peace to his people,
   to his faithful, to those who turn to him in
      their hearts.
Surely his salvation is at hand for those who
      fear him,
   that his glory may dwell in our land.

The Lord speaks of peace to his people.

READING
Romans 12:9–10; 13:8–10

A reading from the Letter of Paul to the Romans.

Let love be genuine; hate what is evil, hold fast to what is good; love one another with mutual affection; outdo one another in showing honor. Owe no one anything, except to love one another; for the one who loves another has fulfilled the law. The commandments, "You shall not commit adultery; You shall not murder; You shall not steal; You shall not covet";

and any other commandment, are summed up in this word, "Love your neighbor as yourself." Love does no wrong to a neighbor; therefore, love is the fulfilling of the law.

The Word of the Lord.

◆ All observe silence.

FOR SILENT REFLECTION

Think about this silently in your heart. If you don't like someone, how can you follow God's law and love that person? Perhaps the Holy Spirit can help you think about that.

CLOSING PRAYER

Let us pray to God for our needs and the needs of others: our family, neighborhood, and the world. For each need we say, "Lord, hear our prayer."

◆ All may add their own prayers here.

Let us pray: **Our Father . . . Amen.**

Come, Holy Spirit,
fill our hearts with the fire of your love!
Show us how to love
even those we do not like.
We ask this in Jesus' name.

Amen.

✚ All make the Sign of the Cross.

OPENING

It is the memorial of St. Anthony of Padua, a Franciscan priest who is the patron saint of Padua, Italy; the country of Portugal, and San Antonio, Texas. Today's Scripture is hard to understand when we first hear it. St. Paul wants us to know that we're all weak in praying; that is, we find it hard to pray or are not sure for what to pray. But we can be sure the Holy Spirit always knows what our heart wants to say to God.

✦ All make the Sign of the Cross.

In the name of the Father, and of the Son, and of the Holy Spirit. Amen.

PSALM
(For a longer psalm, see page xv.) Psalm 85:8–9

The LORD speaks of peace to his people.

The LORD speaks of peace to his people.

Let me hear what God the LORD will speak,
 for he will speak peace to his people,
  to his faithful, to those who turn to him in
   their hearts.
Surely his salvation is at hand for those who
  fear him,
 that his glory may dwell in our land.

The LORD speaks of peace to his people.

READING
Romans 8:26–28

A reading from the Letter of Paul to the Romans.

The Spirit helps us in our weakness; for we do not know how to pray as we ought, but that very Spirit intercedes with sighs too deep for words. And God, who searches the heart, knows what is the mind of the Spirit, because the Spirit intercedes for the saints according to the will of God. We know that all things work together for good for those who love God, who are called according to his purpose.

The Word of the Lord.

✦ All observe silence.

FOR SILENT REFLECTION

Think about this silently in your heart. How often do you pray outside of Mass or school? Do you ever specifically pray to God the Holy Spirit?

CLOSING PRAYER

Let us pray to God for our needs and the needs of others: our family, neighborhood, and the world. For each need we say, "Lord, hear our prayer."

✦ All may add their own prayers here.

Let us pray: **Our Father . . . Amen.**

Come, Holy Spirit,
fill our hearts with the fire of your love!
Teach us how to pray.
We ask this in Jesus' name.

Amen.

✦ All make the Sign of the Cross.

PRAYER FOR
FRIDAY, JUNE 14, 2019

OPENING

After Pentecost, the disciples found they had new gifts. When we are faithful followers of Jesus and believe the Holy Spirit is with us, extraordinary things can happen. Sts. Peter and John were strong in their confidence and trust in the Spirit.

✦ All make the Sign of the Cross.

In the name of the Father, and of the Son, and of the Holy Spirit. Amen.

PSALM   (For a longer psalm, see page xv.) Psalm 85:8–9

The LORD speaks of peace to his people.

The LORD speaks of peace to his people.

Let me hear what God the LORD will speak,
    for he will speak peace to his people,
    to his faithful, to those who turn to him in
        their hearts.
Surely his salvation is at hand for those who
        fear him,
    that his glory may dwell in our land.

The LORD speaks of peace to his people.

READING   Acts 3:1a, 2a, 3–8, 10b

A reading from the Acts of the Apostles.

One day Peter and John were going up to the temple at the hour of prayer. And a man lame from birth was being carried in. When he saw Peter and John about to go into the temple, he begged them for alms. Peter looked intently at him, as did John, and said, "Look at us." And he fixed his attention on them, expecting to receive something from them. But Peter said, "I have no silver or gold, but what I have I give you; in the name of Jesus Christ of Nazareth, stand up and walk." And he took him by the right hand and raised him up; and immediately his feet and ankles were made strong. Jumping up, the man stood and began to walk, and he entered the temple with them, walking and leaping and praising God; and all the people were filled with wonder and amazement at what had happened to him.

The Word of the Lord.

◆ All observe silence.

FOR SILENT REFLECTION

Think about this silently in your heart. What events in Scripture fill you with wonder and amazement?

CLOSING PRAYER

Let us pray to God for our needs and the needs of others: our family, neighborhood, and the world. For each need we say, "Lord, hear our prayer."

◆ All may add their own prayers here.

Let us pray: **Our Father . . . Amen.**

Come, Holy Spirit,
fill our hearts with the fire of your love!
Fill us with the wonder of God.
We ask this in Jesus' name

Amen.

✦ All make the Sign of the Cross.

PRAYER FOR THE WEEK
WITH A READING FROM THE GOSPEL FOR **SUNDAY, JUNE 16, 2019**

OPENING

Today we celebrate the Most Holy Trinity; that is, God the Father, God the Son, and God the Holy Spirit. The idea of the Holy Trinity (or three persons in one God) is hard to think about, so we say it is a mystery. However, we do understand that God the Father created us in love; God the Son loved us so much he died for us; and God the Holy Spirit lovingly dwells in us every day. The Most Holy Trinity is all about God's amazing love!

✦ All make the Sign of the Cross.

In the name of the Father, and of the Son, and of the Holy Spirit. Amen.

PSALM   (For a longer psalm, see page xv.) Psalm 85:8–9

The LORD speaks of peace to his people.

The LORD speaks of peace to his people.

Let me hear what God the LORD will speak,
   for he will speak peace to his people,
   to his faithful, to those who turn to him in
      their hearts.
Surely his salvation is at hand for those who
      fear him,
   that his glory may dwell in our land.

The LORD speaks of peace to his people.

✦ All stand and sing **Alleluia.**

GOSPEL   John 16:12-15

A reading from the holy Gospel according to John.

"I still have many things to say to you, but you cannot bear them now. When the Spirit of truth comes, he will guide you into all the truth; for he will not speak on his own, but will speak whatever he hears, and the Spirit will declare to you the things that are to come. He will glorify me, because he will take what is mine and declare it to you. All that the Father has is mine. For this reason I said that he will take what is mine and declare it to you."

The Gospel of the Lord.

✦ All sit and observe silence.

FOR SILENT REFLECTION

Think about this silently in your heart. What are the signs of God's amazing love in your life?

CLOSING PRAYER

Let us pray to God for our needs and the needs of others: our family, neighborhood, and the world. For each need we say, "Lord, hear our prayer."

✦ All may add their own prayers here.

Let us pray: **Our Father . . . Amen.**

God, Most Holy Trinity,
help us believe in you firmly,
trust in you completely and
love you with full hearts.
We ask this in Jesus' name.

Amen.

✦ All make the Sign of the Cross.

PRAYER FOR
MONDAY, JUNE 17, 2019

OPENING

This week we will hear Scriptures that tell us how, after Jesus' Ascension, the early Christians continued his mission to teach about God's love. Today Jesus teaches the Twelve Apostles how to do his mission. The word "apostle" means "one who is sent."

✝ All make the Sign of the Cross.

In the name of the Father, and of the Son, and of the Holy Spirit. Amen.

PSALM   (For a longer psalm, see page xv.) Psalm 85:8–9

The LORD speaks of peace to his people.

The LORD speaks of peace to his people.

Let me hear what God the LORD will speak,
    for he will speak peace to his people,
        to his faithful, to those who turn to him in
            their hearts.
Surely his salvation is at hand for those who
        fear him,
    that his glory may dwell in our land.

The LORD speaks of peace to his people.

◆ All stand and sing **Alleluia.**

GOSPEL   Luke 9:1–7a

A reading from the holy Gospel according to Luke.

Then Jesus called the twelve together and gave them power and authority over all demons and to cure diseases, and he sent them out to proclaim the kingdom of God and to heal. He said to them, "Take nothing for your journey, no staff, nor bag, nor bread, nor money—not even an extra tunic. Whatever house you enter, stay there, and leave from there. Wherever they do not welcome you, as you are leaving that town shake the dust off your feet as a testimony against them." They departed and went through the villages, bringing the good news and curing diseases everywhere.

The Gospel of the Lord.

◆ All sit and observe silence.

FOR SILENT REFLECTION

Think about this silently in your heart. The Apostles trusted Jesus. They also trusted that the towns would feed and house them. How well do we trust Jesus?

CLOSING PRAYER

Let us pray to God for our needs and the needs of others: our family, neighborhood, and the world. For each need we say, "Lord, hear our prayer."

◆ All may add their own prayers here.

Let us pray: **Our Father . . . Amen.**

Show us how to continue Jesus' mission,
O God.
May we trust you and the Church
to support us in doing our part of your work.
We ask this in Jesus' name.

Amen.

✝ All make the Sign of the Cross.

OPENING

Jesus now sends seventy more people out to proclaim that the Kingdom of God is near. In the towns where Jesus' message is welcome, the closeness of the Kingdom brings healing. But for the towns who do not welcome Jesus' message, the Kingdom's closeness is a warning!

✚ All make the Sign of the Cross.

In the name of the Father, and of the Son, and of the Holy Spirit. Amen.

PSALM   (For a longer psalm, see page xv.) Psalm 85:8–9

The LORD speaks of peace to his people.

The LORD speaks of peace to his people.

Let me hear what God the LORD will speak,
   for he will speak peace to his people,
   to his faithful, to those who turn to him in
      their hearts.
Surely his salvation is at hand for those who
      fear him,
   that his glory may dwell in our land.

The LORD speaks of peace to his people.

◆ All stand and sing **Alleluia.**

GOSPEL   Luke 10:1, 3a, 4abc, 7a, 8–11

A reading from the holy Gospel according to Luke.

After this the Lord appointed seventy others and sent them on ahead of him in pairs to every town and place where he himself intended to go. Jesus said, "Go on your way. Carry no purse, no bag, no sandals. Remain in the same house. Whenever you enter a town and its people welcome you, eat what is set before you; cure the sick who are there, and say to them, 'The kingdom of God has come near to you.' But whenever you enter a town and they do not welcome you, go out into its streets and say, 'Even the dust of your town that clings to our feet, we wipe off in protest against you. Yet know this: the kingdom of God has come near.'"

The Gospel of the Lord.

◆ All sit and observe silence.

FOR SILENT REFLECTION

Think about this silently in your heart. What would the world look like if the Kingdom of God were fully in place?

CLOSING PRAYER

Let us pray to God for our needs and the needs of others: our family, neighborhood, and the world. For each need we say, "Lord, hear our prayer."

◆ All may add their own prayers here.

Let us pray: **Our Father . . . Amen.**

Holy God, help us to do our part
to spread the good news of your Kingdom.
We ask this in Jesus' name.

Amen.

✚ All make the Sign of the Cross.

OPENING

Sts. Paul and Barnabas are continuing Jesus' mission in Antioch. They are preaching to the Gentiles, or non-Jews, and many believe. But some powerful people are jealous and try to hurt them. Paul and Barnabas did as Jesus instructed the Apostles, so they "shook the dust off their feet." That means they would not waste time arguing with nonbelievers.

✛ All make the Sign of the Cross.

In the name of the Father, and of the Son, and of the Holy Spirit. Amen.

PSALM   (For a longer psalm, see page xv.) Psalm 85:8–9

The LORD speaks of peace to his people.

The LORD speaks of peace to his people.

Let me hear what God the LORD will speak,
  for he will speak peace to his people,
    to his faithful, to those who turn to him in
      their hearts.
Surely his salvation is at hand for those who
    fear him,
  that his glory may dwell in our land.

The LORD speaks of peace to his people.

READING   Acts 13:43ab, 44–45ab, 46abd, 50ab, 51

A reading from the Acts of the Apostles.

When the meeting of the synagogue broke up, many Jews and devout converts to Judaism followed Paul and Barnabas. The next sabbath almost the whole city gathered to hear the word of the Lord. But when the Jews saw the crowds, they were filled with jealousy. Then both Paul and Barnabas spoke out boldly, say-ing, "It was necessary that the word of God should be spoken first to you. Since you reject it we are now turning to the Gentiles." But the Jews incited the devout women of high standing and the leading men of the city, and stirred up persecution against Paul and Barnabas. So they shook the dust off their feet in protest against them, and went to Iconium (eye-COH-nee-uhm).

The Word of the Lord.

◆ All observe silence.

FOR SILENT REFLECTION

Think about this silently in your heart. Do you ever refuse to listen even when you know you should?

CLOSING PRAYER

Let us pray to God for our needs and the needs of others: our family, neighborhood, and the world. For each need we say, "Lord, hear our prayer."

◆ All may add their own prayers here.

Let us pray: **Our Father . . . Amen.**

Help us to listen to your word, O God,
and to be your faithful disciples.
We ask this in Jesus' name.

Amen.

✛ All make the Sign of the Cross.

OPENING

Paul and Barnabas are doing a lot of travelling to continue Jesus' mission. People in the town of Derbre [derb] become believers in Jesus. When people compliment Paul and Barnabas on their success, they give all the credit to God. We need to remember that God is also working through us!

✚ All make the Sign of the Cross.

In the name of the Father, and of the Son, and of the Holy Spirit. Amen.

PSALM   (For a longer psalm, see page xv.) Psalm 85:8–9

The LORD speaks of peace to his people.

The LORD speaks of peace to his people.

Let me hear what God the LORD will speak,
   for he will speak peace to his people,
      to his faithful, to those who turn to him in
         their hearts.
Surely his salvation is at hand for those who
         fear him,
   that his glory may dwell in our land.

The LORD speaks of peace to his people.

READING   Acts 14:21–22, 26–28

A reading from the Acts of the Apostles.

After Paul and Barnabas had proclaimed the good news to that city and had made many disciples, they returned to Lystra [LĬS-truh], then on to Iconium [eye-COH-nee-uhm] and Antioch [AN-tee-och]. There they strengthened the souls of the disciples and encouraged them to continue in the faith, saying, "It is through many persecutions that we must enter the kingdom of God." From there they sailed back to Antioch, where they had been commended to the grace of God for the work that they had completed. When they arrived, they called the church together and related all that God had done with them, and how he had opened a door of faith for the Gentiles. And they stayed there with the disciples for some time.

The Word of the Lord.

◆ All observe silence.

FOR SILENT REFLECTION

Think about this silently in your heart. How can you let God's love and mercy work through you today?

CLOSING PRAYER

Let us pray to God for our needs and the needs of others: our family, neighborhood, and the world. For each need we say, "Lord, hear our prayer."

◆ All may add their own prayers here.

Let us pray: **Our Father . . . Amen.**

Show us how to continue Jesus' mission,
O God.
May we trust you and trust the Church
to support us in doing our part of your work.
We ask this in Jesus' name.

Amen.

✚ All make the Sign of the Cross.

OPENING

St. Paul calls those who believe in Jesus "ambassadors." An ambassador has authority to speak for someone. God has given us the authority to do Jesus' mission. Today is the memorial day of St. Aloysius [al-oh-ISH-us] who died very young. It is said that his first words were "Jesus and Mary" and that his last word was the name of Jesus.

✚ All make the Sign of the Cross.

In the name of the Father, and of the Son, and of the Holy Spirit. Amen.

PSALM   (For a longer psalm, see page xv.) Psalm 85:8–9

The LORD speaks of peace to his people.

The LORD speaks of peace to his people.

Let me hear what God the LORD will speak,
    for he will speak peace to his people,
    to his faithful, to those who turn to him in
        their hearts.
Surely his salvation is at hand for those who
        fear him,
    that his glory may dwell in our land.

The LORD speaks of peace to his people.

READING   2 Corinthians 5:14a, 15, 20; 6:1–2de, 11–12

A reading from the Second Letter of Paul to the Corinthians.

For the love of Christ urges us on. And he died for all, so that those who live might live no longer for themselves, but for him who died and was raised for them. So we are ambassadors for Christ, since God is making his appeal through us; we entreat you on behalf of Christ, be reconciled to God. As we work together with him, we urge you also not to accept the grace of God in vain. See, now is the acceptable time; see, now is the day of salvation! We have spoken frankly to you Corinthians; our heart is wide open to you. There is no restriction in our affections, but only in yours.

The Word of the Lord.

◆ All observe silence.

FOR SILENT REFLECTION

Think about this silently in your heart. Are you a good ambassador for Jesus Christ?

CLOSING PRAYER

Let us pray to God for our needs and the needs of others: our family, neighborhood, and the world. For each need we say, "Lord, hear our prayer."

◆ All may add their own prayers here.

Let us pray: **Our Father . . . Amen.**

Show us how to continue Jesus' mission,
O God.
Make us ambassadors for Christ.
We ask this in Jesus' name.

Amen.

✚ All make the Sign of the Cross.

✝ All make the Sign of the Cross.

ALL: In the name of the Father, and of the Son, and of the Holy Spirit. Amen.

LEADER:
Loving God,
you created all the people of the world,
and you know each of us by name.
We thank you for N., who today
    celebrates his/her birthday.
Bless him/her with your love and friendship
that he/she may grow in wisdom, knowledge,
    and grace.
May he/she love his/her family always
and be faithful to his/her friends.

Grant this through Christ our Lord.

ALL: Amen.

LEADER:
Let us bow our heads and pray for N.

◆ All observe silence.

LEADER:
May God, in whose presence our ancestors walked, bless you.

ALL: Amen.

LEADER:
May God, who has been your shepherd from birth until now, keep you.

ALL: Amen.

LEADER:
May God, who saves you from all harm, give you peace.

ALL: Amen.

✝ All make the Sign of the Cross.

In the name of the Father, and of the Son, and of the Holy Spirit. Amen.

PRAYER SERVICE
FOR SAD DAYS

The following prayer can be used when there is a sad or tragic event in the school community. This may be an illness or death of a student, faculty, or staff member, or a parent of a student. It may also be used at a time of a local or national crisis when the school gathers to pray. For this prayer, an adult should take the part of the leader as it is important to offer a few words that describe the particular need or concern.

✚ All make the Sign of the Cross.

ALL: In the name of the Father, and of the Son, and of the Holy Spirit. Amen.

LEADER:
We gather today to pray for [name the person or concern].
We trust, O God, that you hear us.
We trust that you understand the suffering and pain of your people.
We trust that you are with all those in need.
Let us listen to the Word of God.

READER: Matthew 11:28–30
A reading from the holy Gospel according to Matthew.

"Come to me, all you that are weary and are carrying heavy burdens, and I will give you rest. Take my yoke upon you, and learn from me; for I am gentle and humble in heart, and you will find rest for your souls. For my yoke is easy, and my burden is light."

LEADER:
Let us take a few moments to pray in our hearts for [name the person or concern].

LEADER:
Let us pray:
God of all,
help us to remember that your son Jesus suffered, died, and rose so that we might know of your great love.

He invites us to bring our cares and concerns to you in prayer, and so we ask you to be with [name the persons]. Give them courage and peace.

We ask you also to be with us during this time of difficulty. Help us to trust that you are always with us.

◆ [If appropriate, invite spontaneous prayers from those gathered.]

LEADER:
Assured of your great love, we pray:
Our Father . . . Amen.

◆ Pause and say:
As we conclude our prayer, let us offer one another the sign of Christ's peace.

◆ All offer one another a sign of peace.

LEADER:
May God the Creator bless us:

✚ All make the Sign of the Cross

In the name of the Father, and of the Son, and of the Holy Spirit. Amen.

CHILDREN'S DAILY PRAYER 2018–2019, © 2018 Archdiocese of Chicago: Liturgy Training Publications. All rights reserved. Orders: 800-933-1800 or www.LTP.org.

Prepare a leader, reader, intercessor, and song leader (if the group will sing). Mark the passage in the Bible with a ribbon or bookmark. Prepare the class for the commissioning by talking about anointing. Mention that the oil we use is not holy oil but a reminder of the holy oil used in our Baptism and/or Confirmation anointing. Place a clear glass bowl of olive oil in the environment with a small cloth (to wipe the fingers). The teacher or another adult should do the anointing. You may wish to begin with the song "In the Lord I'll Be Ever Thankful."

LEADER:

We will soon go separate ways during the break, so we take some time to think about how we have grown in God's love and how God will continue to work through us.

✛ All make the sign of the Cross.

In the name of the Father, and of the Son, and of the Holy Spirit. Amen.

Let us pray.
God of all goodness,
we thank you
for this time together
where we have been challenged
to be your very good people.
As we prepare to start our summer break,
we ask you to keep us close to one another
and to you.
We ask this through Jesus Christ our Lord.

LEADER: Psalm 119:1–3, 10–11, 41–49, 89–90, 105

Let us repeat the Psalm Response: Your word is a lamp to my feet and a light to my path.

ALL: Your word is a lamp to my feet and a light to my path.

Happy are those whose way is blameless,
    who walk in the law of the LORD.

Happy are those who keep his decrees,
    who seek him with their whole heart,
who also do no wrong,
    but walk in his ways.

ALL: Your word is a lamp to my feet and a light to my path.

With my whole heart I seek you;
    do not let me stray from your
        commandments.
I treasure your word in my heart,
    so that I may not sin against you.

ALL: Your word is a lamp to my feet and a light to my path.

Let your steadfast love come to me, O LORD,
    your salvation according to your promise.
Then I shall have an answer for those who
        taunt me,
    for I trust in your word.

ALL: Your word is a lamp to my feet and a light to my path.

The LORD exists forever;
    your word is firmly fixed in heaven.
Your faithfulness endures to all generations;
    you have established the earth, and it
        stands fast.

ALL: Your word is a lamp to my feet and a light to my path.

READER: Romans 12:16–21

A reading from the Letter of St. Paul to the Romans.

◆ Read the Scripture passage from the Bible.

The Word of the Lord.

◆ All observe silence.

PRAYER SERVICE
LAST DAY OF SCHOOL

TEACHER:

We are Jesus' face, hands, and feet in our families and our neighborhoods. We are called by God to be people of kindness, justice, and peace. I invite you to come forward and be commissioned in Jesus' work.

◆ Students come forward with hands open. The teacher makes a cross on the hands with the oil saying:

You are part of the Body of Christ everywhere you go.

STUDENT: Amen.

INTERCESSOR:

Part of our work is to pray for the world and those in need. Our response to our prayers is "Lord, hear our prayer."

May all children everywhere be given access to education.

We pray to the Lord . . .

May our school's teachers, administrators, staff, and volunteers be refreshed by this break.

We pray to the Lord . . .

May all of us, and all in our school, have fun and be safe.

We pray to the Lord . . .

May our families grow closer together as we spend more time together.

We pray to the Lord . . .

May those who are suffering—from job loss, illness, the death of a loved one, or other difficulties—find the help they need and experience the presence of Christ.

We pray to the Lord . . .

Lord Jesus, your gentle Spirit has guided us these past months. Knowing how much you love us, may we follow you with all our hearts.

ALL: Amen.

LEADER:

Let us pray:
Bless us, O God,
as we go forth to new adventures
knowing you are always with us.
May we cherish the time we have had together.

✚ All make the sign of the Cross.

Let us offer one another a sign of Christ's peace.

◆ All offer one another a sign of peace.

CHILDREN'S DAILY PRAYER 2018–2019, © 2018 Archdiocese of Chicago: Liturgy Training Publications. All rights reserved. Orders: 800-933-1800 or www.LTP.org.

PSALMS AND CANTICLES

PSALMS

PSALM 23

*This psalm is appropriate during all liturgical seasons. It may
be prayed in times of difficulty or stress, when comfort is needed,
or to meditate on Christ's presence in the sacraments.*

The LORD is my shepherd, I shall not want.
   He makes me lie down in green pastures;
he leads me beside still waters;
   he restores my soul.
He leads me in right paths
   for his name's sake.

Even though I walk through the darkest valley,
   I fear no evil;
for you are with me;
   your rod and your staff—
   they comfort me.

You prepare a table before me
   in the presence of my enemies;
you anoint my head with oil;
   my cup overflows.
Surely goodness and mercy shall follow me
   all the days of my life,
and I shall dwell in the house of the LORD
   my whole life long.

PSALM 27

Psalm 27:1, 4–5, 7–9, 13–14

Use this psalm during times of darkness, anxiety, or uncertainty.
This psalm is also an affirmation of God's goodness at any
moment in life.

The LORD is my light and my salvation;
   whom shall I fear?
The LORD is the stronghold of my life;
   of whom shall I be afraid?

One thing I asked of the LORD,
   that will I seek after:
to live in the house of the LORD
   all the days of my life,
to behold the beauty of the LORD,
   and to inquire in his temple.

For he will hide me in his shelter
   in the day of trouble;
he will conceal me under the cover of his tent;
   he will set me high on a rock.

Hear, O LORD, when I cry aloud,
   be gracious to me and answer me!
"Come," my heart says, "seek his face!"
   Your face, LORD do I seek.
   Do not hide your face from me.

I believe that I shall see the goodness of the LORD
   in the land of the living.
Wait for the LORD;
   be strong, and let your heart take courage;
   wait for the LORD!

PSALM 34

Psalm 34:1–8

This psalm of trust in God's power may be prayed by anyone seeking to wonder and rejoice in Christ's presence in the Eucharist. It is especially appropriate for those preparing to celebrate first Holy Communion.

I will bless the LORD at all times;
   his praise shall continually be in my mouth.
My soul makes its boast in the LORD;
   let the humble hear and be glad.
O magnify the LORD with me,
   and let us exalt his name together.

I sought the LORD, and he answered me,
   and delivered me from all my fears.
Look to him, and be radiant;
   so your faces shall never be ashamed.
This poor soul cried, and was heard by the LORD,
   and was saved from every trouble.
The angel of the LORD encamps
   around those who fear him, and delivers them.
O taste and see that the LORD is good;
   happy are those who take refuge in him.

PSALM 46

Psalm 46:1–5

This psalm may be used during times of suffering, confusion, or fear. Its offer of comfort and renewal will give cause for hope in any extremity.

God is our refuge and strength,
    a very present help in trouble.
Therefore we will not fear, though the earth should change,
    though the mountains shake in the heart of the sea;
though its waters roar and foam,
    though the mountains tremble with its tumult.

There is a river whose streams make glad the city of God,
    the holy habitation of the Most High.
God is in the midst of the city; it shall not be moved;
    God will help it when the morning dawns.

PSALM 51

Psalm 51:1–2, 6, 10, 12, 15

*This is a penitential psalm that is especially appropriate during
a communal celebration of the Sacrament of Reconciliation.
It can also be incorporated into any Lenten prayer service.*

Have mercy on me, O God,
   according to your steadfast love;
according to your abundant mercy
   blot out my transgressions.
Wash me thoroughly from my iniquity,
   and cleanse me from my sin.

You desire truth in the inward being;
   therefore teach me wisdom in my secret heart.

Create in me a clean heart, O God,
   and put a new and right spirit within me.
Restore to me the joy of your salvation,
   and sustain in me a willing spirit.

O LORD, open my lips,
   and my mouth will declare your praise.

PSALMS

PSALM 84

Psalm 84:1–2, 10–12

This is a good psalm to pray when preparing to enter a church.
It helps to foster a great love for God's dwelling place.

How lovely is your dwelling place,
    O LORD of hosts!
My soul longs, indeed it faints
    for the courts of the LORD;
my heart and my flesh sing for joy
    to the living God.
For a day in your courts is better
    than a thousand elsewhere.
I would rather be a doorkeeper in the house of my God
    than live in the tents of wickedness.
For the LORD God is a sun and shield;
    he bestows favor and honor.
No good thing does the LORD withhold
    from those who walk uprightly.
O LORD of hosts,
    happy is everyone who trusts in you.

PSALM 100

This is a joyful psalm of thanksgiving that helps orient the heart to God.

Make a joyful noise to the LORD, all the earth.
　Worship the LORD with gladness;
　come into his presence with singing.
Know that the LORD is God.
　It is he that made us, and we are his;
　we are his people, and the sheep of his pasture.
Enter his gates with thanksgiving,
　and his courts with praise.
　Give thanks to him, bless his name.
For the LORD is good;
　his steadfast love endures forever,
　and his faithfulness to all generations.

PSALM 103

Psalm 103:1–5, 19–22

*This is a deeply meditative psalm of grateful acknowledgment
of God's gifts and God's mercy.*

Bless the Lord, O my soul,
   and all that is within me,
    bless his holy name.
Bless the Lord, O my soul,
   and do not forget all his benefits—
who forgives all your iniquity,
   who heals all your diseases,
who redeems your life from the Pit,
   who crowns you with steadfast love and mercy,
who satisfies you with good as long as you live
   so that your youth is renewed like the eagle's.

The Lord has established his throne in the heavens,
   and his kingdom rules over all.
Bless the Lord, O you his angels,
   you mighty ones who do his bidding,
    obedient to his spoken word.
Bless the Lord, all his works,
   in all places of his dominion.
Bless the Lord, O my soul.

PSALMS

PSALM 139

Psalm 139:1–6, 13–16

This psalm expresses the wonder and awe of our mysterious relationship to the God who knows us intimately and loves us completely.

O Lord, you have searched me and known me.
You know when I sit down and when I rise up;
 you discern my thoughts from far away.
You search out my path and my lying down,
 and are acquainted with all my ways.
Even before a word is on my tongue,
 O Lord, you know it completely.
You hem me in, behind and before,
 and lay your hand upon me.
Such knowledge is too wonderful for me;
 it is so high that I cannot attain it.

For it was you who formed my inward parts;
 you knit me together in my mother's womb.
I praise you, for I am fearfully and wonderfully made.
 Wonderful are your works;
that I know very well.
 My frame was not hidden from you,
when I was being made in secret,
 intricately woven in the depths of the earth.
Your eyes beheld my unformed substance.
In your book were written
all the days that were formed for me,
 when none of them as yet existed.

PSALM 148

Psalm 148:1-4; 7-13

This is a psalm praising God for the glory of creation. It is a good prayer to use especially during the weeks in which the Scripture readings focus on creation of the earth.

Praise the LORD!
Praise the LORD from the heavens; praise him in the heights!
Praise him, all his angels; praise him all his host!

Praise him, sun and moon; praise him, all you shining stars!
Praise him, you highest heavens, and your waters below the heavens!

Praise the LORD from the earth,
   you sea monsters and all deeps,
fire and hail, snow and frost, stormy wind fulfilling his command!

Mountains and all hills, fruit trees and all cedars!
Wild animals and all cattle, creeping things and flying birds!

Kings of the earth and all peoples,
   Princes and all rulers of the earth1
Young men and women alike, old and young together.

Let them praise the name of the LORD,
   For his name alone is exalted;
His glory is above earth and heaven.

PSALMS

PSALM 150

Psalm 150

This psalm praises God, suggesting that we use all sorts of musical instruments to offer our praise. It is a song of great joy and rejoicing.

Praise the LORD!
Praise God in his sanctuary; praise him in his mighty firmament!
Praise him for his mighty deeds; praise him
   according to his surpassing greatness!

Praise him with trumpet sound; praise him with lute and harp!
Praise him with tambourine and dance;
   praise him with strings and pipe!
   Praise him with clanging cymbals;
      Praise him with loud clashing cymbals!
   Let everything that breathes praise the LORD!
   Praise the LORD!

THE *MAGNIFICAT* OF MARY

Luke 1:46–55

Mary prayed with these words when she visited her relative, Elizabeth, after Elizabeth declared, "Blessed are you among women and blessed is the fruit of your womb!" For centuries, this beautiful song of praise and trust has been the Church's evening prayer.

And Mary said,
"My soul magnifies the Lord,
    and my spirit rejoices in God my savior,
for he has looked with favor on the lowliness of his servant.
    Surely, from now on all generations will call me blessed;
for the Mighty One has done great things for me,
    and holy is his name.
His mercy is for those who fear him
    from generation to generation.
He has shown strength with his arm;
    he has scattered the proud in the thoughts of their hearts.
He has brought down the powerful from their thrones,
    and lifted up the lowly;
he has filled the hungry with good things,
    and sent the rich away empty.
He has helped his servant Israel,
    in remembrance of his mercy,
according to the promise he made to our ancestors,
    to Abraham and to his descendants forever."

CANTICLES

THE *BENEDICTUS* OF ZECHARIAH

Luke 1:68–79

Zechariah had been struck mute during the pregnancy of his wife, Elizabeth. After their baby was born, on the day when they gave him his name, Zechariah's voice was restored and he spoke these prophetic words over his child, John the Baptist. His prophecy is part of the Church's traditional morning prayer.

"Blessed be the Lord God of Israel,
   for he has looked favorably on his people and redeemed them.
He has raised up a mighty savior for us
   in the house of his servant David,
as he spoke through the mouth of his holy prophets from of old,
    that we would be saved from our enemies and from the hand
      of all who hate us.
Thus he has shown the mercy promised to our ancestors,
   and has remembered his holy covenant,
the oath that he swore to our ancestor Abraham,
    to grant us that we, being rescued from the hands
      of our enemies,
might serve him without fear, in holiness and righteousness,
   before him all our days.
And you, child, will be called the prophet of the Most High;
   for you will go before the Lord to prepare his ways,
to give knowledge of salvation to his people
   by the forgiveness of their sins.
By the tender mercy of our God,
   the dawn from on high will break upon us,
to give light to those who sit in darkness and in the shadow
    of death,
   to guide our feet into the way of peace."

THE CANTICLE OF SIMEON

Luke 2:29–32

The canticle, or song, of Simeon is often called the Nunc Dimittis, from the first lines of the song. This is the prayer that Simeon offered when he recognized the infant Jesus as the Messiah. Simeon was an old man, and for many years he had prayed for the Messiah to come. It is a wonderful prayer that is said each evening in Compline, the evening prayer of the Church. It is especially fitting to pray the Canticle of Simeon at the time of the Feast of the Presentation of the Lord on February 2.

"Master, now you are dismissing your servant in peace,
    according to your word;
for my eyes have seen your salvation,
    which you have prepared in the presence
    of all peoples,
a light for revelation to the Gentiles
    and for glory to your people Israel."

RESOURCES FOR PRAYING WITH CHILDREN

In addition to *Children's Daily Prayer*, teachers, principals, and catechists may find these LTP resources to be helpful in their work of developing prayer services and preparing children for Mass and reception of the sacraments.

PREPARING MASSES WITH CHILDREN: 15 EASY STEPS

A resource to assist teachers and catechists in preparing children to participate fully in the Mass.

FROM MASS TO MISSION

A small guide that explains the significance of the Mass for living a Christian life. There is a guide for children and a guide for teens; each has a leader's guide to accompany the book.

THE YEAR OF GRACE LITURGICAL CALENDAR

This annual circular calendar displays the liturgical year. It highlights the color for each liturgical season and provides a visual guide to the major feasts and saints' days throughout the year. Each year, the calendar has beautiful art to illustrate a particular theme or liturgical focus.

CHILDREN'S LITURGY OF THE WORD

An annual publication that offers a guide to help prepare a Liturgy of the Word for children on Sundays and Holydays of Obligation.

BLESSINGS AND PRAYERS THROUGH THE YEAR: A RESOURCE FOR SCHOOL AND PARISH

This is an illustrated collection of prayers and blessings and prayer services, which includes two CD-ROMS of music with vocal instruction and musical accompaniment to facilitate singing.

COMPANION TO THE CALENDAR: A GUIDE TO THE SAINTS, SEASONS, AND HOLIDAYS OF THE YEAR.

An invaluable resource for learning more about the particular saint or feast of the day. This book could be used to help children learn more about their patron saint or saints of special interest.

SCHOOL YEAR, CHURCH YEAR: CUSTOMS AND DECORATIONS FOR THE CLASSROOM

Teachers and catechists who wish to create an environment in the classroom that reflects the liturgical season will find many creative and doable ideas in this book.